Communications in Computer and Information Science 353

Tai-hoon Kim   Jeong-Jin Kang
William I. Grosky   Tughrul Arslan
Niki Pissinou (Eds.)

Computer Applications for Bio-technology, Multimedia, and Ubiquitous City

International Conferences
MulGraB, BSBT and IUrC 2012
Held as Part of the Future Generation
Information Technology Conference, FGIT 2012
Gangneug, Korea, December 16-19, 2012
Proceedings

Springer

Volume Editors

Tai-hoon Kim
GVSA and University of Tasmania, Hobart, TAS, Australia
E-mail: taihoonn@hanmail.net

Jeong-Jin Kang
Dong Seoul University, Seongnam-si, Korea
E-mail: jjkang@du.ac.kr

William I. Grosky
University of Michigan – Dearborn, MI, USA
E-mail: wgrosky@umich.edu

Tughrul Arslan
Edinburgh University, UK
E-mail: tughrul.arslan@ee.ed.ac.uk

Niki Pissinou
Florida International University, Miami, FL, USA
E-mail: pissinou@fiu.edu

ISSN 1865-0929   e-ISSN 1865-0937
ISBN 978-3-642-35520-2   e-ISBN 978-3-642-35521-9
DOI 10.1007/978-3-642-35521-9
Springer Heidelberg Dordrecht London New York

Library of Congress Control Number: 2012953703

CR Subject Classification (1998): C.2, H.4, I.2, H.3, K.6.5, D.4.6

Typesetting: Camera-ready by author, data conversion by Scientific Publishing Services, Chennai, India

Printed on acid-free paper

Springer is part of Springer Science+Business Media (www.springer.com)

Foreword

Multimedia, computer graphics and broadcasting, bio-science and bio-technology, and intelligent urban computing are areas that attract many academics and industry professionals. The goal of the MulGrab, the BSBT, and the IUrC conferences is to bring together researchers from academia and industry as well as practitioners to share ideas, problems, and solutions relating to the multifaceted aspects of these fields.

We would like to express our gratitude to all of the authors of submitted papers and to all attendees for their contributions and participation.

We acknowledge the great effort of all the Chairs and the members of Advisory Boards and Program Committees of the above-listed events. Special thanks go to SERSC (Science & Engineering Research Support Society) for supporting this conference.

We are grateful in particular to the following speakers who kindly accepted our invitation and, in this way, helped to meet the objectives of the conference: Zita Maria Almeida do Vale, Hai Jin, Goreti Marreiros, Alfredo Cuzzocrea and Osvaldo Gervasi.

We wish to express our special thanks to Yvette E. Gelogo for helping with the editing of this volume.

December 2012

Chairs of MulGraB 2012
BSBT 2012
IUrC 2012

Preface

We would like to welcome you to the proceedings of the 2012 International Conference on Multimedia, Computer Graphics and Broadcasting (MulGraB 2012), the 2012 International Conference on Bio-Science and Bio-Technology (BSBT 2012), and the First International Conference on Intelligent Urban Computing (IUrC 2012), which were held during December 16–19, 2012, at the Korea Woman Training Center, Kangwondo, Korea.

MulGraB 2012, BSBT 2012, and IUrC 2012 provided a chance for academics and industry professionals to discuss recent progress in related areas. We expect that the conference and its publications will be a trigger for further research and technology improvements in this important field. We would like to acknowledge the great effort of all the Chairs and members of the Program Committee.

We would like to express our gratitude to all of the authors of submitted papers and to all attendees for their contributions and participation. We believe in the need for continuing this undertaking in the future.

Once more, we would like to thank all the organizations and individuals who supported this event and helped in the success of MulGraB 2012, BSBT 2012, and IUrC 2012.

December 2012   Tai-hoon Kim on behalf of the Volume Editors

Organization

Honorary Chair

Jeong-Jin Kang   Dong Seoul University, Korea

General Co-chairs

Ed Rothwell	Michigan State University, USA
Hoon Ko	Institute of Engineering-Polytechnic of Porto, Portugal
Niki Pissinou	Florida International University, USA
Timothy K. Shih	National Taipei University of Education, Taiwan
Tughrul Arslan	Engineering and Electronics, Edinburgh University, UK
Wai-chi Fang	National Chiao Tung University, Taiwan
William I. Grosky	University of Michigan-Dearborn, USA

Program Co-chairs

Byeongho Kang	University of Tasmania, Australia
Goreti Marreiros	Institute of Engineering-Polytechnic of Porto, Portugal
Kyungjin An	Newcastle University, UK
Lidia Ogiela	AGH University of Science and Technology, Poland
Marek R. Ogiela	AGH University of Science and Technology, Poland
Tai-hoon Kim	GVSA, Australia
Xiaofeng Song	Nanjing University of Aeronautics and Astronautics, China

Workshop Chair

Byungjoo Park   Hannam University, Korea

Publication Chair

Yongho Choi   Jungwon University, Korea

Publicity Co-chairs

Muhammad Khurram Khan	King Saud University, Saudi Arabia
Aboul Ella Hassanien	Cairo University, Egypt

International Advisory Board

Andrea Omicini	DEIS, Università di Bologna, Italy
Bozena Kostek	Gdansk University of Technology, Poland
Byoung-Tak Zhang	Seoul National University, Korea
Cao Jiannong	Hong Kong Polytechnic University, SAR China
Cas Apanowicz	Ministry of Education, Canada
Ching-Hsien Hsu	Chung Hua University, Taiwan
Claudia Linnhoff-Popien	Ludwig-Maximilians-Universität München, Germany
Daqing Zhang	Institute for Infocomm Research (I2R), Singapore
Diane J. Cook	University of Texas at Arlington, USA
Frode Eika Sandnes	Oslo University College, Norway
Guoyin Wang	CQUPT, Chongqing, China
Hamid-R Arabnia	The University of Georgia, USA
Han-Chieh Chao	National Ilan University, Taiwan
Ing-Ray Chen	Virginia Polytechnic Institute and State University, USA
Jae-Sang Cha	Seoul National University of Science and Technology, Korea
Jian-Nong Cao	Hong Kong Polytechnic University, SAR China
Joseph Kolibal	University of Southern Mississippi, USA
Krzysztof Marasek	PJIIT, Warsaw, Poland
Krzysztof Pawlikowski	University of Canterbury, New Zealand
Lionel Ni	The Hong Kong University of Science and Technology, SAR China
Mahmut Kandemir	Pennsylvania State University, USA
Matt Mutka	Michigan State University, USA
Mei-Ling Shyu	University of Miami, USA
Philip Maini	University of Oxford, UK
Rajkumar Buyya	University of Melbourne, Australia
Robert Young Chul Kim	Hongik University
Sajal K. Das	University of Texas at Arlington, USA
Sajid Hussain	Acadia University, Canada
Saman Halgamuge	University of Melbourne, Australia
Sankar K. Pal	Indian Statistical Institute, India
Schahram Dustdar	Vienna University of Technology, Austria
Seng W. Loke	La Trobe University, Australia
Seung-Jung Shin	Hansei University, Korea
Stefanos Gritzalis	University of the Aegean, Greece

Yang Xiao   University of Alabama, USA
Yong-Gyu Jung   Eulji University, Korea
Zbigniew W. Ras   University of North Carolina, USA

Program Committee

Abdelwahab Hamou-Lhadj   Concordia University, Canada
Ahmet Koltuksuz   Izmir Institute of Technology, Turkey
Alexander Loui   Eastman Kodak Company, USA
Alexei Sourin   Nanyang Technological University, Singapore
Alicja Wieczorkowska   PJIIT, Poland
Andrew Kusiak   University of Iowa, USA
Andrzej Dzielinski   Warsaw University of Technology, Poland
Anthony Lewis Brooks   Aalborg University, Denmark
Atsuko Miyaji   JAIST, Japan
Biplab K. Sarker   Primal Fusion Inc., Canada
Ch. Z. Patrikakis   National Technical University of Athens,
                                   Greece
Chantana Chantrapornchai   Silpakorn University, Thailand
Chao-Tung Yang   Tunghai University, Taiwan
Chengcui Zhang   University of Alabama at Birmingham, USA
Chi Sung Laih   National Cheng Kung University, Taiwan
Ching-Hsien Hsu   Chung Hua University, Taiwan
Christine Fernandez-Maloigne   Université de Poitiers, France
Dae-Hyun Ryu   Hansei University, Korea
Daniel Thalmann   EPFL VRlab, Switzerland
Dieter Gollmann   Hamburg University of Technology, Germany
Dimitris Iakovidis   University of Athens, Greece
Do-Hyeun Kim   Jeju University, Korea
Eung-Nam Ko   Baekseok University, Korea
Fabrice Mériaudeau   IUT Le Creusot, France
Fangguo Zhang   Sun Yat-sen University, China
Francesco Masulli   University of Pisa, Italy
Federica Landolfi   Università degli Studi del Sannio, Italy
Gérard Medioni   USC/IRIS, Los Angeles, USA
Hae-Duck Joshua Jeong   Korean Bible University, Korea
Hai Jin Huazhong   University of Science and Technology, China
Hiroaki Kikuchi   Tokai University, Japan
Hironori Washizaki   National Institute of Informatics, Japan
Hongji Yang   De Montfort University, UK
Hyun-Sung Kim   Kyungil University, Korea
Hyun-Tae Kim   Dongeui University, Korea
Jacques Blanc-Talon   DGA/MRIS, Arcueil, France
Jalal Al-Muhtadi   King Saud University, Saudi Arabia
Jang Sik Park   Kyungsung University, Korea
Javier Garcia-Villalba   Complutense University of Madrid, Spain

Table of Contents

Semantic Description and Recognition of Human Body Poses and Movement Sequences with Gesture Description Language

Tomasz Hachaj[1] and Marek R. Ogiela[2]

[1] Pedagogical University of Krakow, Institute of Computer Science and Computer Methods,
2 Podchorazych Ave, 30-084 Krakow, Poland
tomekhachaj@o2.pl
[2] AGH University of Science and Technology, 30 Mickiewicza Ave, 30-059 Krakow, Poland
mogiela@agh.edu.pl

Abstract. In this article we introduce new approach for human body poses and movement sequences recognition. Our concept is based on syntactic description with so called Gesture Description Language (GDL). The implementation of GDL requires special semantic reasoning module with additional heap-like memory. In the following paragraphs we shortly describes our initial concept. We also present software and hardware architecture that we created to test our solution and very promising early experiments results.

Keywords: Pose recognition, movement sequences recognition, syntactic description, semantic reasoning, natural interface.

1 Introduction

The researches on human - computer interaction have been conducted for many years. The concept of human-device interaction based on human senses, mostly focused on hearing and vision is now known under term Natural Interaction or Natural User Interface (NI). Lately appearing of affordable by a single consumer multimedia sensor resulted in commercialization of NI techniques and intensification of studies on that subject. The vision communication with computer program is mainly based on exposing some predefined body poses and movement sequences. Many methods have been yet proposed for extraction and interpretation of those communicates from video stream. In [1] authors propose a method to quickly and accurately predict 3D positions of body joints from a single depth image using no temporal information. The method is based on body part labeling, extracting depth image features and randomized decision forests. In [2] system for estimating location and orientation of a person's head, from depth data acquired by a low quality device is presented. Approach is based on discriminative random regression forests: ensembles of random trees trained by splitting each node so as to simultaneously reduce the entropy of the class labels distribution and the variance of the head position and orientation. Most of the gesture recognition approaches are based on statistical modeling, such as principal component analysis or hidden Markov models [3]. The concept of modeling the

T.-h. Kim et al. (Eds.): MulGraB/BSBT/IUrC 2012, CCIS 353, pp. 1–8, 2012.

dynamic hand gesture using a finite state machine has been proposed in [4]. In [5] a radial basis function network architecture is developed that learns the correlation of facial feature motion patterns and human expressions. The recognition techniques have many applications not only in games entertainment but also in medicine for example during rehabilitation presses [6]. In this article we introduce new approach for human body poses and movement sequences recognition for NI. Our concept is based on syntactic description with so called Gesture Description Language (GDL) which is LALR(1) grammar. The implementation of GDL requires special semantic reasoning module with additional heap-like memory. In the following paragraphs we shortly describe our initial concept. We also present software and hardware architecture that we created to test our solution and very promising early experiments results.

2   Methods

We have developed the system that allow us initially tests our approach (Figure 1). It is consisted of sensor for data acquisition, image processing library for tracking user and semantic reasoner with GDL language interpreter that is our novel and original contribution. In our solution we utilized the Kinect sensor for data capture and Open-NI Framework software for image processing. We have chosen that software because it has low hardware and software requirements comparing to other solutions with similar capabilities.

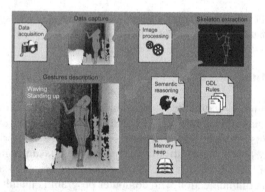

Fig. 1. System architecture. The detailed description is in the text.

2.1   Sensor for Data Acquisition

The Kinect controller was preliminary design to use with the video game and entertainment system. It is consisted of: depth camera, RGB camera and Audio sensors.

2.2   Image Processing (Tracking) Software

The OpenNI framework [7] provides an application programming interface (API) for writing applications utilizing natural interaction. The API enables modules to be registered in the OpenNI framework and used to produce sensory data. PrimeSense NITE Middleware [8] is a module for OpenNI providing gesture and skeleton tracking. Skeleton tracking functionality enables detection and real-time tracking of fifteen key points on human body (see Figure 2). Those key points will be called joints in the rest of the article. After processing of depth sensor data NITE returns joint positions and orientations are given in the real world coordinate system.

Fig. 2. Skeleton joints and the coordinate system. All body parts are mirrored because user is facing the camera.

2.3   Semantic Reasoner

Semantic reasoner implements our GDL specification. GDL language is used for syntactic description human body poses and movement sequences. The GDL script consists of rules set. Each rule has the logical expression and conclusion. If that expression is satisfied the conclusion is added on the top of memory heap. The conclusion from one rule can be present in logical expression of another rule. Multiple rules can have same conclusion. The determination of truthfulness of all rules is made with forward chaining inferring schema by semantic reasoning module. On each level of the memory heap semantic reasoner keeps information about input data (coordinates of skeleton joints of tracked user) and satisfied rules for given state of memory heap. Each heap level keeps also timestamp informing (how much time passed since last data addition to the top of the heap). Using this time stamp program can easily check how much time has passed from now to the moment when data was added to the chosen heap level simply by summing up all time stamps from to the top to the chosen heap level. GDL gives an access to heap memory by direct access to actual / previous joint coordinate value (the level of the heap must be specified) or by indirect checking if some of possible conclusions was satisfied in the given time period. All possible elements of GDL are presented and described in Table 1. In GDL letter case does not matter. The GDL gives direct access to joint data tracked by OpenNI Framework but our algorithm is not limited to this particular software solution or sensor type. The GDL implementation can be easily adapted to any other image processing framework as long as it generates three dimensional joint-based user tracking data.

Table 1. Elements of GDL

Type	Symbols	Description
Rule definition	**RULE** logicalValue **THEN** conclusion	If logical values equals true the conclusion occurs and it is added on the top of the memory heap.
Relational operators	<,<=,>,>=,=,!=	Binary relational operators between numeric values. If the condition is satisfied it returns logical value true, if not false.
Aritmetic operators	+,-,*,/,%	Binary arithmetic operators between numeric values. "-" can also be an unary operator.
Logical operators	**&, |**	Logical operators between logical values.
Brackets	()	Bracket can be used for changing the order of operators' execution (arithmetic and logical).
Logical functions	**not()**	Negation of logical value.
Numeric functions	**abs(), sqrt()**	Absolute value and square root of numeric value. If the numeric value in sqrt function parameter is negative it generates programming language exception.
Sequence checking functions	**sequenceexists**("movementSequence")	Returns true if given "movementSequence" exists in the memory heap. Return false in not.
Movement sequence	"[conclusion1,!conclusion2,timeRestriction1] …[conclusion3,timeRestriction2]"	Sequence of sets of conclusions. Each set of conclusions is in the square brackets. Each conclusion in the set has to be present in the memory heap by the time period specified in field timeRestriction (so the first time period is from current time to current time – timeRestriction1, next period is from current time – time by which all conclusion occurred to current time – time by which all conclusion occurred – timeRestriction2 and so on). If ! precede conclusion that means that given conclusion cannot be present in given time period. If all conditions are satisfied function returns logical value true. If not function returns false.
Existence of the conclusion	conclusion	If conclusion with the given name is present on the top of memory heap it returns logical value true. In not it returns false.

Table 1. (*continued*)

Joint coordinate value	joint-Name.**x**[heapPosition], joint-Name.**y**[heapPosition], joint-Name.**z**[heapPosition]	Returns numeric value of one of joint coordinates (x, y or z). Names of possible joints are presented in Fig. 2. Numeric value heapPosition determinates position of joint to be retrieved from the memory heap (zero means top of the heap). If joint does not exist in the given position of the heap (for example it was not detected by the image processing library) this expression returns 0.
Commentary	// /* */	Single and multiline commentary.

3 Experiment and Results

In order to check the usefulness of proposed semantic description we have created set of scripts that recognize some common behavior that might be present in human - computer interaction. Because of the article space limitation we will only described three of them that represents different capabilities of GDL: detection of movement, recognition of hand clapping and recognition of waving gesture. Our intention was to present not very complex examples to make that approach easier to clarify. It should be remembered that GDL does not limit the number and complexity level or rules in the script. The first example is detection movement along horizontal axis of the tracked user. In that case we assumed that movement means changing position of torso skeleton joint so we have to check if absolute difference value between torsos horizontal coordinates has changed in last two tracking sequences (see Appendix - example 1). The second example is detection of hand clapping along horizontal axis. The proposed implementation is consisted of two frames: with hands separate (the difference between vertical coordinates of hands has to be under given threshold) and hands close to each other - the difference between vertical and horizontal coordinates of the hands are under given threshold (Figure 3, Appendix - example 2). The third rule checks if previous rules have occurred in the specific order in given time constraints. The GDL script example can be easily modified to make recognition independent of coordinate axis by applying Euclidean distance between points.

Fig. 3. Two gestures that have been used for description of hand clapping sequence along horizontal axis. In first column user holding his hands separately, the difference between vertical coordinates of hands has to be under given threshold. In second column user holding his hands close to each other - the difference between vertical and horizontal coordinates of the hands are under given threshold. First column – image from RGB camera, second column - image from depth camera with region of interest (user body) and skeleton detected, third column - tracked skeleton.

The third example is gesture of waving with right hand. It has been partitioned to three poses: with right hand over the right elbow, right hand on the left from an elbow and right hand on the right from elbow. The whole sequence should appear in the given time period (Figure 4, Appendix - example 3).

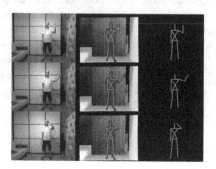

Fig. 4. First column - image from RGB camera, second column - image from depth camera with region of interest (user body) and skeleton detected, third column - tracked skeleton. The detailed description is in the text.

Our experiment has proved that GDL scripts processed by our reasoning framework is capable for real time recognition of the considered gestures. That is because any body position can be expressed by inequalities between selected skeleton joints. The sequenceexists function restricts the time period in which the sequence should appear. The noises generated by tracking software can be compensated by abs function. Our early experiments has also showed that some well know gestures (like those we proposed in this section) are easily reproduced (and recognize by our system) by new users who did not have any previous experiences with tracking software.

4   Discussion

Our preliminary proposition of human body poses and movement sequences recognition system has yet proven to be reliable in recognition of user behavior consisted of few skeleton joints and poses. The main advantages of our approach are simplicity and intuitiveness of GDL scripts. What is more the application of forward chaining inferring schema with memory stack concept is straightforward to any computer programmer and makes development of movement sequences fast and effective. That type of description does not require any training and gathering of huge movement databases. The GDL architect has to decide which skeleton joints can be omitted to simplify the description without affecting resemblance to exact movement recording. Also GDL does not limit the number and complexity level or rules in the script and because semantic analysis of once parsed script is not time demanding our approach can potentially has very large rules databases. The main drawback of the methodology is that complex movement sequences might need many key frames. That problem might be solved by finding solution of reverse problem - automatic generation of GDL from filmed movement sequences (similarly to [9]). With proper computed aided tool that would guide the user in process of removing needles joints and setting tolerance level it might be quite effective. From the other hand it should also be remembered that many multimedia vision systems for natural user interfaces use one camera for capturing the movement of user. That fact strongly limits the field of view of the device leading to limitation in observation of some gestures in particular body positions. In those situations some key points of the body might be invisible and difficult to predict by the software. Because of that in many cases one can omit dependences of skeleton joint towards selected axis because the moving sequence will not be proper reiterated by sensor and tracking software.

5   Conclusion

Our goals for the future will be comparison of our approach to other existing methods and validation its sensitivity on test datasets. We also want to include the functionality that will supply the user with possibility of interacting with virtual object and environment (for example three dimensional visualizations of medical images [10]). That would require adding new procedures to GDL and more complex memory stack architecture. We should also consider adding some languages semantic that would allow user to define parts of code that are used multiply times (for example possibility of variables definition).

Acknowledgments. We kindly acknowledge the support of this study by a Pedagogical University of Krakow Statutory Research Grant.

References

1. Shotton, F., et al.: Real-time human pose recognition in parts from single depth images. In: CVPR 2011 (March 2011)
2. Fanelli, G., Weise, T., Gall, J., Van Gool, L.: Real Time Head Pose Estimation from Consumer Depth Cameras. In: Mester, R., Felsberg, M. (eds.) DAGM 2011. LNCS, vol. 6835, pp. 101–110. Springer, Heidelberg (2011)
3. Mitra, S., Acharya, T.: Gesture recognition: A survey. IEEE Transactions on Systems, Man, and Cybernetics, Part C: Applications and Reviews 37(3) (2007)
4. Yeasin, M., Chaudhuri, S.: Visual understanding of dynamic hand gestures. Pattern Recognition 33, 1805–1817 (2000)
5. Rosenblum, M., Yacoob, Y., Davis, L.S.: Human expression recognition from motion using a radial basis function network architecture. IEEE Trans. Neural Netw. 7(5), 1121–1138 (1996)
6. Obdrlek, S., Kurillo, G., Han, J., Abresch, T., Bajcsy, R.: Real-Time Human Pose Detection and Tracking for Tele-Rehabilitation in Virtual Reality. Studies in Health Technology and Informatics 173, 320–324 (2012)
7. OpenNI homepage, http://www.openni.org

8. Prime Sensor NITE 1.3 Algorithms notes, Version 1.0, PrimeSense Inc. (2010),
   http://pr.cs.cornell.edu/humanactivities/data/NITE.pdf
9. Hong, P., Turk, M., Huang, T.S.: Gesture modeling and recognition using finite state
   machines. In: Proc. 4th IEEE Int. Conf. Autom. Face Gesture Recogn., Grenoble, France,
   pp. 410–415 (2000)
10. Hachaj, T., Ogiela, M.R.: Visualization of perfusion abnormalities with GPU-based vo-
    lume rendering. Computers & Graphics 36(3), 163–169 (2012)

Appendix

Example 1. GDL scripts that detect movement along horizontal axis of the tracked user.

```
RULE abs(torso.x[0] - torso.x[1]) > 10 THEN Moving
```

Example 2. GDL scripts that detect hand clapping along horizontal axis.

```
RULE abs(RightHand.x[0] - LeftHand.x[0]) < 80 & abs(RightHand.y[0] -
LeftHand.y[0]) < 80 THEN HandsTogether
RULE abs(RightHand.x[0] - LeftHand.x[0]) > 80 & abs(RightHand.y[0] -
LeftHand.y[0]) < 80 THEN HandsSeparate
RULE sequenceexists( "[HandsSeparate,0.5] [HandsTogether,0.5] [HandsSep-
arate,0.5]" ) THEN HandClap
```

Example 3. GDL scripts that detect waving with right hand.

```
RULE RightElbow.x[0] > Torso.x[0] & RightHand.x[0] > Torso.x[0] &
RightHand.y[0] > RightElbow.y[0] & abs(RightHand.x[0] - RightElbow.x[0])
< 50 THEN WavingGestureCenter
RULE RightElbow.x[0] > Torso.x[0]& RightHand.x[0] > Torso.x[0] &
RightHand.y[0] > RightElbow.y[0] & RightHand.x[0] - RightElbow.x[0] <= -
50 THEN WavingGestureLeft
RULE RightElbow.x[0] > Torso.x[0] & RightHand.x[0] > Torso.x[0] &
RightHand.y[0] > RightElbow.y[0] & RightHand.x[0] - RightElbow.x[0] >=
50 THEN WavingGestureRight
RULE sequenceexists ( "[WavingGestureLeft,1] [WavingGestureCenter,1]
[WavingGestureRight,1]" ) THEN WavingRight
RULE sequenceexists ( "[WavingGestureRight,1] [WavingGestureCenter,1]
[WavingGestureLeft,1]" ) THEN WavingLeft Rule WavingRight | WavingLeft
THEN Waving
```

Core-Shell Detection in Images of Polymer Microbeads[*]

Yeonggul Jang, Byunghwan Jeon, and Yoojin Chung[**]

Department of Computer Science and Engineering
Hankuk University of Foreign Studies
Kyonggi, 449-791, Republic of Korea
{jyg1722,xpsxm85,chungyj}@hufs.ac.kr

Abstract. Microbeads of various size with complex core-shell structures are widely used in many applications such as drug delivery. During synthesis, it is important to characterize the beads' size such that uniform properties can be obtained from uniform size. The core-shell structures can be imaged with SEM (scanning electron microscope) or TEM (transmission electron microscope) but there are no available methods to quantitatively analyze the size and distribution automatically. In this paper, we propose two automated core-shell detection methods using Hough transform and generalized Hough transform. We show the capabilities of these methods using OpenCV and compare the relative advantages and limitations.

Keywords: Counting core-shells, Hough transform, OpenCV.

1 Introduction

Uniform sized polymer particles are widely used in many engineering and clinical applications such as drug delivery. In all applications, it is important to have tight control over the size and chemistry of the particles. For particles or beads with core-shell structure, this requirement is stricter such that the measurements and distribution should be analyzed for each set of experiment. As the particles are imaged with SEM (scanning electron microscope) and TEM (transmission electron microscope), an automated method that can measure and various parameters such as size of the bead, relative size of the core-shell structure, standard deviation and other parameters would be useful for the synthetic chemists.

The Hough transform is a feature extraction technique used in image analysis, computer vision, and digital image processing [1-5]. The Hough transform was initially developed to detect analytically defined shapes (e.g., lines, circles, ellipse etc.). The generalized Hough transform [2] is the modification of the Hough transform using the principle of template matching. This modification enables the Hough transform to be used for the detection of an arbitrary shape (i.e., shapes having no simple analytical form). OpenCV (Open Source Computer Vision Library) [6] is a library of programming functions mainly aimed at real-time computer vision, developed by Intel.

---

[*] This research was supported by Hankuk University of Foreign Studies Research Fund of 2012.
[**] Corresponding author.

T.-h. Kim et al. (Eds.): MulGraB/BSBT/IUrC 2012, CCIS 353, pp. 9–15, 2012.
© Springer-Verlag Berlin Heidelberg 2012

In this paper, we propose two automated core-shell detection methods in image of polymer chemistry using Hough transform and generalized Hough transform. We show their experimental results using OpenCV and discuss their limitations.

2   Methods

2.1   Hough Transform

We first used Hough transform to perform the characterization. The steps are as follows.

Step 1) Image input: Any type of image can be used, B/W or color. If input image is a color with 3 channels (red, green, blue), it is transformed into 1channel mode.

Step 2) Smoothing: Noise in an image can be removed using smoothing to improve the signal to noise (S/N) ratio.

Step 3) Edge detection: Canny edge detection is performed using the matrix in Figure 1.

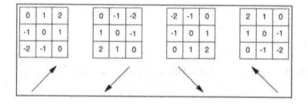

Fig. 1. The matrix for Canny edge detection

Step 4) Determining threshold value: Figure 2 shows the SEM micrograph of polymer core-shell structures. Each image has a characteristic value such as bead radius. When performing Hough transform, the number of core-shells in image depends on radius R. Thus this step can be used to automatically determine the threshold value for each image.

Fig. 2. SEM micrograph of polymer core-shell structures

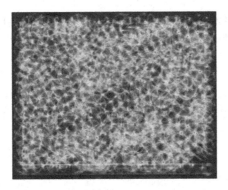

Fig. 3. Image after Hough transform

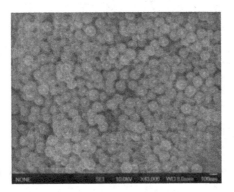

Fig. 4. Overlap image of Fig. 2 and Fig. 3

Step 5) Hough Transform: Each circle in SEM micrograph of polymer core-shell structures in Fig. 2 has slightly different radius value R. The center of each circle is determined after performing edge detection using threshold value. Thus the total number of the circles depends on threshold value. Figure 3 shows the image after performing Hough Transform. Figure 4 is the overlap image of Figure 2 and Figure 3. In Figure 4, red dots with higher intensity indicate point of intersection for higher number of circles.

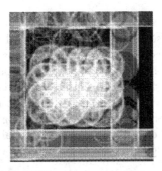

Fig. 5. Traces of circles after Hough transform

For circle detection in Hough transform, three dimensional parameter space ($x0$, $y0$, r) is used, where $x0$ and $y0$ are the coordinates of a circle center, r is the radius of a circle and its equation is in (1).

$$2(x - x_0) + 2(y - y_0) = 2r \qquad (1)$$

The parameter vector is $p = (x_0, y_0, r)$ \qquad (2)

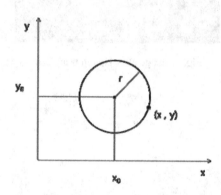

Fig. 6. Definition of circle in Hough Transform

The pseudo code for circle detection in Hough transform is as follows.

```
For each edge point (x0, y0)
   For (x0 = x0_min ; x0< x0_max x0++)
      For(y0= y0_min ; y0<= y0_max ; y0++)
         R=sqrt((x-x0)^2 + (y- y0)^2);
         Accumulator[r][x0][ y0]++;   //Voting
         Find local maxima in accumulator [r][x0][y0]
   that higher than threshold
```

Step 6) Selecting the correct peak: A red peak or a point indicates high frequency of matches for a circle. These points are the centers of the core-shells and therefore the number of red points is equal to the number of core-shells. Using this approach, we can also reduce the total number and remove some spurious noise while keeping the bright spots. If the core-shell's size is increased, the edge's size will increase as well and there will be many points clustered around the real point. Therefore, it is important to obtain correct threshold values by removing the noise around the real center point. Next task is to determine the number of real center points by counting the number of overlapping edges. In some cases, only half of the edges might show up due to overlapping images. In addition, as a core-shell's size increases, the number of pixels that are at the edge of a core-shell will increase as well.

2.2   Generalized Hough Transform

As shown in Figure 2, because of the high density of core-shells in an image, there are many overlapping cores, showing only those that are in foreground. Those in the back appear as partial spheres as they are shadowed. In order to account for those that are partially blocked, we will need to implement a method to count them even if they do not show complete outline. In such cases, a template is needed to count incomplete crescent-shaped objects using generalized Hough transform, which consists of modeling and detection steps.

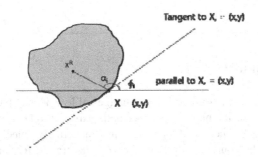

Fig. 7. Target shell modeling for non-symmetric shaped shells

Figure 7 shows an example of non-symmetric shaped object. In modeling step, after detecting the edge, following algorithm is performed to generate an R-Table. We need to build a separate R-table for each different object. The pseudo code for making R-Table (modeling step) is as follows. The R-table allows us to use the contour edge points and gradient angle to re-compute the location of the reference point.

Pick a reference point : $X^R=(x_c,y_c)$
For each edge point, $X_i = (x_i, y_i)$
  Calculate tangential angle ϕ_i
  Calculate $V_i=X^R-X_i$ and find norm r_i
  Direction angle α_i of v_i
  Store r_i, α_i in R-Table with an index of
  Ψ_i, quantized value of Φ_i
End for

Its detection step is described in the following pseudo code. At first, it calculates Φ_i for each pixel as in modeling step. Acc[][] in the pseudo code is the accumulated array (vector) of the candidate reference points X^R for a given model. Then it adds the vector to coordinate (x_i, y_i) of current edge pixel and finds out candidate standard point. Finally, possible locations of the object contour are given by local maximum in the array Acc[][].

Clear accumulator array : Acc[][] =0
For each edge point : $E_i =(x_i, y_i)$
   Calculate tangential angle Φ_i
   For every item in R-Table indexed by Ψ_m quantized value of Φ i
      Find $X^R_{m,j} =E_i+V^j_m$, where $V^j_m=r^j_m \angle \alpha^j_m$
      $X^R_{m,j}=E_i+V^j_m=(x^R_{m,j}, y^R_{m,j})$
      $Acc[y^R_{m,j}][x^R_{m,j}]<- Acc[y^R_{m,j}][x^R_{m,j}]+1$
   End For
End For

---

3   Experiments

When the data contain non-overlapping images of low density particles, it is relatively simple to determine the number of core-shells using straight forward methods. This is shown in Figure 8, where each particle can be accurately detected and the number of core-shells can be counted with high accuracy in straight forward manner. However, when the images contain high density of core-shells (shown in Figure 9), there are many overlapping particles making the determination of total number and size of particles difficult. For these types of images, we have successfully implemented Hough transform for irregularly shaped particles and successfully taken into account of non-symmetric crescent shaped particles.

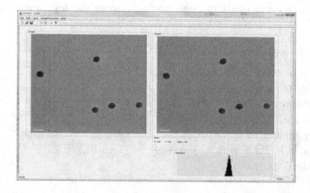

Fig. 8. Result of simple shaped core-shell structures without overlapping

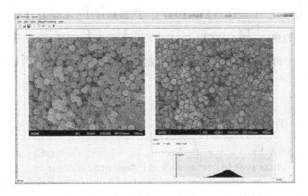

Fig. 9. Result of high density number of core-shells

4   Conclusion

We have developed a robust method for accurately analyzing the total number and size of particles from images. Using appropriate edge detection protocol together with generalized Hough Transform, we have successfully analyzed the images of uniform polymer particles synthesized by polymer chemists.

Improvements to accuracy may result from better edge detection methods using GHT based on pixel domain. Using generalized Hough transform references R-table, it is possible to generate templates automatically by using another algorithm and reference R-tables of template for each case.

References

1. Shapiro, L., Stockman, G.: Computer Vision. Prentice-Hall, Inc. (2001)
2. Ballard, D.H.: Generalizing the Hough Transform to Detect Arbitrary Shapes. Pattern Recognition 13(2), 111–122 (1981)
3. Basça, C.A., Taloş, M., Brad, R.: Rondomized Hough transform for ellipse detection with result clustering. In: Proceedings of International Conference on Computer as a Tool, vol. 2, pp. 1397–1400 (2005)
4. Ogawa, K., Ito, Y., Nakano, K.: Efficient Canny edge detection using a GPU. In: Proceedings of International Workshop on Advances in Networking and Computing, pp. 279–280 (2010)
5. Duda, R.O., Hart, P.E.: Use of the Hough Transformation to Detect Lines and Curves in Pictures. Comm. ACM 15, 11–15 (1972)
6. http://opencv.org/

A Gaussian Mixture Models Approach to Human Heart Signal Verification Using Different Feature Extraction Algorithms

Rasha Wahid[1,5], Neveen I. Ghali[1,5], Hala S. Own[2,5],
Tai-hoon Kim[3], and Aboul Ella Hassanien[4,5]

[1] Al-Azhar University, Faculty of Science, Cairo, Egypt
{rashawahid,neveen.ghali}@egyptscience.net
[2] National Research Institute of Astronomy and Geophysics, Helwan, Cairo, Egypt
[3] School of Information Science, University of Tasmania, Australia
taihoonn@empas.com
[4] Cairo University, Faculty of Computers and Information, Cairo, Egypt
[5] Scientific Research Group in Egypt (SRGE)
http://www.egyptscience.net

Abstract. In this paper the possibility of using the human heart signal feature for human verification is investigated. The presented approach consists of two different robust feature extraction algorithms with a specified configuration in conjunction with Gaussian mixture modeling. The similarity of two samples is estimated by measuring the difference between their negative log-likelihood of the features. To evaluate the performance and the uniqueness of the presented approach tests using a high resolution auscultation digital stethoscope are done for nearly 80 heart sound samples. The experimental results obtained show that the accuracy offered by the employed Gaussian mixture modeling reach up to 100% for 7 samples using the first feature extraction algorithm and 6 samples using the second feature extraction algorithm and varies with average 85%.

Keywords: Heart Sounds, Human verification, Gaussian Mixture Models, Feature Extraction.

1 Introduction

The need to identify persons correctly and irrevocably has existed for a very long time. The authorization to enter a building, to open a cupboard, to cross a border, to get money from a bank etc. is always connected to the identity of a person. It is therefore necessary to prove this identity in one way or the other. We call this procedure Verification. A person claims to be authorized or to have a certain identity, and this must then be verified. The problem is known to the police e.g. persons presenting an ID card which is doubtful. However the police are frequently confronted with another problem: Who is the person who has left a certain trace, e.g. a fingerprint, or who is this dead body? In this case we ask for the identity of an unknown person, we do Identification.

T.-h. Kim et al. (Eds.): MulGraB/BSBT/IUrC 2012, CCIS 353, pp. 16–24, 2012.

Knowledge-based and possession-based authentication mechanisms imply that users need to carry or remember the authenticator in order to be granted access to a system, building, or service. For comparing these traditional authenticators with authentication through biometrics, it is often argued that keys could be lost, stolen or easily duplicated and passwords could be forgotten. A serious problem is that the link between the legitimate individual and the authenticator is weak, and the authentication system has no means to distinguish between a designated owner of the authenticator and an impostor or a guesser. On the other hand, the general view is that biometric traits have an advantage in that they cannot be stolen, easily guessed or forgotten [1], [2], [4].

Biometrics are commonly categorized as either physiological or behavioral trait. Physiological traits (sometimes called passive traits) refer to fixed or stable human characteristics, such as fingerprints, shape and geometry of face, hands, fingers or ears, the pattern of veins, irises, teeth, the heart sound as well as samples of DNA. Physiological traits are generally existent on every individual and are distinctive and permanent, unless accidents, illnesses, genetic defects, or aging have altered or destroyed them. Behavioral traits (active traits) measure human characteristics represented by skills or functions performed by an individual. These include gait, voice, key-stroke and signature dynamics [3], [4].

Biometric recognition can be defined as automated methods for accurately recognizing individuals based on distinguishing physiological and/or behavioral traits. The technology of biometrics, in many different forms, is currently being used very widely for identification and authentication of individuals. In a non-automated way and on a smaller scale, parts of the human body and aspects of human behavior have been used for decades as a means of interpersonal recognition and authentication. For example, face recognition has been used for a long time in (non-automated) security and access applications. Safety, quality and technical compatibility of biometric technologies can be promoted through standards and standardization activities. Standards are essential for the deployment of biometric technologies on large-scale national and international applications.

The most salient feature in using the heart sound as a biometric is that it cannot be easily simulated or copied, as compared to other biometrics such as face, fingerprint or voice. Also, if the authorized user is not living, the system will not authorize him even if his fingerprint is still available or his iris is still valid. Furthermore, the proposed framework is relatively economical to install and maintain as it requires only an electronic stethoscope and a simple processor and database server for carrying out the identification task [5]. In this paper Gaussian mixture model is used to investigate the possibility of using the human heart signal feature for human verification, with two different robust feature extraction algorithms with a specified configuration.

The rest of the paper is organized as follows. Section (2) gives a brief introduction to the Gaussian mixture model technique used in the presented approach. Section (3) presents heart signal human verification approach in detail. Experimental results are discussed in Section (4) while Section (5) concludes and presents future work.

2   Gaussian Mixture Model: Preliminaries

Gaussian Mixture Models (GMM) is conventional and successful method for the speaker recognition approach [5]. Here, we will evaluate the suitability of this method for the proposed heart-sound-based identification. A Gaussian mixture density is a weighted sum of M component densities and is given by

$$p(\overrightarrow{x} \mid \lambda) = \sum_{i=1}^{M} P_i b_i(\overrightarrow{x}) \tag{1}$$

where $\overrightarrow{x}$ is a D-dimensional random vector, $b_i(\overrightarrow{x})$ are the component densities and P_i are the mixture weights, where $i = 1, ..., M$. Each component density is a D-variate Gaussian function of the form

$$b_i(\overrightarrow{x}) = \frac{1}{(2\pi)^{\frac{D}{2}} \Sigma_i^{\frac{1}{2}}} exp\{-\frac{1}{2}(\overrightarrow{x} - \overrightarrow{\mu_i})^T \Sigma_i^{-1} (\overrightarrow{x} - \overrightarrow{\mu_i})\} \tag{2}$$

with $\overrightarrow{\mu_i}$ mean vector and covariance matrix Σ_i. The mixture weight satisfies the constraint that

$$\sum_{i=1}^{M} P_i = 1 \tag{3}$$

The complete Gaussian mixture density is parameterized by the mean vector, covariance matrix and mixture weights from all component densities. These parameters are collectively represented by the notation

$$\lambda = P_i, \overrightarrow{\mu_i}, \Sigma_i, i = 1, ..., M \tag{4}$$

3   Heart Signal Human Verification Approach

The proposed heart signal human verification approach is composed of three main phases; Capturing heart signals phase, feature extraction and verification. These three phases are described in detail in the following section along with the steps involved and the characteristics feature for each phase.

3.1   Capturing Heart Signals

Using a Thinklabs Rhythm Digital Electronic Stethoscope (ds32a) [7] different heart sound samples had been collected from 80 different persons (40 Male, 40 Female), with different age range and cases of pregnant women, in addition to cases suffering different heart diseases and healthy people forming a general dataset.

3.2 Feature Extraction Phase

The goal of the heart sound feature extraction is to convert the original wave heart sound sample into a relatively low dimensional feature space matrix. Also, it used to filter the noise caused by the other internal organs (e.g lung) which may overlap the heart sound.This work used two feature extraction algorithms.

In feature extraction algorithm 1(FEal1), the heart sound wave sample is transformed using Fast Fourier transformation (FFt) use hamming window with length 256ms. Next, heart sound is filtered using Mel-spaced filer bank (Melfb). Then the spectral magnitude is calculated. Later the output filtered signal is compressed in the logarithm domain, followed by the discrete cosine transform with 24 coefficients.

In feature extraction algorithm 2(FEal2), the heart sound wave sample is transformed using short time discrete Fourier transformation (STDFT) use non-overlap system, with frame length 256ms and window length 500ms. Then the spectral magnitude is calculated. Then , heart sound spectrum is simply processed by filtering out the frequencies outside the range of 20-100Hz. Later the output filtered signal is compressed in the logarithm domain, followed by the discrete cosine transform with 24 coefficients. After that, hard thresholding with T=6 as a threshold value is applied. Finally, cepstral mean subtraction is applied.

3.3 Heart Sound Verification

For heart sound human verification, each heart signal is represented by a GMM. The expectation maximization (EM) algorithm is usually used due to its simplicity and quick convergence. The GMM model is trained for each person to calculate negative log-likelihood and then in testing by comparing with the Negative log-likelihood of all trained previously samples. The model can have one covariance matrix per Gaussian component *nodal covariance* , one covariance matrix for all Gaussian components in a model *grand covariance*, or a signal covariance matrix shared by all models *global covariance*. The covariance matrix can also be full or diagonal [6]. In this work, nodal diagonal covariance matrices are used for heart sounds models .

4 Experimental Results and Discussion

The heart sounds used in our experiments were recorded using a Thinklabs Rhythm Digital Electronic Stethoscope (ds32a). The digital stethoscope was placed on the chest of the participant seated in a relaxed position. The heart signal was captured using the Thinklabs phonocardialogy [7] software application via the sound card of the computer with a sampling rate of 2KHz and 16 bits. A Pentium IV 2 GHz Intel Core2 Duo personal computer is used. A total of 80 heart sounds were recorded from 80 participants (40 male and 40 female). Each heart sound recording is approximately 30sec. The training phase used the first 10sec while the testing used the next 10sec after a 10sec interval. These heart sounds are analyzed using MATLAB R2008a.

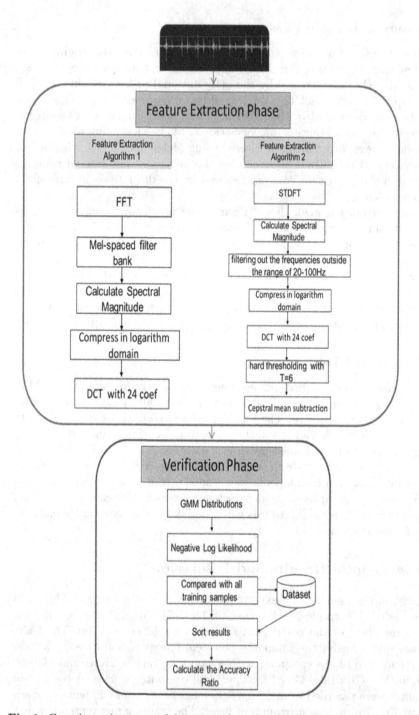

Fig. 1. Gaussian mixture models approach to human heart signal verification using different feature extraction algorithms

---

Algorithm 1. Classification and Verification

Input Feature extracted matrix $FEMx$

1: Distributed GMM using EM algorithm
2: Compute Negative log-likelihood ($Nlogl$).
   Verification stage:
3: Compare with $Nlogl$ of all trained samples and get the difference.
4: Sort the result.
5: Determine the order of the testing sample.
   accuracy measure (acc) using the following form:

$$Acc = \frac{Tn - (Ort - 1)}{Tn} \times 100\% \qquad (5)$$

Where Tn, is the total number of samples while Ort represents the order of tested samples.

Standard EM for mixture learning shows weakness which also affects the EM algorithm it requires knowledge of the number of components for reaching good local optimum. To overcome this difficulty, many deterministic criteria are proposed to estimate the appropriate number of components in GMM. Some examples of such model selection criterion are the Akaike information criterion (AIC), the minimum description length (MDL), the Bayesian inference criterion (BIC), etc [8]. In this study (AIC) is used to determine the best number of component. When samples was trained with 50, 40, 20, 10, 4, 2 components, It found that AIC decreased as number of component decreased. Since the number of components $m \geq 2$,so $m = 2$ is an optimal number of components.

The training sample of each person was compared with all training samples in the dataset. Comparison using $Nlogl$ was established. Then the result was sorted. Table(1) shows deferent accuracy ratios and the number of samples verified using feature extraction algorithm1 FEal1, and feature extraction algorithm FEal2.

Table 1. Comparison results of GMM with FEal1 and FEal2

Ratio	FEal1	FEal2
Recognized 100%	7	6
Over 95%	25	13
Between 95% and 90%	10	14
Between 90% and 80%	18	22
Less than 80%	20	25

Figure (2) shows the accuracy ratio of all samples.

Then samples categorized according to age. Figure (3) shows the accuracy ratio of different heart samples classified according to age.

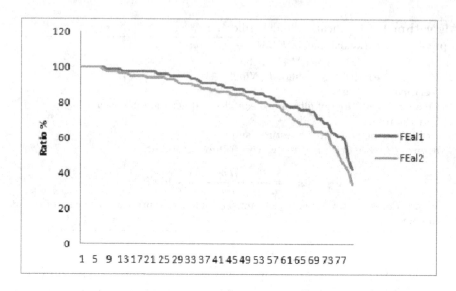

Fig. 2. Accuracy ratio for heart sound taken samples using FEal1 and FEal2

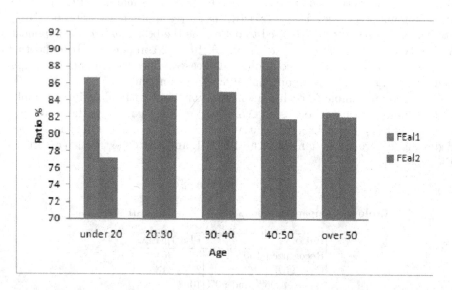

Fig. 3. Accuracy ratio according to the age of the taken samples using FEal1 and FEal2

Further investigation was done to detect the accuracy ratio for the collected heart sound samples according to the gender, figure (4) shows the accuracy ratio for the samples according the gender.

Fig. 4. Accuracy ratio according to the gender of the taken samples using FEal1 and FEal2

5   Conclusion and Further Scope of Research

In this work, the possibility of using human heart sound as a biometric for human identity verification was investigated. After a preliminary study for nearly 80 heart sound samples which were collected from 80 different persons. In our experiments, AIC was used to determine the best number of components. It found that AIC decreased as number of component decreased. So, using two components gave promising results.

Two different feature extraction algorithms were used. For the feature extraction algorithm1 the accuracy ratio was nearly the same for both male and female. But, it appeared to be more accurate in age under 50, specially between 20 and 50. The accuracy ratio reached 100% for 7 samples, over 95% for 25 samples, over 90% for 10 samples, over 80% for 18 and the rest samples accuracy ratio less than 80%. For the feature extraction algorithm2 the accuracy ratio was nearly the same for both male and female. But, it appeared to be more accurate in age over 20, specially between 20 and 40. The accuracy ratio reached 100% for 6 samples, over 95% for 13 samples, over 90% for 14 samples, over 80% for 22 and the rest samples accuracy ratio less than 80%.

Future work will concentrate on combining other biometric to achieve a more reliable authentication and identification, the effect of heart diseases or taking certain drags which effect on heart beats will be also tested. Finally, the change in heart rates caused by sporting or stop sporting after long interval of time.

References

1. Phua, K., Dat, T.H., Chen, J., Shue, L.: Human identification using heart sound. In: Workshop on Multimodal User Authentication, Toulouse, France, pp. 1–7 (May 2006)
2. du Preez, J.F., Von Solms, S.H.: Personal identification and authentication by using the way the heart beats. In: Electronic Proceedings of Information security, South Africa (ISSA), pp. 1–12 (July 2005)
3. Beritelli, F., Serrano, S.: Biometric identification based on frequency analysis of cardiac sounds. IEEE Transactions on Information Forensics and Security 2(3), 596–604 (2007)
4. El-Bendary, N., Al-Qaheri, H., Zawbaa, H.M., Hamed, M., Hassanien, A.E., Zhao, Q., Abraham, A.: HSAS: Heart Sound Authentication System. In: Second IEEE World Congress on Nature and Biologically Inspired Computing, Japan, NaBIC 2010, pp. 351–356 (December 2010)
5. Phua, K., Dat, T.H., Chen, J., Shue, L.: Heart sound as a biometric. Pattern Recognition 41, 906–919 (2008)
6. Reynolds, D.A., Rose, R.C.: Robust text-independent speaker identification using Gaussian mixture speaker models. IEEE Trans. Speech Audio Process 3, 72–83 (1995)
7. Thinklabs Rhythm Digital Electronic Stethoscope (ds32a), http://www.thinklsbamedical.com/
8. Yu, J.: Pattern recognition of manufacturing process signals using Gaussian mixture models-based recognition systems. Computers and Industrial Engineering 61, 881–890 (2011)

Design and Implementation of Real-Time Monitoring System Based on CPS for Telemedicine in Disaster Areas

Moonwon Choi, Jaesung Lee, and Inwhee Joe

Division of Computer Science and Engineering,
Hanyang University, Seoul, Korea
iwjoe@hanyang.ac.kr

Abstract. In this paper, we design and implement a real-time monitoring system based on CPS (Cyber Physical System) for telemedicine in disaster areas where the infrastructure is destroyed. In this situation, our monitoring system relies on a wireless sensor network (WSN) in ad-hoc mode, which provides a very low data rate. There are several types of real-time traffic to transmit over the low-rate WSN: voice, bio data, and pictures of victims or disaster scenes. First, network quality is judged by the delay of voice packets. Also, priority is given to voice packets over bio data or pictures, because they are critical for telemedicine. Voice packet sampling is performed at intervals of 100ms, because voice packets must arrive at the receiving side in 100ms at least. According to the network quality, one image is segmented in a different size. As a result, real-time voice, bio data & segmented pictures can be transmitted in a low-rate WSN network in 100ms. Furthermore, the health diagnosis center is able to identify the site conditions. Through this study, if the system is applied to a real disaster situation, it will be effectively utilized for rescue activities by rescue workers.

Keywords: Telemedicine, Cyber Physical System, Voice Communication, Packet Scheduling, Packet Segmentation.

1 Introduction

The world is constantly damaged by disaster situations like fire, explosions, collapses, traffic accidents and environmental pollution. In Korea, nevertheless, there is infrastructure for an emergency network; many casualties were caused by loss of communication in, for example, Yeonpyeong Island attack, and the Daegu subway ire. Therefore, telemedicine system suitable for destroyed-infrastructure environment is essential for survivors.

Current infrastructure technologies are easy to destroy in real disaster situations and it is difficult to utilize rescue activity and grasp the situation. Therefore we present a suitable telemedicine system for emergency patients and survivors in disaster areas based on ad-hoc system.

A CPS (Cyber Physical System) is defined as a system featuring a tight link between the computational and physical elements. Our monitoring system is based on

T.-h. Kim et al. (Eds.): MulGraB/BSBT/IUrC 2012, CCIS 353, pp. 25–32, 2012.
© Springer-Verlag Berlin Heidelberg 2012

CPS for telemedicine in disaster areas where the infrastructure is destroyed. In this situation, it relies on an ad-hoc WSN in order to interact with the physical world for real-time monitoring. Also, our monitoring system is a computational system developed to work for telemedicine over the Internet cyber world.

Table 1. Number of Regional Earthquakes

	Regions	Number of earthquakes	Proportion (%)
1	Asia	19	65.5
2	Europe	4	13.8
3	Africa	4	13.8
4	Latin America	2	6.8
5	North America	0	0
6	Oceania	0	0
Total		29	

Table 2. .Number of Regional Floods

	Regions	Number of floods	Proportion (%)
1	Asia	50	50
2	Europe	19	19
3	Africa	18	18
4	Latin America	7	7
5	North America	3	3
6	Oceania	3	3
Total		100	

Through the system, real-time voice & bio data can be transmitted to a health diagnosis center. To overcome the low data rate of WSN, video streams will be captured and transferred to a high-quality image packet. Also, the image packet will be transmitted to a health diagnosis center.

2   System Design and Implementation

The goal of performing telemedicine monitoring is to take appropriate action for survivors by communication between the disaster area and health diagnosis center. For this action, we need independent WSN devices suitable for disaster status and a consolidated system for telemedicine monitoring, a packet scheduling for reliable and effective communication in low-rate WSN environment. For this reason, first we designed the telemedicine monitoring system as shown in Figure 1. Second, we improved the throughput by applying the packet scheduling.

2.1   Telemedicine Monitoring System

System Overview: A telemedicine monitoring system was designed for survivors in disaster areas. It can transmit information about the disaster area accurately and it is possible to communicate with rescue people and health diagnosis center through voice data. As shown in Figure 1, we divided the system into two parts, disaster area and health diagnosis center. Between the two parts, there are relay sensors for the

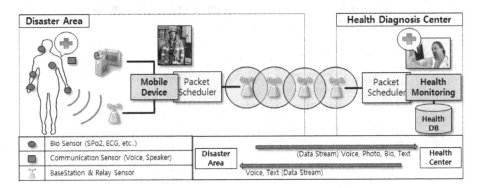

Fig. 1. Architecture of telemedicine monitoring system

independent WSN network. First, in the disaster area, rescue workers find survivors and transmit the collected data through sensors. In detail, all data (bio, voice, and video) is collected by the relevant sensor and collected by the mobile device. Also, packet scheduling and segmenting is performed by packet scheduler, because of the low-bandwidth in WSN environment. It will badly affect real-time voice & bio data by transmitting the video data of high volume. Second, health diagnosis center serve rescuers through the communication by voice & text data and it can estimate the situation through the received data.

The Method of Communication Settings Suitable for Disaster: The disaster area may have communication difficulties with other places because of destroyed infrastructure. Therefore we utilize the independent WSN networks. To perform the telemedicine monitoring, collect four kinds of data, video, voice, bio, and text data. Among these, video data is most influential data for communication. To transmit the video data in real-time, networks need about 30 MB/s bandwidth, which is standard for high-quality 960x544. However, 802.15.4 WSN cannot accommodate such bandwidth that has a maximum bandwidth of 256kps. Therefore we propose a snapshot method of transmission for transmitting visual information at a low-rate. It transmits the snapshot only at critical points or when the user needs it. Because video data has unnecessary information such as repetitive data, if we apply the system, communication resources can be used effectively. Also snapshotted data is segmented according to network status; it can be more effective communication.

2.2   Packet Scheduling Based on Packet Segmentation

As mentioned above, packet scheduling is essential for WSN. Therefore, we applied the priority queuing method for real-time data & non-real-time data and segmented only high-volume video data according to network status. Figure 2 shows the method of the packet scheduling and packet segmentation flow for telemedicine monitoring system.

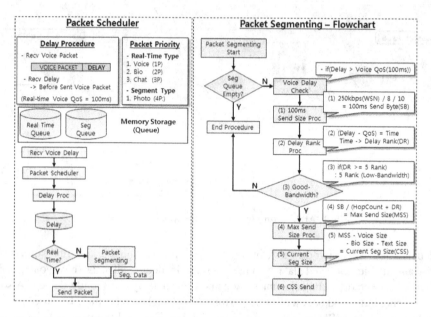

Fig. 2. Method of the packet scheduling & packet segment flow for telemedicine monitoring system

In the voice packet, a network status delay report is enveloped because voice data is the most frequently transmitted. Delay information is used to photo packet segmentation later. There are two kinds of queue storing the packet, real time queue and segment queue. The reason for dividing the queue into packets is the real time queue has high priority conditions that have to be sent immediately and packets in the segment queue have fewer time limits and are transmitted according to network status. Also, segment queue includes the image data for effective usage of resources. Packet segment size is determined by the delay report in the audio packet. As above in Figure 3, segment size is determined by calculation of the transmission bandwidth moment according to the delay rank of current network status. To explain further, (1) is determined to packet size (SB) possible to be transmitted in 100ms. (2) is measured the delay in ms unit and the set delay time rank 1,2,3,4,5 in 100ms intervals. In (3), if the rank is higher than rank 5, packet is not transmitted, because is not a proper bandwidth. In (4), Max Send Size (MSS) is calculated using hop-count and delay rank, because delay is different according to hop-count of the routing path. Finally in (5), sizes of high-priority packets are subtracted from MSS. It is CSS (Current Segment Size). Then, the image data segmentation is performed as much as CSS. To prevent drop & delay of real time packet as much as possible, delay the larger, giving priority to real-time data transmission.

3   Performance Evaluation

In this section we detail the implementation of the real-time monitoring system based on CPS for telemedicine in the disaster area.

3.1   Simulation Model

We utilize the Windows 7 OS as a system development environment and development tool is Visual C 6.0, MySql. Also, Intel 8051 8 bit Micro-Controller is used to voice sensor processor and ATmega128 is used to bio sensor processor. Also, the RF Chip is a CC2420 2.4GHz ZigBee/IEEE 802.15.4 Protocol. Finally, data rate is maximum 250Kbps. The system development structure is shown below in Fig 3.

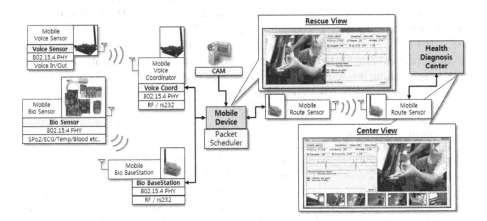

Fig. 3. Development architecture of telemedicine system

As shown above in Figure 3, we designed the system. First, there is a coordinator for sensing the voice data. Second, bio data is collected by multiple sensors and then integrated by the base-station. Third, video data is collected by CAM and then directly transmitted to mobile device through the USB. At this moment, the mobile device displays the collected data in U.I and then transmits the data to the health diagnosis center according to network status.

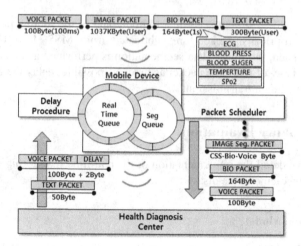

Fig. 4. Method of implemented packet scheduling

Also, the mobile device performs a role in that it receives collected data from health diagnosis and then sends it to UI (User Interface) or voice sensor, functioning as a router. Shown above in Figure 4, is the implemented queuing method. There are four kinds of packets; video, voice, bio, and text packet. These pickets' real transmission capacity and generation cycle are 100 bytes (100ms), 1037 Kbytes (user), 164 bytes (1 second), 300 bytes (user). Delay information which is enclosed in the audio packet is the difference between transmission time and arrival time. Based on this information, image is segmented as same as CSS (MSS - voice size - bio size - text size), and then transmit with real-time data.

3.2 Simulation Results

In Figure 5, we performed the simulation by OPNET modeler 14.5. We composed the two source nodes and two route nodes. Also, to change the network status, inflicted the delay every 30 seconds about 10%, 20% and 30%. And we composed the treads, packet scheduler and packet segmenting process in the SRC node. Figure 5 is a simulation result confirming the packet drop and loss. On the left side, it performs the proposed packet segmentation. On the opposite side there is no segmentation.

As shown in the results, the left side transmits the packet more than right side, relatively, because the high-quality image packet was segmented less. Therefore, the number of packets was greater than on the right side. As shown in Recv Packet Count of the left side, almost all the packets were no drop & loss. However, the other side is shown that it did not guarantee the Quality of Service (QoS). The following Figure 6, compared the ETE (end to end) delay and delay of voice and image

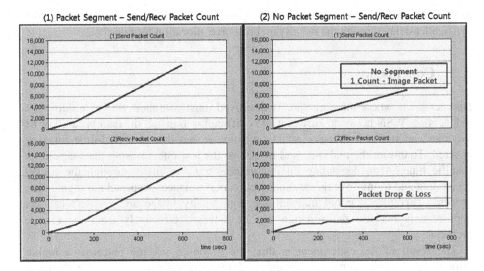

Fig. 5. Comparison of Packet Drop & Loss in proposed segmentation environment and non-segmentation environment

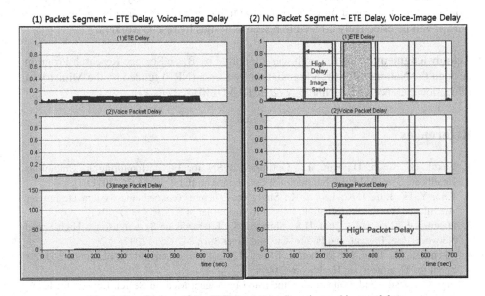

Fig. 6. Comparison of the ETE (end to end), voice and image delay

As shown in the result, voice QoS shows the delay under the 100ms. Therefore, there is no effect to audio-communication and can be transmitted the high quality images. Despite the changing of the network status, the delay was controlled by the delay report enclosed in the audio packet. The conclusion is that telemedicine monitoring was very difficult in low-rate of WSN when there was an ability to adapt to the low bandwidth and constantly changing network environment. Also, it shows the smaller delay through the priority and resource allocation for real-time.

4   Conclusion

Disaster areas where infrastructure is destroyed must communicate by building the independent WSN network. However, it is difficult to transmit the data because of its low-rate and it has a decisive effect on voice & bio data that real-time must be ensured. To ensure the real-time and overcome the low-rate, transmit the snapshot in specific time. Also, depending on importance, transmit firstly through the packet scheduling and to improve the communication performance, proposed the segmenting process. Therefore it could transmit the high-quality image and rescuers can act appropriately because the situation can be assessed effectively from the remote location.

The result of the experiment is this; the proposed scheme performs a higher throughput than the common scheme, and the data drop is lower than common scheme. It is possible to transmit important voice & bio data without interruption, because the image data of high-volume is segmented according to network status and transmitted to control center. Therefore, through this study, if the real-time monitoring system based on CPS for telemedicine in a disaster area is applied in real time, it will be effectively utilized in rescue activities by rescue workers.

Acknowledgments. This research was supported by Basic Science Research Program through the National Research Foundation by Korea (NRF) funded by the Ministry of Education, Science and Technology (2012R1A1A3012227).

References

1. Bakul, G., Singh, D., Kim, D.: Optimized WSN for ECG Monitoring in Ubiquitous Healthcare System. In: 4th International Conference on ICIS, pp. 23–26 (2011)
2. Kim, Y.-H., Lim, I.-K., Lee, J.-K.: Study on Efficient Telemedicine System Design for Ambulance Emergency Situation. International Journal of KIMICS 9(1) (2011)
3. Hahm, J.-S., Lee, H.L., Choi, H.S., Shimizu, S.: Telemedicine System using a High-Speed Network. Past, Present, and Future: Gut and Liver 3(4), 247–251 (2009)
4. Akematsu, Y., Tsuji, M.: Economic: Effect of eHealth: Focusing on the Reduction of Days Spent for Treatment. In: Healthcom (2009)
5. Luo, G.: Design and Evaluation of the iMed Intelligent Medical Search Engine. In: ICDE IEEE 25th International Conference on DOI, pp. 1379–1390 (2009)
6. Iantovics, B.: The CMDS Medical Diagnosis System. In: International Symposium on DOI, pp. 246–253 (2007)
7. Lu, X.-L.: System Design and Development for a CSCW Based Remote Oral Medical Diagnosis System. In: ICLMC, vol. 6, pp. 3698–3703 (2005)

High-Capacity Blind Binary Text Document Watermarking Scheme Robust to Print-and-Scan Operations

De Li[1], Mo You[1], and JongWeon Kim[2,*]

[1] Dept. of Computer at Yanbian University, China
`leader1223@ybu.edu.cn`, `947664337@qq.com`
[2] Dept. of Copyright Protection at Sangmyung University, Korea
`jwkim@smu.ac.kr`

Abstract. An algorithm of high-capacity blind text watermarking is presented that is robust to print-and-scan operations. First, binary images of Chinese text characters are segmented depends on the complexity of the characters: each character image is segmented to embedded part, adjust part, and dislodge part. After segmentation, a quantization function is built on the basis of invariables during printing-scanning. The watermark is embedded via the strategy of flipping pixels at the characters boundaries. This method exploits human visual masking characteristics to reduce the distortion degree in the text image. Experimental results indicate that the method is robust to common attacks and the watermark can be extracted without original document.

Keywords: text watermark, print-scan, quantification, high-capacity.

1   Introduction

With the development of national information in many countries, more and more government and other relevant departments have begun to distribute contracts and other important documents directly in digital form. This has brought needs for strong digital watermarking schemes that can guarantee the integrity and authenticity of such documents. However, many files are spread through printing and scanning, which can disrupt the watermark.

Digital watermarking embedded information through the redundant data in such strategy that it cannot be perceived by the human senses [1-4]. However, the conventional frequency-domain watermarking schemes [5-6] do not produce good results with plain text image documents. Instead, better visual results can be obtained by flipping single pixel in each text character, but such scheme has very low embedding capacity. It depends on the number of characters directly in the text image document. Thus, there is urgent need to improve the embedding capacity for individual characters.

---

* Corresponding author.

T.-h. Kim et al. (Eds.): MulGraB/BSBT/IUrC 2012, CCIS 353, pp. 33–40, 2012.

This paper present a high embedding capacity for text image watermarking that can resistive to print-and-scan operations. Experimental results show that the algorithm has well imperceptible, it has very good robustness and can resist attack of print and scan.

This paper is organized as follows. Section 2 presents the fundamental theory about the scheme. Section 3 describes the text image algorithms for watermark embedding and extraction. Section 4 presents the results of experiments on the robustness against various common attacks. Finally, the main conclusions are presented in the last section.

2   Invariants During Print and Scanning

2.1   Invariants in Printing and Scanning

The process of printing and scanning will import random noise [7], Fig. 1 is the compare of Chinese text before-and-after print and scan. The process of import noise can be described as convolution process approximately. With this assumption, preference [8] and [9] concluded that the proportion of the black pixels in a single character, then the average number of black pixels among all characters remain invariant during printing and scanning. We employ the same assumption in the design of the present algorithm.

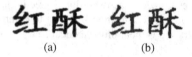

(a)   (b)

Fig. 1. Comparison of original text (a) with printed-and-scanned text (b)

2.2   Data Hiding in Character Boundaries

A binary text image has the only pixel value 0 or 1, so few pixels changed would cause highly perceivable distortion in the character images. Therefore, many binary image watermarking algorithms only flip the boundaries pixels of characters. Furthermore, to identify pixels flipped that can be modified with the least visual distortion, Wu and Liu defined a function f(x) for 3×3 window centered on each boundary pixel x as Fig. 2 , we only modify the simple boundary points[10].

y_1	y_8	y_7
y_2	x	y_6
y_3	y_4	y_5

Fig. 2. Boundary pixel points of pixel x

Table 1 presents the scores of boundary points in a binary text image according to the Ref.[10] from Mrs. WU. Larger scores indicate pixels that can be changed with less visual distortion. In our paper, we use the pixel whose score is higher than 0.1.

Table 1. Scores for the boundary points of a binary image

template	11W	12W	31W	4W	51W	71W	6W	52W
score	0.01	0.01	0	0.62	0.38	0.38	0.8	0
template	2W	32W	72W	11B	12B	2B	31B	
score	0.125	0.38	0.25	0.38	0.25	0.38	0.38	
template	32B	4B	51B	52B	6B	71B	72B	
score	0	0.625	0	0.8	0.125	0.01	0.01	

The flipping strategy for boundary points as follows: 1) Find the simple boundary points. 2) For white boundary points, first flip the types of 51W, 6W, 71W, and 72W and then flip the types of 4W and 32W. 3) When need to minus point, flip the black boundary point, first flip the types of 11B, 12B, 2B, and 31B and then flip the types of 4B and 52B. 4) For improving the visual quality, when a neighboring pixel of the same color has been flipped, that point could not been flipped. The strategy does not degrade the visual quality of the final embedded image.

3 Proposed Watermarking Algorithm

3.1 Embedding of Watermark

First, the binary text image is processed to segmented characters. Character with less pixels should not be flipped, otherwise it would influence the visual effect. Thus, characters with fewer pixels could not embedded watermark. In order to keep the ratio of black and white pixels invariant, we divided the whole text image to embedded part, adjust part and dislodge part. The number of pixel flipped in embedded part, the same number pixel should flipped opposite in adjust part. A threshold T is set to balance complex of the character pixel, and it is a parameter as dislodge the image of character. Define A as the embedded part of the text image, B as the adjust part, C as the dislodge part. Suppose the pixels in parts A and B are $x_1, x_2, ... x_{N_A}$ and $y_1, y_2 ... y_{N_B}$ in single character image, then we compute the average value for all the pixels in character image as follows:

$$m = 1/(N_A + N_B + N_c)\left(\sum_{i=1}^{N_A} x_i + \sum_{i=1}^{N_B} y_i + \sum_{i=1}^{N_c} c_i\right) \tag{1}$$

1. Segment each character image into four parts and processing the pixels in each block.
2. For a watermark comprising the binary sequence $w_1, w_2...w_{N_A}$, where the value of w_i is zero or one. Set the value of x_i to $\tilde{x}_i$ such that the value of $\tilde{x}_i$ is an odd or even multiple of k (k > 0) which is the closest step length. In this part k is a step length we selected. Then, compute the value of the flipped black pixels $\Delta x_A^{'}$, for each four parts of the character image in embedded part A. Next, compute the value of Δ_i for all pixels changed in the embedded part.
3. In order to keep the total number of pixels as a constant, the flipped pixels in the embedded part must be flipped back in the adjust part. The number of adjust pixel as follows:

$$\sum_{i=1}^{N_B} \tilde{y}_i - \sum_{i=1}^{N_B} y_i = -\Delta_i \qquad (2)$$

4. If the number of flipped pixels is greater than zero, flip corresponding number of white boundary points. If the number of flipped pixels is less than zero, flip corresponding number of black boundary points.

3.2   Extraction of Watermark

The proposed scheme realized blind extraction of the watermark as follows:

1. Segment the watermarked text image to identify all character images that are in the embedded part, adjust part, and dislodge part.
2. Segment each character image into four parts and process the pixels in each four character image.
3. Compute the number of black pixels in each character of image A and B, which are $\tilde{x}_1, \tilde{x}_2,...\tilde{x}_{N_A}$ and $\tilde{y}_1, \tilde{y}_2...\tilde{y}_{N_B}$. Compute the average value for the entire character image as follows:

$$\tilde{m} = 1/(N_A + N_B + N_c)\left(\sum_{i=1}^{N_A}\tilde{x}_i + \sum_{i=1}^{N_B}\tilde{y}_i + \sum_{i=1}^{N_c}\tilde{c}_i\right) \qquad (3)$$

4. Extract the watermark of each single character image: if the value of $\tilde{x}/(K\tilde{m})$ is an even number, then the watermark bit is zero, otherwise it is one.

3.3   Performance Evaluation

The performance of watermarking system mainly reflected on the aspects of imperceptibility and robustness. However, there is no standard and objective method could

evaluate the visual distortion. We evaluate the performance by the visual effect sub-
jectively. We estimate the robustness by the bit error rate (BER) when to extract
watermark from attacked text image.

4   Results and Discussion

For the binary text image with 160 Chinese characters, the dislodge part has 40 character images, the adjust part has 33 character images, and the embedded part has 87
character images. The algorithm segments the embedded part into three sections and
repeat embeds a random sequence three times. Four bits of the watermark are embedded in each character image, and the length of the step is 0.095.

In order to improve the robustness, the watermark is extracted three times, and the
finally value depends on the probability pixel value is 0 or 1.

In contrast with the scheme proposed in Ref. [10] where a single bit is embedded in
each character image, our scheme can embed four bits, as shown in Fig. 3.

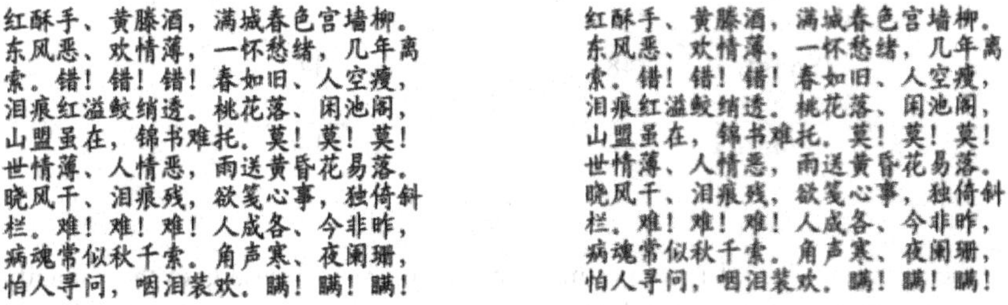

Fig. 3. Embedded a single bit and four bits in a single character image

We can see that the text image with four bits embedded has not greatly distorted.
Thus, our scheme has four times in the capacity than the scheme proposed in Ref [10].

In addition, when compared with the original text, the text embedded four bits watermark has little influence on visual distortion, as in Fig. 4.

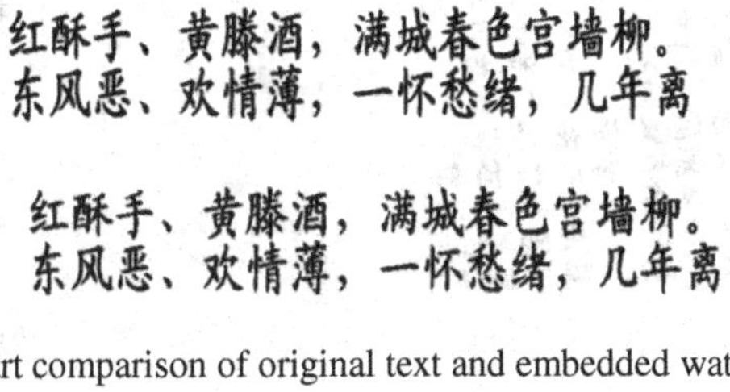

Fig. 4. The part comparison of original text and embedded watermark text

We can see some coarsening or thinning of individual strokes in some characters.
However, the difference is hardly obvious. It shows that the embedded watermark is
sufficiently imperceptible.

Compared the capacity of the algorithm for different text images (Fig. 3 as text 1 and Fig. 2 as text 2) and for different character fonts, the experiment result as shown in Tables 2 and 3.

Table 2. Comparison of capacity

	Proposed algorithm (four bits per character)	Ref. [10]
Text 1	100	25
Text 2	392	99

Table 3. Test results for different character fonts

Font	Number of embedded bits	Number of bits extracted
Kaiti 4	348	342
Songti 4	348	340
Songti 5	348	336

For the number of pixel in some image material has decreased, so the capacity of our algorithm may less than four times in some text material experience, but the number is closed to four times. Because extract process has some degree of lost, so the extract data would have some loss, but the loss is very little.

The proposed algorithm also can resist rotation attacks, as shown in Fig. 5, where the image was scanned at an angle.

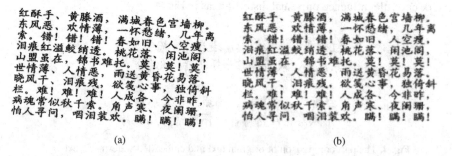

(a)   (b)

Fig. 5. Rotation attack (a) and rectified image (b)

In addition, as shown in Fig. 6, the proposed algorithm is robust to many attacks, such as the attack of salt-and-pepper noise and Gaussian noise.

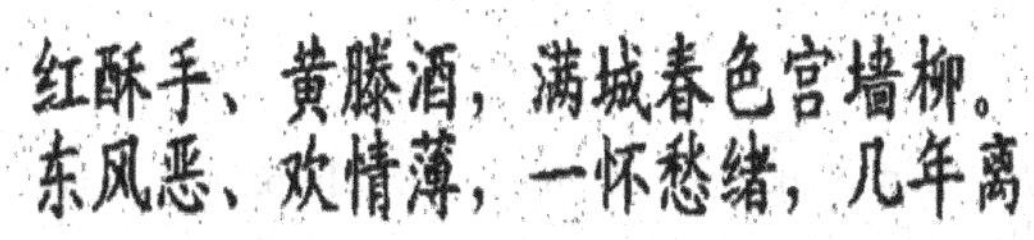

红酥手、黄藤酒，满城春色宫墙柳。
东风恶、欢情薄，一怀愁绪，几年离

Fig. 6. Text image with salt-and-pepper noise addition

With noise added at different image positions, the BER of the extracted watermark will vary. Hence, we show the average BER for five repetitions of each attack parameter, as shown in Fig. 7.

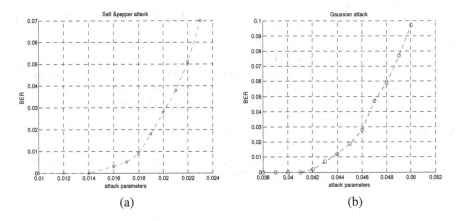

(a)　　　　　　　　　　　　　　(b)

Fig. 7. Average BER of image with salt-and-pepper (a) and Gaussian (b) noise addition

As shown in Fig. 7, the watermark can still be extracted with low BER after different type attacks of noise. Furthermore, scaling the image to 85%, the BER is 0.081 in the extracted watermark, which is quite low.

5　Conclusions

This paper proposed a high-capacity text watermarking algorithm, with the pixel flipping strategy, it produces better visual results than the algorithm based on the frequency domain. It can reasonably resist most attacks such as noise addition, rotation, and scaling. And it also achieves four times in embedding capacity per character as that of the scheme of Wu and Liu [10]. Thus, the proposed scheme achieves higher embedding capacity with little reduction in robustness.

Acknowledgements . This research project was supported by the Ministry of Culture, Sports and Tourism (MCST) and the Korea Copyright Commission in 2011.

References

1. Petitcolas, F.A.P., Anderson, R.J., Kuhn, M.G.: Information Hiding-a survey. Proc. IEEE 87, 1062–1078 (1999)
2. Kim, H.Y., Mayer, J.: Data hiding for binary document robust to print-scan, photocopy and geometric distortion. In: Proc. 10th Brazilian Symposium on Computer Graphics and Image Processing, Washington, DC, USA, pp. 105–112 (2007)
3. Cox, I., Kilian, J., Leighton, T., Shamoon, T.: Secure spread spectrum watermarking for multimedia. IEEE Trans. Image Processing 6, 1673–1687 (1997)
4. Kim, J., et al.: Watermarking two dimensional data object identifier for authenticated distribution of digital multimedia contents. Signal Processing: Image Communication 25, 559–576 (2010)
5. Brassil, J., Low, S., Maxemchuk, N.: Copyright protection for the electronic distribution of text documents. Proc. IEEE 87, 1181–1196 (1999)
6. Liu, Y., Sun, X., Gan, C.: An efficient linguistic steganography for Chinese text. In: Proc. ICME 2007, Beijing, pp. 2094–2097 (2007)
7. Sun, X., Chen, H.: Mathematical representation of a Chinese character and its applications. International Journal of Pattern Recognition and Artificial Intelligence 16, 735–747 (2002)
8. Qi, W., Li, X., Yang, B., Cheng, D.-F.: Document watermarking scheme for information tracking. Journal of Communications 29, 183–190 (2008)
9. Yang, H., Kot, A.C.: Pattern-based data hiding for binary image authentication by connectivity preserving. IEEE Transactions on Multimedia 9, 475–486 (2007)
10. Wu, M., Liu, B.: Data hiding in binary image for authentication and annotation. IEEE Transactions on Multimedia 6, 528–538 (2004)

A Study on the Subjectivity of Sensibility Quality Factors Affecting the Selection of the Smart-Phone

Young Ju Lee

Chungwoon University, Department of Multimedia, Namjang-ri. 21,
HongSeong, ChungNam, Republic of Korea
yjlee@chungwoon.ac.kr

Abstract. This study analyzed the sensitivity quality factors that are important in choosing smart-phone using PQ method of Q methodology. It was possible to find representative types such as sensibility focusing type, use-convenience focusing type and stability focusing type by the analysis. The discriminative sensibility focusing type thinks personality expression and social pride as important and this type prefers differentiation from others. The sensibility quality causes of sensibility focusing type are uniqueness, fun, curiosity, surprise, fashion, attracting others' view, ostentation and emotional attachment. The use-convenience focusing type prefers convenience cumulated by personal experience. This type thinks the sensibility quality causes such as comfort, freedom, expandability and control of device as important. The stability focusing type prefers familiarity by use experience, attachment by intimacy and harmony with personal image as important. This type thinks the sensibility quality causes such as experience, habits, intimacy, conciseness and fun as important.

Keywords: Subjectivity, Sensibility Quality factor, Selection of the smart-phone.

1   Introduction

Ericsson is the world's largest communication equipment manufacturer. It its recent report, Ericsson stated that worldwide smart-phone users were 700 million in 2011 and it will quadruple to 3.1 billion six years later in 2017. Ericsson forecasts mobile communication user in 2017 shall reach 8.9 billion in 2017; therefore, 30% of mobile communication user will use smart-phone in 2017. According to Gartner survey, the market share of Samsung smart-phone in the 2nd quarter of 2012 was 21.6%. Nokia 19.9% and Apple 6.9% followed Samsung [1].

The number of smart-phone users in Korea had been just 0.75 million in 2009. However, it became 7.2 million in 2010, 20 million in 2011 and it will be more than 35 million in 2012. According to another forecast by Roa Consulting, there will be more than 42 million smart-phone users in Korea in the end of 2012. The smart-phone users are rapidly increasing like above; however, only limited brands of smart-phone are being sold in the market. As anyone can easily expect, Galaxy series of Samsung

T.-h. Kim et al. (Eds.): MulGraB/BSBT/IUrC 2012, CCIS 353, pp. 41–48, 2012.

and I-Phone series of Apple established two-top structure in the second half of 2011. HTC had launched premium grade smart-phones several times in Korea; however, they eventually withdrew from Korean market. Other foreign phones such as Sony Ericsson and Motorola even have difficulty in establishing launching plan in Korea for late 2012 except the launching of one Mp3 player.

Consumer choice always changes. Renowned design scholar Professor Donald Norman said that "Sensibility design that moves the emotion of consumers has the biggest and immediate impact on the purchase decision of consumers. A product cannot succeed just because it has beautiful outlook design or it has excellent functions". There are many smart-phone manufacturers home and abroad; however, only a few of them are chosen by consumers. The curiosity on the cause of this inevitably and directly led us to the question on why consumers buy certain brands of smart-phone. Accordingly, this study explores the subjectivity of consumer regarding the factors that have impact on their smart-phone choice.

2   Theoretical Review

The design quality causes that users perceive are not systemized yet because they are different dependent on researcher. The quality cause study in the area of interactive design has been done mostly on websites [2]. The most representative website quality cause classification is classifying the causes into functional causes and non-functional causes. Herzberg classified the needs of organization in human behavior dimension into hygiene causes and motivator causes [3].

J.H, Seo and G.P, Lee drew the sensibility quality vocabularies of users on mobile phone by way of card-sorting method with a specialist group. Seo and Lee classified the quality dimension into six dimensions such as usefulness, ease of use, aesthetic, stimulation, identity and harmony after statistical test process [4].

Kano approached the subject from the perspective of user expectation. Kano's classification is three dimensions; which are basic causes, performance causes and interest causes dependent on product and service quality model [5]. Zhang & von Dran evaluated actual websites using Kano's model. They established a ranking of quality points by applying 42 detail causes on 6 kinds of websites [6].

2.1   Q Methodology to Learn Subjectivity

Q methodology had been created by William Stevenson. The subjective areas such as attitude, belief, conviction and value had been ignored in science before Stevenson. He created a methodology integrating the concepts related to philosophical, psychological and statistical measurement in order to study them from objective viewpoint. It is a statistical method that can analyze the subjectivity of men with tactics. Since it can objectively study the concepts like awareness, values, attitude and conviction of consumers, it is possible to apply it to confirmative studies such as explorative studies and theoretical tests that generate hypothesis. Compared to the R methodology which has transverse characteristic by having large number of samples,

Q methodology is quite useful in the study of consumer behaviour because it enables in-depth study on individuals and small groups.

The Q methodology also satisfies overall and qualitative approach method which complements existing quantitative studies; therefore, it can remove the relation between subjectivity and objectivity. H.G, Kim, Chairman of Korean Society for Scientific Study on Subjectivity (Korea Q Society), said on the difference between qualitative study method and Q methodology that "the qualitative study method includes subjectivity dependent on the capability of researcher; while the Q methodology is finding the subjectivity of men from study object". Q methodology also scientifically measures the subjectivities of men such as values, attitude and conviction. It begins from the definition of doer, not from the hypothesis of researcher, and it finds the hypothesis instead of testing the hypothesis. Psychology is a research/analysis method widely used in social science. Now, the Q methodology has been proved of its appropriateness and usefulness in all areas where men's subjectivity is involved.

2.2   PQ Method

PQ method is one of the analysis programs used in Q research with Quanl. The PQ method is a program devised for easy entry of Q Sort data. PQ method has the advantage that the cause analysis is possible by Centroid method in addition to PCA, primary cause analysis. With PQ method, it is possible to draw the causes by Varimax method, when the cause is in rotation, or, by judgmental rotation through two-dimensional plotting [7].

3   Design of Study

3.1   Selection of Q Sample and Q Statement

More than 300 Q samples had been collected from books, newspaper articles, Internet articles and the content of FGI (Focus Group Interview) with a user group consisting of 55 persons. Then 47 Q statements related to smart-phone which fit with study purpose were finally extracted using unstructured method.

Table 1. 47 Q Statement

No	Statement	No	Statement
1	Method familiar to use	2	having many convenient functions
3	OS being stable	4	A/S being easy
5	grip being good	6	speech quality being excellent
7	screen conversion sliding being smooth	8	updating being easy
9	data transmission being fast	10	design with personality
11	being large	12	thin and slim design
13	luxurious design	14	diverse colours being offered
15	neat design	16	refined design

Table 1. (*continued*)

17	simple design	18	charming design
19	glamorous design	20	fresh design
21	beautiful design	22	stylish design
23	glossy design	24	angular design
25	round-shaped square containing a curve	26	plastic appearance material
27	metallic appearance material	28	appearance design with bends
29	appearance design with a pattern	30	flat design
31	natural touch	32	keypad size being large
33	screen and color being sharp	34	appl being diversified
35	being sturdy	36	being light weighted
37	importance of charging method and time	38	new functions being plenty
39	storage capacity being large	40	Loading speed being fast
41	foreign product	42	unique design
43	dignified design	44	heavy design
45	superior feeling	46	manufacturer
47	diverse accessories		

3.2   Selection of P Samples

P samples are males and females in their 10s to 40s who use smart-phones now, who want to buy new smart-phone, or, who want to change smart-phone. Their demographic characteristics are as following.

Table 2. P Samples

Teen's	20's	30's	40's	Male	Female
2	23	4	1	10	20

3.3   Q Sorting

Q Sorting has 'most positive' (+4) and 'most negative' (-4). The Q sorting of this study is as following.

Table 3. Q Sorting Table

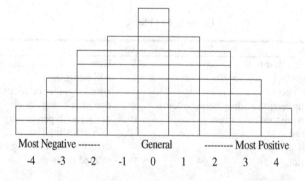

Most Negative -------   General   --------- Most Positive

-4   -3   -2   -1   0   1   2   3   4

4   Analysis

This study used PQ Method Version 2.11. The data from Q sorting went through cause analysis by Centroid method. Then judgmental rotation was performed. Among the relations with causes, optimum causes were found and rotation results that show high loading values were obtained. Then the rotation was finished and three causes with unique value bigger than 1 were selected as significant causes.

Table 4. Eigen Value

	1st Type	2nd Type	3rd Type
Eigen Value	10.2391	2.0298	1.0457
Loding's Percentage(%)	34	7	3

The correlation coefficient matrixes among 30 Q Sorts were no. 14 and no. 15 ($r=0.52$), no. 26 and no. 27 ($r=0.53$), and, no. 28 and no. 29 ($r=0.66$). It suggested that the possibility of their belonging to same cause in the future is very high. After the judgmental rotation had been finished, Q Sort 1 and 5 were allocated to cause 1, Q Sort 12 and 14 were allocated to cause 2, and, Q Sort 16 and 18 were allocated to cause 3 in the cause-loading value flagging. The correlations between factor-scores were as following; however, the Q methodology does not rely on correlation coefficients, different from R methodology.

Table 5. Factor scores

	1st Type	2nd Type	3rd Type
1	1.0000	0.655	0.2791
2	0.6552	1.0000	0.2582
3	0.2791	0.2582	1.0000

5   Interpretation of Analysis

The Q causes calculated by study result can be seen as common opinion or value-set of test objects that judge or think on specific subject in similar way. The classified data from 30 test objects on 47 Q statements regarding smart-phone preference were analyzed to get following cause values.

5.1   Discriminative Sensibility Focusing Type

The discriminative sensibility focusing type looks like they have keen interest in aesthetic elements; however, they think personality expression and social pride as important and prefer differentiation from others. It has been learned that they want to have a sense of superiority by having a product. According to Kano's study, this type thinks interest cause as important. The test objects belonging to this type think that the message transmitted to others by way of personal image and owned product is important. They develop logics through reflective process on own concern. (42, 18, 22) Since they focus on the discriminative sensibility, this type thinks the sensibility aspect of non-functional quality dimension as important. This type overcomes the boredom caused by simplicity and pursues proper stimulation by interest and tension caused by the richness and novelty of interface elements in addition to outlook element. The sensibility quality causes of sensibility focusing type are uniqueness, fun, curiosity, surprise, fashion, attracting others' view, ostentation and emotional attachment.

Table 6. Discriminative sensibility focusing type

No	Z-Score	No	Z-Score
7	2.088	28	-1.042
43	2.024	5	-1.047
45	2.024	44	-1.239
42	1.565	8	-1.437
18	1.437	30	-1.437
22	1.239	32	-1.437
		26	-1.501
		41	-1.565
		25	-1.698

5.2   Use-Convenience Focusing Type

The use-convenience focusing type excludes the aesthetic elements and awareness on individual sensibility taste. Instead, they pursue the convenience accumulated by individual experience and they think the performance element is most important. They use more application programs ('app') than basic phone functions. They cumulate or consume data by way of various apps provided by smart-phone. (9, 40, 37) They also think the lifestyle of self is important. The sensibility quality causes of this type are more based on mechanical elements excluded of visual attraction, or, convenience such as comfort, freedom, expandability and control of device.

Table 7. Use-convenience focusing type

No	Z-Score	No	Z-Score
9	1.900	28	-1.252
40	1.900	19	-1.308
6	1.548	26	-1.308
31	1.365	24	-1.365
37	1.365	44	-1.365
3	1.252	45	-1.365
8	1.126	47	-1.365
2	1.126	29	-1.900
39	1.069		

5.3   Stability Focusing Type

The stability focusing type thinks that harmony and identity excluded of stimulation are important. They think the basic cause is the most important. (22, 13, 1) They think that familiarity by use experience, attachment by intimacy and harmony with personal image are important. This type has the characteristic of including self into people. They tend to show similar characteristics with use-convenience focusing type; however, they also share certain characteristics with discriminative sensibility focusing type. However, they have conflict between the burden of attracting gaze of others and internal tendency of rejecting common things. In other words, they do not give up both usability and aesthetic. The sensibility quality causes of this type are experience, habits, intimacy, conciseness and fun.

Table 8. Stability focusing type

No	Z-Score	No	Z-Score
31	1.721	38	-1.017
2	1.656	14	-1.082
7	1.532	3	-1.082
22	1.467	25	-1.147
13	1.402	30	-1.147
1	1.33	37	-1.212
42	1.277	8	-1.402
18	1.147	27	-1.467
		41	-1.532
		26	-1.721
		28	-1.786

6   Discussion and Conclusion

The craze on smart-phone is not limited in Korea. It is a global trend and the impact of smart-phone craze on industry is rapidly increasing. The domination of Samsung and Apple even created mania class that has very high brand loyalty. They do not change their smart-phones until their favorite brand, Samsung or Apple, would launch a new product. In this situation, a type analysis study to learn the sensibility quality causes that have impact on smart-phone choice has certain significance in setting up the direction of future smart-phone design.

This study analyzed the sensibility quality causes that have important impact on smart-phone choice by way of Q methodology. As the result, it was possible to find three representative types as following. The discriminative sensibility focusing type thinks personality expression and social pride are important and this type prefers differentiation from others. The sensibility quality causes of sensibility focusing type are uniqueness, fun, curiosity, surprise, fashion, attracting others' view, ostentation and emotional attachment. The use-convenience focusing type prefers convenience cumulated by personal experience. This type thinks the sensibility quality causes such as comfort, freedom, expandability and control of device are important. The stability focusing type prefers familiarity by use experience, attachment by intimacy and harmony with personal image as important. This type thinks the sensibility quality causes such as experience, habits, intimacy, conciseness and fun are important.

References

1. http://www.fnnews.com/view?ra=Sent0901m_View&corp=fnnews&arci
   d=201208270100216030012824&cDateYear=2012&cDateMonth=08&cDate
   Day=27
2. Schmidt, K.E., Liu, Y.L., Sridharan, S.: Webpage Aesthetics, Performance and Usability: Design Variables and Their Effects. Ergonomics 52, 631–643 (2009)
3. Herzberg, F.: Work and the nature of man. World Publishing, NY (1966)
4. Lee, J.H., Lee, G.P.: A Study on the Emotional Quality Design Framework for Improvement of the User Experience -with emphasis on the User Interface Design. Korean Society for Emotion & Sensibility 13(3), 523–532 (2010)
5. Kano, N., Seraku, N., Takahashi, F., Tsuji, S.: Attractive and normal quality. Quality 14(2), 39–48 (1984)
6. Zhang, P., von Dran, G.: User expectations and rankings of quality factors in different web site domains. International Journal of Electronic Commerce, 9–33 (2002)
7. Kim, H.K.: Q Methodology, p. 192. Communication Books, Seoul Korea (2008)

A New Method for Tangerine Tree Flower Recognition

Ulzii-Orshikh Dorj, Malrey Lee[*], and Diyan-ul-Imaan

Center for Advanced Image and Information Technology,
School of Electronics & Information Engineering,
Chon Buk National University, 664-14, 1Ga, Deokjin-Dong,
Jeonju, Chon Buk, 561-756, South Korea
ulzii158@hotmail.com, mrlee@chonbuk.ac.kr,
diyanulimaan@gmail.com

Abstract. Different machine vision strategies are adapted for performing auto-mated real time agricultural tasks in order to increase more productivity with less cost. Based on this notion, a new method is developed and implemented for detecting white color flowers in Tangerine tree and counting Tangerine fruit flowers to yield better outputs with regard to the existing schemes. Gaussian fil-ter is employed to reduce unwanted noise in Tangerine tree flower recognition for Tangerine yield mapping system. It is observed that the newly developed method gives better valid output for tangerine tree flower detection in natural outdoor lighting, with different lighting condition without any alternative light-ing source to control the luminance. The simulation result reveals that the new method is reliable, feasible and efficient compared to other existing methods.

Keywords: Tangerine tree flower, yield estimation, color detection, Gaussian smoothing, counting algorithm, machine vision.

1 Introduction

From literature study, it is noticed that related research is still being carried out in diversified areas but not in Tangerine tree flower recognition. It is observed that, lot of potential applications for automated agricultural tasks are found using machine vision system; therefore, we introduced new method for new Tangerine tree flower recognition. But, recently, many researchers are engaged in fruit recognition system for automated harvesting and for educational purpose to enhanced learning. Lak et al. [1] used edge detection and combination of color and shape analysis to segment im-ages of red apples obtained under natural lighting using machine vision, Arivazhagan et al. [2] proposed fusion of color and texture features for fruit recognition by color and texture feature, Jun Zhao et al. [3] studied ways of locating both red and green apples in a single image frame. Song Wan-Gan et al. [4] studied a method of fruits recognition based on SIFT characteristics, Gabriel Gatica et al. [5] presented a model for the recognition of the diameter of olives, Yang et al. [6] presented a method to detect and recognize mature tomato fruit clusters on a complex-structured tomato for

---

[*] Corresponding author.

T.-h. Kim et al. (Eds.): MulGraB/BSBT/IUrC 2012, CCIS 353, pp. 49–56, 2012.
© Springer-Verlag Berlin Heidelberg 2012

automatic harvesting purpose using stereo vision camera. Libing Zhang et al. [7] studied a method for cucumber fruit recognition in greenhouse using neural network and Wan Ishak Wan Ismail et al. [8] presented the development of outdoor image analysis for oil palm fruit fresh bunches (FFB). Also, Urena et al. [9] presented an automatic system for monitoring seed germination by means of a software tool incorporating an artificial vision system and a fuzzy logic-based classifier. Jingtao Lei et al. [10] presented a method used for fruit category recognition based on machine vision and total matching degree of fruit's multi characteristics. Arguenon, et.al. [11] proposed a multiagents system for the simulation of prototypes for different agriculture robots that can be employed in the harvesting of a vineyard. Patel et al. [12] presented automatic segmentation and yield calculation of fruit based on shape analysis. Palaniappan Annamalai [13] presented a machine vision algorithm to identify and count the number of citrus fruits in an image and finally to estimate the yield of citrus fruits in a tree.

The yield potential of a tangerine field depends on a number of factors, such as 1) the numbers of trees in the field; 2) weather conditions in both the sprout and crop years; 3) insect and disease incidence; 4) soil fertility; 5) soil moisture, as well as 6) the number of flowers which result in a fruit. There are a few methods for determining the percent fruit set. One such method is counting number of flowers of tangerine tree. It is important to point out that, Tangerine trees bloom on May, and during that time one can estimate yield. If there are too many blooms in one tangerine tree, it is not suitable for high quality yield, because tangerine can be too small. Also, if take too much yield, price can be down, because tangerines market is not too large. Therefore one can count the tangerine tree flowers and control yield of the tangerine every year by manually. In order to overcome the existing problems a new method has been introduced and executed to obtain better solution. The paper is arranged as follows. Section 2 discusses about the objectives and newly proposed methodology. Results and discussion is presented in section 3. Finally, conclusion and future work is given in section 4.

2   Objectives and New Methodology

The aim is to develop an image analysis system which is able to identify flowers in natural tangerine tree with the following needs:

1. The system should be able to recognize tangerine tree flowers.
2. Pictures should be taken on May, when flowers of tangerine tree are blooming.

A flow diagram for Tangerine tree processing is shown in Figure 1 which gives a better idea on the new methodology to be incorporated to obtain better output. For developing a Tangerine tree flower recognition algorithm, images were taken in the Tangerine tree field, which is in Jeju Island. A total of 21 tree images were taken on May during Tangerine tree flower blooming season. The Tangerine tree images were taken in natural outdoor lighting condition. Each tree picture was taken from four sides. The tree images were noisy and different lighting conditions. Flowers in some images were under the shadow of the leaves and branches. Also, there were too many flowers in the one tree for counting. So the input image was first removed noise, divided many sections (from ten into thirty five) before image processing steps. Figure 2 shows the input / original image of a Tangerine tree with background noise and figure 3 illustrates the ground noises are removed manually i.e. output image of a Tangerine tree without blurred noise.

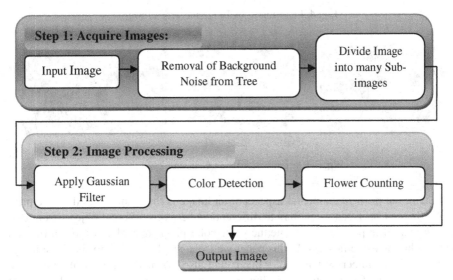

Fig. 1. Flow Diagram for Tangerine tree Processing

Fig. 2. Original image of Tangerine tree with background noise

Fig. 3. Output image of Tangerine tree without background noise

Image processing was carried out using 28 calibration images and tested on the 172 images. Also, the preprocessing of the input image was performed first. A Gaussian Filter was used to reduce the noise as much as possible. Input image of Tangerine tree flower is presented in figure 4, which is divided into sections. Filtering of an image cause blurring (noise) therefore, Gaussian 2x2 Filter is employed to reduce noise as shown in figure 5.

Fig. 4. Input Image of Tangerine Tree Flower

Fig. 5. Blurred Image using Gaussian 2x2 Filter

One of the most fundamental aspects of an image is the colors. Based on the principle, the end user can use colors to differentiate between different objects from others. Further, it is possible to isolate the white color pixels from the image and find out the number of white flowers. In this paper we isolated white color pixels of the image and counted a number of white color pixels and also, counted a number of white color pixels of the one flower. However, flower counting was performed by dividing a total number of white color pixels of the image to a total number of white color pixels of the one flower as following

$$N_{flowers} = \frac{N_{total\,flower\,pixels}}{N_{one\,flower\,pixels}} \tag{1}$$

where

$N_{flowers}$ – a total number of flowers of the input image

$N_{total\,flower\,pixels}$ - a total number of white color pixels of the image

$N_{one\,flower\,pixels}$ - a total number of white color pixels of the one flower.

Input picture was included with different kinds of flowers, like small, bloomed and mixed (small and bloomed). Accordingly, white color pixels of the one flower were calculated by using 10 images for two kinds of flower images: small and bloomed. In order to perform optimal counting of flowers, flower counting algorithm was employed as follows:

-     Input image was checked by manually and was classified for three types: small (s), bloomed (b), mixed (m)
-     White color pixels of the one small type flowers were calculated by 253 pixels

- White color pixels of the one bloomed type flowers were calculated by 601 pixels
- Almost all mixed type flower images were included 50%   small   and   50% bloomed flowers. Then mixed input image flowers were counted by 50% white color pixels of the one small type flowers and 50% white color pixels of the one bloomed type flowers and tested on the 28 calibration images.

In order to evaluate the performance of the algorithm, flowers were counted by the flower counting algorithm should have been compared with the actual number of flowers. The flowers were counted manually from an input image by two different persons for three times. The percentage error of images was defined as percentage error between the number of flowers counted by the machine vision algorithm, and the average number of flowers counted by manually as carried out by Palaniappan Annamalai [2].

$$\text{Error}_{\text{image}}(\%) = \frac{MV-MC}{MC} \times 100 \tag{2}$$

where

MV - number of fruits counted by the machine vision algorithm

MC – average number of fruits counted manually

3   Results and Discussion

The aim of this paper was to develop color detection and counting algorithm of the tangerine fruit flowers under various natural lighting conditions. As a result, total of 200 images of tangerine tree flowers was detected by this algorithm. White flowers of tangerine tree were presented in the resultant image by black color. A snapshot of window program implementation is presented in figure 6.

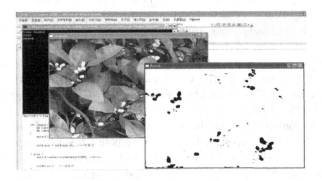

Fig. 6. Program Implementation Window

A sub-module of program source code as shown below. We used RGB color code from 190 to 220.

```
if( (data[i*step+j*channels+2]>190)   //R
            && (data[i*step+j*channels+1]>190)   //G
            && (data[i*step+j*channels]>190) )  //B
    {             datar[i*stepr+j*channelsr]=0;  //black
            cntBlack = cntBlack +1;
    } else {
            datar[i*stepr+j*channelsr]=255;  //white
            cntWhite++;
    }
```

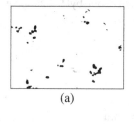

(a)

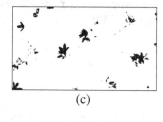

(c)

(b)

Counted Flower Pixels: 7048
Flower Type: Small (s) Total
Number of Flowers: 28

Counted Flower Pixels: 10241
Flower Type: Mixed (m)
Total Number of Flowers: 29

Counted Flower Pixels: 11825
Flower Type: Bloomed (b)
Total Number of Flowers: 20

Fig. 7. Output image of Tangerine tree using Color Detection Algorithm

In specific, color detection algorithm was performed and the output image of a Tangerine tree is presented in figures 7(a)-7(c) for better understanding. Patel et al. [12] presented automatic segmentation and yield calculation of fruit based on shape analysis. They applied Guassian Low Pass Filter, converted RGB to L*a*b space, selected the range of "a" for coarse detection, extracted the fruit regions by adding the input image with the binary mask, used morphological operations for remove noise, generated a binary image, labeled the pixels, applied Sobel Edge Detection, for each labeled region edge points are used for fitting of appropriate circle. A total of 100 images of different fruit were collected from internet. Finally, a minimum error of 0%, maximum error of 72%, mean absolute error of 31.4% and the Regression analysis value (R^2)= 0.79 is obtained.

A machine vision algorithm to identify and count the number of citrus fruits in an image and finally to estimate the yield of citrus fruits in a tree was discussed by Palaniappan Annamalai [13]. They Converted RGB to HIS, binarizated of color image in hue-saturation color plane, pre-processing (threshold using area, dilation, erosion, extracted features of fruits) to remove noise and to fill gaps, and, finally, counting the number of fruits. The fruit counting algorithm was applied to the 329 images. Finally, a minimum error of 0%, maximum error of 100%, mean absolute error of 29.33% and the Regression analysis value (R^2)= 0.79 is obtained.

It is noticed from above discussion that Patel et al. [12], and Palaniappan Annamalai [13] methods gives less significant results. Therefore, in order to yield better results we introduced our new machine vision method, there by percentage error was as low 0% and as high as 55% for all input images. The mean of absolute error was determined to be 17% for all input images. The main reason for this error was due to the fact that there were many and, small flowers or were in a shaded place and clear to the human eye. The algorithm would have treated them as noise or would not recognize well and left them while counting the flowers.

A regression analysis is performed between the number of flowers counted by flower recognition algorithm and the number of flowers counted by human observation for 200 images as shown in figure 8. Regression analysis value was $R^2=0.94$.

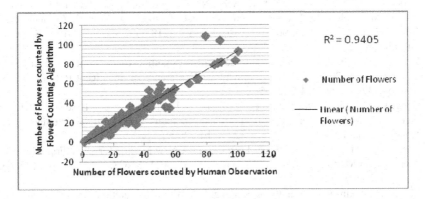

Fig. 8. Regression analysis between the number of flowers counted by flower recognition algorithm and the number of flowers counted by human observation

The white color pixels of the one small and bloomed type flowers were calculated to the 10 images and tested 28 calibration images. The white color pixels of the one small type flowers were calculated by 253 pixels. The percentage error was as low 4% and as high as 27% for all images. The mean of absolute error was determined to be 27%. The white color pixels of the one bloomed type flowers were calculated by 601 pixels. The percentage error was as low 1% and as high as 63% for all images. The mean of absolute error was determined to be 30%.

4   Conclusions and Future Work

The goal of this paper is to propose a general algorithm under different natural lighting conditions without any additional lighting source to control the luminance. A new method for tangerine tree flower recognition by computer vision using Tangerine yield mapping system is introduced to obtain better results in comparison with other existing methods. It is important to point out that the newly introduced method gives better output of tangerine tree flower detection in natural outdoor lighting, in different lighting condition and found to be efficient and effective. Future work is to develop yield prediction model for estimation yield information of the Tangerine grove and mobile system for counting Tangerine fruit, and its related applications.

Acknowledgement. This paper was supported by research funds of "Chon Buk National University in 2011".

References

1. Lak, M.B., Minaei, S., Amiriparian, J., Beheshti, B.: Apple Fruits Recognition Under Natural Luminance Using Machine Vision. Advance Journal of Food Science and Technology 2(6), 325–327 (2010); ISSN: 2042-4876, © Maxwell Scientific Organization 2010
2. Arivazhagan, S., Newlin Shebiah, R., Selva Nidhyanandhan, S., Ganesan, L.: Fruit Recognition using Color and Texture Features. Journal of Emerging Trends in Computing and Information Sciences 1(2), 90–94 (2010); E-ISSN 2218-6301 © 2009-2010 CIS Journal. All rights reserved
3. Zhao, J., Tow, J., Katupitiya, J.: On-tree Fruit Recognition Using Texture Properties and Color Data. In: 2005 IEEE/RSJ International Conference on Intelligent Robots and Systems, pp. 3993–3998. IEEE (2005)
4. Song, W.-G., Guo, H.-X., Wang, Y.: A Method of Fruits Recognition Based on SIFT Characteristics Matching. In: 2009 International Conference on Artificial Intelligence and Computational Intelligence, pp. 119–122. IEEE (2009)
5. Gatica, C.G., Best, S.S., Ceroni, J., Lefranc, G.: A New Method for Olive Fruits Recognition. In: San Martin, C., Kim, S.-W. (eds.) CIARP 2011. LNCS, vol. 7042, pp. 646–653. Springer, Heidelberg (2011)
6. Yang, L., Dickinson, J., Wu, Q. M. J., Lang, S.: A Fruit Recognition Method for Automatic Harvesting. 1-4244-1358-3/07/$25.00 ©2007 IEEE, pp. 152–157
7. Zhang, L., Yang, Q., Xun, Y., Chen, X., Ren, Y., Yuan, T., Tan, Y., Li, W.: Recognition of greenhouse cucumber fruit using computer vision. New Zealand Journal of Agricultural Research 50(5), 1293–1298
8. Ismail, W.I.W., Razali, M.H.: Outdoor colour recognition system for oil palm fresh fruit bunches (ffb). International Journal of Machine Intelligence 2(1), 01–10 (2010) ISSN: 0975-2927
9. Urena, R., Rodriguez, F., Berenguel, M.: A machine vision system for seeds germination quality evaluation using fuzzy logic. Elsevier Science B.V. (2001); All rights reserved. PII: S0168-1699(01)00150-8
10. Lei, J., Wang, T., Gong, Z.: Study on Machine Vision Fuzzy Recognition Based on Matching Degree of Multi-characteristics. In: Li, K., Jia, L., Sun, X., Fei, M., Irwin, G.W. (eds.) LSMS/ICSEE 2010. LNCS, vol. 6330, pp. 459–468. Springer, Heidelberg (2010)
11. Arguenon, V., Bergues-Lagarde, A., Rosenberger, C., Bro, P., Smari, W.: Multi-Agent Based Prototyping of Agriculture Robots. 0-9785699-0-3/06/$20.00©2006 IEEE
12. Patel, H.N., Jain, R.K., Joshi, M.V.: Automatic Segmentation and Yield Measurement of Fruit using Shape Analysis. International Journal of Computer Applications 45(7), 0975–8887 (2012)
13. Annamalai, P.: Citrus Yield Mapping System Using Machine Vision. A Thesis Presented to the Graduate School of the University of Florida in Partial Fulfillment of the Requirements for the Degree of Master of Science (2004)

Quality Assessment of Sound Signals in Multimedia and Communication Systems

Wongeun Oh and Sung-Keun Lee

Dept. of Multimedia Engineering, Sunchon National University,
255 Jungang-ro, Suncheon, Jeonnam, Korea
{owg,sklee}@sunchon.ac.kr
http://multi.sunchon.ac.kr

Abstract. Assessing the perceptual quality of speech and audio signals is an important consideration in multimedia networks and devices. This paper constitutes an introduction to the standardized speech and audio quality assessment methods in ITU recommendations and other international organizations. A brief survey on the subjective and objective quality evaluation methods for the speech and the audio is provided. Recent developments as well as new topics for future developments are also outlined.

Keywords: Sound Quality, Audio Quality, Intelligibility.

1 Introduction

Sound is an important application area in many multimedia systems. Examples of such systems are streaming audio, VoIP (Voice over Internet Protocol), DAB (Digital Audio Broadcasting), mobile phones and various audio codecs. Assessing perceptual quality of sound signals is an important consideration for overall multimedia systems. Therefore, technical organizations and scientific societies have made consistent efforts towards standardization on sound quality assessment methods since 1990s.

The assessment can be done using subjective listening test and/or objective methods. The subjective test involves comparisons of the original and the processed signals by human listeners. The method is traditional and widely used to evaluate the sound quality, but has several constraints in test environments e.g. the number of subjects, listening room conditions, the test procedures, etc. Since these issues make the subjective tests expensive and time consuming, several computer based objective algorithms have been developed. The objective algorithms are different than the traditional physical measurements like the signal-to-ratio or bit-error rate. The algorithms model the psychoacoustic principles of the human auditory system, and automatically estimate the subjective scores of the human listeners.

There are several excellent survey works for quality of sound signals, but they focused only part of all assessment methods (e.g., objective method or audio

T.-h. Kim et al. (Eds.): MulGraB/BSBT/IUrC 2012, CCIS 353, pp. 57–64, 2012.

quality) [1]-[4]. This paper presents a brief review of various sound quality assessment methods including subjective and objective methods, speech and audio, the international standards, the recent developments, and some future trends. The paper is organized as follows: Section 2 and 3 review the speech intelligibility and speech quality. Section 4 discusses audio quality and the conclusion is provided in section 5.

2   Speech Intelligibility

The evaluation of speech signal is conducted two different points of view, e.g. the intelligibility and the quality. Intelligibility measures assess the content of the spoken words, while quality measures assess the good or bad impression of the sound. The relationship between the two measures is not clearly understood yet. Poor quality speech can be intelligible or good quality speech cannot be completely intelligible. The examples of the former are synthesized speech using a small number of sine waves or a small number of noise bands. Conversely, if a large number of packets are lost in certain time slot on the VoIP network, the average quality might be good but some word would not be intelligible [5].

2.1   Subjective Testing

The subjective methods of intelligibility can be measured by presenting speech material to a group of listeners and asking them to identify the word (or sentence) spoken. Then the intelligibility is measured by counting the correctly identified materials. Depending on the speech materials the tests can be categorized into the nonsense syllable tests, word tests, and sentence tests. The nonsense syllable tests are one of the earliest methods to evaluate intelligibility. Their materials consist of a group of nonsense monosyllables which have consonant-vowel-consonant (C-V-C) format. The word tests use a set of single meaningful words which are phonetically balanced or have rhyme, while the sentence tests use real sentences in which the phonetic content is balanced.

The testing materials used in the tests should be phonetically balanced and equally difficult to recognize. For these reasons, different test lists are used depending on the languages. For American English, ANSI S3.2 [6] includes the measurement of the intelligibility of speech over entire communication systems and the evaluation of the contributions of elements of speech communication systems for evaluations. The standard specified the PB (phonetically balanced) test, MRT (modified rhyme) test, and DRT (Diagnostic rhyme) test. The PB lists consist of a set of twenty phonetically balanced words, which was developed during World War II and has been used widely since then. PB test requires more training of listeners and talkers than other statistical tests, and is particularly sensitive to noise. The MRT uses 50 six-word lists of rhyming monosyllabic English words. Each word is constructed from a consonant-vowel-consonant sound sequence, and the six words in each list differ only in the initial or final consonant sound. The DRT test uses 192 words, which are arranged in 96 rhyming pairs which differ only in their initial consonants [6][7].

For Korean language, several Korean PB word lists were proposed by many investigators, however, there is not yet a standard PB word list [8]-[10]. Byun et al [11] pointed out total 13 lists are used in 80 training hospitals in Korea, among them Hahm's list [10] was most commonly used. Another study [12] showed that the existing Korean PB words lists need to be modified to reflect actual frequencies of phonemes.

2.2   Objective Testing

The subjective tests are complicated to set up, time-consuming to conduct and require extensive statistical analysis to interpret. For these reasons, the objective methods have been investigated that yield meaningful intelligibility scores. They estimate intelligibility from the measured acoustical parameters.

AI (Articulation Index) is one of the earliest objective methods to measure the intelligibility of a speech transmission system, but it does not effectively account for all the impairments that can degrade the intelligibility [7]. The AI method has recently been updated to SII (Speech Intelligibility Index) which is documented in an ANSI standard (S3.5-1997) [13]. The SII method accounts for several of the factors that the AI ignored, such as reverberation.

STI (Speech Transmission Index) was developed in the early 1970s by Houtgast and Steeneken [14]. In STI testing, speech is modeled by a special test signal with speech-like characteristics. Then it transmits the test signal to the system or the communication channel under test. At the receiving end of the communication system, the depth of modulation of the received signal is compared with that of the original signal in each of a number of frequency bands. Reductions in the modulation depth are associated with loss of intelligibility. The estimated intelligibility score varies from 0 (completely unintelligible) to 1 (perfect intelligibility). RASTI (Rapid Speech Transmission Index) is a simpler version of STI, and has been implemented in a simple and portable instrument that can make rapid intelligibility measurements. Both STI and RASTI have been adopted for a number of international standards and civil system specifications, e.g. IEC60286-16 [15] and NFPA72 [16]. In Table 1, three subjective methods and three objective methods are compared. In the table, ALcons(%) means Percentage Articulation Loss of Consonants that is closely related with the TEF analyzer [17].

In the recent literature, some new approaches are founded. Li and Cox [20] developed extract STI from running speech using neural networks. Eggenschwiler and Machner [21] investigated the relationship between room acoustical parameters and speech intelligibility. Han and Mak [22] conducted a case study for improving speech intelligibility in classrooms.

3   Speech Quality Assessment

The quality assessment of speech is to evaluate the general quality of a given set of speech signals. In the subjective tests, human listeners listen to the test

Table 1. Speech Intelligibility Rating[7][18][19]

Intelligibility Rating	Objective Methods			Subjective Methods		
	STI	ALcons(%)	SII	Syllable	Word	Sentence
Excellent	0.75-1.0	<3		90-96	94-96	96
Good	0.6-0.75	3-8	>0.75	67-90	87-94	95-96
Fair	0.45-0.6	8-11		48-67	78-87	92-95
Poor	0.3-0.45	11-15	<0.45	34-48	67-78	89-92
Bad	0-0.3	>15		0-34	0-67	0-89

signals and are asked to score the speech quality. Objective tests use machine-based algorithms, which model the human ears and perceptions.

3.1   Subjective Testing

The most common subjective tests were standardized in ITU-T P.800 recommendations [23], where three methods are described for the listening tests : ACR (absolute category rating), DCR (degradation category rating), and CCR (comparative category rating).

In ACR test, typically each stimulus consisted of two sentences of around 5s 8s duration from a single speaker. The material is played and then evaluated by 24-32 listeners using a 5-point scale (Table 2(a)), and the average score indicates the MOS (Mean Opinion Score). The DCR method compares the system output with an original signal (reference) and the degradation is rated on a five-point scale (Table 2(b)). This method is suitable for assessing in noise or when the impairment is small. It may therefore be particularly useful for evaluating similar digital speech processing algorithms. The CCR method compares the original and the reference as in the DCR. The difference of two tests is the order where the signals are presented. In the DCR, the degraded signal immediately follows the reference, whereas in the CCR the order is random. In addition, they use different scales (Table 2(b), (c)). The CCR procedure may be particularly suitable for systems that improve the quality of the input speech (e.g. noise cancellation systems).

In the subjective tests, the test environments are critical factors for correct evaluation and should meet the conditions in the norm. For example, in the recording room, the talker should be seated in a quiet room with volume between $30m^3$ and $120m^3$ and a reverberation time less than 500ms (preferably in the range 200-300ms). The room noise level must be below 30 dBA with no dominant peaks in the spectrum [23].

3.2   Objective Testing

The standard objective method for speech quality in ITU is the ITU-T P.862 PESQ (Perceptual Evaluation of Speech Quality) [24]. The algorithm compares the original signal and the system output under test, and estimates the degradation estimation score. The estimation algorithm is based on the perceptual

Table 2. The Opinion Scales in ITU-T P.800

(a) ACR scale	(b) DCR scale	(c) CCR scale
Listening quality is	Degradation is	The quality of the second is
5 : Excellent	5 : inaudible	3 : much better
4 : Good	4 : audible but not annoying	2 : better
3 : Fair	3 : slightly annoying	1 : slightly better
2 : Poor	2 : annoying	0 : about the same
1 : Bad	1 : very annoying	-1 : slight worse
		-2 : worse
		-1 : much worse

and cognitive model of human. It is well correlated to the subjective test results with the average around 0.935 [24]. The PESQ method is suited for 300-3400Hz narrowband speech signals. For the wideband speech (50-7000Hz), the wideband PESQ version (W-PESQ) is described in the ITU-T P.862.2 [25]. The ITU-T P.863 [26] is the most recent recommendation for super-wideband (50 14000Hz) speech, representing current digital telephony. P.863 was known as the POLQA (Perceptual Objective Listening Quality Assessment) in the developing stage.

The ITU-T P.563 is another type of objective test algorithm. It does not compare the original and the system output. It attempts to perform the quality evaluation with based only on the corrupted signal. This single-end approach is commonly referred to as the non-intrusive method [27].

4   Audio Quality Assessment

Assessing the quality of audio signal is an important factor in audio codecs and multimedia networks. Both subjective methods and objective testing methods are standardized in the ITU-R recommendations.

4.1   Subjective Testing

The subjective audio quality test methods defined by ITU can be found in ITU-R BS.1284, BS.1116, and BS.1534 recommendations [28]-[30]. The BS.1284 summarizes previous ITU standards and is intended as a guide to the general assessment of sound quality. The subject methods of BS.1116 focus on small impairments as in the high quality audio codecs. Tests are performed by at least 20 expert listeners with the method called double-blind triple-stimulus with hidden reference which has been found to be especially sensitive. The listeners are presented to stimuli (A, B, C) where A is the known reference and B, C are either degraded signal or just copy of A with a random order. Then the listeners grade the impairments of B, C against A, according to a scale from 5(imperceptible) to 1(very annoying).

However, the BS.1116 is not suitable for the applications where lower quality audio is acceptable. The BS.1534 targets intermediate impairments which occur in the Internet audio services, digital AM, etc. Test set consists of maximum 15 signals including a reference, degraded audio signals, a hidden anchor, and a hidden reference. This method provides the benefits of a full paired comparison test between various types of degradations. The test employs a continuous scale from 0(bad) to 100(excellent).

4.2   Objective Testing

The ITU-R standardized method for audio quality is PEAQ (Perceptual Evaluation of Audio Quality), or ITU-R BS.1387 [31]. It is the objective counterpart of BS.1116, and can generate similar to those derived from the subject tests using the psychoacoustic model and the cognitive model.

There are two versions of the PEAQ algorithm. The basic version has a FFT-based, less complex ear model, and is suitable for real-time application. While the advanced version employs filter bank based complex, but accurate ear model. The reference and the degraded signal are processed by these ear models and compared internally. The result of the comparison is a set of MOVs (Model Output Variables) which are perceptual metrics based on signal characteristics. The MOVs are the inputs to a neural network which is trained to map them to a single ODG (Overall Difference Grade). The ODG score corresponds to the subjective score by human listeners, and can range from 0(imperceptible) to -4(very annoying). The correlation coefficient was 0.837 for the basic version and 0.851 for the advanced version [31][32].

The PEAQ works well for many applications, but is not entirely reliable under the untested cases because of the pre-trained neural network. Also, it is not suitable for assessing the quality of the lower bit-rate codecs, the multichannel audio, and the intermediate quality audio signal. Currently, ITU Study Group 6 is investigating a possible revision of PEAQ, specifically investigating the quality assessment of multichannel audio and intermediate quality audio.

Recent research related to objective assessment methods includes improvements to PEAQ by including new parameters or a new cognitive model [33][34]. PEMO-Q [35] and Rnonlin [36] are alternative approaches for evaluation of audio along the entire audible band, and George [37] and Zielinski [38] developed the assessment methods for multichannel audio. Besides improving PEAQ, development of nonintrusive measurement methods is highly required because there are many possible applications for audio quality assessment, e.g. real time evaluation of teleconferencing, sound reinforcement systems and public address systems.

5   Conclusions

This paper presents a brief survey on the various sound quality assessment methods, mainly within a framework based on several International standards. The topics discussed here included the current international standards of subjective and objective assessment of speech intelligibility, speech quality and audio quality. Recent developments and future trends were also provided.

Acknowledgments. This work was supported by Research Foundation of Engineering College, Sunchon National University.

References

1. Campbell, D., Jones, E., Glavin, M.: Audio Quality Assessment Techniques-A Review, and Recent Developments. Signal Processing 89, 1489–1500 (2009)
2. de Lima, A.A., Freeland, F.P., de Jesus, R.A., Bispo, B.C., Biscainho, L.W.P., Netto, S.L., Said, A., Kalker, A., Schafer, R., Lee, B., Jam, M.: On the quality assessment of sound signals. In: 2008 IEEE International Symposium on Circuits and Systems, vol. 3, pp. 416–419 (2008)
3. AES: Measuring and Predicting Perceived Audio Quality. J. of Audio Engineering Society 53, 443–448 (2005)
4. Rix, A., Beerends, J., Kim, D.-S., Kroon, P., Ghitza, O.: Objective Assessment of Speech and Audio Quality - Technology and Applications. IEEE Transactions on Audio, Speech and Language Processing 14 (2006)
5. Loizou, P.C.: Speech Enhancement. CRC Press (2007)
6. ANSI S3.2-1989(R1999): Method for Measuring the Intelligibility of Speech over Communication Systems
7. Meyer Sound: Speech Intelligibility Papers,
   http://www.meyersound.com/support/papers
8. Yoon, C., Kim, S., Oh, Y.: A Study on the Standardization of Articulation Testing Method and Its Evaluation Suitable for Korean Language(I). J. AIK. 20, 117–125 (1988)
9. Yoon, C., Kim, S., Oh, Y.: A Study on the Standardization of Articulation Testing Method and Its Evaluation Suitable for Korean Language(II). J. AIK. 21, 95–108 (1989)
10. Hahm, T.: Complementary Study on Construction of Korean Word Lists for Speech Audiometry. Inje Medical J. 7, 1–19 (1986)
11. Byun, S., Chung, S., Kim, H., Go, Y.: A Survey of Phonetically Balanced Words Lists Used in Training Hospitals in Korea. Korean J. Otolaryngol 48, 1086–1090 (2005)
12. Byun, S.: Frequencies of Korean Phonemes and Reliability of Korean Phonetically Balanced Word Lists. Korean J. Otolaryngol 44, 485–489 (2001)
13. ANSI S3.5-1997(R2012): American National Standard Methods for Calculation of the Speech Intelligibility Index
14. Steeneken, H.J., Houtgast, T.: A physical method for measuring speech-transmission quality. The J. of the Acoustical Society of America 67, 318–326 (1980)
15. IEC 60268-16: Sound system equipment - Part 16: Objective rating of speech intelligibility by speech transmission index
16. NFPA 72: National Fire Alarm and Signaling Code,
    http://www.nfpa.org/aboutthecodes/AboutTheCodes.asp?DocNum=72
17. Everest, F.A., Pohlmann, K.C.: Master Handbook of Acoustics. McGraw-Hill (2009)
18. Steeneken, H.J.M.: Standardisation of Performance Criteria and Assessments Methods for Speech Communication
19. Ballou, G.: Handbook for Sound Engineers. Elsevier (2008)

20. Li, F.F., Cox, T.J.: Speech transmission index from running speech: A neural network approach. The J. of the Acoustical Society of America 113, 1999–2008 (2003)
21. Eggenschwiler, K., Machner, R.: Intercomparision Measurements of Room Acoustical Parameters for Speech Intelligibility in a Room with a Sound System. J. of Audio Engineering Society 53 (2005)
22. Han, N., Mak, C.M.: Improving speech intelligibility in classrooms through the mirror image model. Applied Acoustics 69, 945–950 (2008)
23. ITU-T P.800: Methods for Subjective Determination of Transmission Quality (1996)
24. ITU-T P.862: Perceptual Evaluation of Speech Quality (PESQ): An Objective Method for End-to-End Speech Quality Assessment of Narrow-band Telephone Networks and Speech Codecs (2001)
25. ITU-T P.862.2: Wideband extension to Recommendation P.862 for the assessment of wideband telephone networks and speech codecs (2007)
26. ITU-T P.863: Perceptual Objective Listening Quality Assessment (2011)
27. ITU-T P.563: Single-ended method for objective speech quality assessment in narrow-band telephony applications (2004)
28. ITU-R BS.1284-1: General Methods for the Subjective Assessment of Sound Quality (1997)
29. ITU-R BS.1116-1: Methods for the subjective assessment of small impairments in audio systems including multichannel sound systems (1994)
30. ITU-R BS.1534-1: Method for the subjective assessment of intermediate quality level of coding systems (2001)
31. ITU-R BS.1387-1: Method for Objective Measurements of Perceived Audio Quality (1998)
32. Kabal, P.: An Examination and Interpretation of ITU-R BS.1387: Perceptual Evaluation of Audio Quality (2003)
33. Creusere, C.D., Hardin, J.C.: Assessing the Quality of Audio Containing Temporally Varying Distortions. IEEE Transactions on Audio, Speech and Language Processing 19, 711–720 (2011)
34. Creusere, C.D., Member, S., Kallakuri, K.D., Vanam, R., Member, S.: An Objective Metric of Human Subjective Audio Quality Optimized for a Wide Range of Audio Fidelities 16, 129–136 (2008)
35. Huber, R., Kollmeier, B.: PEMO-Q: A New Method for Objective Audio Quality Assessment Using a Model of Auditory Perception. IEEE Transactions on Audio, Speech and Language Processing 14, 1902–1911 (2006)
36. Tan, C.-T., Moore, B.C.J., Zacharov, N., Mattila, V.-V.: Predicting the perceived quality of nonlinearly distorted music and speech signals. J. of AES 52, 699–711 (2004)
37. George, S., Zielinski, S., Rumsey, F.: Feature Extraction for the Prediction of Multichannel Spatial Audio Fidelity. IEEE Trans. Audio, Speech, Lang. Process. 14, 1994–2005 (2006)
38. Zielinski, S., Rumsey, F., Kassier, R., Bech, S.: Development and Initial validation of a Multichannel Audio Quality Expert System. J. of AES 53, 4–21 (2005)

A Study on the Generation of Artificial Fish's Behavior Using Elasticity Force

Chong Han Kim[1], Seung Moon Jeong[1], Im Chul Kang[1], and Byung Ki Kim[2]

[1] Dong Shin University, Digital Contents Cooperative Research Center
Naju, Jeollanamdo, Republic of Korea
[2] Dept.Computer Science, Chonnam National University
Gwang ju, Youngbong-Dong 77 - Korea
{chkim,jsm,softkang}@dsu.ac.kr, bgkim@chonnam.ac.kr

Abstract. Objects can interact with each other in accordance with the events considering certain conditions. However, to express the interactive behaviors, the event conditions and behavioral patterns need to correspond with each other almost on a one-to-one basis. Thus, if the number of patterns which have been already defined is insufficient, the realistic actions cannot be accomplished and the event conditions to be considered increase for the expression of diverse behavioral patterns, which will in turn increase the complexity of the whole system. Thus, this study suggests a new method which will facilitate more realistic expression of artificial fishes and the creation of diverse behavioral patterns for one evasion event by applying a physical approach utilizing elastic momentum and using variable multi-sensors.

Keywords: Virtual Space, Artificial Fish, Elasticity, Sensory System.

1 Introduction

Digital creatures refer to the digitally restored characters of the animals and plants in a real world or of the imaginary creatures and are used as the contents library such as videos or games.

An artificial fish is a type of digital creature which transforms to an automatic agent form which is used in interactive media such as computer animations or computer games. Those behaviors are controlled by the data generated by definite logic rules and generate dynamic mutual communication rules and algorithms. The complexity of the automatic behaviors generated in this manner is regulated by the degree of the expression of correlation with the environmental variables on the basis of the artificial variables acting given to the early artificial fishes and the force acting under the sea. Tu expressed the behaviors according to an event by combining motion mechanisms and also expressed the behaviors, combining motions according to Fear, Hunger, and Libido by giving intention attributes to artificial fishes. When each attribute is given fishes, the behaviors matching the situations are generated by using muscular system for realistic motion. However, the same motions tend to repeat due to the insufficient consideration of the variables determined by environmental factors.

T.-h. Kim et al. (Eds.): MulGraB/BSBT/IUrC 2012, CCIS 353, pp. 65–72, 2012.

Fishes behave according to sensors and the state of fishes without considering the variables such as the distance between predator fishes and prey fishes, the weight of fishes, and the approaching velocity, which results in the same behavioral patterns under the same conditions. Thus, to express more realistic behaviors, this study suggests a behavior generation method based on physics by considering environmental factors. This method leads to another behavior of artificial fishes by the given environmental factors even under the same input conditions and state attributes. To do this, the initial momentum and direction is defined, the direction vector and evasion direction of predator fishes and prey fishes are determined by applying force as an environmental variable, and then the distance between them and the evasion velocity are determined.

2   Basic Elements of the Existing Artificial Fishes

2.1   Modeling

Tu, having designed the early artificial fishes, suggested the fishes based on a spring-mass model with elasticity. This fish model based on this force was composed of 23 point masses and 91 springs and these springs were named "Muscles". These fishes generate the motion by changing the rest length of these springs.

2.2   Sensory System

Artificial fishes need sensor systems to detect other dynamic or stationary objects in a virtual undersea space. A sensor system detects the objects reacting in a certain distance and generates events depending on the objects. Reynolds detects other fishes or obstacles using a ray tracing method using a ray from the fish heads. This method is the most primitive method which can detect the object in the direction of the fish heads only. To compensate this, Tu suggested a sensor system with 300 degree viewing angle by using the vision of above 3 typical sensing. Fig. 1 is a ray tracing sensor system suggested by Tu.

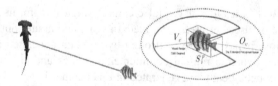

Fig. 1. A method suggested by Reynolds, A sensory system suggested by Tu

2.3   Artificial Fish-Motion Generation and Behavioral Pattern Algorithms

Grey provides a formula to indicate the velocity of fishes through the vertical velocity of fish tails by a central axis in the water. Equation (1) shows the travel speed according to the velocity of the fish tails.

$$(V_{fish}/V_{tail}) = (2\pi a^2 / \lambda^2)[1/((1+[4\pi a^2 / \lambda^2]))] \tag{1}$$

In equation (1), a is the amplitude of the tails, λ is the wave length, and V_{fish} and V_{tail} indicate the travel speed and the propagation velocity of fishes. Artificial fishes are divided into predators, preys, and pacifists. Predators hunt preys and preys escape from predators. Predators and preys act in response to sensors. In case there is no input value to detection sensors, individual object wanders. Predators pursue preys when preys are detected within the radius of a sensor. Preys with relatively small radius flee when predators appear within a certain distance. Table 1 describes each behavior.

2.4   Problems of the Previous Studies and Solutions

The early artificial fishes were designed in the order of sensing, choosing the behavior defined to match each object, and fleeing when preys detected predators in terms of the relationship between predators and preys. Thus, each object could express only monotonous behaviors because the same event (sensing) could generated the same behavior. As solutions to this problem, the previous studies were conducted on a method triggering behavioral patterns by considering the state of preys and predators such as the weight and the velocity and the environmental condition such as the velocity of fluid, frictional force, and buoyance when preys detected predators. However, this also has the disadvantages in the sense that it increases the complexity in design and implementation of system because the output value matching each input value needs to be generated in advance for triggering behaviors. Fig. 2 is the comparison between the behavior inducing algorithms considering the previous simple behaviors inducing algorithms and all the input variables and the algorithms suggested in this study. The simple behavioral patters are pointed out as a problem in respect of the evasion after the early detection. In respect of the input parameter analysis after the detection and the generation of output values according to the input values, a measure that brings each fish's approaching velocity, approaching distance, and early evasion velocity which has been defined earlier is taken according to the combination of input values. The elastic momentum method suggested in this study can immediately determine the above approaching velocity, approaching distance, and early evasion velocity by utilizing the output values numerically after simplifying the correlation between these input values and output values.

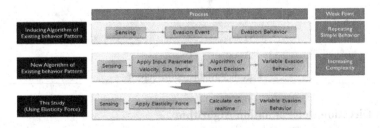

Fig. 2. Comparison between the previous behavior inducing algorithms and the improved algorithms

3   Improvement of an Artificial Fish Sensor System and Design of a Free Behavior Inducing System

To build a realistic virtual undersea space, preys and predators have variable sensors. More realistic behaviors can be induced by changing the size of sensors according to the size of objects and the degree of hunger. Furthermore, the forces acting on the dynamic objects in a 3D virtual space include the propulsion, buoyancy, gravity, and friction force due to the water viscosity. These are the important parameters in expressing natural behaviors when preys are found by predators. The distance between two objects approaching at rapid rate decreases sharply immediately before fleeing and an object which moves slowly flees in the distance equivalent to the size of the sensor. This study generates elastic momentum to this basic force for natural behavior. Elastic moment is generated by a virtual spring between preys and predators. A spring contracted by the inertia resulted from the momentum of a dynamic object reacts beyond the critical point, which will give the different elastic force to the objects approaching at rapid rate or a slow rate and generates evasion velocity according to the size and weight of fishes. Furthermore, the adjustment of the elastic modulus facilitates realistic fish behavior.

3.1   Variable Sensor and Evasion Direction Deciding System

Variable Multi-sensor
Real fishes control their ability to detect preys. Thus, this study has designed variable sensors and set the early pursuit velocity and evasion velocity differently. The predators which feel more hunger over time expand the sensor size and increase the velocity of early pursuit. Furthermore the predators have separate sensors which detect preys or the ordinary obstacles such as rocks and seaweed. Fig.3 shows the sensors of artificial fishes.L_f, a prey detection sensor or predator detection sensor, varies depending on the state of objects and L_o, an obstacles detection sensor, detects the floor conditions or surrounding rocks depending in the state of Wander, Flee, and Pursuit.

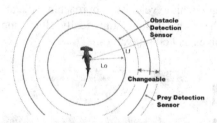

Fig. 3. Variable multi-sensor

Evasion Direction Determination Algorithm
When the sensors of prey and predators react to each other, preys flee at the velocity of $V_{evasion}$ and the evasion direction $D_{evasion}$ is determined by considering predators and

surrounding obstacles. In case there is no obstacle within the sensing rage of prey, preys have the same direction as that of predators. In case there are obstacles or other predators within the sensing range, the direction of preys is determined in the following manner. $P_{predator}$ is the location of Predator 1 and $P_{obstacle}$ is the location of Predator 2(or obstacle).

$$P_{predator} = (x_{predator}, y_{predator}, z_{predator}) \, , P_{obstacle} = (x_{obstacle}, y_{obstacle}, z_{obstacle}) \, , P_{prey} = (x_{prey}, y_{prey}, z_{prey})$$

At this time, if the location of a prey is P_{prey}, $P_{predator} - P_{prey}$ is the direction of an predator for an prey and the direction of an obstacle for a prey is $\overrightarrow{P_{Obstacle} - P_{Prey}}$. The evasion direction of a prey is $D_{evasion}$, which is the opposite direction of the total of the vectors of these two directions.

$$\vec{D}_{evasion} = -((x_{predator} + x_{obstacle} - 2x_{prey}), (y_{predator} + y_{obstacle} - 2y_{prey}) \, , (z_{predator} + z_{obstacle} - 2z_{prey}))$$

Fig. 4 shows the evasion direction of prey and predators against obstacles.

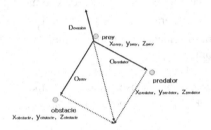

Fig. 4. Evasion direction vector

Virtual Spring Generation for the Application of Elastic Force

Preys which respond to a sensor immediately evade upon the receipt of an event, yet a sensor incurs an event generating a elastic spring and moves a certain distance x to achieve the equilibrium between the inertia forces and the elastic forces, and then shows evasion event when having maximum x value. At this time, the elastic force is reflected in the velocity after converting elastic force into kinetic energy. Fig 5 shows a virtual spring generated between two objects.

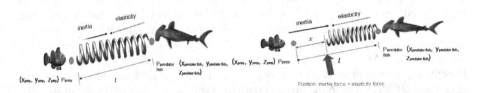

Fig. 5. Generation of a virtual elastic spring

When the location of an predator is $P_{predator}$ and the location of a prey is P_{prey}, the distance between a predator and a prey becomes l.

$$l = \sqrt{(x_{predator} - x_{prey})^2 + (y_{predator} - y_{prey})^2 + (z_{predator} - z_{prey})^2} \tag{2}$$

When the reciprocal detection state of a prey and a predator becomes True, a spring with length l and the modulus of elasticity k is generated between the two. The potential energy of this spring V_e is shown in Equation 3.

$$V_e = \int_0^x F dx = \int_0^x kx\,dx \tag{3}$$

The reason why the sensor length of a prey is not equal to the length is because the length of a spring which is shorter than the length of a sensor can be generated at some point of time because of obstacles. F is the momentum by a fish, k is spring constant, and constant x is the modulus of strain. At this time, when assuming the size of predators is infinitely larger than that of preys, the compression by predators is not achieved and only the whole location is changed, so it is set as a partition. Thus, the relative momentum to predators is not considered. The modulus of stain x for predators' momentum $F_{positive}$ is generated. At this time, as $\int_0^x kx\,dx = \frac{1}{2}kx^2$, the energy of a fish on a spring W has been changed into potential energy. Thus, the maximum of modulus of strain x becomes $x_{\max}$.

In other words, when x becomes $x_{\max}$, evasion event will be given and then the evasion direction obtained from a sensor system becomes ($x_{Predator}$ + $x_{Obstacle}$ - $2x_{Prey}$), - ($yx_{Predator}$ + $y_{Obstacle}$ - $2y_{Prey}$), - ($z_{Predator}$ + $z_{Obstacle}$ - $2z_{Prey}$).

$$\frac{1}{2}mv^2 = \frac{1}{2}kx^2 \tag{4}$$

As the initial evasion velocity v_{escape} is the velocity after the elastic energy restored as the kinetic energy, v_{escape} can be calculated by Equation 5.

$$v_{escape} = \frac{\sqrt{m_{prey}k}(Cv_{p/p} - m_{prey}a_{prey})}{m_{prey}k} \tag{5}$$

4   Experiments and Result

In this paper, the relationship between fishes is limited to the relationship between preys and predators. Predators have the attribute of Pursuit and Wander and preys have the attribute of Flee and Wander. These behaviors are generated and become extinct by the interaction between preys and predators. To implement the behaviors of an artificial fish, this study has modeled a prey after a back porgy and a predator after a hammerhead. As for the behaviors, to express the behavior of Flee, Wander, and Pursuit, animations in units such as Swimming, Turning, Rapid Swimming were produced and set according to the given situations. Table 2 indicates the event of individual object in accordance with the reaction of sensors.

O and X indicating the occurrence of sensor detection were set for the case where one party detected the other party first because the detection sensor sizes of preys and predators were different. As for the behaviors of preys and predators, the following 3 behaviors are defined: 1) a case where both do not detect the other, 2) a case where a predator detects a prey because it has a larger detection sensor than a prey, 3) a case where a pry detects a predator after the predator pursues the prey. For the target object, a black porgy and a hammerhead were produced by 3Ds Max 8.0 and their behaviors were expressed by this animation. VR environment was implemented by Virtools 4.0.

Table 1. Events according to the sensor response

Condition		Predator	Prey	Object's reaction		Object Behavior
Sensor Detection	1	X	X	Predator	Wander	Random Move(Wander)
				Prey	Wander	
	2	O	X	Predator	Pursuit	Variation of a predator ' s orientation value (target : prey)
				Prey	Wander	
	3	O	O	Predator	Pursuit	Application of elasticity momentum through the calculation of the distance between a predator and a prey.
				Prey	Flee	Application of flee determination direction of a rey

Fig.6(a) shows the detection sensor of a black porgy. The detection sensor was made as a globe with consistent radius and was designed to be proportional to the size of objects. As mentioned earlier, the detection sensor for preys and predators were designed to be larger than the evasion sensors for obstacles. Fig.6(b) shows the behaviors that a prey determines the evasion direction after detecting a predator.

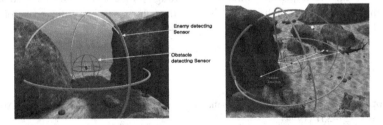

Fig. 6. (a)Variable multi-detection sensors, (b) Evasion behavior of a prey

Fig.7 shows the changes in velocity and direction of a fish applied with and without the existing elastic moment. The graph Fig.7(a) indicates the change of the velocity of a prey in respect of time t. A prey changes the direction or shifts to the evasion velocity at t_6. At this time, the animation is not naturally connected. In Fig.7(b), a prey detects a predator at $t_{4,5}$ and then reduces its velocity due to the elastic force against the inertial force and approaches a predator closer by x than the existing fish. When x has the maximum value, the velocity becomes 0, the minimum value, and the opposite evasion direction is taken. At this time, the elastic force has maximum value.

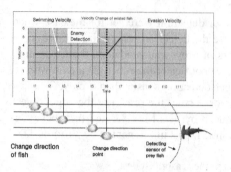 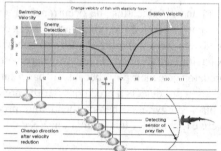

Fig. 7. (a)Velocity and directional change of a prey which is not applied with elastic momentum, (b) Velocity and directional change of a prey applied with elastic momentum

5   Conclusion

This study has suggested a method to generate a natural behaviors of artificial fishes in a 3D virtual space rendered on a real-time basis. These behaviors are different from each other because the response time by the environmental variables such as the size and weight of target objects are calculated on a real-time beyond the limitation of one-to-one correspondence rules. Furthermore the study designed the similar phenomena to a real world by applying variable multi-sensors. To do this, the study has suggested a method for evasion direction determination, calculation of approaching distance of preys and predators, and evasion velocity determination. The expression of realistic behaviors of digital creatures is controlled by precision motion control. This study has suggested a method to process behaviors followed in accordance with a formal framework calculated on a real-time basis. Thus, for the generation of less artificial fishes, the improved intelligence through objects' learning as well as the environmental variables such as the changes in water's viscosity due to velocity of fluid and temperature will be needed.

References

1. Terzopoulos, D., Tu, X., Grezeszczuk, R.: Artificial Fishes. Published in Artificial Life 1(4), 327–351 (1994)
2. Stephens, K., Pham, B., Wardhani, A.: Modlling Fish Behaviour, pp. 71–78. ACM Press/ ACM SIGGRAPH (2003)
3. Helfman, G.S.: The Diversity of Fishes, 3rd edn. Blackwell Science (1994)
4. Grey, J.: Aniamal Locomotion, Weidenfield and Nicolson, UK, pp. 18–83 (1968)
5. Beer, F.P.: Vector Mechanics for Engineers, 2nd edn. McGraw Hill (1990)
6. Clarke, E.M., Grumberg, O., Long, D.E.: Checking and Abstraction. In: Proceedings of the Nineteenth Annual ACM Symposium on Principles of Programming Languages (January 1992)
7. Reynolds, C.: Flocks, Herds, and Schools: A Distributed behavioral model, Computer Graphics. In: Proceedings of ACM SIGGRAPH 1987. ACM Press/ACM SIGGRAPH (1987)

A Software Implementation for Quality Management of Mobile VoIP Services

Chin-Chol Kim[1] and Beomjoon Kim[2,*]

[1] National Information Society Agency (NIA) of Korea, NIA Bldg., 77, Mugyo-Dong,
Jung-Gu, Seoul, 110-775, Korea
cckim@nia.or.kr
[2] Department of Electronic Engineering, Keimyung University, Daegu, 704-701,
Korea
bkim@kmu.ac.kr

Abstract. This paper proposes a new quality management scheme for the successful deployment of the mobile voice over internet protocol (VoIP) service. The proposed scheme can support the quality monitoring by measurement at any time with a software installed at every user terminal. As the first step toward the proposed scheme, a software is developed to measure the quality of the mobile VoIP service. The reliability of the developed software is verified by experiments in which the measurement results are compared between the developed software and the commercial proven softwares.

Keywords: mobile VoIP service, quality management, E-Model, MOS.

1 Introduction

The recent technical progress in wireless communication facilitates a packet-based voice service to be serviced over wireless networks. Considering its cheap cost and convenience such as mobility, the mobile voice over internet protocol (VoIP) service that is a telephony service provided over a wireless IP network adopting VoIP technology is likely to become popular in near future.

The national information society agency (NIA), an organization under the government of Korea, has been making an effort to establish a policy to promote the quality of the services provided over the Internet. As such an effort, an intensive research has been carried out to understand and judge the possibility and feasibility of commercialized mobile VoIP services.

Due to the innate best-effort property of IP, the quality of voice service using VoIP technology can be degraded comparing to the conventional telephone service over a circuit-based network [1]. The quality degradation would be severer when it comes to a wireless network supporting terminal mobility [2]. How to manage its service quality, therefore, is a key issue for the successful deployment of the mobile VoIP service.

---

* Corresponding author: Beomjoon Kim, Dept. Electronic Engineering, Keimyung University, 1095 Dalgubeol-daero, Dalseo-Gu, Daegu, 704-701, Korea.

T.-h. Kim et al. (Eds.): MulGraB/BSBT/IUrC 2012, CCIS 353, pp. 73–80, 2012.
© Springer-Verlag Berlin Heidelberg 2012

It has been concluded that an appropriate management scheme should appear for the quality management of mobile VoIP service. In addition, the proposed scheme should meet the requirement - the service quality monitoring should be supported by measurement initiated by user himself at any time. [1] Thus, this paper proposes a new service quality management scheme for mobile VoIP service that can be realized by a software installed in every user terminals.

2   Existing Voice Quality Models

2.1   PESQ

The perceptual evaluation of speech quality (PESQ) algorithm[3] predicts the speech quality of narrowband speech transmission. It compares the original and the degraded version of a speech sample to assess the speech quality with a mean opinion score value (MOS), which scales from 1 (bad) to 5 (excellent).

PESQ compares an original speech sample with its transmitted and hence degraded version. It implements a cognitive model which emulates the psychoacoustics of human hearing. First PESQ adjusts the degraded version to be time aligned. Then a psychoacoustic model assesses the distortion between original and degraded sample. PESQ can identify both constant delay offset and variable delay jitter. Constant delays are not considered in the calculation of the MOS value, but delay variations change the rating of the speech quality.

Even though the PESQ model can be downloaded free of charge from the ITU web page, using PESQ requires an expensive license agreement. Furthermore the computational complexity of PESQ is high. Thus, PESQ cannot be used in real-time nor it can be integrated into open-source software.

2.2   E-Model

The E-Model[4] takes into account various other impairments like delay and echoes to calculate the so-called R factor. The E-Model is a computational model that can be used as a transmission-planning tool for telecommunication systems.

One novel feature of the E-Model is the assumption that sources of impairment which are not correlated to each other can be added on a psychological scale. This allows to trade off different sources of impairment (e.g. loss versus delay) against each other.

The transmission rating factor R-Score range from 0 to 100, and a higher R-Score corresponds to a better telephone quality, zero being the worst value, 70 toll quality, and 100 excellent quality. The R-Score can be computed by the following simplified equation [2]

$$R = 94.2 - I_d(d) - I_e(c,l). \tag{1}$$

---

[1] This requirement is learned from our past experience with the Internet access service. In Korea, every ISP is recommended to build a website in which a user can measure the current transmission rate by himself at any time.

I_d is derived from the one-way delay (d) and given by

$$I_d(d) = 0.024d + 0.11(d - 177.3)H(d - 177.3) \tag{2}$$

where $H(x) = 1$ if $x \geq 0$, and 0 otherwise. I_e is derived from the used codec (c) and the packet loss rate (l) and given by

$$I_e(c, l) = \gamma_1 + \gamma_2 \cdot log(1 + \gamma_3 \cdot l) \tag{3}$$

where $\gamma_1, \gamma_2, \gamma_3$ are specified by the codec. Finally, MOS can be derived from the relationship given by

$$MOS = 1 + 0.035R + 7 \cdot 10^{-6}R(R - 60)(100 - R). \tag{4}$$

3   The Proposed Scheme

3.1   Basic Concept

Usually most Internet service providers (ISPs) depend on measurement equipments for their service quality management. For example, if a service provider is reported that a problem occurred with the service quality, it attempts to identify the cause of the problem by measuring a number of transmission conditions over its network. The approach in which an action is taken after a problem happens is inappropriate to manage the quality of mobile VoIP service that is being provided in real-time and affected by a lot of time-varying characteristics over a wireless channel. In particular, it is almost impossible to recognize the network conditions at the very moment when the problem occurred.

The only way to overcome the limitation due to 'the equipment-based management' is to enable every user terminals to measure the service quality by themselves. Then, the service quality can be measured while actual service is being provided; that is, the service quality can be monitored in real-time.

In Fig. 1, the basic concept of the proposed management scheme is shown. It requires a software installed in every user terminal. The software has the function to monitor the quality of mobile VoIP service by real-time measurement so that it can facilitate the user-friendly management satisfying the requirement of 'the measurement by user himself at any time' mentioned above.

Furthermore, if it is configured to report the measurement result to the management server, a database can be constructed containing a variety of

Fig. 1. The basic concept of the proposed management scheme

information on the service quality of mobile VoIP service. The information in the database can be utilized in many ways such as statistical analysis of the correlation between the service quality and transmission condition.

3.2   Software Development

The measurement software plays an essential role in implementing the proposed quality management scheme. The first version of the software has been developed for the mobile VoIP service is provided over the wireless broadband (WiBro) network [2] that is currently available in Korea.

The developed software consists of measurement function, reporting function, and user interface (UI). In developing the measurement function, it has to be decided which quality metric is applied. Since there are a number of metrics that have been introduced so far, we have selected typical ones considering their impact on the service quality of mobile VoIP service.

The selected quality metrics are summarized in Table 1. According to the communication layer that they belong, the selected metrics are classified into three groups: wireless metrics, networks metrics, and VoIP metrics.

Table 1. The selected service quality metrics

	Quality metrics
Wireless quality metrics	RSSI (Received Signal Strength Indicator)
	Tx Power (Transmission power)
	CINR (Carrier to Interference Noise Ratio)
Network quality metrics	Bandwidth, One-way delay, Jitter, Packet loss rate
VoIP quality metrics	R-Score, MOS (Mean Opinion Score)

3.3   Measurement Methodology

Once the quality metrics are selected, the detailed measurement method should be defined for each selected metric. For a metric, the measured value may differ according to the algorithm applied for its measurement. In order to avoid such an undesirable situation, the standardized measurement algorithm should be obeyed.

The wireless quality metrics are measured based on the information obtained from the standard interface and commands provided by the modem manufacturer. The RFCs are referred to for the network quality metrics; i.e., one-way

---

[2] WiBro is a broadband wireless access (BWA) system based on IEEE 802.16e standard. It is also known as mobile WiMax globally.

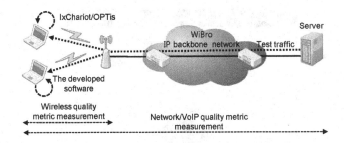

Fig. 2. The experimental environment

delay [6], packet loss ratio [7], and jitter [8]. For the VoIP quality metrics, we follow the E-Model[4] that derives R-Score using the measured values of network quality metrics.

4   Experiment

For the purpose of verifying the measurement capability and reliability of the developed software, a large-scale experiment was conducted.

4.1   Experimental Environment

The experimental environment is established as shown in Fig. 2. A server and two test terminals are connected through a commercial WiBro network.

The server generates test traffic based on ITU-T G.729 codec [9] with the transmission rate of 8 kb/s. For G.729, we have $\gamma_1 = 10$, $\gamma_2 = 47.82$, and $\gamma_3 = 0.18$ [1]. The generated traffic is configured to be downloaded to the two test terminals simultaneously.

The developed software operates on one test terminal and the commercial software does on the other test terminal. Two commercial software is used; Ix-Chariot [10] for network and VoIP metcris and OPTis [11] for wireless metrics. The measurement results can be compared between the two test terminals.

In this experiment, a laptop is used as a test terminal to minimize the effect of the performance of terminal on the measurement result. The laptop is equipped with a CPU of Intel Core 2 Duo T8300 2.4GHz*2 and a memory of 1 Gbytes. The operating system (OS) running at the laptop is Windows XP.

In order to reflect various transmission characteristics over a wireless link, the measurement is performed under the following five conditions:

- condition 1: indoor-stationary
- condition 2: indoor-walk
- condition 3: outside-stationary
- condition 4: outside-walk
- condition 5: outside-moving

Fig. 3. A screen capture of the measurement result by the developed software.

A measurement period lasts for 300 seconds. A data sample is made from averaging 60 values measured in every 5 seconds during the measurement period. Fig. 3 is a screen shot showing a data sample obtained from the developed software.

4.2   Measurement Result Comparison

In Fig. 4, we show the measurement results for four quality metrics: RSSI, delay, jitter, and R-Score. Although the other service quality metrics excluding these four indicators are also measured, their results are not included because they are redundant. The left-hand four figures show the measurement results by the developed software while the right-hand four figures show the the measurement results by IxChariot and OPTis.

The x-axis of each figure indicates the number of sample data. There are 1,000 data samples included in each figure. The 1,000 data samples are comprised of 5 sets of 200 data samples measured under the 5 measurement conditions above; e.g., the data samples [1, 200] are measured under the condition 1. The y-axis indicates the measured values corresponding to the target service quality metrics such as RSSI, delay, jitter, and R-Score. For comparison, the average (AVE), standard deviation (STDEV), maximum (MAX) and minimum (MIN) of the measured values are marked in each figure.

Overall, the results shown in left-hand four figures are very similar to those shown in right-hand four figures. For example, the measured values of one-way delay in both Fig 4-(c) and 4-(d) increase as terminal mobility increases. The 200 samples 801 through 1,000 correspond to the condition 5 in which one-way delay is measured in subway. Under the condition 5, therefore, the increase in one-way delay is very straightforward and the developed software captures

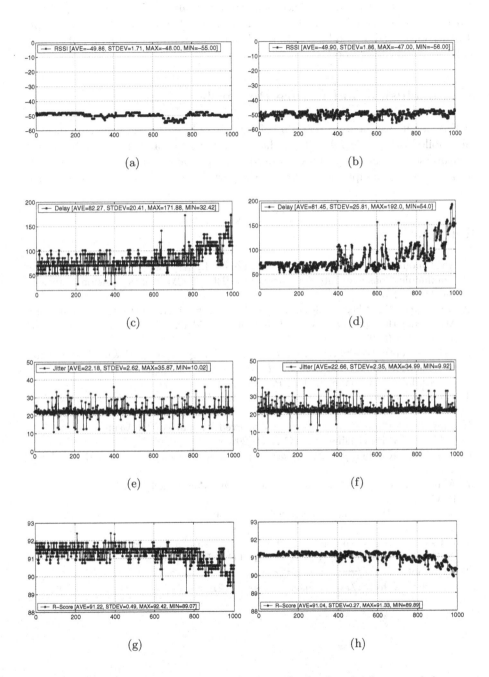

Fig. 4. Measurement results comparison between the developed software and the commercial software (x-axis: number of sample, y-axis: the measured value.)

it clearly as IxChariot does. Since one-way delay always remains under 177.3, $I_d(d)$ has almost no effect on the R-Score in Fig. 4-(g) and 4-(h). Based on the R-Score measured, it can be concluded that the current service quality of mobile VoIP service is quite good.

5   Conclusion and Future Research

In this paper, we have proposed a software-based quality management scheme for mobile VoIP service. A software has been developed and the reliability of its measurement capability has been proved by experiment. Currently, further work is in progress to adapt the software for a portable user device such as a smart phone.

References

1. Markopoulou, A.P., Tobagi, F.A., Karam, M.J.: Assessing the Quality of Voice Communications over Internet Backbones. IEEE/ACM Transactions on Networking 11(5) (2003)
2. Scalabrino, N., Pellegrini, F.D., Riggio, R., Maestrini, A., Costa, C., Chlamtac, I.: Measuring the Quality of VoIP Traffic on a WiMAX Testbed. In: Proceeding of Tridentcom (2007)
3. ITU, Perceptual evaluation of speech quality (PESQ): An objective method for end-to-end speech quality assessment of narrow-band telephone networks and speech codecs. ITU-T Recommendation P.862 (2001)
4. ITU, The E-Model, A Computational Model for Use in Transmission Planning: ITU-T Recommendation G.107 (1998)
5. Ding, L., Goubran, R.A.: Speech Quality Prediction in VoIP in Using the Entended E-Model. In: Proceeding of GTC 2003 (2003)
6. Almes, G., Kalidindi, S., Zekauskas, M.: A One-way Delay Metric for IPPM. RFC 2679 (1999)
7. Almes, G., Kalidindi, S., Zekauskas, M.: A One-way Packet Loss Metric for IPPM. RFC 2680 (1999)
8. Schulzrinne, H., Casner, S., Frederick, R., Jacobson, V.: RTP: A Transport Protocol for Real-Time Applications. RFC 3550 (2003)
9. ITU-T, Coding of speech at 8 kbit/s using conjugate-structure algebraic-code-excited linear prediction (CS-ACELP). ITU-T Recommendation G.729 (2007)
10. IxChariot, http://www.ixchaiot.com
11. Innowireless, http://www.innowireless.co.kr

Evaluation of User Sensibility Experience by Comparing the Product Use

Young Ju Lee

Chungwoon University, Department of Multimedia, Namjang-ri. 21,
HongSeong, ChungNam, Republic of Korea
yjlee@chungwoon.ac.kr

Abstract. This study drew user sensibility experience causes in the three dimensions of usability, perception and stimulation from smart-phone users who do not have use experience of I-Phone 4 or Galaxy S2. There were 10 cause factors that have impact on the sensibility experience of smart-phone users. They were; usefulness, ease of use, shortening capability, intuitive, orderly, similarity, aesthetic, difference, sensibility and fun. Among them, six causes had significant differences between the users of I-Phone 4 and Galaxy S2. These six causes were; usefulness, ease of use, intuitive, orderly, aesthetic and sensibility. Galaxy S2 received higher evaluation in usefulness, ease of use and sensibility. On the other hand, I-Phone received higher evaluation in intuitive, orderly and aesthetic.

Keywords: Sensibility Experience, Comparing the Product Use, Smart-phone.

1 Introduction

According to the market survey specialist IDC, the worldwide smart-phone market share of Samsung is 29.1% and I-Phone is 24.2%. However, according to recent information from NPD Co., in United States smart-phone market, Apple has market share of 31% and Samsung has 24% [1]. According to the survey results from comScore, mobiLens and Nielsen, the market shares of Samsung and Apple are slightly different by quarter dependent on new product launching; however, the fact that Samsung and Apple are top two is definite. Especially, Samsung and Apple forced HTC to withdraw from Korea and Motorola is also reducing their Korean operation now [2].

At present, the biggest issue in smart-phone market is the patent war between Samsung and Apple, in addition to the performances of two companies. The renowned design scholar Professor Donald Norman said that "Sensibility design that moves the emotion of consumer has the biggest and immediate impact on consumer's purchase decision. A product cannot succeed just because it has beautiful outlook design or it has excellent functions". Then it would be quite interesting to know the differences in sensibility response of I-Phone and Galaxy users, the two representative brands of Samsung and Apple. Accordingly, this study compares and analyzes the user sensibility experience causes on I-Phone and Galaxy, the two representative brands of Samsung and Apple.

T.-h. Kim et al. (Eds.): MulGraB/BSBT/IUrC 2012, CCIS 353, pp. 81–87, 2012.
© Springer-Verlag Berlin Heidelberg 2012

2   Previous Studies

K.D, Woo worked on design model building for the development of sensitivity type GUI. Woo drew the design-determining causes for user sensitivity GUI and classified them into four types (easy-shopping type, design-focusing type, new-product aiming type, price-sensitive/health-focusing type). He then built a user sensibility type GUI design development model by analyzing the similarities and differences among four lifestyle types [3].

S.K, Ihm worked on the relationship between fun sensibility and visual elements of touch phone GUI icon design. Ihm identified the relationship between fun and user preference on the main menu icon design type, which is the most important communication tool between user and mobile phone among the touch phone graphic elements. Ihm verified the differences in preference and fun regarding the icon design types dependent on the socio-demographic characteristics such as gender, age, occupation and design education. Ihm drew the visual constitution elements that are highly related to fun sensibility and explained the relationships by verifying the relationship between visual constitution elements and fun sensibility [4].

J.H, Byeon worked on the impact of mobile phone sensibility GUI design on users focusing on full touch screen phones. Byeon believed that mobile phone with various contents and additional functions is the basic specification of mobile phones these days and verified the impact of design considering sensibility on the usability of users [5].

J.H, Ahn worked on the enhancement of UI design usability for mobile phone integrated service. Ahn did survey on the satisfaction of users on nine menus of Samsung, LG, Pentech and Motorola. Based on the user satisfaction on current mobile phone UI, Ahn suggested future service direction which can enhance the satisfaction and meet the psychological/behavioral demand of users by way of efficiency tests [6].

H.W, Jeong worked on sensibility measurement and evaluation methods. Jeong focused on visual/tactile sensibility evaluation of interior finishing material and studied the synaesthesia design evaluation method by establishing the vocabulary and concepts of sensibility. Jeong pointed out the issues in sensibility studies and tried to build basic theory. Jeong finally suggested synaesthesia interface guideline by redefining the concept of sensibility and building the Korean language sensibility vocabulary system [7].

J.M, Pyeon worked on the optimization of mobile phone GUI design usability evaluation method. In order to develop optimum GUI design that fits with mobile environment, Pyeon recombined the existing usability evaluation methods from the viewpoint of mutual complementation. Pyeon suggested optimum evaluation method which can analyze mobile GUI usability from various viewpoints [8].

J.R, Kim suggested user forecast model by way of design sensibility measurement. Kim explored the definitions and standards in Enneagram, MBTI and G-sensibility, which are the representative design sensibility measuring methods. Kim reviewed the characteristics, measurement method, classification criteria and utilization of each type. Kim finally suggested user forecast model by design sensibility measurement on three characteristics and classification methods on sensibility measurement [9].

The sensibility design theory gets impact from the development and characteristic of self. For example, modernism design theory intensely encouraged production efficiency in terms of standardization and rationalization to meet the mass production demand caused by industrialization; however, the rigid and simple design form could not appeal to the aesthetic taste of many people.

In other words, modernism design theory needs change to fit with time. At present, the advance of modern sensibility design has not reached the stage of definition with universal properness acknowledged by everybody. Meanwhile, the sensibility design theory is an efficiency design method that gives certain sensibility/characteristic to product and meets the consumer spirit by being based on men's sensibility and cognition [10].

Sensibility is an internal matter of men and it has been an important study subject mainly in philosophy and psychology. After the sensibility engineering has appeared, approach on sensibility from the perspective of engineering became active and this change gave birth to the sensibility design methodology [11].

2.1   User Experience Design

User experience is overall experience of user feeling and thinking while directly/indirectly using certain system, product or service. It is not limited to the satisfaction in certain function or procedure. It is a valuable experience which user gets by participating, using, observing and interacting in all perceptive aspect of product. The creation of positive user experience is an important task in industrial design, software engineering, marketing and business administration.

This is very important matter in meeting the needs of user, enhancing the brand loyalty and succeeding in market. When user cannot achieve intended purpose, or, even when user has achieved the intended purpose, if the user had negative experience, or, if the user felt it was not emotionally, rationally or economically convenient, negative user experience occurs.

User experience design is developing and creating positive user experience on theoretical level or practical level. User experience design is mainly studied and developed in the areas of product design, interactive design, user interface design, information architecture and usability. However, user experience is based on core principle, which should be approached from wider and inter-study viewpoint in various fields.

User experience is a concept which was used in computer user interaction study. Still many user experience principles are coming from the software and hardware development in computer engineering. However, now the user experience concept has spread to and applied in many areas such as industrial service, goods, process, society and culture, in addition to computer products.

E. C. Edwards and D. J. Kasik first used the terminology of user experience in their paper. Since then, there had been many studies in 1970s and 1980s mainly in the context of human-centered design, which tried to create positive experience value from interaction between men and machine [12]. Apple Computer employee Donald Norman designed UX (User experience) in 1993 and he gave big impact on Apple computer design and researches on men-computer interaction.

In 1998, B. Joseph Pine II and James Gilmore gave their paper 'Welcome to the Experience Economy' to Harvard Business Journal. In 1999, they published it and it attracted interest on user experience in the field of economics and business management [13]. Pine and Gilmore said that the leading companies created unique experiences in their products and experiences in order to differentiate their products from others as superior products while agricultural economy advanced to industrial economy.

Especially entertainment companies like Walt Disney Co. put higher weight on the value of experience. They emphasized the positive aspect of consistent theme and removed negative aspect before they give visual-audio message to customers. They made the memories of such experience worthwhile to remember and ultimately tried to make products and service that can intensify the experience and memory through five senses.

3   Survey Method and Test Objects

Tests were done with 40 intensive smart-phone users in their 20s (average age 21.7 years old) in order to compare the sensibility of Apple I-Phone users and Samsung Galaxy phone users. 20 of the test objects used I-Phone only and another 20 used Galaxy phone only. The average use time of I-Phone users was 1 year and 3 months while that of Galaxy phone users was 1 year and 1 month. The two groups used smart-phone everyday for 7 hours and 7.5 hours respectively.

Regarding smart-phones to be used in the test, two iPhone-4s and two Galaxy-S2s were reset to original state immediately after purchase. We did not install any applications. Two I-Phone users and two Galaxy users entered the designated place for evaluation. Testing time for one team made of 4 users, was 90 minutes. In order to remove the familiarity effect, the I-Phone users were given Galaxy S2 and the Galaxy users were give iPhone-4.

Test objects answered the questionnaire on personal information and smart-phone use before the test. After the smart-phones were given, they performed the given tasks during given time limitation in accordance with the instruction given by test coordinator. After the task has been finished, they answered the questionnaire again.

3.1   Questionnaire Content and Measurement

Evaluation of user experience sensibility awareness of smart-phone user was done on 10 detail causes in 3 dimensions using 7 points Likert scale. The usability dimension had three causes of usefulness, ease of use and shortening capability. The perception had three causes of intuitive, orderly and similarity. The simulation had three causes of aesthetic, discriminative and sensibility and fun.

Table 1. Dimension and factors

Dimension	Factors	Questionnaire statement
Usability	Usefulness	It is easy to find desired function immediately
	Ease of use	It is easy to resolve an error
	Shortening	It provides with shortened path in major function execution
Perception	Intuitive	It is easy to visually recognize and understand
	Orderly	It is arranged in orderly manner
	Similarity	Similar functions are well grouped in menu
Stimulation	Aesthetic	It is visually attractive
	Discriminative	It is visually high-class and discriminative
	Sensibility	I feel homogeneity with others
	Fun	It stimulates curiosity without boring

4 Analysis Result

Users of Apple's I-Phone and the Samsung Galaxy smart-phone users sensibility comparative analysis results are as follows.

4.1 Usability Dimension Causes

In order to test the statistical differences among the items, matching sample t-test was done. There were statistically significant differences in usability (p<.001) and ease of use (* p<.05); however, there was no significant difference in shortening capability. In all three usability causes, Galaxy S2 had higher evaluation than I-Phone 4. Galaxy S2 was noticeably high in finding desired function immediately, in other words in usefulness, than I-Phone. The usefulness average of Galaxy S2 was 5.70 (s.d. = 1.19) while that of I-Phone was 4.98 (s.d.=.97). Regarding the ease of use for error resolving, Galaxy S2 was 5.09 (s.d. =1.15) and I-Phone 4 was 4.73 (s.d. = 1.08).

Table 2. Font sizes of headings. Table captions should always be positioned *above* the tables

	I-Phone 4	Galaxy S2	T
Usefulness	4.98 (.97)	5.70(1.19)	4.53 ***
Ease of use	4.73 (1.08)	5.09(1.15	2.03 *
Shortening	4.36 (1.27)	4.84(1.29	1.97

4.2 Perception Dimension Causes

In all three perception dimension causes, I-Phone 4 had higher evaluation than Galaxy S2. The intuitive average of I-Phone 4 was 5.77 (s.d.=1.13), average 1.04 higher than Galaxy S2 (m=4.73, s.d.=1.56). In orderly, I-Phone 4 (m=5.89, s.d.=1.26) was again higher than Galaxy S2 (m=5.09, s.d.=1.36). I-Phone was also higher in similarity; however, its evaluation point was relatively lower than other items. According to the statistical test on average differences by matching sample, intuitive (p<.001) and orderly (p<.001) had high statistical difference. There was no significant statistical difference in the average of grouping of similar functions in menu.

Table 3. Font sizes of headings. Table captions should always be positioned *above* the tables.

	I-Phone 4	Galaxy S2	T
Intuitive	5.77 (1.13)	4.73 (1.56)	4.26 ***
Orderly	5.89 (1.26)	5.09 (1.36)	3.93 ***
Similarity	4.75 (1.12)	4.43 (1.35)	1.70

4.3   Simulation Dimension Causes

In aesthetic, discriminative and fun, I-Phone 4 had higher evaluation than Galaxy S2. However, in sensibility, Galaxy S2 was higher than I-Phone 4. In aesthetic, the visual attraction, I-Phone 4 (m=4.20, s.d.=1.51) was higher. The differences in discriminative and fun were negligible. On the other hand, Galaxy S2 (m=5.39, s.d.=1.08) had average 1.04 higher in sensibility than I-Phone 4. In the t-test result, there were statistical differences between I-Phone 4 and Galaxy S2 in sensibility (p<.001) and aesthetic (p<.05). There were no significant differences in discriminative and fun.

Table 4. Font sizes of headings. Table captions should always be positioned *above* the tables.

	I-Phone 4	Galaxy S2	T
Aesthetic	4.20 (1.51)	3.68 (1.23)	2.21 *
Discriminative	4.02 (1.19)	3.90 (1.12)	.67
Sensibility	4.34 (1.59)	5.39 (1.08)	4.79 ***
Fun	4.93 (1.60)	4.86 (1.30)	.35

5   Conclusion

This study drew and compared user experience sensibility causes in the three dimensions of usability, perception and stimulation with test objects that do not have use experience of I-Phone 4 and Galaxy S2 respectively. Regarding the causes that have impact on the smart-phone user experience sensibility, there are ten detail causes in three dimensions. The usability had three causes of usefulness, ease of use and shortening capability. The perception had three causes of intuitive, orderly and similarity. The simulation had four causes of aesthetic, discriminative and sensibility and fun.

Among them, six causes had significant differences between the users of I-Phone 4 and Galaxy S2. These six causes were; usefulness, ease of use, intuitive, orderly, aesthetic and sensibility. Galaxy S2 received higher evaluation in usefulness, ease of use and sensibility. On the other hand, I-Phone received higher evaluation in intuitive, orderly and aesthetic.

After the test had been finished, the test objects were asked about their impression in using I-Phone 4 and Galaxy S2 for the first time. The I-Phone users said that they were not much confused or felt difficult in using Galaxy S2 for the first time; however, the Galaxy S2 users said that they had difficulty in finding desired functions in I-Phone 4. Galaxy S2 had higher evaluation than I-Phone 4 in usefulness and ease of use. The reason is believed that the UX of Galaxy S2 did not change a lot from the UX of previous feature phones, which the test objects had used before. Also, users who had used any smart-phone before seem to be capable of guessing the use method of new smart-phone, even it is their first time use.

References

1. http://www.appleinsider.com/articles/12/05/01/samsung_overtakes
   _apple_to_claim_smartphone_market_share_lead.html
2. http://snswow.com/82
3. Woo, K.D.: The Research on the Development Modal of Users' Emotional GUI Design. JeonBuk University (2009)
4. Ihm, S.K.: A study on the relationship between desig elements of GUI icons in the thouch phone and fun. YeonSei Uiversity (2009)
5. Byeon, J.H.: The study of the influence of sensational design of GUI design of mobile phones on the user. KeMyeong University (2010)
6. Ahn, J.H.: A study to improve the usability of UI design for the mobile integral service. HanYang University (2010)
7. Jeong, H.W.: A study on the evaluation method for the symesthetic design through the meaning of sensibility and vocabulary system. HongIk University (2008)
8. Pyeon, J.M.: The Optimization of the Graphic User Interface Usability Evaluation for Mobile Phone. DanKuk University (2005)
9. Kim, J.R.: A proposal of prediction model by design emotion measurement. KukMin University (2009)
10. Jin, J.M.: The study on Factors of Structure fir the Notebook Emotional Design. DongSoe University (2008)
11. Son, J.P.: A Study on emotional design in the digital era. Korean Society of Communication Design 8 (2005)
12. Edwards, E.C.: User Experience With the CYBER Graphics Terminal. In: Proceedings of VIM-21, pp. 284–286 (October 1974)
13. Joseph Pie II, B., Gilmore, J.: Welcome to the Experience Economy. Havard Business Journal (1998)

Better Decision Tree Induction
for Limited Data Sets of Liver Disease

Hyontai Sug

Division of Computer & Information Engineering, Dongseo University,
47 Jurye-ro, Sa-sang-gu, Busan 617-716, Korea
sht@gdsu.dongseo.ac.kr

Abstract. Decision trees can be very useful data mining tools for human experts to diagnose the disease, because the knowledge structure is represented in tree shape. But we may not get satisfactory decision tree, if we do not have enough number of consistent instances in the data sets. Recently two kinds of relatively small data sets of liver disorder from America and India are available, so in order to generate more accurate and useful decision trees for the disease this paper suggests appropriate sampling for the data instances that are in the class of higher error rate. Experiments with the two public domain data sets and a representative decision tree algorithm, C4.5, shows very successful results.

Keywords: Decision trees, C4.5, liver disorder, sampling.

1   Introduction

Data mining tools have been being adapted more and more in the domain of medicine to diagnose disease more accurately based on clinical test data. Liver is one of the most important internal organs in the human body, and it is known that the organ is responsible for more than one hundred functions of human body. The complexity of this organ makes it not easy to diagnose the disease of disorder in the organ [1]. A lot of attention has been given to build more accurate models based on public domain data of liver disorder since the data set is available in 1990 [2], and most recent research is based on some artificial neural network based approach for better accuracy. But, even though trained neural networks can be transformed into some rule forms, because the rules are in flat structure, identifying major factors in classification can be difficult [3]. On the other hand, tree structures can give information on what are major factors of the disease. But, unfortunately the accuracy of trained decision trees may not be as good as that of neural networks. This is especially true when we do not have enough number of instances for training. But, because we can easily understand the knowledge structures of decision trees, they have been considered very good data mining tools in medicine domain [4, 5].

The training algorithms of decision trees have the tendency of neglecting minor class in tree building process to achieve maximum accuracy with respect to the whole

T.-h. Kim et al. (Eds.): MulGraB/BSBT/IUrC 2012, CCIS 353, pp. 88–93, 2012.

data set. Minor class is the class that has smaller number of instances and relatively higher error rates than the other classes. Therefore, we may need some means to compensate the property of decision trees for better utilization.

Related issues in generating decision trees are random sampling. Because we usually do not have a perfect data set for data mining, and we don't have exact knowledge about the property of data sets, we use random sampling [6]. Each random sampling could generate different training and test data sets, so each random samples could generate slightly different results. Moreover, since our target data sets have limited information, random sampling like over-sampling could generate more different results. More recently, another data set called 'Indian liver patient data set' becomes available since 2012 [17], so it'll be interesting to compare the results of the two data sets. In order to see over-random sampling is effective, we want to do experiment based on the two different data sets of liver disorder disease and 10-fold cross validation for better objectivity in the experiment.

2   Related Work

A decision tree generation method, C4.5 [8], can be a representative decision tree algorithm, because the algorithm has been referred frequently and ranked number one by a survey in ICDM'06 [9]. When we build a decision tree, as each subtree in the tree is being built, each node will have smaller number of instances, so the reliability of lower part of the tree becomes worse than upper part of the tree. This problem is called fragmentation problem. Fragmentation problem can affect the training of decision tree, especially the data set has class imbalance in data composition. Class imbalance has different effect on over-sampling and under-sampling. Over-sampling means more duplicate instances are sampled from minor classes, while under-sampling means less number of instances are sampled from major classes than normal. In [10] five data sets that are mostly in large size are experimented using C4.5, and preferred under-sampling. In [11] four data sets consisting of 208~840 instances are experimented, and preferred under-sampling because it produced better sensitivity in misclassification cost. On the other hand, SMOTE [12] used synthetic data generation method as a way of over-sampling for minor classes, and showed that it is effective for nine different data sets in small to very large size. A weak point of the approach is that we need to understand the characteristics of data sets to synthesize the data. In [13] over-sampling was preferred for more accurate classification. In [14] an ensemble of neural networks are used to create new instances having different class values with original instances, and C4.5 with the 100% new instances of liver disorder data set showed worse accuracy of 67.8%, while C4.5 with the original data set showed the accuracy of 68.1%. From the reports of different results, we can conclude that for some data sets under-sampling can be more desirable, but for some other data sets, over-sampling can be more desirable.

For the liver disorder data set many researchers reported their results of experiments. In [15] sparse gird based approach achieved the accuracy of 72.5% for test data, but the approach does not consider symbolic representation of found models like artificial neural networks. In [16] artificial neural network based approach called artificial immune algorithm is used to find more accurate model, and achieved the accuracy of 94.8% for training data, and generated rules. In [17] four different data mining algorithms like Naïve Bayes classifier, C4.5, neural networks, and support vector machines were tried, and the accuracy of the algorithms ranges 56.52% ~ 71.59% in 10-fold cross-validation. Even though some artificial neural network based approach achieved high accuracy on training data, and we may drive rules from trained artificial neural networks, the rules are in flat structure so that determining major factors can be difficult, and moreover, we might confront with over-fitting problem.

3   Experimentation

We want to find better decision trees for the two liver disorder data sets of America and India. The size of data sets is relatively small. In this sense over-sampling the instances in the class of higher error rate or minor class to generate decision trees could improve our decision trees. In other words, because the splitting criterion of decision tree is heavily dependent on the number of instances, we increase the number of instances in the class of higher error rate by duplication to find decision trees of better accuracy. The following is the process.

Begin
    Do random sampling of 10-fold cross validation;
    Determine the class of higher error rate by generating decision tree of C4.5;
    For each fold **Do**
      R := 10%;
    Repeat
      Do R% more sampling for class of higher error rate;
      Generate decision trees of C4.5;
      Increase R by 10%;
    Until R = 200%;
    End For;
End.

The two data sets in UCI machine learning repository [18] called 'liver disorder' [2] and 'Indian liver patient data set' [7] were used. The liver disorder data set has the following properties: The number of instances is 345. There are 145 instances in class 1 and 200 instances in class 2 (disorder). Class 1 is the class of higher error rate, because its error rate is 50.1%, while the error rate of class 2 is 20.1% based on 10-fold cross-validation with C4.5. There are six continuous attributes as independent attributes. There are no missing values in all attributes. Table 1 shows the results of experiment. The averages of conventionally sampled data and the best of 20 over-sampled data are presented in 10-fold cross validation. The average accuracy of the liver disorder data set is slightly lower than the accuracy reported in other papers which is 64.6% ~ 68.9% in 10-fold cross validation [19]. Anyway, this difference comes from random sampling effect, so it doesn't matter for our experiment of over-sampling. As we can see in table 1, over-sampling gives 7% better accuracy with increase of 16 leaf nodes in the tree. In the table '±' symbol means standard deviation.

Table 1. Comparison of conventional and over-sampling for the liver disorder data set

Sampling method	Average accuracy	Average no. of leaves
Conventional	66.67%±5.94%	23.9±5.8
Over-sampling	73.35%±2.84%	39.9±15.7

'Indian liver patient data set' has the following properties; the number of instances is 583, and there are 167 instances in class 2 and 416 instances in class 1 (disorder). Note that class value has opposite meaning in the two data sets. There are nine continuous attributes as independent attributes, and one attribute has gender value. Small number of missing values exists in the data set. Class 2 is the class of higher error rate, because its error rate is 52.3%, while the error rate of class 1 is 17.8% based on 10-fold cross-validation with C4.5. As we can see in table 2, oversampling gives 5% better accuracy with increase of 26 leaf nodes in the tree.

Table 2. Comparison of conventional and over-sampling for Indian liver data set

Sampling method	Average accuracy	Average no. of leaves
Conventional	69.64%±7.39%	33.1±8.3
Over-sampling	74.63%±7.0%	58.9±14.3

4   Conclusions and Future Work

Decision trees have been considered one of the best data mining tools of understandability. But, weakness of decision trees arises due to the fact that their branching criteria give higher priority to the classes of majority. Two different data sets related to liver disorder attract our interest for data mining. The data sets are relatively small and have some error rates so that decision trees in conventional means may not generate good results due to the property.

In order to generate more accurate trees we used over-sampling technique for the data instances of the class of higher error rates. Experiments with a decision tree algorithm, C4.5, showed very good results. But, the trees become larger, so we may want to apply severer pruning for better understandability. Because pruning can generate smaller trees, we want to apply appropriate pruning parameters to generate comprehensible and accurate trees for the data sets.

A branch will be pruned, if predicted error rate decreases by pruning the branch. The upper limit of predicted error rate P for a leaf is calculated by $U_{CF}(e, t)$ function that is in binomial distribution. In the function e is the number of incorrectly classified instances and t is the number of training instances in a node. CF is confidence level of the predicted error rate. The number of predicted error for the leaf is $t \times P$. This number is summed for each leaf in a subtree to calculate the number of predicted errors for the subtree. The number of predicted error is calculated for both of pruned state and unprunned state of a subtree, and if pruned state generates smaller number of predicted errors, the subtree will be pruned. Because P value is proportional to CF value, lower CF value can generate smaller predicted error rate. Default CF value in C4.5 is 25% and this values was set based on C4.5 developer's experience [8]. Moreover, as we can see in table 1 and 2, the standard deviations are somewhat large in our trees. Therefore, we have room to find proper CF value for accurate and understandable trees from the results of the experiment.

References

1. Ribeiro, R., Marinho, R., Velosa, J., Ramalho, F., Sanches, J.M.: Chronic liver disease staging classification based on ultrasound, clinical and laboratorial data. In: Proceedings of 2011 IEEE International Symposium on Biomedical Imaging from Nano to Macro, pp. 707–710 (2011)
2. UCI Machine Learning Repository,
   http://archive.ics.uci.edu/ml/datasets/Liver+Disorders
3. Zhou, Z., Jiang, Y., Chen, S.: Extracting symbolic rules from trained neural network ensembles. AI Communications 16(1), 3–15 (2003)
4. Podgorelec, V., Kokol, P., Stiglic, B., Rozman, I.: Decision trees: an overview and their use in medicine. Journal of Medical Systems 26(5), 445–463 (2002)
5. Lin, Y.C.: Design and Implementation of an Ontology-Based Psychiatric Disorder Detection System. WSEAS Transactions on Information Sciences and Applications 7(1), 56–69 (2010)
6. Tryfos, P.: Sampling for Applied Research: Text and Cases, Willy (1996)
7. Ramana, B.V., Babu, M.S.P., Venkateswarlu, N.B.: A Critical Comparative Study of Liver Patients from USA and INDIA: An Exploratory Analysis. International Journal of Computer Science, 506–516 (2012)
8. Quinlan, J.R.: C4.5: Programs for Machine Learning. Morgan Kaufmann Publishers, Inc. (1993)
9. Wu, X., Kumar, V., Quinlan, J.R., Ghosh, J., Yang, Q., Motoda, H., McLachlan, G.J., Ng, A., Liu, B., Yu, P.S., Zhou, Z., Steinbach, M., Hand, D.J., Steinberg, D.: Top 10 Algorithms in Data Mining. Knowledge Information System 14, 1–37 (2008)
10. Chawla, N.V.: C4.5 and Imbalanced data sets : Investigating the effect of sampling emthod, probalistic estimate, and decision tree structure. In: Workshop on Learning from Imbalanced Datasets II, ICML, Washington DC (2003)
11. Drummond, C., Holte, R.C.: C4.5, Class Imbalance, and Cost Sensitivity: Why Under-sampling beats Over-sampling. In: Workshop on Learning from Imbalanced Datasets II, ICML, Washington DC (2003)
12. Chawla, N.V., Bowyer, K.W., Hall, L.O., Kegelmeyer, W.P.: SMOTE: Synthetic Minority Over-sampling Technique. Journal of Artificial Intelligence Research 16, 341–378 (2002)
13. Japkowicz, N., Stephen, S.: The class imbalance problem: A systematic study. Intelligent Data Analysis 6(5), 429–449 (2002)

14. Zhou, Z., Jiang, Y.: NeC4.5: Neural Ensemble Based C4.5. IEEE Transactions on Knowledge and Data Engineering 16 (2004)
15. Garcke, J., Griebel, M.: Classification with sparse grids using simplicial basis function. Intelligent Data analysis 6 (2002)
16. Kahramanli, H., Allahverdi, N.: Mining Classification Rules for Liver Disorders. International Journal of Mathematics and Computers in Simulation 3(1), 9–19 (2009)
17. Ramana, B.V., Babu, M.S.P., Venkateswarlu, N.B.: A Critical Study of Selected Classification Algorithms for Liver Disease Diagnosis. International Journal of Database Management Systems 3(2), 101–114 (2011)
18. Frank, A., Suncion, A.: UCI Machine Learning Repository. University of California, School of Information and Computer Sciences, Irvine (2010), http://archive.ics.uci.edu/ml
19. Zheng, Z.: Scaling up the Rule Generation of C4.5. In: Wu, X., Kotagiri, R., Korb, K.B. (eds.) PAKDD 1998. LNCS, vol. 1394, pp. 348–359. Springer, Heidelberg (1998)

Expert System Based on Neural-Fuzzy Rules
for Thyroid Diseases Diagnosis

Ahmad Taher Azar[1,3], IEEE Member, Aboul Ella Hassanien[2,3],
and Tai-hoon Kim[4]

[1] Misr University for Science & Technology (MUST), 6th of October City, Egypt
[2] Faculty of Computers and Information - Cairo University
[3] Scientific Research Group in Egypt (SRGE)
Ahmad_t_azar@ieee.org, aboitcairo@gmail.com
http://www.egyptscience.net
[4] Hannam University, Korea
taihoonn@empas.com

Abstract. The thyroid, an endocrine gland that secretes hormones in the blood, circulates its products to all tissues of the body, where they control vital functions in every cell. Normal levels of thyroid hormone help the brain, heart, intestines, muscles and reproductive system function normally. Thyroid hormones control the metabolism of the body. Abnormalities of thyroid function are usually related to production of too little thyroid hormone (hypothyroidism) or production of too much thyroid hormone (hyperthyroidism). Therefore, the correct diagnosis of these diseases is very important topic. In this study, Linguistic Hedges Neural-Fuzzy Classifier with Selected Features (LHNFCSF) is presented for diagnosis of thyroid diseases. The performance evaluation of this system is estimated by using classification accuracy and k-fold cross-validation. The results indicated that the classification accuracy without feature selection was 98.6047% and 97.6744% during training and testing phases, respectively with RMSE of 0.02335. After applying feature selection algorithm, LHNFCSF achieved 100% for all cluster sizes during training phase. However, in the testing phase LHNFCSF achieved 88.3721% using one cluster for each class, 90.6977% using two clusters, 91.8605% using three clusters and 97.6744% using four clusters for each class and 12 fuzzy rules. The obtained classification accuracy was very promising with regard to the other classification applications in literature for this problem.

1   Introduction

The thyroid gland is the biggest gland in the neck [1]. The thyroid gland is placed in the anterior neck. It has the shape of a butterfly with the two wings being represented by the left and right thyroid lobes. The thyroid provides the thyroid hormones. The thyroid gland produces two active thyroid hormones, levothyroxine (abbreviated T4) and triiodothyronine (abbreviated T3). These hormones are important in the production of proteins, in the regulation of body temperature, and in overall energy production and regulation. The thyroid gland has many diseases. The most of these are goiters, thyroid cancer, solitary thyroid nodules, hyperthyroidism,

T.-h. Kim et al. (Eds.): MulGraB/BSBT/IUrC 2012, CCIS 353, pp. 94–105, 2012.

hypothyroidism, thyroiditis, etc [2]. The hypothyroidism is too little thyroid hormone. It is a common problem. Hypothyroidism can even be associated with pregnancy. The diagnosis and treatment for all types of hypothyroidism is usually straightforward. The goiter is a dramatic enlargement of the thyroid gland. Goiters are often removed due to cosmetic reasons. Moreover, these compress other vital structures of the neck including the trachea and the esophagus making breathing and swallowing difficult. The thyroid nodules can take on characteristics of malignancy. Therefore, these require biopsy or surgical excision. In addition to, these contain risks of radiation exposure. The thyroid cancer is a fairly common malignancy. Therefore the diagnosis of this disease is very difficult. The hyperthyroidism is too much thyroid hormone. The radioactive iodine, anti-thyroid drugs, or surgery are common methods used for treating a hyperthyroid patient. The thyroiditis is an inflammatory status for the thyroid gland. This can give with a number of symptoms such as fever and pain, but it can also give as subtle findings of hypo or hyperthyroidism. Accurate prediction of the thyroid data besides clinical examination and complementary investigation is an important issue in the diagnosis of thyroid disease. Various new methods have been used for diagnosis of thyroid diseases like Artificial Neural Network [3-8], Linear Discriminant Analysis (LDA) [9], decision trees [9, 10], Fuzzy expert systems and neuro-fuzzy classification [11-16], Support Vector Machines [15-20]. This paper presents a fuzzy feature selection (FS) method based on the linguistic hedges (LH) concept [21, 22] for thyroid diseases classification. This classifier is used to achieve a very fast, simple and efficient computer aided diagnosis (CAD) system. The rest of this paper is organized as follows: Section 2 provides subjects and methods that are used in this study. In Section 3, a review of the classifier that is considered in thyroid diseases diagnosis is presented. Section 4 reports the results of experimental evaluations of the adaptive neural-fuzzy classifier and finally, in Section 5, conclusion and directions for future research are presented.

2   Subjects and Methods

Classification of data from the University of California, Irvine (UCI) machine learning data set repository was performed to evaluate the effectiveness of the Neural-fuzzy classifier on real-world data, and to facilitate comparison with other classifiers. [23]. The dataset contains 3 classes and 215 samples. These classes are assigned to the values that correspond to the hyper-, hypo-, and normal function of the thyroid gland. All samples have five features. These are [23]:

1. T3-resin uptake test (A percentage).
2. Total serum thyroxin as measured by the isotopic displacement method.
3. Total serum triiodothyronine as measured by radioimmuno assay.
4. Basal thyroid-stimulating hormone (TSH) as measured by radioimmuno assay.
5. Maximal absolute difference of TSH value after injection of 200 µg of thyrotropin-releasing hormone as compared to the basal value.

The 150 samples of 215 belong to hyper-function class namely class-1. The 35 samples of 215 belong to hypo-function class namely class-2. The 30 samples of 215 belong to normal-function class namely class-3 [23].

3   Adaptive Neuro-Fuzzy Classifiers

The usage of ANFIS [24-26] for classifications is unfavorable. For example, if there are three classes labeled as 1, 2 and 3. The ANFIS outputs are not integer. For that reason the ANFIS outputs are rounded, and determined the class labels. But, sometimes, ANFIS can give 0 or 4 class labels. These situations are not accepted. As a result ANFIS is not suitable for classification problems. In this section, adaptive neuro-fuzzy classifier is discussed in details. In these models, k-means algorithm is used to initialize the fuzzy rules. Also, Gaussian membership function is only used for fuzzy set descriptions, because of its simple derivative expressions.

3.1   Adaptive Neuro-Fuzzy Classifier with Linguistic Hedges (ANFCLH)

Adaptive neuro-fuzzy classifier (ANFC) with Linguistic hedges [21] is based on fuzzy rules. Linguistic hedges are applied to the fuzzy sets of rules, and are adapted by Scaled Conjugate Gradient (SCG) algorithm. By this way, some distinctive features are emphasized by power values, and some irrelevant features are damped with power values. The power effects in any feature are generally different for different classes. The using of linguistic hedges increases the recognition rates. A fuzzy classification rule that has two inputs $\{x_1, x_2\}$ and one output y is defined with LHs as IF x_1 is A_1 with p_1 hedge AND x_2 is A_2 with p_2 hedge THEN y is C_1 class, where A_1 and A_2 denote linguistic terms that are defined on X_1 and X_2 feature space; p_1 and p_2 denote linguistic hedges, respectively; C_1 denotes the class label of the output y. Fig. 1 shows the ANFCLH architecture. The feature space with two inputs $\{x_1, x_2\}$ is partitioned into three classes $\{C_1, C_2, C_3\}$, in the Figure. The feature space $X_1 \times X_2$ is separated into fuzzy regions (Jang et al. 1997). This technique is based on zero-order Sugeno fuzzy model [27]. The crisp outputs of fuzzy rules are determined by weighted average operator [26].

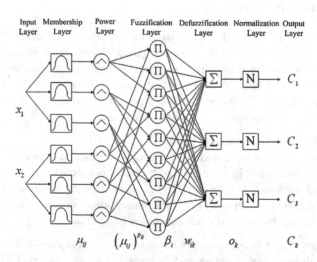

Fig. 1. A neuro-fuzzy classifier with LHs. [21]

In this classifier, the nodes in the same layer have the same type of node functions. The layers and their properties are given as follows:

Layer 1: In this layer, the membership grade of each input to specified fuzzy region is measured. Gaussian function is employed as MF due to smooth partial derivatives of its parameters, and has less parameter. The Gaussian MF is given as follows [21]:

$$\mu_{ij}(x_{sj}) = \exp\left(-0.5\frac{(x_{sj}-c_{ij})^2}{\sigma_{ij}^2}\right) \tag{1}$$

where $\mu_{ij}(x_{sj})$ represents the membership grade of the ith rule and the jth feature; x_{sj} denotes the sth sample and the jth feature of input matrix $X\{X \in R^{NxD}\}$; c_{ij} and σ_{ij} are the center and the width of Gaussian function, respectively.

Layer 2: In this layer, the secondary meanings of fuzzy sets are calculated with their LHs as in Eq. (2) [21].

$$\alpha_{ijs} = [\mu_{ij}(x_{sj})]^{p_{ij}} \tag{2}$$

where α_{ijs} denotes the modified membership grades of $\mu_{ij}(x_{sj})$; p_{ij} denotes the LH value of the ith rule and the jth feature.

Layer 3: The degree of fulfillment of the fuzzy rule for x s sample is determined in this layer. It is also called as the firing strength of rule. So, the B_{is} firing strength of the ith rule for D number of features is defined as in Eq. (3) [21].

$$B_{is} = \prod_{j=1}^{D} \alpha_{ijs} \tag{3}$$

Layer 4: In this layer, the weighted outputs are calculated as in Eq. (4) [21], and every rule can affect each class according to their weights. However, if a rule controls a specific class region, the weight between this rule output and the specific class is to be bigger than the other class weights. Otherwise, the class weights are fairly small:

$$O_{sk} = \sum_{i=1}^{U} B_{is} w_{ik} \tag{4}$$

where w_{ik} represents the degree of belonging to the kth class that is controlled with the ith rule; O_{sk} denotes the weighted output for the sth sample that belongs to the kth class, and U is the number of rules.

Layer 5: If the summation of weights is bigger than 1, the outputs of the network should be normalized in the last layer as follows [21]:

$$h_{sk} = \frac{O_{sk}}{\sum_{l=1}^{k} O_{sl}} = \frac{O_{sk}}{\delta_s}, \delta_s = \sum_{l=1}^{k} O_{sl} \tag{5}$$

Where h_{sk} represents the normalized degree of the sth sample that belongs to the kth class; and K is the number of classes. After then, the class label (C_s) of sth sample is determined by the maximum h_{sk} value as in Eq. (6) [21].

$$C_s = \max_{k=1,2,\ldots,k} \{h_{sk}\} \qquad (6)$$

The antecedent parameters of the network $\{c, \sigma, p\}$ could be adapted by any optimization method. In this study, scaled conjugate gradient (SCG) method is used to adapt the network parameters [28]. The cost function that is used in the SCG method is determined from the least mean squares of the difference target and the calculated class value [26, 29]. According to the above definition, the cost function E is defined as in Eq. (7) [21].

$$E = \frac{1}{N} \sum_{s=1}^{N} E_s, \; E_s = \frac{1}{2} \sum_{k=1}^{K} (t_{sk} - h_{sk})^2 \qquad (7)$$

3.2   Linguistic Hedges Neural-Fuzzy Classifier With Selected Features (LHNFCSF)

Cetişli (2010) presented a fuzzy feature selection (FS) method based on the LH concept. It uses the powers of fuzzy sets for feature selection [21, 22]. The values of LHs can be used to show the importance degree of fuzzy sets. When this property is used for classification problems, and every class is defined by a fuzzy classification rule, the LHs of every fuzzy set denote the importance degree of input features. If the LHs values of features are close to concentration values, these features are more important or relevant, and can be selected. On the contrary, if the LH values of features are close to dilation values, these features are not important, and can be eliminated. According to the LHs value of features, the redundant, noisily features can be eliminated, and significant features can be selected. In this technique, [22], if linguistic hedge values of classes in any feature are bigger than 0.5 and close to 1, this feature is relevant, otherwise it is irrelevant. The program creates a feature selection and a rejection criterion by using power values of features. There are two selection criteria, one is the selection of features that have the biggest hedge value for any class and the other is the selection of features that have a bigger hedge value for every class, because any feature cannot be selective for every class. For that reason, a selective function should be described from the hedge values of any feature as in Eq. (8) [22]:

$$P_j = \prod_{i=1}^{k} P_{ij} \qquad (8)$$

where P_j denotes the selection value of the jth feature, and K is the number of classes. The Feature selection and classification algorithms were discussed in detail in [22].

4 Results and Discussions

4.1 Training and Testing Phases of Classifier

The collection of well-distributed, sufficient, and accurately measured input data is the basic requirement in order to obtain an accurate model. The classification process starts by obtaining a data set (input-output data pairs) and dividing it into a training set and testing data set. The training data set is used to train the NFC, whereas the test data set is used to verify the accuracy and effectiveness of the trained NFC. Once the model structure and parameters have been identified, it is necessary to validate the quality of the resulting model. In principle, the model validation should not only validate the accuracy of the model, but also verify whether the model can be easily interpreted to give a better understanding of the modeled process. It is therefore important to combine data-driven validation, aiming at checking the accuracy and robustness of the model, with more subjective validation, concerning the interpretability of the model. There will usually be a challenge between flexibility and interpretability, the outcome of which will depend on their relative importance for a given application. While, it is evident that numerous cross-validation methods exist, the choice of the suitable cross-validation method to be employed in the NFC is based on a trade-off between maximizing method accuracy and stability and minimizing the operation time. To avoid overfitting problems during modeling process, k-fold cross-validation was used for better reliability of test results [30]. In k-fold cross-validation, the original sample is randomly partitioned into k subsamples. A single subsample is retained as the validation data for testing the model, and the remaining k - 1 subsamples are used as training data. The cross-validation process is then repeated k times (the 'folds'), with each of the k subsamples used exactly once as the validation data. The average of the k results gives the validation accuracy of the algorithm [31]. The advantages of k-fold cross validation are that the impact of data dependency is minimized and the reliability of the results can be improved [32]. In the first phase, NFC is trained using all data instances without feature reduction. In this study, 60–40% partition was used for training-test of the NFC for diagnosis of thyroid disease. According to this proportion, 129 of 215 samples in thyroid gland database were used for training of NFC while 86 of 215 samples in thyroid gland database were used for testing. The number of training and test data for each of classes can be given as in Table 1.

Table 1. The number of training and test data for each of class

Class	The number of training data (60%)	The number of testing data (40%)
Class-1: The hyper-function class	90	60
Class-2: The hypo-function class	21	14
Class-3: The normal-function class	18	12
Total	129	86

The error convergence curve of NFC achieved mean RMSE values of 0.0233 in the training phase as shown in Fig. 2. In feature reduction stage of the ANFCLH for diagnosis of thyroid disease, the feature extraction and the feature reduction processes are performed. In the validation phase, 4-fold cross validation is used to compute the recognition rates. The number of fuzzy rules is determined according to the number of classes. The LH values of selected features for thyroid gland dataset after the training are given in Table 2. The total LH values for every class and every feature are shown in Fig. 3.

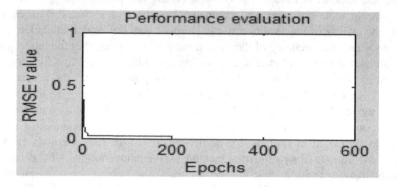

Fig. 2. Performance Evaluation of NFC during training phase without feature reduction

According to the feature selection algorithm, T3-resin uptake test (Feature 1), total serum thyroxin (Feature 2), Total serum triiodothyronine (Feature 3) and Maximal absolute difference of TSH (Feature 5) are common relevant features for each class. The basal thyroid-stimulating hormone (TSH) (Feature 4) is irrelevant for each class. It can be seen from Table 2 that malignant class is easily distinguished from the other class.

Table 2. The LH values of Thyroid Disease dataset for every class and every feature

Class/Features	Feature 1	Feature 2	Feature 3	Feature 4	Feature 5
Class-1: The hyper-function class	0.7147	0.5382	0.2665	5.68e-11	0.3119
Class-2: The hypo-function class	0.4052	1	0.3439	0.2792	0.8821
Class-3: The normal-function class	0.6538	1	0.4367	0.3828	0.5506
Total LH values	1.7738	2.5383	1.0471	0.6619	1.7446

If the classification rules are expressed for each class, then the rules are:

R1: IF T3-resin uptake test is A_{11} with $p_{11} = 0.7147$ AND total serum thyroxin is A_{12} with $p_{12} = 0.2665$ AND Total serum triiodothyronine is A_{13} with $p_{13} = 0.2665$ AND Basal thyroid-stimulating hormone (TSH) is A_{14} with $p_{14} = 5.6802e-11$ AND Maximal absolute difference of TSH is A_{15} with $p_{15} = 0.3119$ THEN class is hyper-function.

R2: IF T3-resin uptake test is A_{21} with p_{21} = 0.4052 AND total serum thyroxin is A_{22} with p_{22} = 1 AND Total serum triiodothyronine is A_{23} with p_{23} = 0.3439 AND Basal thyroid-stimulating hormone (TSH) is A_{24} with p_{24} = 0.2792 AND Maximal absolute difference of TSH is A_{25} with p_{25} = 0.8821 THEN class is hypo-function.

R3: IF T3-resin uptake test is A_{31} with p_{31} = 0.6538 AND total serum thyroxin is A_{32} with p_{32} = 1 AND Total serum triiodothyronine is A_{33} with p_{33} = 0.4367 AND Basal thyroid-stimulating hormone (TSH) is A_{34} with p_{34} = 0.3828 AND Maximal absolute difference of TSH is A_{35} with p_{35} = 0.5506 THEN class is normal-function.

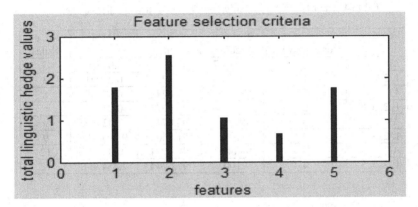

Fig. 3. Total LH values of thyroid gland dataset for every class and every feature

After the classification step, it can be seen from Table 3, using one cluster for each class, that some of the hedge values are bigger than 1, because the hedge values are not constrained in the classification step [22]. It's clear from the results that T3-resin uptake test (Feature 1) is very important feature for hyper-function and normal-function classes while total serum thyroxin (Feature 2) is very important feature for hypo-function class. As shown in Table 3, the discriminative powers of the selected features are better than all features.

Table 3. The LH values of thyroid disease dataset for every class after selection of relevant features

Class/Features	Feature 2	Feature 1	Feature 5	Feature 3
Class-1: The hyper-function class	0.6966	1.0668	0.5294	1.0210
Class-2: The hypo-function class	1.3054	1.0393	1.0142	1.1147
Class-3: The normal-function class	1.3278	1.4968	1.1150	0.9845

The classification results of the training and testing phases obtained from the neural-fuzzy classifier are displayed in Table 4 and also represented graphically in Fig. 4. Here, each class for LHNFCSF is intuitively defined with 3, 6, 9 and 12 fuzzy rules based on the cluster size for each class ranged from 1-4 clusters. The results indicated that the classification accuracy without feature selection was 98.6047% and 97.6744% during training and testing phases, respectively with RMSE of 0.02335. After applying feature selection algorithm, LHNFCSF achieved 100% for all cluster sizes during training phase. However, in the testing phase LHNFCSF achieved 88.3721% using one cluster for each class, 90.6977% using two clusters, 91.8605% using three clusters and 97.6744% using four clusters for each class and 12 fuzzy rules. The classifier achieved mean RMSE values of 7.4547e-8 in the training phase using four clusters as shown in Fig. 5.

Table 4. The LHNFCSF classification results of thyroid disease dataset

Features	Cluster size for each class	Training Accuracy	Testing Accuracy	RMSE	No. of Rules
All	1	98.6047	97.6744	0.02335	3
1, 2, 3, 5	1	100	88.3721	0.00091	3
All	2	98.6047	97.6744	0.02335	6
1, 2, 3, 5	2	100	90.6977	0.00072	6
All	3	98.6047	97.6744	0.02335	9
1, 2, 3, 5	3	100	91.8605	9.374e-11	9
All	4	98.6047	97.6744	0.02335	12
1, 2, 3, 5	4	100	97.6744	7.4547e-8	12

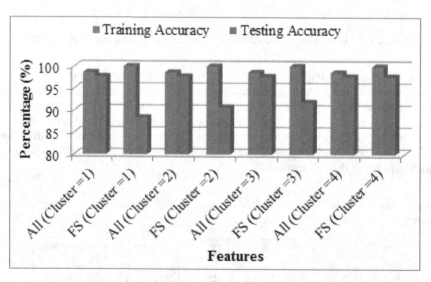

Fig. 4. LHNFCSF Classification Results of thyroid disease based on feature selection and cluster size for each class

The results indicated that, the selected features increase the recognition rate for test set. It means that some overlapping classes can be easily distinguished by selected features. The neural fuzzy classifier surface of feature 1 and feature 2 using 12 fuzzy rules is shown in Fig.

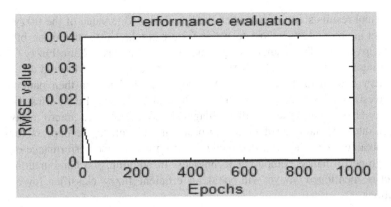

Fig. 5. Performance Evaluation of LHNFCSF during training phase after selection of relevant features using two clusters for each class

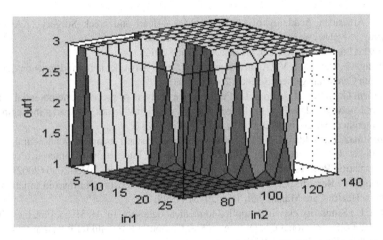

Fig. 6. Neural Fuzzy classifier surface using four clusters for each class

5   Conclusion

Nowadays, CAD systems are getting more and more popular. Because with the help of the CAD systems, the possible errors experts made in the course of diagnosis can be avoided, and the medical data can be examined in shorter time and more detailed as well. In fact, thyroid function diagnosis can be formulated as the classification problem, so it can be automatically performed with the aid of the CAD systems. Machine learning techniques are increasingly introduced to construct the CAD systems owing to its strong capability of extracting complex relationships in the bio- medical data. Recently, various methods have been presented to solve this problem. In this study, the positive effect of linguistic hedges on adaptive neural-fuzzy classifier is presented. According to the proposed method of Cetişli [21, 22], linguistic hedges are used in fuzzy classification rules, and adapted during the training of the system.

Experimental results showed that when the linguistic hedge value of the fuzzy classification set in any feature is close to 1, this feature is relevant for that class, otherwise it may be irrelevant. The results strongly suggest that Adaptive Neuro-Fuzzy Classifier with Linguistic Hedges (ANFCLH) can aid in the diagnosis of thyroid disease and can be very helpful to the physicians for their final decision on their patients. The future investigation will pay much attention to evaluate Neuro-Fuzzy Classifier with Linguistic Hedges in other medical diagnosis problems like micro array gene selection, internet, and other data mining problems. Therefore, the impressive results may be obtained with the proposed method and improving the performance of NFCs using high-performance computing techniques. In addition, the combination of the approaches mentioned above will yield an efficient fuzzy classifier for a lot of applications.

References

[1] The American Academy of Otolaryngology—Head and Neck Surgery (AAO-HNS), http://www.entnet.org/HealthInformation/ Thyroid-Disorders.cfm (accessed June 2012)
[2] Zhang, G., Berardi, L.V.: An investigation of neural networks in thyroid function diagnosis. Health Care Management Science, 29–37 (1998)
[3] Serpen, G., Jiang, H., Allred, L.: Performance analysis of probabilistic potential function neural network classifier. In: Proceedings of Artificial Neural Networks in Engineering Conference, St. Louis, MO, vol. 7, pp. 471–476 (1997)
[4] Özyilmaz, L., Yildirim, T.: Diagnosis of thyroid disease using artificial neural network methods. In: Proceedings of ICONIP 2002 Nineth International Conference on Neural Information Processing, Orchid Country Club, Singapore, pp. 2033–2036 (2002)
[5] Zhang, G., Berardi, V.L.: An investigation of neural networks in thyroid function diagnosis. Health Care Manag. Sci. 1(1), 29–37 (1998)
[6] Pasi, L.: Similarity classifier applied to medical data sets. In: 10 Sivua, Fuzziness in Finland 2004 International Conference on Soft Computing, Helsinki, Finland & Gulf of Finland & Tallinn, Estonia (2004)
[7] Hoshi, K., Kawakami, J., Kumagai, M., et al.: An analysis of thyroid function diagnosis using Bayesian-type and SOM-type neural networks. Chem. Pharm. Bull (Tokyo) 53(12), 1570–1574 (2005)
[8] Erol, R., Ogulata, S.N., Sahin, C., Alparslan, Z.N.: A radial basis function neural network (RBFNN) approach for structural classification of thyroid diseases. J. Med. Syst. 32(3), 215–220 (2008)
[9] Temurtas, F.: A comparative study on thyroid disease diagnosis using neural networks. Expert Syst. Appl. 36(1), 944–949 (2009)
[10] Margret, J.J., Lakshmipathi, B., Kumar, A.S.: Diagnosis of Thyroid Disorders using Decision Tree Splitting Rules. International Journal of Computer Applications 44(8), 43–46 (2012)
[11] Keles, A., Keles, A.: ESTDD: Expert system for thyroid diseases diagnosis. Expert Systems with Applications 34(1), 242–246 (2008)
[12] Polat, K., Sahan, S., Günes, S.: A novel hybrid method based on arti?cial immune recognition system (AIRS) with fuzzy weighted pre- processing for thyroid disease diagnosis. Expert Systems with Applications 32, 1141–1147 (2007)

[13] Polat, K., Gunes, S.: A hybrid medical decision making system based on principles component analysis, k-NN based weighted pre-processing and adaptive neuro-fuzzy inference system. Digital Signal Processing 16(6), 913–921 (2006)

[14] Polat, K., Gunes, S.: An expert system approach based on principal component analysis and adaptive neuro-fuzzy inference system to diagnosis of diabetes disease. Digital Signal Processing 17(4), 702–710 (2007)

[15] Shariati, S., Haghighi, M.M.: Comparison of anfis Neural Network with several other ANNs and Support Vector Machine for diagnosing hepatitis and thyroid diseases. In: Proceedings of IEEE IACSIT 2010, pp. 596–599 (2010)

[16] Liu, D.Y., Chen, H.L., Yang, B., et al.: Design of an Enhanced Fuzzy k-nearest Neighbor Classifier Based Computer Aided Diagnostic System for Thyroid Disease. J. Med. Syst. (2011), doi:10.1007/s10916-011-9815-x

[17] Chen, H.L., Yang, B., Wang, G., Liu, J., Chen, Y.D., Liu, D.Y.: A three-stage expert system based on support vector machines for thyroid disease diagnosis. J. Med. Syst. 36(3), 1953–1963 (2012)

[18] Dogantekin, E., Dogantekin, A., Avci, D.: An automatic diagnosis system based on thyroid gland: ADSTG. Expert Syst. Appl. 37(9), 6368–6372 (2010)

[19] Dogantekin, E., Dogantekin, A., Avci, D.: An expert system based on Generalized Discriminant Analysis and Wavelet Support Vector Machine for diagnosis of thyroid diseases. Expert Syst. Appl. 38(1), 146–150 (2011)

[20] Li, L.N., Ouyang, J.H., Chen, H.L., Liu, D.Y.: A Computer Aided Diagnosis System for Thyroid Disease Using Extreme Learning Machine. J. Med. Syst. (2012), doi:10.1007/s10916-012-9825-3

[21] Cetişli, B.: Development of an adaptive neuro-fuzzy classifier using linguistic hedges: Part 1. Expert Systems with Applications 37(8), 6093–6101 (2010)

[22] Cetişli, B.: The effect of linguistic hedges on feature selection: Part 2. Expert Systems with Applications 37(8), 6102–6108 (2010)

[23] UCI Machine Learning Repository, http://archive.ics.uci.edu/ml/index.html (accessed June 2012)

[24] Jang, J.S.R.: ANFIS: Adaptive-Network-Based Fuzzy Inference System. IEEE Transactions on Systems, Man, and Cybernetics 23(3), 665–685 (1993)

[25] Jang, J.S.R., Sun, C.T.: Neuro-fuzzy modeling and control. Proceedings of the IEEE 83(3), 378–406 (1995)

[26] Jang, J.S.R., Sun, C.T., Mizutani, E.: Neuro-Fuzzy and soft computing. Prentice-Hall, Englewood Cliffs (1997)

[27] Takagi, T., Sugeno, M.: Fuzzy identification of systems and its applications to modeling and control. IEEE Trans. Syst. Man Cybern. 15(1), 116–132 (1985)

[28] Moller, M.F.: A scaled conjugate gradient algorithm for fast supervised learning. Neural Networks 6, 525–533 (1993)

[29] Sun, C.T., Jang, J.S.R.: A neuro-fuzzy classifier and its applications. In: Proc. of IEEE Int. Conf. on Fuzzy Systems, San Francisco, vol. 1, pp. 94–98 (1993)

[30] Francois, D., Rossi, F., Wertz, V., Verleysen, M.: Resampling methods for parameter-free and robust feature selection with mutual information. Neurocomputing 70, 1276–1288 (2007)

[31] Diamantidis, N.A., Karlis, D., Giakoumakis, E.A.: Unsupervised stratification of cross-validation for accuracy estimation. ArtifIntell 116, 1–16 (2000)

[32] Salzberg, S.L.: On comparing classifiers: Pitfalls to avoid and a recommended approach. Data Mining and Knowledge Discovery 1, 317–327 (1997)

Texture Feature Extraction and Classification by Combining Statistical and Neural Based Technique for Efficient CBIR

Siddhivinayak Kulkarni and Pradnya Kulkarni

School of Science, Information Technology and Engineering,
University of Ballarat,
Mount Helen, Victoria-3353, Australia
{S.Kulkarni,P.Kulkarni}@ballarat.edu.au

Abstract. This paper presents a technique based on statistical and neural feature extractor, classifier and retrieval for real world texture images. The paper is presented into two stages, texture image pre-processing includes downloading images, normalizing into specific rows and columns, forming non-overlapping windows and extracting statistical features. Co-occrance based statistical technique is used for extracting four prominent texture features from an image. Stage two includes, feeding of these parameters to Multi-Layer Perceptron (MLP) as input and output. Hidden layer output was treated as characteristics of the patterns and fed to classifier to classify into six different classes. Graphical user interface was designed to pose a query of texture pattern and retrieval results are shown.

Keywords: Texture images, Multi Layer Percptron, Classifier, image retrieval.

1 Introduction

Image databases are becoming very popular due to the large amount of images that are generated by various applications and due to the advancement in storage devices, image compression, scanning, networking etc. Retrieving the specific images based on their content has become an important research area for the last decade. These images are retrieved based on their content such as global colour, texture, shape as low level features.

An image database may contain thousands of textured images. The main problem user that user is facing of locating the images having similar texture pattern in the given query. More specifically, this problem is considered in two main parts: a. finding the images having the similar texture given in query and b. specifying a texture in query.

A good image retrieval system dealing with textures must provide solutions to both problems. In posing a query in terms of texture, it is not realistic to expect the user to draw a texture that he or she wants to retrieve. Therefore, all the textures which are extracted from the database are classified into different clusters and to pose a query in

T.-h. Kim et al. (Eds.): MulGraB/BSBT/IUrC 2012, CCIS 353, pp. 106–113, 2012.

terms of these textures. While retrieving the texture patterns, those are similar to the query, only that particular cluster has been considered. The similarity is calculated based on the query pattern and all the texture images which belong to the same class. This technique reduces the search only for that particular class and effectively reduces the searching time. This similarity is calculated based on weighted Euclidean distance and presented to the user. This is the effective way to express the texture query and getting the result based on that particular query.

In this paper, gray level single textured images are used to extract the texture features and construct a feature vector by using co-occurrence matrix for each textured image. These statistical based extracted features are used an input and output to the Multi Layer Perceptron and characertics was taken from hidden layer, which is then fed to classifier to classify these features into six different classes for efficient retrieval. The results obtained are very promising and some of the results are illustrated in this paper.

The rest of the paper is organised as follows: Section 2 gives the brief idea regarding analysis of prominent texture feature extraction techniques, Section 3 details the proposed research methodology for extracting texture features based on statistical-neural technique, Section 4 describes experimental results and analysis and the paper is finally concluded in Section 5.

2   Analysis of Prominent Texture Feature Extraction Techniques

In texture feature representations such as pixel neighborhood [1], a simple texture feature can be constructed by comparing suitable properties of current pixel with the properties of neighboring pixels. But the disadvantage of this technique is that these features are not very accurate as the feature vectors entirely depend upon the center pixel. In tamura features [2], all the six texture properties are visually meaningful so this texture representation becomes attractive in image retrieval. These properties of texture are easy to recognize by human but elusive when to be described quantitatively by a machine.

Markov random fields are attractive because they yield local and parsimonious texture descriptions. But MRF model use individual pixels based measurements and are hence not easily flexible to change in image resolution [3], [4], [5]. With SAR models, there are major difficulties in selecting the size of the dependent pixel neighborhood and the appropriate window size in which texture is regarded homogenous. MRSAR model was developed to overcome this problem. But MRSAR is computationally a very expensive set of features [6]. The wold decomposition model avoids the actual decomposition of images and tolerates a variety of in-homogeneities in natural data, making it suitable for use in large collections of natural patterns [7]. The statistical properties such as mean and variance are extracted from the wavelet sub-bands as texture representations. To explorer the middle band characteristics, tree structured wavelet transform is used to improve the classification accuracy. The wavelet transform when combined with other techniques such as Kohonen map achieves better results. Gabor transform provides an attractive approach [8], which is well suited to texture classification and database retrieval. These are far superior compared to co-occurrence features and less sensitive to noise. But there are possibilities for either mistreatment or adaptation to suit specific data. This technique is not generally applicable for segmentation or image analysis.

3   Research Methodology

This section deals with the retrieval of texture images in detail. To retrieve texture images, it is important to pre-process these images. This preprocessing includes the formation of a texture image database, extraction of texture features from these images, classifying these features in appropriate classes for retrieval. Research methodology is divided broadly into two sections: Section-I Texture images pre-processing and section-II Feature Extraction and Classification. Figure 1 shows the block diagram of the proposed technique.

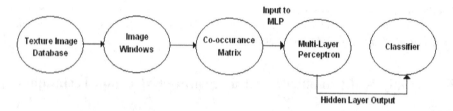

Fig. 1. Block diagram of proposed statistical-neural technique for texture image classification

3.1   Texture Image Database

Texture image database was created by downloading images from World Wide Web and consists of 500 texture images. Each image is re-arranged as 512 x 512 pixels. These images consist of textures of both statistical and structural natures. Structural textures are considered to be consists of texture primitives which are repeated systematically within the texture. In statistical texture usually no repetitive texture can be identified. These texture images mainly contain the texture of brick wall, wood, sky, grass, glass and fire. Each image is divided into 16 non-overlapping sub-images each 128×128 pixels in size, thus creating a database of (500×16) 8000 texture images.

3.2   Co-occurance Matrix

Gray Level Co-occurrence Matrix (GLCM) is one of the texture feature extraction methods, estimates the image properties related to the second order statistics. It contains the information about grey levels (intensities) of pixels and their neighbours, at fixed distance and orientation. Each entry (i, j) in GLCM corresponds to the number of occurrences of the pair of gray levels i and j which are a distance d in direction θ apart in original image. Figure 2 shows the distances and orientations of pixel p for co-occurrence matrix.

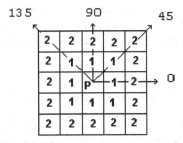

Fig. 2. Distances and directions of pixel p for co-occurrence matrix

In order to estimate the similarity between the different gray level co-occurrence matrices, Haralick [9] proposed 14 statistical features extracted from them. To reduce the computational complexity, only some of these features were selected. The description of four most relevant features that are widely used in the literature [10] [11] are given in Table 1.

Energy is a measure of textual uniformity of an image. Energy reaches its highest value when grey level distribution has either a constant or a periodic form. A homogenous image contains very few dominant grey tone transitions, and therefore the P matrix for this image will have fewer entries of larger magnitude resulting in larger value of energy feature. Also, energy feature have smaller value if P matrix contains large number of smaller entries.

Table 1. Features extracted from grey level co-occurance matrix

Energy	$\sum_i \sum_j P_d^2(i,j)$
Entropy	$\sum_i \sum_j P_d(i,j) \log P_d(i,j)$
Contrast	$\sum_i \sum_j (i-j)^2 P_d(i,j)$
Inverse Difference Moment	$\sum_i \sum_j \dfrac{P_d(i,j)}{|i-j|^2}, i \neq j$

Entropy measures the disorder of an image and it achieves its largest value when all the elements in P matrix are equal. When the image is not textually uniform many GLCM elements have a very small value, which implies the entropy is very large. Entropy is inversely proportional to GLCM energy.

Contrast measures the difference between the highest and lowest values of a contiguous set of pixels. In other words, Contrast is a difference moment of the P and it measures the amount of local variations in an image. Low contrast images features low special frequencies.

Inverse Difference Moment (IDM) measures image homogeneity. This parameter achieves its largest value when the most of the occurrences in GLCM are concentrated near the main diagonal. IDM is inversely proportional to GLCM contrast.

3.3   MLP as Feature Extractor and Classifier

Multi Layer Perceptron is proposed to extract more features of these texture images. For input and output, features (energy, entropy, contrast and inverse difference moments) are used and output of the hidden layer is taken as the characteristics of texture patterns. This MLP learns the same pattern to provide typical features at the hidden layer. The network is trained using a supervised learning algorithm. The feature vector is fed to another MLP feature classifier.

This stage describes the capability of the Multi-layer Perceptron for the classification tasks and the implementation of a trainable MLP and presents a suitable kind of MLP structure for classification of texture data. In order to discuss classification capabilities of the MLP, it is necessary to define what "classification" means in the ANN context. Here it is defined in the broadest possible sense as the process which gives an output when a pattern is presented to the input of the network.

An MLP texture feature classifier is used to classify the textures in appropriate classes. It has p inputs which are the same as the number of hidden units in an MLP feature extractor. The output of the hidden layer that was obtained from MLP was used as input to the classifier. There were 6 texture classes, so the number of outputs was 6.

4   Experimental Results and Analysis

The objective of these experiments is to illustrate that the proposed texture feature extraction provides a powerful tool to aid in image retrieval. The image data set used in these experiments was texture images downloaded from the Internet. The experiments were conducted separately for feature extraction using co-occurance matrix, feed them to MLP and classifying these texture patterns. After segmenting the images into 16 sub-images, the four texture features based on co-occurrence matrix is extracted and applied to MLP.

4.1   Training of Multi-Layer Perceptron

The experiments were conducted in two stages, firstly the training of the MLP and secondly the training of the classifier. Before training of an MLP, different training parameters were used. The total number of images used for the experiments was 500. After segmenting the images into 16 non-overlapping sub-images, the first 12 sub-images were used for training and the last 4 sub-images were used for testing. The number of training and testing sub-images were 6000 (500 x 12) and 2000 (500 x 4). In the case of the MLP, the same patterns were applied to the output. The values of the learning rate (η) and momentum (α) were 0.9 and 0.8 respectively.

The auto-associator was trained different numbers of hidden units and iterations to improve feature extraction. It was very important to train the auto-associator properly so that the classification of these features became an easy task. Table 2 shows the effect of varying the hidden units and iterations on RMS error.

Table 2. Effect of varying the number of hidden units and iterations on RMS error

Hidden units	Iterations	RMS error
4	1000	0.00576
6	1000	0.00312
8	1000	0.00077
10	5000	0.00064
12	10000	0.00011

4.2   Training of the Classifier

The classifier was trained after obtaining the output from the hidden layer from the MLP. The hidden layer output was given as input to the classifier. The output of the hidden layer of an MLP depends upon the number of units in the hidden layer and the number of training pairs. The number of inputs to the classifier is the same as the number of hidden units used to train the MLP.

4.3   Classification Results for the Testing Set

Table 3 shows the results obtained by the feature classifier on the testing set. The experiments were conducted by altering the number of units in hidden layer and the number of iterations for training. The best classification rate (92.65%) was obtained with number of 16 hidden units and 7500 iterations. Table 3 shows that as the number of hidden units increased, the classification rate also increased. The number of testing pairs was 2000.

Table 3. Results of classification of texture features on testing set

Hidden units	Iterations	RMS error	Classification rate (2000)	Classification rate [%]
16	500	0.0393	1469	73.45
16	1000	0.0670	1503	75.15
16	5000	0.0094	1742	87.10
16	7500	0.0034	1853	92.65

4.4   Graphical User Interface for Texture Query

Graphical user interface was designed to pose the query in terms of texture feature of the image. The user can select the texture from the six textures used for experiments and submit the query.

The Figure 3 shows the results obtained after selecting the texture as "Brick." The confidence factor for each image is the actual output obtained after classifying the extracted features on testing set. All the images of the brick texture are retrieved and top 14 images are shown in Figure 3. The first image appearing at the top left corner has the confidence factor 0.999962, which is highest among all other brick texture images. The confidence factor of the images goes on decreasing from left to right and from top to bottom.

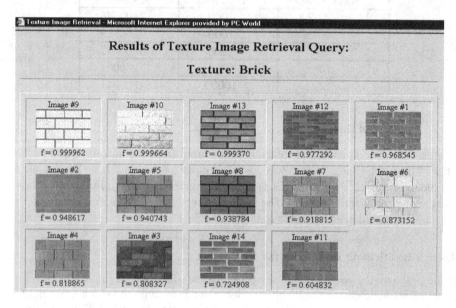

Fig. 3. Graphical Results of the query: brick texture

The query was tested for all the textures and found satisfactory results. All the images for each particular query were retrieved.

5   Conclusion

For texture image retrieval, a novel technique for extracting the texture features from the images was investigated in this paper. Statistical Co-occurance based texture features are used as input and output to the MLP and output of the hidden layer was treated as detailed characeristics of the texture patterns. These texture featurs are classified into six different prominent classes to retrieve texture images based on query. The performance of MLP was evaluated on real world texture images. The results obtained from the classifier showed that statistical-neural feature extractor to be a promising feature extractor using only single hidden layer. For the classifier, the highest classification rate was obtained as 92.65% which was significant. This classification rate can be improved by varying number of hidden units in hidden layer and number of iterations. As texture patterns are classified into specific classes, it is efficient for image retrieval to compare the images in that particular class. Future research combines texture and shape features for retrieving images based on multi-modal features in an image.

References

1. Smith, J.: Integrated Spatial and Feature Image Systems: Retrieval, Analysis and Compression, PhD Dissertation, Columbia University (1997)
2. Tamura, H., Mori, S., Yamawaki, T.: Texture Features Corresponding to Visual Perception. IEEE Transactions on Systems, Man and Cybernetics 8(6), 460–473 (1978)
3. Gimelfarb, G., Jain, A.: On Retrieving Textured Images from an Image Database. Journal of Pattern Recognition Society 29(9), 1461–1483 (1996)
4. Andrey, P., Tarroux, P.: Unsupervised Segmentation of Markov Random Field Modeled Textured Images using Selectionist Relaxation. IEEE Transactions on Pattern Analysis and Machine Intelligence 20, 252–262 (1998)
5. Chellappa, R., Chatterjee, S.: Classification of Textures using Gaussian Markov Random Fields. IEEE Transactions on Accoustics, Speech and Signal Processing 33(4), 959–963 (1985)
6. Mao, J., Jain, A.: Texture Classification and Segmentation using Multiresolution Simultaneous Autoregressive Models. Journal of Pattern Recognition 25(2), 173–188 (1992)
7. Rao, A., Lohse, G.: Towards a Texture Naming System: Identifying Relevant Dimensions of Texture. In: Proceedings of IEEE Conference on Visualization, San Jose, USA, pp. 220–227 (1993)
8. Daubechies, I.: The Wavelet Transform, Time-Frequency Localisation and Signal Analysis. IEEE Transactions on Information Theory 9(36), 961–1005 (1990)
9. Haralick, R., Shanmugam, K., Dinstein, I.: Textural Features for Image Classification. IEEE Transactions on System, Man and Cybernetics 6, 610–621 (1973)
10. Partio, M., Cramariuc, B., Gabbouj, M., Visa, A.: Rock Texture Retrieval using Gray Level Co-occurrence Matrix. In: Nordic Signal Processing Symposium, Norway (2002)
11. Gonzalez, R., Woods, R.: Book on Digital Image Processing (1993)

Towards Efficient Security Services
in Wireless Sensor Networks[*]

Mohammed Faisal, Jalal Al Muhtadi, and Abdullah Al-Dhelaan

College of Computer and Information Sciences, King Saud University, Saudi Arabia
{Mfaisal@ksu.edu.sa, jalal@ksu.edu.sa, Dhelaan@ksu.edu.sa}

Abstract. Wireless Sensor Networks (WSNs) are infrastructure-less and fully distributed systems of self-configurable and self-organizing nodes that wish to exchange information over the air. Security in WSN is challenging, because of its special characteristics, and due to the scarcity of energy and processing power. Many WSN scenarios demand authentication, confidentiality and integrity services. In this paper, we introduce a framework to address these main security services based on a special protocol that integrates public key and symmetric key algorithms to ensure optimal usage of sensors' energy and processing power, and provide adequate security. The proposed framework utilizes Elliptic Curve Cryptography (ECC) and AES to achieve a reasonable tradeoff.

Keywords: WSNs, Confidentiality, Integrity, Authentication, Security, Public Key Infrastructure, Elliptic Curve Cryptography.

1 Introduction

WSNs are being applied in many scenarios, including environmental observation, patient monitoring, military sensing and tracking, etc. Security in wireless sensor network is challenging, because of its special characteristics (dynamic topology, lack of infrastructure, variable capacity, limited bandwidth and computing power, scarce energy, and so on.) Thus, many research proposed security services for WSNs [1, 2]. Many of these schemes use symmetric cryptography and some use asymmetric cryptography. In this paper, we combine both public key and symmetric key cryptography to ensure reasonable security while optimizing energy use. The proposed framework aims to ensure authentication, confidentiality, integrity, and redundancy in WSNS. This is done by proposing a Light Public-Key Infrastructure model (L-PKI), and a Secure, Energy-efficient Cluster-based Multipath Routing (SECMRP) protocol. L-PKI proposes a light implementation of Public Key Infrastructure (PKI) for WSNs. L-PKI sets up secure links between a node and its neighbors, each node and its cluster head, and each cluster head and the base station. SECMRP is used to ensure secure route discovery, and secure data transmission in

---

[*] This research work is funded by the National Plan for Science and Technology at King Saud University, Project number: 11-INF1500-02.

T.-h. Kim et al. (Eds.): MulGraB/BSBT/IUrC 2012, CCIS 353, pp. 114–123, 2012.
© Springer-Verlag Berlin Heidelberg 2012

WSN. SECMRP is trying to enhance the security issue of SEEM [7]. The remainder of the paper is organized as follows. In Section 2, we present related work. In Section 3, we clarify the expected WSN architecture. Section 4 explains the L-PKI Protocol. Section 5 explains the SECMRP protocol. Section 7 concludes.

2   Related Work

TinyPK designs and implements a public-key-based protocol that allows authentication and key exchange between an external party and a sensor network [3]. TinyPK uses RSA [4], using e=3 as the public exponent and Diffie-Hellman key agreement algorithm [5] to deliver the secret. µPKI [6] is a lightweight implementation of PKI for WSN. In this protocol, two handshake are used the first handshake between the base station and each sensor in the network and the second handshake between each pair of node in the network intended to secure sensor to sensor communication. In µPKI, only the base station needs to be authenticated. µPKI uses the public key cryptography in the key distribution operation. µPKI supposes that an off-line dealer distributes the public key of the base station to each sensor in the network. Thus, µPKI uses the public key in the handshake between the base station and sensors. In this handshake, each sensor generates and encrypts the session key using the public key of the base station. Secure and Energy-Efficient Multipath Routing protocol (SEEM) [7] uses the base station to discover the route. The base station discovers multi-paths for data transmissions, and periodically selects one of these paths based on current energy levels of nodes along each path. Our work improves on existing works by integrating a light PKI with a redundant and secure data transmission services via multipath in an efficient manner in terms of resource consummation. The proposed framework enhances the security of WSN by providing mutual authentication between neighbor nodes, and sending the data via multipath, which are not available in µPKI, and SEEM.

3   WSN Architecture

In our scenario, we divide the sensor network into different clusters, and assume the existence of three types of nodes:

1- Normal sensor nodes.
2- One or more Cluster Heads (CH).
3- One or more Base Stations (BS).

The proposed architecture introduces CHs, which are equipped with more embedded energy, storage, and computation capabilities. Digital Certificates are issued during the pre-deployment phase. Nodes which are not CH are considered normal nodes. Since CHs have more resources, we offload processing to them to reduce resource consumption on normal nodes. Figure 1 illustrates the proposed architecture.

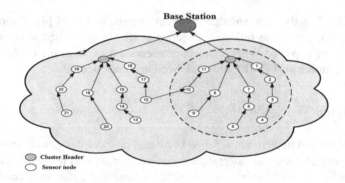

Fig. 1. The proposed architecture

4   L-PKI Protocol

L-PKI proposes a protocol to implement PKI only in authentication and generation of session keys between the cluster header and each node in the cluster. So, L-PKI sets up a secure links between each node and its neighbors, each node and its cluster head, and each cluster header and the base station. These secure links are used to transmit data to the base station via the cluster heads. There are several assumptions for L-PKI: (1) CHs have more computational and energy power compared to other nodes which allow them to work as a Certification Authority (CA) and Registration Authority (RA), (2) the Base Station and Cluster Heads are trusted entities, and (3) each sensor node has the capability to use symmetric encryption and the relatively light Elliptic Curve cryptography (hardware or software).

Several works show that ECC is the most efficient public-key crypto that can be used with WSNs [8, 9, 10, 11]. L-PKI uses ECC with 160 keys bits [12]. L-PKI is divided into two phases. (1) Initial authentication and key-establishment and addition new node phases.

4.1   Initial Authentication and Key Establishment Phase

Initial authentication and Key establishment has two steps. Pre-deployment step and Authentication and Key Establishment step.

Step 1: Pre-deployment Step. The initial step starts before deploying operation, L-PKI protocol supposes many pre-deployment works which the BS and CHs have to do as the initial step.

1- Each CH and Node generate its private & public keys "160 bits"(CH_{Kpub}, CH_{Kprv}), (N_{Kpub}, N_{Kprv}) using ECC-160 [12].
2- Each CH delivers its Public key to BS and each node delivers its Public key to CH.

3- BS issues digital certificates for each CH (CH_cer), signs and delivers them to each corresponding CH.

4- CHs issue digital certificates for each sensor nodes (N_cer)), sign and deliver them to each corresponding node.

According to the FRC of X.509 certificates [13], many fields can use in the certificate. L-PKI uses node's ID, node's public key, Timestamp, and signature. L-PKI uses these fields in order to ensure the security with lowest cost. L_PKI used Elliptic Curve Digital Signature Algorithm ECDSA-160 as a signatures algorithm [10, 12], so the size of signature will be 320. Figure 2 illustrates the signature operation.

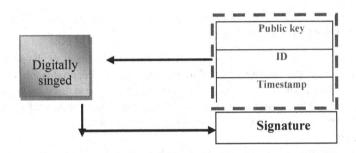

Fig. 2. Signature operation

Step 2: Authentication and Key establishment. After the pre-deployment step and at the first step of the lifetime of the network, L-PKI initiates the authentication step. At this step, each node in the same cluster must authenticate each other. Fig. 3 illustrates the authentication operation. Actually, the security of the WSN starts by making a network of trusted nodes in the clusters. After the authentication step, each node will trust its neighbors.

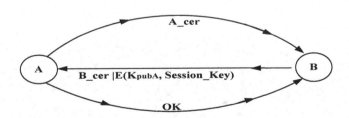

Fig. 3. Authentication operation

After the pre-deployment step, each node has its own digital certificate, N_cer, Public key N_{Kpub}, private key, N_{Kprv}, and also knows the public key (CH_{Kpub}) of its cluster head. The authentication step uses the outputs of the pre-deployment step in order to authenticate each node.

Each node must do the following steps in order to authenticate its neighbors.

1- Sends its N_cer to its neighbors.
2- Each neighbor receives the certificate of node, verifies it by using the public key of its CH.
3- At the neighbor node, if the certificate is valid, the neighbor node creates and encrypts session key SH_ABK AES-128 using the corresponding public key.
4- The neighbor node sends its digital certificate with the encrypted session key "SH_ABK".
5- Source node receives the certificate of the neighbor node and verifies it by using CH_{Kpub}.
6- If the certificate is valid, source node decrypts SH_ABK by using its private key.
7- If both nodes successfully validate the certificate, each node adds each neighbor to its neighbors list.

Now, each node trusts its neighbor nodes. After the establishment of the session keys between nodes in the network, we can ensure the confidentiality in the WSN. According to the L-PKI, the public key cryptography is just used to validate the certificates of each node and to encrypt and decrypt the session key of each pair of nodes. After that, nodes can use symmetric cryptography in order to ensure the confidentiality.

After applying the initial authentication and key establishment phase, each node has a unique ID N_ID, a digital certificate, N_cer signed by its CH, list of all authenticated neighbors, NBR_LIST, public keys of cluster head, CH_{Kpub}, and a shared key with each neighbor node SH_XYK.

4.2   Adding New Node Phase

To insure the scalability in the proposed framework L-PKI allows a new node to join the network, but it must follow the authentication and key establishment step. After that preparation, the new node is deployed to the network.

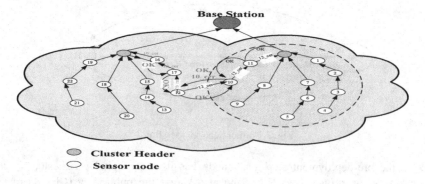

Cluster Header
Sensor node

Fig. 4. Authentication of Nodes in Different Clusters

5   SECMRP Protocol

SECMRP is a protocol that is used to ensure secure route discovery, and secure data transmission in WSN. SECMRP tries to enhance the security of SEEM [7]. SECMRP assumes that each node knows its neighbors, and has a shared key with each neighbor. This assumption is met by deploying L-PKI protocol.

SECMRP has three phases Secure Route Discovery, Secure Data Transmission and Route Maintenance. Secure route discovery phase is responsible for finding secure disjoint multipath or partially disjoint multipath between each node and its cluster head CH. In this phase CH is the responsible of discovering these paths Data transmission phase is responsible for transmitting the sensing data. Route maintenance phase each cluster header updates available energy on each node, which is participating in the communication, and according to the available energy on each node re-selects a new path to the source node.

5.1   Secure Route Discovery Phase

Secure route discovery phase starts applying the L-PKI. Thus, each node has a unique ID, a digital certificate signed by its CH, list of all authenticated neighbors, public keys of cluster head, and shared key with each neighbor node. Secure route discover has three steps: NBR_LIST Requesting, NBR_LIST Sending, and NBR_LIST Receiving and paths creation steps.

Step 1: NBR_LIST Requesting. Each CH of each cluster starts the routing discover operation by sending NBR_SEN "Neighbor sending" packet to each node on its cluster. NBR_SEN packet contains packet sequence number "P_SEQ_NUM" cluster header ID "CH_ID", and MAC values of the cluster head id "CH_ID" and P_SEQ_NUM as the following format.

$\forall i$ where i is a neighbor of CH

CH→i:NBR_SEN|P_SEQ_NUM|CH_ID|MAC(SH_CHiK,CH_ID| P_SEQ_NUM) (1)

Each node receiving NBR_SEN packet does that:

1. Checks if node received this NBR_SEN.
2. Computes the MAC value of CH_ID and P_SEQ_NUM and compares it with the MAC value of the NBR_SEN packet.
3. Computes the MAC value of CH_ID and P_SEQ_NUM by using the shared key of each neighbor node and replaces it with the old one.

    $\forall j$ where j is a neighbor of i ,MAC (SH_ijK , CH_ID I P_SEQ_NUM)).
4. Rebroadcasts the NBR_SEN packet to its neighbors.

    $\forall j$ where j is a neighbor of i
    i→j : NBR_SEN I P_SEQ_NUM I CH_ID |MAC(SH_ijK, CH_ID| P_SEQ_NUM)| (2)

Step 2: NBR_LIST Sending. After each node has received the NBR_SEN packet and completed all operations related to the NBR_SEN packet, it becomes able to send the

NBR_LIST packet. Each node prepares the NBR_LIST packet and sends it directly to the node which has sent the NBR_SEN packet. Each node will have a neighbor list as a result from applying the L-PKI protocol. NBR_LIST packet contains packet sequence number, "P_SEQ_NUM", node ID, "N_ID", MAC values of the node id, "N_ID", and P_SEQ_NUM, encrypted session key of the source node, CH E(CHKpub , SH_iCHK), encrypted neighbor list and power state of the source node E(SH_iCHK, i_NBR| Powe_state), and MAC value between source and CH MAC(SH_ijK, P_SEQ_NUM |i_ID | E(SH_iCHK, i_NBR)) in the following format.

$\forall$ i where i is any node in the cluster, j is the node which has sent the NBR_SEN packet to the node i.

i→j: NBR_LIST | P_SEQ_NUM |i_ID | MAC(SH_ijK,i_ID| P_SEQ_NUM)| E(CH$_{Kpub}$, SH_iCHK)|E(SH_iCHK, i_NBR| Powe_state) | MAC(SH_ijK, P_SEQ_NUM |i_ID | E(SH_iCHK, i_NBR))

Each node receiving NBR_LIST packet does the following steps:

1. Checks if node has received NBR_LIST packet.
2. Computes the MAC value of i_ID, P_SEQ_NUM and compare it with the MAC value of the NBR_LIST, if equal move to next step, otherwise drop the packet.
3. Computes the MAC value of j_ID and P_SEQ_NUM by using the shared key between the j node and the node which send the NBR_SEN packet and replaces it with the old one.
4. Sends the NBR_LIST packet to node which sent the NBR_SEN packet, until the packet reaches the CH.

If the current node is the CH, then it decrypts "E(CH$_{Kpub}$, SH_iCHK)" by using its private key and checks the integrity by computing the MAC of (SH_iCHK, P_SEQ_NUM |i_ID | E(SH_iCHK, i_NBR)) and compares it with the MAC value of the NBR_LIST packet. If the MAC values are equal then CH decrypts neighbor information using the session key between the sender node and the CH, otherwise it drops the packet.

Step 3: BR_LIST Receiving and path creation. After each CH has received neighbors' information and the state of the power of all nodes on the cluster, each cluster head will be aware of the general topology of the cluster nodes, and as a result, all CHs have a vision of the topology of the whole network as illustrated in figure 4. Thus, CH is able to find secure disjoint multipath or partially disjoint multipath between each node and CH. It then can select one of them according to the specific algorithm.

Finding secure disjoint/partially disjoint multipaths: According to the neighbors' information received from the nodes, the CH constructs a weighted directed graph and finds multipath from the CH to every node. SECMRP finds disjoint/partially disjoint multipath and selects N (N=2 in our case) of them according to the minimum hops or the maximum energy available for each node on the path. In order to search for the desired path, SECMRP uses the modified Breadth First Search BFS algorithm in [7] with some modification (MBFS).BFS [14] is an algorithm that is used to find the shortest paths between two nodes. It is not necessary for the MBFS algorithm to select the absolute shortest path, but instead choose the efficient path according to energy levels.

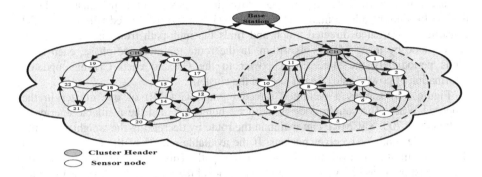

Fig. 5. Topology of whole wireless sensor network

5.2   Secure Data Transmission Phase

In the Secure Route Discovery phase, each CH is responsible for finding secure disjoint multipath or partially disjoint multipath between each node and its CH. Thus, each node becomes able to transmit its sensed data securely. After the secure route discover phase and upon the application .CH has sent the best "N=2" energy efficient paths to each node. Now, nodes become able to send the sensed data to the cluster header.

Secure data transmission phase has two steps. In the first step, the source sensor node sends data packets to the CH via the secure paths that CH established with each node.We are going to assume that the number of paths which we need to send data are two (N=2). According to the paths, the source node divides the data to N parts, makes the following two packets and sends them to nodes which are in the head of the paths. The data packet (DATA_PACKET) has the following formats, assuming that the head nodes are X, and Y, and the source is S:

S →X: P_SEQ_NUM|S_ID|Mac (SH_SXK,P_SEQ_NUS_ID|Path)|
  (SH_SCHK,DATA_PART1|MAC(SH_SCHK,P_SEQ_NUM|S_ID|E(SH_SCHK,
  DATA_PART1)

S →Y:P_SEQ_NUM|S_ID|Mac(SH_SYK,P_SEQ_NM|S_ID|Path)|(SH_SCHK,DAT
  A_PART2)|AC(SH_SCHK, |P_SEQ_NUM |S_ID |E(SH_SCHK, DATA_PART2)

The second step starts after the data becomes available at the CH. CH becomes able to aggregate and compress the received data, which can come from more than one node. After the aggregation and compression operation, the CH encrypts the aggregated data and sends it to BS.

5.3   Route Maintenance

In SECMRP, each CH is aware of the topology of its members, knows the available energy of each node via the weight of each node (the power of each node was sent with NBR_LIST packet at the beginning or is sent periodically from each node to the CH), and uses a matrix which corresponds to the weighted graph. All this information allows the CH to become able to maintain the route easily. As we discussed before, each CH constructs a weighted directed graph and finds the multipath from the CH to every source node by using MBFS algorithm. In the route maintenance phase, each node sends periodically the state of its power to the CH, so each CH has updated information of power state of each node in the cluster.

Figure 5 illustrates a weighted directed graph G (V,E) of one cluster in the proposed WSN. The source node is the node number 4, and the available energy of each node is 700. SECMRP can maintain the route by decreasing the weight when the source node sends or receives packets. If the available energy of the node reaches to the energy limitation level, then it uses another path. This means that if one node on the shortest path has energy less than a specific level then the MBFS discards this path and continues searching the second shortest path that satisfy the specific level of energy to avoid exhausting energy of nodes. It will then send the new path to the node so it will become able to send the data via that new path. SECMRP uses five different levels of energy. Each level is twice the lower level. Thus, MBFS ensures balancing the power consumption in the whole cluster. If MBFS cannot find any shortest path under current levels of the energy limitation, it means that each path has at least one node whose energy is less than current energy limitation as in Figure 6. Thus, MBFS algorithm uses the lower energy limitation and resumes the searching operation with the new level of energy limitation, and sends the new paths to the node. If MBFS algorithm cannot find any path with any level of energy limitation, it means that this node is unreachable and the CH cannot get the sensing data from it.

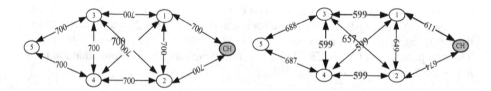

Fig. 6. Weighted directed graph of one cluster in the WSN

Fig. 7. All paths has at least one node which its weight less than first energy limitation

6   Conclusion

The proposed framework protects against the internal and the passive attacks by encrypting data using AES-128 and distributing the encrypted data using multipath. Also, the proposed framework protects against the external and the Impersonation (spoofing) attacks by employing mutual authentication through lightweight certificates.

Modification of the protocol messages can be avoided by authenticating nodes through their certificates. The proposed framework clusters the network and uses the certifications to avoid routing table overflow attacks. We describe the details of both protocols. In future work, we plan to enhance the MBFS algorithm to find more power efficient algorithms for route discovery, as well as simulating full aspects of the proposed protocols.

References

[1]   Zhang, J., Varadharajan, V.: Wireless sensor network key management survey and taxonomy. Journal of Network and Computer Applications 33(2), 63–75 (2010)

[2]   Sen, J.: A survey on wireless sensor network security. Arxiv preprint arXiv:1011.1529 (2010)

[3]   Watro, R., Kong, D., Cuti, S., Gardiner, C., Lynn, C., Kruus, P.: TinyPK: securing sensor networks with public key technology. In: Proceedings of the 2nd ACM Workshop on Security of Ad Hoc and Sensor Networks, pp. 59–64 (2004)

[4]   Rivest, R.L., Shamir, A., Adleman, L.: A method for obtaining digital signatures and public-key cryptosystems. Communications of the ACM 21(2), 120–126 (1978)

[5]   Diffie, W., Hellman, M.E.: 'New directions in cryptography. Secure Communications and Asymmetric Cryptosystems, 143–180 (1982)

[6]   Kadri, B., Feham, M., M'hamed, A.: Lightweight PKI for WSN uPKI. Presented at I. J. Network Security, 194–200 (2010)

[7]   Nasser, N., Chen, Y.: SEEM: Secure and energy-efficient multipath routing protocol for wireless sensor networks. Computer Communications 30(11-12), 2401–2412 (2007)

[8]   Amin, F., Jahangir, A., Rasifard, H.: Analysis of public-key cryptography for wireless sensor networks security. In: Proceedings of World Academy of Science, Engineering and Technology, vol. 31 (2008)

[9]   Gura, N., Patel, A., Wander, A., Eberle, H., Shantz, S.C.: Comparing elliptic curve cryptography and RSA on 8-bit CPUs. In: Cryptographic Hardware and Embedded Systems, CHES 2004, pp. 925–943 (2004)

[10] Wander, A.S., Gura, N., Eberle, H., Gupta, V., Shantz, S.C.: Energy Analysis of Public-Key Cryptography for Wireless Sensor Networks, pp. 324–328

[11] Noroozi, E., Kadivar, J., Shafiee, S.H.: Energy analysis for wireless sensor networks. In: 2010 2nd International Conference on Mechanical and Electronics Engineering (ICMEE), vol. 2, pp. V2–382 (2010)

[12] Hankerson, D., Menezes, A.J., Vanstone, S.: Guide to elliptic curve cryptography. Springer, New York (2004)

[13] RFC of x.509, http://www.ietf.org/rfc/rfc3280.txt

[14] Gormen, T.H., Leiserson, C.E., Rivest, R.L., Stein, C.: Introduction to algorithms. MIT Press, Cambridge (1990)

Ubiquitous Monitoring System
for Critical Cardiac Abnormalities

Uvais Qidwai[1], Junaid Ahsenali Chaudhry[1], Mohamed Shakir[1],
and Robert G. Rittenhouse[2]

[1] Dept. of Computer Science and Engineering, Qatar University, Doha, Qatar
{uqidwai,junaid,shakir}@qu.edu.qa
[2] Keimyung Adams College, Keimyung University, Daegu 704-701 Korea
rrittenhouse@acm.org

Abstract. In many critical cardiac abnormalities, it is desirable to have a monitoring system that can keep a constant surveillance on the conditions of the heart and its related patterns. This can be very convenient in clinical settings but may not be a possibility for individuals who are not in the hospital and are in their day-to-day activities. Wearable ECG-based systems have been proposed for such situations and can perform such monitoring in real life. However, detecting the abnormality in near-real-time is still a challenge in these systems. Similarly, what information should be relayed to the doctors or other care-givers and how soon this can be achieved is a very hot area of research at present. This paper presents a monitoring system that embeds an intelligent wearable data acquisition system with unique identification algorithms requiring very little computational time and simple threshold based classification. Once this is done, the related information is passed to a gateway system that can communicate the criticality flags as well as the actual ECG waveform data to the pre-defined data node that connects it to the doctor and/or other clinical representatives. We have used Android based cellphone for as the gateway. The morphological features of mobile devices and their use in our daily lives create an opportunity to connect medical informatics systems with the main stream. The presented system focuses on intelligent health monitoring with possible wearable application for long-term monitoring and updating in real-time about the patient's ECG conditions to the physician.

Keywords: component, Ubiquitous Computing, Embedded Systems, Energy levels, Finite Impulse Response (FIR) filters, Electrocardiogram (ECG), Atrio-Ventricular Block, Premature Ventricular Contraction, Fibrillation, Healthcare, WBAN, Android System Programming.

1   Introduction

The recent development of high performance microprocessors and novel processing materials has stimulated great interest in the development of wireless sensor nodes for Wireless Body Area Network (WBAN) application [1]. It allows physiological signals

T.-h. Kim et al. (Eds.): MulGraB/BSBT/IUrC 2012, CCIS 353, pp. 124–134, 2012.
© Springer-Verlag Berlin Heidelberg 2012

such as electroencephalography (EEG), electrocardiogram (ECG), blood pressure, glucose to be easily monitored wirelessly and attached to the patient's body. The wireless sensor nodes in WBAN application can be classified into several types, which are the swallowed capsule pill sensor, wired sensor with the wireless sensor node, portable sensors mounted on the surface of human body, implantable physiological sensor and Nano-physiological sensors [2]. Due to increasing numbers of people with illnesses and high clinical costs associated with managing and treating them, two mission-critical schemes can be enforced in order to ensure that low-cost and qualitative health services can be delivered. Firstly, the usual hospital-based healthcare should be transformed to personal-based healthcare, which can lead to the prevention of illnesses or early prediction of diseases. Secondly, cutting-edge technologies have to be developed with the aim of reducing medical costs in the following aspects:

(1) Innovative & low-cost medical device without professional involvements;
(2) Precise and reliable automatic diagnosis system to avoid unnecessary clinical visits and medical tests; and
(3) Telecommunication technologies to support caregivers in remote accessing and diagnosing the patients' status.
(4) Embedded, wearable, reliable and cost effective system.

One such solution is a wearable heartbeat monitor. While a number of such gadgets are available in the market today and are successfully used by athletes as well as for simpler fitness workouts, the main objective of these devices is to get the heartbeat count only [3]. The other solutions comprise of wearable and (Wireless Body Area Networks) WBAN-based health monitoring systems that combine automatic diagnosis system and wireless application protocol (WAP) into ubiquitous telemedicine system [3-11]. The importance of such systems can be understood by their significant contribution to healthcare and to patients' lifestyles.

This paper presents an intelligent system incorporating the ECG measured values corresponding to different types of cardiac health conditions. The system analyzes these ECG signals (including various types of healthy waveforms; slower or faster heart rates) with certain selected cardiac problems and issues the decisions to the Android gateway cellphone for relaying the information and the related waveforms to the doctor or the related healthcare unit for possible immediate actions.

2   Proposed System

A new system for this purpose is being built by the authors and their team to alleviate the existing system from the limitations related to the mode of heavy processing, range of access to the healthcare facilities, and correct diagnosis. Figure 1 shows the overall proposed system as block diagram giving a bird's eye view of the system.

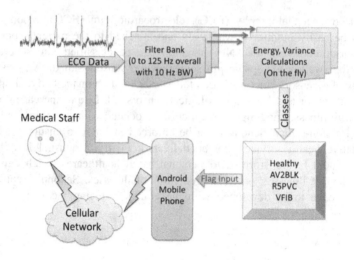

Fig. 1. Overall block diagram of the system

2.1   Hardware Details

Essentially, a mobile phone (or similar device) is needed with cellular connectivity in order to transmit the necessary information to the doctors or other medical staff.

The ECG signals are obtained from the patient by connecting two ECG probes on the chest. Hence a wearable system has been developed for convenient usage. However, for classification purposes, a heartbeat simulator is used in this work [10] so that the exact known waveforms can be utilized for classification purposes. Under normal conditions, the mobile phone is not interrupted to do anything extraordinary. However, as soon as the classification system detects the anomaly, then it indicates this to the phone which then changes its role to a Data Gateway and issues an indication to the concerned doctor or the related medical staff for possible actions to be taken. Simultaneously, the cellphone also initiates ECG waveform transmission to the doctors with time stamps so that further investigations can be performed in the given scenario.

This paper presents one simple technique in this context that has been implemented in a microcontroller for detecting healthy vs. diseased heartbeats. Specifically, three abnormal conditions are selected in this work as a major finding towards the initial development of the algorithm;

- Second degree Atrio-Ventricular block type (referenced as <u>A1</u> in the paper representing Abnormality 1),
- Premature Ventricular Contraction (referenced as <u>A2</u> in the paper representing Abnormality 2), and
- Ventricular Fibrillation (referenced as <u>A3</u> in the paper representing Abnormality 3).

Two specific reasons for selecting only these for the time being are (a) their more frequent occurrences, and (b) the fact that when the first two conditions appear, the patient has a good chance of reaching the hospital or other healthcare facilities since the embedded system can predict the condition in time. The third condition is usually very serious and the patients have only a few minutes before it could become fatal. However, nowadays many public places such as malls, airports, etc. have defibrillators available for such emergencies. If the A3 condition is detected by the microcontroller system, then the proper instrument can be requested (by a direct call to the location based emergency service and at the same time displaying the information on the cellphone). This would enable the immediately available help personnel to quickly attach the defibrillator or similar devices in order to save the life of the patient.

Figure 2 shows the modular block diagram of operation of the test hardware for this system. Essentially, the ECG data from the ECG simulator will come to the microcontroller board, Lilypad, [12], via 3-pole stereo cable. This board has an Atmega-328P from Atmel Corporation. This microcontroller board has 14 digital input/output, 6 analog inputs, an 8 MHz crystal oscillator and a separate Bluetooth module, which is used for serial data transmission and reception, with a data transfer rate of 2400bps-115200bps. This data is transmitted from the Lilypad to the Bluetooth enabled user console [13]. Some of the highlighted features of this module are:

- Federal Communications Commission (FCC) recognized Class 1 Bluetooth module.
- Efficient power usage , with an average of   25mA
- Works even if there are other radio frequencies like the Wi-Fi or Zigbee
- Encoded connectivity,
- Operating Frequency between 2.4~2.524 GHz,
- Operating Temperature between -40 ~ +70C and
- Built-in antenna.

This board can be powered between 2.7 to 5.5 Volts, which is ideal for prototyping wireless patient monitoring and portable and high-end electrocardiogram (ECG) applications. This data after processing will be transmitted to the user console, ideally to a Bluetooth enabled mobile phone. After many experimental observations, the system utilizes only the first chest lead from the standard ECG monitoring protocol and still provides sufficient information in the signal. However, before using real patients' data, a test bed was developed using CARDIOSIM-II [14], an ECG Arrhythmia Simulator (Biometric Cables).

2.2   Android Implementation

The Android SDK paired in the standard Android Development Kit (ADT) is used on the third generation smart phone i.e. Samsung Galaxy S2 for implementation on the mobile devices. The extendibility and Java's compatibility with the XML are solely the two most important factors in choosing Android as the client Operating System.

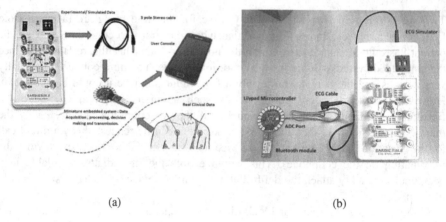

(a)   (b)

Fig. 2. Modular diagram for the proposed system. (a) various modules used, and (b) embedded system used in the paper.

The ECG data is transferred to the mobile device, in our case a smart phone, through a fast Bluetooth interface. The ECG data contains reading records in bulk i.e. 1 million records per second. After scaling the ECG data set size is considerably reduced. As discussed above, there are the following different conditions where mobile device shows different behavior upon reception of critical codes. The critical codes indicate the disease type and the urgency of reactionary measured as a result.

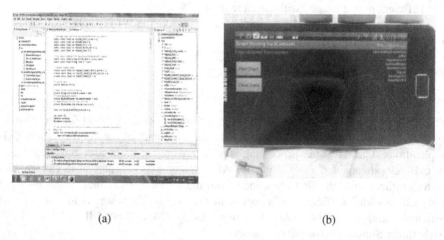

(a)   (b)

Fig. 3. (a) The Android Standard Development Kit and implementation environment, and (b) the user interface developed in this work

The following pseudo code depicts the condition of the system as per different conditional context.

```
LISTEN Bluetooth Client on Port XX
IF ( critical_code == 00)
DO Nothing
Patient_Condition == Normal
        IF ( critical_code == 12)
        RECEIVE ECG_Data FROM Bluetooth Port
        AFTER X1 seconds UNTILL X2 min.
        PLOT ecg_graph
        TAKE Snapshot
         AND
        TRANSMIT ecg_picture_segmants
        Patient_Condition == Needs Attention
        IF ( critical_code == 19)
        RECEIVE ECG_Data FROM Bluetooth Port
        AFTER X1 seconds UNTILL X2 min.
        PLOT ecg_graph
        TAKE Snapshot
        AND
        TRANSMIT ecg_picture_segmants
        Patient_Condition == Needs Attention
        IF ( critical_code == 29)
        ALERT CALL AND MESSAGE AND EMAIL
        Caregivers (Doctors, Kin, Healthcare Unit)
        LOCATE Nearest DEFIB UNIT and Seek Help
        Broadcast LOCATION
        Patient_Condition == Critical Attention
```

Fig. 4. The Pseudo Code for ECG Alert Program

The medical data exchange that is promised in the code above cannot be transmitted in a non-standardized format or else it will not be scalable and understandable for the Health Information System (HIS) in the hospital where the patient history and other personal data is stored. Moreover, since there is personal data attached to the healthcare data, one has to follow industrial standards while dealing with 'airing' data. The Healthcare Level 7 (HL7) is a standard that used for standardizing the healthcare data.

Commonly, in HL7 v3, a Reference Information model (RIM) is created where the actors, procedures, and devices are defined that are authorized in dealing with the healthcare data. The Packetization of the ECG segments in the experiments we conducted is shown in Figure 5 below.

In the normal course of operation, as far as the ECG signals from the patient are concerned, a periodic update is sent to the HIS at remote location regarding patient's

PID	CNo	TSTMP	LOC	PCGID	CDN
IPiD	CPNo	HL7No	INo	CSCG	CDFiB

Multimedia Service Contents

MSH|^~\&|PID|1|||2012071300987645504
||ADT^INO|786786786|HL7NO|2.3|||
EVN|INO|2012071300987645504|||||
PID|1||10006579^^^1^MRN^1||AHMAD^K
HALID^D||00987645504|M||1|111 AHMAD
CNO^^QATARI^CA^786786786^^M|1|8885
551212|8885551212|1|2||40007716^^^PC
GID^VN^1|123121234|||||||||||NO
LOC|1|AHMAD^LOAY|SO|00987645504
AHMAD
RD^^QATARI^CNO^786786786|1231.2123.4
342.4543||Y|||||||||||||||
GT1|1|8291|AHMAD^KHALID^D||111^AH
MAD
ST^^QATARI^CA^786786786|8885551212||
00987645504|M||1|123121234|||||#CART
OON AHMADS INC|111^AHMAD
CNO^^QATARI^CA^786786786|8885551212
||PT| DG1|1|I9|71596^
|ARTERIOVENTRICULAR BLOCKAGE ||A|
IN1|1|QCARE|3|
CNO^^QATARI^CA^786786786|||||||||||||
|||||123121234A||||||PT|M|111 AHMAD
SENDMMS.SENDMMMS(MMS_SAMPLEACTI
VITY.THIS, BYTESTOSEND)

PID – Patient Identifier | CNo – Case Number | TSTMP – Time Stamp | LOC – Location | PCGID – Primary Caregivers Identifier | CDN – Cellular Device Number | IPiD – Initial Packet Identifier | CPNo – Current Packet Number | CRC – Cyclic Redundancy Check | HL7No – Healthcare Level 7 Version Number | CSCG - Contact Secondary Care Giver | CDFiB - Contact De-fibliration | INo – Instance Number

Fig. 5. An HL7 Standard Packet along with its HL7 v3 code for transmission from mobile device to the HIS.

health condition to be normal. As soon as the microcontroller present in the healthcare vest worn by the patient detects an anomaly i.e. it sends an alert to the mobile device with an alert code (These alert codes are transmitted at the initial handshaking level). Upon reception of an alert, the data is transmitted to the mobile device carrying ECG signal data along with the meta data mentioned in the figure above e.g. if the alert code is 22 or 29, it means that patient is suffering from cardio ventricular blockage and articular blockage respectively. In these cases, the device plots and sends the ECG signals in the wave formats to the HIS. Upon reception of code 29, which means that the patient is going through a major heart attack, nearest de-fibliration unit is alerted along with the remote HIS, caregivers etc. with the patient's current location and a history of all the events is maintained.

3   Testing and Results

The simulator produces 10 different healthy ECG signals with different rates in order to mimic various physical situations such as walking, running, lying down, etc. One of these, sitting posture waveform, has been used as the reference healthy signal in the presented work. The three arrhythmia cases selected for this study are briefly described in the following:

3.1   Second Degree Block Type I (A1)

This is a disorder of the cardiac conduction system in which some atrial impulses do not get conducted to the ventricles. Electrocardiographically, some P waves are not followed by a QRS complex. This is also accompanied with progressive lengthening of the PR interval and ultimately leading to the failure of conduction of an atrial beat. This is followed by a conducted beat with a short PR interval and then the cycle repeats itself.

3.2   Premature Ventricular Contraction (A2)

This is a compound condition which has a combination of five waveforms, called A2s, and is then followed by 36 normal beats. This sequence is then repeated.

3.3   Ventricular Fibrillation (A3)

A3 is the result of highly irritable ventricle(s), which begin to send out rapid electrical stimuli. The stimuli are chaotic resulting in no organized ventricular depolarization. The ventricles do not contract because they never depolarize. Because the ventricles are fibrillating and never contracting, the patient does not have a pulse, cardiac output, or blood pressure.

These signals are shown in Figure 6.

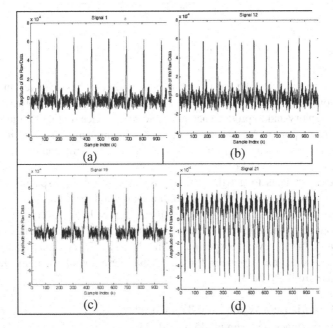

Fig. 6. ECG signals as obtained by the microcontroller system. (a) Healthy person in sitting posture, (b) Class A1, (c) Class A2, and (d) Class A3 scenarios.

These signals are decomposed into various frequency components by using a FIR Filter bank. Initially, six filters were designed in the range of 0 to 62.5 Hz corresponding to the main components of the signal present in the underlying signals. However, after several tests, only one filter range was found to be more effective. The range of this filter is between 10 Hz to 20 Hz, and ultimately corresponds to certain features of the ECG signal, hence, making it possible to classify them. Essentially, for the disease cases presented in this work, the selected filter range works best. However, a similar line of argument can be used for other cases as well where other filter ranges might work better. Figure 7 shows this filter's coefficient plot.

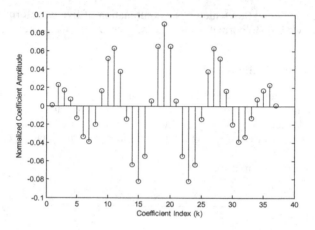

Fig. 7. The 36th order FIR band filter used in this work

In the microcontroller, an array set is initialized as type *Single*, in which the coefficients of the filter are stored. A hardware Timer is enabled in order to check the overflow of memory and to produce accurate Interrupt service routine for data acquisition through the ADC port 1. A small delay of 5ms is intentionally included in the loop in order reduce the processing load on the microcontroller. As the analog signal from the simulator arrives at the ADC of the microcontroller, the values are multiplied with this filter bank's coefficients to get the filtered signal with only the specific components. Figure 8 shows the outcomes of the filter for the signals in Figure 6.

The energy is then calculated for this signal (typically for every 5 seconds) and then the variance of these recurring energy values is calculated (again, in typically 5 seconds). In light of several experiments in diversified situations of noise levels, following ranges of the variances for each case were found as main classification thresholds and are listed below:

1. A3 Variance between :   0.87 and 0.65
2. A2 Variance between : 0.45 and   0.23
3. Normal Variance between   : 0.22 and 0.17
4. A1 Variance between   : 0.13 and 0.05

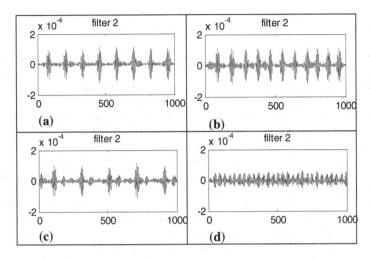

Fig. 8. Filter outputs for the four classes in Figure 6 under study

With respect to these values, the possibility of any arrhythmia cases is determined. Once the classification is for the abnormality, a flag is signaled to the Android phone and following it, the microcontroller transmits the ECG waveform to the user console for further storage and transmission to the doctor and/or the related medical staff.

4   Conclusion

In this work, a cost-effective personal healthcare system is presented to achieve computationally low cost classification for the ECG signals in an embedded microcontroller system with ubiquitous settings. This technique can be used for real-time classification, as the ECG data arrives in the embedded system. Therefore this method can be used not only as classifier but also as a predictor for certain irregular arrhythmia. During all the tests, the algorithm detected the change of waveform in a 100% correct manner. The only limiting factor at the moment is the processing delay which still requires about 13 seconds to have the decision available for the transmission. Even this delay is more than acceptable for the current system, but an improved version for near-real-time operations is being developed on top of the presented system. The actual human interface for the same system has been completed as well and is ready to be put forth for clinical testing in near future.

Acknowledgment. This publication was made possible by a grant from Qatar National Research Fund under its National Priority Research Program, for projects NPRP 09-292-2-113. Its contents are solely the responsibility of the authors and do not necessarily represent the official views of Qatar National Research Fund.

References

1. Qidwai, U., Shakir, M.: Filter Bank Approach to Critical Cardiac Abnormalities Detection using ECG data under Fuzzy Classification. Accepted for Publication in International Journal of Computer Information Systems & Industrial Management Applications (July 2012) ISSN: 2150-7988
2. Qidwai, U., Shakir, M.: Embedded System Design with Filter Bank and Fuzzy Classification Approach to Critical Cardiac Abnormalities Detection. To be Presented at IEEE Symposium on Industrial Electronics and Applications, Indonesia (2012)
3. Qidwai, U., Shakir, M.: Fuzzy Detection of Critical Cardiac Abnormalities using ECG data: A ubiquitous approach. In: IEEE 11th Hybrid Intelligent Systems Conference, Malaysia (2011)
4. Ullah, S., Higgins, H., Braem, B., Latre, B., Blondia, C., Moerman, I., Saleem, S., Rahman, Z., Kwak, K.S.: A Comprehensive Survey of Wireless Body Area Networks: On PHY, MAC, and Network Layers Solutions. Journal of Medical Systems (2010)
5. Chen, M., Gonzalez, S., Vasilakos, A., Cao, H., Leung, V.C.M.: Body Area Networks: A Survey. Mobile Networks and Applications (MONET) 16(2), 1–23 (2011)
6. Schmidt, R., Norgall, T., Mörsdorf, J., Bernhard, J., von der Grün, T.: Body Area Network BAN–a key infrastructure element for patient-centered medical applications. Biomed. Tech. 47(1) (2002)
7. O'Donovan, T., O'Donoghue, J., Sreenan, C., O'Reilly,'P., Sammon, D., O'Connor, K.: A Context Aware Wireless Body Area Network (BAN). In: Proceedings of the Pervasive Health Conference (2009)
8. Yuce, M.R.: Implementation of wireless body area networks for healthcare systems. Sensors and Actuators A: Physical 162, 116–129 (2010)
9. Grajales, L., Nicolaescu, I.V.: Wearable multisensor heart rate monitor. In: International Workshop on Wearable and Implantable Body Sensor Networks, pp. 154–157 (2006)
10. Otto, C., Milenkovic, A., Sanders, C., Jovanov, E.: System Architecture of a Wireless Body Area Sensor Network for Ubiquitous Health Monitoring. Journal of Mobile Multimedia 1(4), 307–326 (2006)
11. Milenkovic, C., Otto, E., Jovanov, E.: Wireless Sensor Networks for Personal Health Monitoring: Issues and an Implementation. Computer Communications Special issue: Wireless Sensor Networks Performance, Reliability, Security, and Beyond (2006)
12. Lily Pad Microcontroller board for embedded applications, http://www.arduino.cc/en/Main/ArduinoBoardLilyPad/
13. Bluetooth module with lily pad microcontroller system, http://www.sparkfun.com/products/9358
14. CardioSim Heartbeat simulator system, http://biometriccables.com/product/ecgsimulatorscardiosim11/

A Study on the Java Compiler
for the Smart Virtual Machine Platform[*]

YunSik Son[1] and YangSun Lee[2]

[1] Dept. of Computer Engineering, Dongguk University
26 3-Ga Phil-Dong, Jung-Gu, Seoul 100-715, Korea
sonbug@dongguk.edu
[2] Dept. of Computer Engineering, Seokyeong University
16-1 Jungneung-Dong, Sungbuk-Ku, Seoul 136-704, Korea
yslee@skuniv.ac.kr

Abstract. SVM(Smart Virtual Machine) is the virtual machine solution that supports various programming languages and platforms, and its aims are to support programming languages like ISO/IEC C++, Java and Objective-C and smart phone platforms such as Android and iOS. Various contents that developed by supported language on SVM can be execute on Android and iOS platforms at no additional cost, because the SVM has the platform independent characteristic by using SIL(Smart Intermediate Language) as an intermediate language. In this paper, we will introduce the Java compiler to support the contents written in Java language on SVM which generates platform independently stack-based SIL code as target code.

Keywords: SVM(Smart Virtual Machine), SIL(Smart Intermediate Language), Java Compiler, Compiler Construction.

1 Introduction

The previous development environments for smart phone contents are needed to generate specific target code depending on target devices or platforms, and each platform has its own developing language. Therefore, even if the same contents are to be used, it must be redeveloped depending on the target machine and a compiler for that specific machine is needed, making the contents development process very inefficient. SVM(Smart Virtual Machine) is a virtual machine solution which aims to resolve such problems, and it uses the SIL(Smart Intermediate Language) code which designed by our research team as an input at the execution time[1-4].

In this study, a compiler for use in a program designed in the Java programming language[5] to be used on a SVM is designed and implemented. In order to effectively

---

[*] This research was supported by Basic Science Research Program through the National Research Foundation of Korea(NRF) funded by the Ministry of Education, Science and Technology(No.20110006884).

T.-h. Kim et al. (Eds.): MulGraB/BSBT/IUrC 2012, CCIS 353, pp. 135–140, 2012.

implement the compiler, it was designed to five modules; syntax analysis, class file loader, symbol information collector, semantic analyzer and code generator.

2   Relative Studies

2.1   SVM(Smart Virtual Machine)

The SVM is a platform which is loaded on smart phones. It is a stack based virtual machine solution which can independently download and run application programs. The SVM consists of three main parts; compiler, assembler and virtual machine. It is designed in a hierarchal structure to minimize the burden of the retargeting process.

The SVM is designed to accommodate successive languages, object-oriented languages and etc. through input of SIL as its intermediate language. It has the advantage of accommodating C/C++ and Java, which are the most widely used languages used by developers. SIL was a result of the compilation/translation process and it is changed into the running format SEF(SIL Executable Format) through an assembler. The SVM then runs the program after receiving the SEF[1-4].

2.2   SIL(Smart Intermediate Language)

SIL[6], the virtual machine code for SVM, is designed as a standardized virtual machine code model for ordinary smart phones and embedded systems. SIL is a stack based command set which holds independence as a language, hardware and a platform. In order to accommodate a variety of programming languages, SIL is defined based on the analysis of existing virtual machine codes such as bytecode[7], .NET IL[8] and etc. In addition, it also has the set of arithmetic operations codes to accommodate object-oriented languages and successive languages.

SIL is composed of meta-code(shows class declarations and specific operations) and arithmetic codes (responds to actual commands). Arithmetic codes are not subordinate to any specific hardware or source languages and thus have an abstract form. In order to make debugging of the languages such as the assembly language simple, they apply a name rule with consistency and define the language in mnemonics, for higher readability. In addition, they have short form arithmetic operations for optimization. SIL's arithmetic codes are classified into seven and each category has its own detailed categories.

3   Java to SIL Compiler

In this study, the Java to SIL compiler was designed as can be seen in Fig. 3 it has five parts and 10 detailed modules.

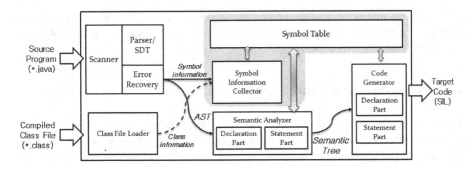

Fig. 1. Java to SIL Compiler Model

The Java to SIL compiler embodies the characteristics of the Java language and therefore was designed with five different parts; syntax analysis, class file loader, symbol information collection module, semantic analysis and code generation. The detailed information for each part is as follows.

The syntax analysis part carries out syntax analysis regarding the given input program(*.java) and converts it into an AST(Abstract Syntax Tree) which holds the equivalent semantics. There are largely three steps in the syntax analysis part; lexical analysis, syntax analysis and error recovery [9-11].

The Class file loader is the module to extract symbol information needed to syntax analysis, semantic analysis and code generation from the pre-compiled class files. The Class file loader extracts class information from the inputted class files(*.class), and stores it in the symbol table through symbol information collector.

The module for symbol information collection consists of symbol information collection routines and a symbol table. First, the symbol information collection routine carries out the job of saving information into the symbol table which is obtained by inserting ASTs and rounding the tree. The routines consist of the interface, protocol, class member, ordinary declarations and others(given the characteristics of the Java language). Next, the symbol table is used to manage the symbols(names) and information on the symbols within a program.

The semantic analysis part is composed of the declarations semantic analysis module and the statements semantic analysis module. The declarations semantic analysis module checks the process of collecting symbol information on the AST level, to verify cases which are grammatically correct but semantically incorrect. Semantic analysis of the declarations part is handled by two parts; semantic error and semantic warning. The statements semantic analysis module uses the AST and symbol table to carry out semantic analysis of statements and creates a semantic tree as a result. A semantic tree is a data structure which has semantic information added to it from an AST[4,10]. It is responsible for all that has not been taken care of during the syntax analysis process and then it is used to generate codes as it has been designed to generate codes easily.

The code generation part receives the semantic tree as an input after all analysis is complete and it generates a SIL code which is semantically equal to the input program (*.java). For this, the SIL code is expressed as symbols so it is convenient to generate and handle them. For type conversion code lists, the same data structure is kept so that the code generation process can take place efficiently. Type conversion code lists are data structures that pre-calculate the process of converting a semantic code into a SIL code when generating a code. A code generator visits each nodes of the semantic tree to convert them into SIL codes[10].

4   Implementation and Experiments

To implement the Java to SIL compiler, first the language's grammar was chosen and then using this a LALR(1) parsing table was created. The grammar used was based on JDK 6.0 and the information on the grammar parsing table can be seen in Table 1.

Table 1. Java Grammar, Parsing Table, Tree Information

Name	Count
Grammar Rules	380
Terminal Symbols	105
Nonterminal Symbols	152
Parsing Table Kernels	650
AST Nodes	153
Semantic Tree Nodes	236

Next, we show the process of converting the source program's code(written in Java language) into the target code, the SIL code, using the implemented Java to SIL compiler. Table 2 has been created so that the characteristics of the declarations and syntax of the example program can be seen using the Java language.

Table 2. Example Program(TicTacToe.java)

```
public class TicTacToe extends Component
{
    ...

    public TicTacToe() {
      this.player = 0;
      this.computer = 0;

      ...
    }

    public void paint( Graphics g) {
      g.setColor( getBackground());
      g.fillRect( 0, 0, getSize().width,
            getSize().height);
```

```
      g.setColor( gridColor);
      int fieldSize = this.getFieldSize();
      g.drawLine( 0, fieldSize, 3*fieldSize,
            fieldSize);
      g.drawLine( 0, fieldSize+1,
            3*fieldSize, fieldSize+1);

      ...
    }
    ...

}

...
```

Table 3 shows the AST structures generated from the input program. You can see that the syntax have been expressed using the AST nodes defined earlier on. Table 4 shows a part of the SIL code that has been generated using a semantic tree.

Table 3. AST for an Example Program Segment

Nonterminal: PROGRAM	Nonterminal: DCL_SPEC
...	Nonterminal: INT_TYPE
Nonterminal: CLASS_DCL	Nonterminal: VAR_ITEM
Nonterminal: PUBLIC	Nonterminal: SIMPLE_VAR
Terminal: TicTacToe	Terminal: player
Nonterminal: EXTENDS	Nonterminal: FIELD_DCL
Nonterminal: CLASS_INTERFACE_TYPE	Nonterminal: PRIVATE
Nonterminal: SIMPLE_NAME	Nonterminal: DCL_SPEC
Terminal: Component	Nonterminal: INT_TYPE
Nonterminal: CLASS_BODY	Nonterminal: VAR_ITEM
Nonterminal: FIELD_DCL	Nonterminal: SIMPLE_VAR
Nonterminal: PRIVATE	Terminal: computer
	...

Table 4. Generated SIL Code for Example Program

%%HeaderSectionStart			%Label	##0		lod.i	1	12
...			lod.i	1	4	lod.i	1	8
%%HeaderSectionEnd			lod.i	1	0	add.i		
%%CodeSectionStart			le.i			str.i	1	12
%FunctionStart			fjp	##1		add.p		
.func_name			ldc.i	0		ldi.p		
&TicTacToe::TicTacToe$			str.i	1	12	...		
0			ldc.i	1		.opcode_end		
.func_type	2		str.i	1	8	%FunctionEnd		
.param_count	0		%Label	##3				
.opcode_start			lod.i	1	8	...		
proc	16	1 1	lod.i	1	4	%%CodeSectionEnd		
lod.p	1	0	ldc.i	2		%%DataSectionStart		
ldc.p	0		div.i			...		
add.p			le.i			%%DataSectionEnd		
ldc.i	0		fjp	##4				
sti.i			lod.i	1	4			
lod.p	1	0	lod.i	1	8			
ldc.p	4		mod.i					
add.p			ldc.i	0				
ldc.i	0		eq.i					
sti.i			fjp	##6				

5   Conclusions and Further Researches

Virtual machines refer to the technique of using the same application program even if the process or operating system is changed. It is the core technique that can be loaded onto recently booming smart phones, necessary as an independent download solution software technique. In this study, the Java to SIL compiler was designed and virtualized to run a program that was originally created for another platform to enable its use on a SVM. In this paper, we defined five modules to create a compiler and generate a SIL code for use on a SVM which is independent of platforms. As a result, programs developed for use as Java contents could be run on a SVM using the compiler developed throughout the study and therefore expenses required when producing such contents can be minimized.

In the future, there is need for research on an Android Java-SIL compiler so that Android contents can be run on a SVM. Further research on optimizers and assemblers for SIL code programs are also needed so that SIL codes that have been generated can run effectively on SVMs.

References

1. Lee, Y.S.: The Virtual Machine Technology for Embedded Systems. Korea Multimedia Society 6, 36–44 (2002)
2. Oh, S.M., Lee, Y.S., Ko, K.M.: Design and Implementation of the Virtual Machine for Embedded Systems. Journal of Korea Multimedia Society 8(9), 1282–1291 (2005)
3. Lee, Y.S., Oh, S.M., Son, Y.S.: Development of C++ Compiler for Embedded Systems. Industry-Academia Cooperation Foundation of Seokyeong University (2006)
4. Son, Y., Lee, Y.: Design and Implementation of an Objective-C Compiler for the Virtual Machine on Smart Phone. In: Kim, T.-H., Gelogo, Y. (eds.) MulGraB 2011, Part I. CCIS, vol. 262, pp. 52–59. Springer, Heidelberg (2011)
5. The Java Language & Virtual Machine Specifications, Oracle, http://docs.oracle.com/javase/specs/index.html
6. Yun, S.L., Nam, D.G., Oh, S.M., Kim, J.S.: Virtual Machine Code for Embedded Systems. In: International Conference on CIMCA, pp. 206–214 (2004)
7. Meyer, J., Downing, T.: JAVA Virtual Machine. O'Reylly (1997)
8. Lindin, S.: Inside Microsoft.NET IL Assembler. Microsoft Press (2002)
9. Aho, A.V., Lam, M.S., Sethi, R., Ullman, J.D.: Compilers: Principles, Techniques, & Tools. Addison-Wesley (2007)
10. Son, Y.S.: 2-Level Code Generation using Semantic Tree, Master Thesis, Dongguk University (2006)
11. Graham, S.L., Haley, C.B., Joy, W.N.: Practical LR Error Recovery. In: Proceedings of the SIGPLAN Sym. on Compiler Construction, SIGPLAN Notices, vol. 13(8), pp. 168–175 (1979)

Advanced Knowledge Sharing Strategies
Based on Learning Style Similarity for Smart Education

Jae-Kyung Kim[1], Won-Sung Sohn[1,*], and YangSun Lee[2]

[1] Dept. of Computer Education, Gyeongin National University of Education, Incheon, Korea
{kimjk,sohnws}@ginue.ac.kr
[2] Dept. of Computer Engineering, Seokyung University, Seoul, Korea

Abstract. The spread of the smart device has led collaborative technologies to valuable applications in developing educational content. Many electronic textbooks provide basic annotation features like sharable bookmarks, notes, highlighting and underlining. These user activities contain important information in the view of education such as user knowledge and students' learning style. In this paper, we proposed annotation-content learning model to analyze learner's annotating behavior on electronic textbooks. Based on the model, we also developed similarity algorithms to find other notes created by students who have similar learning style. The purpose of the proposed system is to encourage students to have their own online communities using smart tablets to pool their knowledge and share ideas and experiences. We also presented the evaluation indicating that the system improved students' knowledge significantly.

Keywords: Annotation, Collaborative learning, Smart education.

1   Introduction

Today's students have been exposed to digital technology from birth and schools move into continuously a digital learning environment. Especially, the usability of digital textbooks in smart devices such as tablets is becoming more important. The usability is very important since digital textbooks are interactive contents and must be designed with the needs of their students in mind[1,2]. Scanned textbooks, HTML contents without interaction and lecture-centered teaching are no longer appropriate, because learning involves high levels of problem-solving tasks by cognitive collaboration and interaction[3,4].

Interactive learning environments should consider each student's abilities and learning styles. E-learning systems should provide expressing students' opinion and knowledge in digital textbooks freely and communicating with group members. This will encourage students to access study material more frequently and find information easily via communication[5,6].

However, it has been difficult to provide such systems for learning in desktop environment. Students had to go to a computer room in school or home, sit down, turn it on and run the application to access the resources. Location and time factor was the big obstacle for increasing usability of interactive and collaborative learning system.

T.-h. Kim et al. (Eds.): MulGraB/BSBT/IUrC 2012, CCIS 353, pp. 141–148, 2012.
© Springer-Verlag Berlin Heidelberg 2012

Fortunately, this structural problem was solved by the wide use of smart devices. Students can access to applications anytime and anywhere they want. Now, our homework is how to design the system properly to increase learning effect in smart device environment.

The factor that students want to create their own annotation in digital textbooks and share their opinion should be considered to enhance the usability of educational contents in smart device. Especially, they want to organize their annotations as a personal collection such as a notebook. Moreover, they are very happy to share it with others and discuss about it[7,8].

Therefore, we designed and implemented the knowledge recommendation interface based on the proposing annotation-contents model. Our system provides note-taking style interface for students to annotate their work. Thus, annotated information in digital textbooks is analyzed and stored in a database according to the model. The similarity algorithms can find other annotations created by students who have top grade or similar learning style. Thus, the student can access other annotation related to his or her learning style. The main idea of the system is to get more information from annotation about our students, and to put students at the center of the learning system.

In this paper, we propose annotation-contents model and algorithm in Section 2, implemented system in Section 3, evaluate it in Section 4. Then we conclude in Section 5.

2   Annotation-Content Model and Similarity Algorithm

In this section, annotation-content model was developed for the interactive and collaborative learning system. The system needs to collect learning activities and build learning profile data for self-directed learning. Thus, the students' activity data is stored according to the model. The model is defined based on the relation of annotation such as note and digital textbook content.

2.1   Annotation Model

In tablets, students make their own annotation by touching their finger on the screen. They reserve an area as a bookmark or note-taking space. They write then a *comment*, *question*, *answer* to other annotation and tags if they want to put. Basically, annotation can be consisted of *area*, *text*, *types* and *tags* in this model.

All annotations are anchored to digital textbook content such as text, image or page itself. In the low-level, they are floating on the screen by coordinates. However, in the abstract level, they are anchored information to book, chapter, section, or text phrase somehow. Therefore, the area is consisted of *book, chapter, section, HTM path* and *coordinates* on the screen. Formula (1) shows the proposed definition of annotation model.

$$Annotation = \{Area, Text, Type, Tags\}$$

$$Area = \{Book, Chapter, Section, HTML\_Path, Coordinates\} \qquad (1)$$

$$Type = \{Memo, Question, Answer\}$$

2.2 Annotation-Content Based Leaner's Profile

According to the annotation model, we propose the learner's profile. It also includes fundamental information such as quiz score or attendance, but it is not sufficient to reflect students' learning behavior. The key characteristic of the model is using dynamic information from students. They make, read, and share their annotation over semesters. The annotation is rich and valuable knowledge in education and all these dynamic activities need to be collected.

Therefore, we defined the annotation-content based learner's profile as shown in table 1. It mainly organizes and manages information occurring among annotation-content-student. The data is then extracted and stored in database based on XML schema.

Table 1. Annotation-content based learner's profile

Category		item	Description
Basic Info.		Name	Basic profile
		Sex	
		Grade/Classroom	
Test Report		Mid/Final Term	Mid/Final Score
		Quiz	Quiz score
Learning Progress		Textbook Progress	Textbook reading progress.
Annotation Activities	Creating	Creating frequency	The number of created annotations
		Annotation types	Ratio of created annotation types
		Anchored content	Semantic location of annotations
		Notebook creating frequency	The number of created notebooks
	Reading	Accessing frequency	Annotation accessing frequency
		Reading types	Ratio of accessed annotation types
		Notebook reading frequency	The number of accessed notebooks
Foxonomy		Tag information	Tag information in each annotations
		Tag frequency	Tag frequency in a tag cloud
		Tag access frequency	The number of hit tags
Attendance		Login info	Login connection information
		Connected time	Total connected time to system

2.3 Similarity Algorithm for Annotation Recommendation

Active sharing of student knowledge is an essential element of effective and meaningful way of learner-centered teaching. Thus, students can access a public notebook, a collection of user annotations, by other learners in the proposed system. The notebooks are displayed on the bookshelf categorized by courses and chapters.

The notebooks in the same category have different weight values of similarity and recommendation calculated by the proposing algorithm. The similarity weight value of a notebook is determined by a vector inner-product of HTML structure and student annotation score.

The format of digital textbooks on the system use ePub3, which is basically based on HTML5. Thus, the structure of textbooks is explicitly divided into chapter, section, paragraph, etc. Every structural element has a generated unique id, and an annotation can be attached to one of the element.

$$Similarity(a, b) = \sum_{i=1}^{n} N_{a,i} \times N_{b,i} \tag{2}$$

If no student(s_n) annotation activity occurs on structural element i, the value, v would be zero. Scores of v for simple comment or memo, question and answer are 1, 2, and 3 respectively. Accumulated annotations on the same i have higher score. table 2 shows the example of annotation-content values. N is normalized value for each v on i_n.

Table 2. Student learning pattern based on annotation-content relation

	i_1		i_2		i_3		i_4	
	v	N	v	N	v	N	v	N
s_1	0	0.00	1	0.41	2	0.82	1	0.41
s_2	3	0.42	2	0.28	6	0.85	1	0.14
s_3	2	0.53	0	0.00	3	0.80	1	0.27
s_4	0	0.00	2	0.55	0	0.00	3	0.83

The similarity between two students can be deducted from the formula (2). The similarity value is sum of multiplying normalized value of each element i and student a, b.

3   Implementation

According to the annotation definition and similarity formula, the system was implemented on iPad on iOS 5.1. Digital textbooks on the system follows ePub3 standard based on HTML5.

Figure 1(left) shows the annotation user interface allowing users to draw annotation area around a target object such as paragraphs, images, tables and etc. When a touch-up event occurs at the new area, the annotation module then recognizes target area information such as *Book, Chapter, Section, HTML_Path, Coordinates*, defined in formula 1. It prompts then the input menu for text comment, note type and tags associated at the new annotation. Users select type of annotation such as *Memo, Question* or *Answer* and fill additional information out (*Text, Tags*).

Detailed steps to process annotation are described in [9]. In this paper, we focus on the model and similarity function.

Swiping through the page with two fingers switches to the notebook page, collection of annotations as shown figure 1(right). All created annotations are gathered here as a form of leaner's personal notebook which stores their own summaries of annotations.

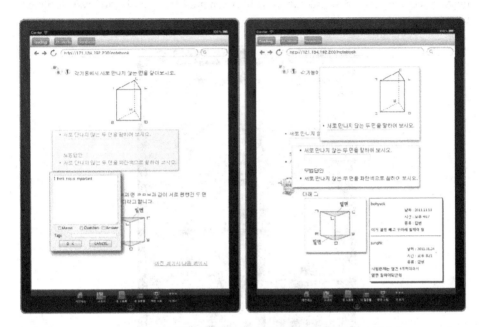

Fig. 1. Annotation creation interface(left) and notebook page(right)

The "note-bookshelf" as shown in figure 2 lets students browses public notebooks shared by other learners. Once students see something that interests them, students can tap a book icon to read the annotations.

As students pile their notebooks in the shelf, there can be lots of different kinds of notebooks available. Even though the note-bookshelf allow students organize them by course category, it would be hard to find something useful. Therefore, the system executes the proposed algorithm to sort the notebooks by learning pattern similarity. Students whose annotation activity is similar to the current login user in application have high similarity scores. The notebook with the highest score in a subject category would be located to the most left side of the row.

As a result, notebooks are sorted by the scores in each subject categories in descending order. Students can access to the most similar notebooks as well as the most not similar ones. By comparing their own work with others, they would find information they had missed, or learn how others study for the subject. Therefore, the notebook-self is interface where learners rely on each other to achieve the same goal.

If students haven't created annotations enough, they are not able to identify the similar notebook yet. As collaborative filtering methods recommend items based on users' past preferences, new users will need to rate sufficient number of items to enable the system to capture their preferences accurately and thus provides reliable recommendations[10]. However, looking on the bright side, it encouraged students to do more annotation activities, which proved us that the fact we mentioned in the introduction section were correct, and the usability feature of the application was designed properly.

Fig. 2. Public notebooks in the 'note-bookshelf' ordered by similarity weight

4   Evaluation

In this evaluation, G_1 represents the experimental group using the proposed application, and G_2 represents the control group using the same application without similarity and recommendation functionality. G_2 still can annotate and share the notebooks, but they are not sorted by the formulas. 40 elementary students (22 male and 18 female, the 6th grade student) participated as evaluators. Enough time were given to be familiar with the application before the evaluation. Our hypothesis is that G_1 will improve student's knowledge more than G_2 after using the application.

First, we took the pre-test to measure students' basic knowledge on the course material. G_1 and G_2 scored average of 68.26 and 69.92, standard deviation of 3.78 and 4.59 respectively. The difference of test results between G_1 and G_2 is not significant ($p = .83$). This ensures that those two groups have a similar level of basic knowledge on the material.

Table 3. A comparison between the post-test of two groups

	N	Avg.	SD	df	t	p
G_1	20	90.12	8.21	17.22	1.017	.000
G_2	20	82.32	12.16	15.18		

After the pre-test, one week was given to both groups for using the application to read, annotate and share them on digital textbooks.

Then, we took the post-test to measure how the proposed functionality affected them. G_1 and G_2 scored average of 90.12 and 82.32 respectively. The significant difference was found($p = .00$) as shown in Table 3. The proposed application improved students' knowledge more than digital textbooks with basic annotation functionalities. Therefore, we found that the use of the proposed notebook application had a positive effect on problem solving skills.

5   Summary

The note-taking and sharing interface based on students learning style was implemented to enrich usability for e-learning system on tablets. Annotation structure and similarity algorithm were developed for collaborative and learner-centered learning. It is deployed on tablet device and evaluated to measure its effectiveness. As a result, students were satisfied with creating their own work by using the proposed note-taking interface, and their knowledge was also improved by sharing notebooks recommended by the similarity module. Therefore, the digital textbooks with the presented features could offer more opportunities to enhance the entire learning experience.

Acknowledgements. This research was supported by Basic Science Research Program through the National Research Foundation of Korea(NRF) funded by the Ministry of Education, Science and Technology(2012-0006751).

References

1. Thayer, A., Lee, C.P., Hwang, L.H., Sales, H., Sen, P., Dalal, N.: The imposition and superimposition of digital reading technology: the academic potential of e-readers. In: Proceedings of the 2011 Annual Conference on Human Factors in Computing Systems, pp. 2917–2926. ACM, Vancouver (2011)
2. Merriënboer, J.G., Ayres, P.: Research on cognitive load theory and its design implications for e-learning. ETR&D 53, 5–13 (2005)
3. Balla, A.: Designing Pedagogical Learning Environment. International Journal of Advanced Science and Technology 6, 1–14 (2009)
4. Sung, J.S.: Design of Collaborative Learning on Mobile Environment. International Journal of Advanced Science and Technology 25, 43–54 (2010)

5. Nagarajan, P., Wiselin Jiji, G.: ONLINE EDUCATIONAL SYSTEM (e- learning). International Journal of u- and e-Service, Science and Technology 3, 37–48 (2010)
6. Tse, E., Schoning, J., Huber, J., Marentette, L., Beckwith, R., Rogers, Y., Muahlhauser, M.: Child computer interaction: workshop on UI technologies and educational pedagogy. In: Proceedings of the 2011 Annual Conference Extended Abstracts on Human Factors in Computing Systems, pp. 2445–2448. ACM, Vancouver (2011)
7. Marshall, C.C.: The future of Annotation in a Digital (paper) world. In: The 35th Annual GSLIS Clinic: Successes & Failures of Digital Libraries, University of Illinois at Urbana-Champaign (1998)
8. Ovsiannikov, I.A., Arbib, M.A., McNeill, T.H.: Annotation technology. International Journal of Human-Computer Study 50, 329–362 (1999)
9. Kim, J.K., Sohn, W.S., Kim, T.H., Lee, Y.S.: Annotation-based Smart User Interface for Digital Textbook. In: The 1st International Conference on Advanced Information Technology and Sensor Application, Daejun, Korea (2012)
10. Collaborative filtering,
    http://en.wikipedia.org/wiki/Collaborative_filtering

Efficient Emotional Factor Extraction Using Moving Average Filter in Digital Sound and LED Color

Jaesang Cha[1] and Seokkee Hong[2,*]

[1] Dept. of Electronic & IT Media Eng., Seoul National Univ. of Science and Tech.,
Seoul, Korea
[2] Converging Technology Insititute of Seoul Technopark, Seoul, Korea
hong@seoultp.or.kr

Abstract. In this paper, as the fusion study of LED lighting and sound based on the emotion, we conducted this study for extraction of Emotional Factor based on LED lighting and sound. The sound received from a microphone through FFT and FIR filter extracts only useful frequency band. And the Emotional Factor possible to be extracted via a Moving Average Filter send data to serial output port. The Moving Average Filter takes an average at time axis. Also it is easy to extract Emotion Factor to maintain overall tendency of the data which strong at noise. We demonstrated the usefulness of the proposed system through the experiment.

Keywords: Digital Sound, Moving average Filter, Emotional Factor.

1 Introduction

Recently, emotional lighting method has been studied through the matching with audible frequency and visible light spectrum of audio signal. Also, LED used to installing and using a car or house, and the product is being sold. The existing methods express the simple emotions, but practical Emotional Factor is incomplete or does not contain not [1][2].

The LED visible light and emotion design algorithm of human actual feel. And construct of the system need emotion expression and more realistic conveying system.

Therefore In this paper, the existing emotional light ways are practical Emotional Factor is incomplete or does not contain not. So we deliver more realistic representation and we applied Design and Application of the Moving Average Filter for Effectively Extract LED color based Emotional Factor[3][4].

2 Emotional Factor Extraction Using Moving Average Filter

Digital sound with frequency domain characteristics change very frequently, and Algorithms are needed to maximize natural emotion flow delivery.

In this paper, we adopt the FFT and the Moving Average Filter. Sudden transits of LED color are mitigated through the classification of frequency characteristic.

We proposed emotional and expressive than in previous studies. We proposed emotional and expressive than in previous studies. The Moving average of nth data is represented by the formula as follows [5].

---

* Corresponding author.

T.-h. Kim et al. (Eds.): MulGraB/BSBT/IUrC 2012, CCIS 353, pp. 149–151, 2012.
© Springer-Verlag Berlin Heidelberg 2012

$$\overline{x}_k = \frac{x_{k-n+1} + x_{k-n+2} + \cdots + x_k}{n} \tag{1}$$

$$\overline{x}_k = \overline{x}_{k-1} + \frac{x_k - x_{k-n}}{n} \tag{2}$$

Formula (2) is a recursive equation.

The Moving Average $\overline{x}_k$ is from k-n+1 data to k th data. It means average in total nth data.

Namely, average in certain time interval changes frequently through and emotional information can be extracted more accurately and effectively.

3   Experiment and Simulation

In this paper, we demonstrate the usefulness of proposed LED emotional lighting algorithms and Digital Sound through the simulation. After processing the FFT transform of Digital Sound, it divides musical range using FIR filter. Then the Moving Average Filter and emotional mapping table are applied. And this data convert to DMX protocol. Finally, RGB control data is acquired. Following simulation results shown, the Moving Average Filter is used according to the LED color has been changed.

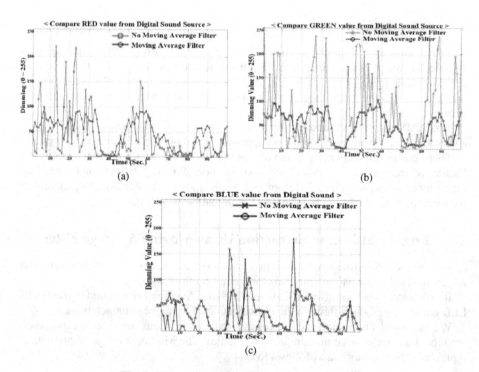

(a)   (b)

(c)

Fig. 1. Compare R, G, B value from Digital Sound

X-axis: Time axis measurements showed a total of 100 seconds. Y-axis: Dimming of the LED's RGB value expressed as a number from 0 to 255. We confirmed that using the Moving Average Filter is possible to decrease the deviation about R, G, B value. We analyzed the results from the simulation numerical value. Dimming value of the average value for R(a), G(b), B(c), each of the Moving Average Filter algorithm when applied: R65.33, G75.4, and B51.26. When do not applied: R62, G 75, and B 48.11. The Moving Average Filter algorithm when applied: R 7.4, G 9.6, and B 7.2. When do not applied: R 61.01, G 72.11, and B 48.11. The standard deviation would be reduced: R is 8 times, G is 7 times, and B is 7times.

4   Conclusion

In this paper, we proposed the algorithm for extracting Emotion Factor in Digital Sound. As the fusion study of LED lighting and sound based on the emotion.

Additionally, for the efficient direction of the LED color which randomly transforms based on the emotion, we proposed The Moving Average filter to LED color matching part on time axis. Also we confirmed that color transition decreased about 7~9 times through the simulation based on the experiment and demonstrated the usefulness of proposed algorithm.

Acknowledgment. This work was partially supported by The Research Institute funded Korea Small and Medium Business Administration as part of Business for The Technology Development with a small & medium Business Convergence ("Integrated monitoring system for the observation of unmanned environment", No. S2023602) from 2012.

References

1. Jang, Y.B., Choe, B.J.: Emotional LED Lighting Using Music. EASKO 2(1), 5–12 (2010)
2. Jang, Y.B., Jang, H., Choe, B.J., Choe, H., Yoo, J., Suk, S.C.: Audio Signal using LED Fixture. EASKO 8(1), 62–65 (2010)
3. Jang, Y.B.: Emotional Lighting Apparatus and Method through Mapping of the Audio Spectrum and the Visible Light Spectrum, Patent application (Application No. 10-2010-0109035) (November 2010)
4. Jang, Y.B.: DSP Real-time processing, Saengnueng (2007)
5. Chou, Y.-l.: Statistical Analysis. In: Holt International (1975) ISBN 0-03-089422-0, section 17.9

Microprocessor Device to Control Lights Using LED Communications for Body Area Networks

Jaesang Cha[1], Soonho Jung[1], Choenil Park[1], Dongha Shim[2], Jason Yi[3],
Hyeungkeun Yu[4], and Junghoon Lee[1],*

[1] Dept. of Electronic & IT Media Eng., Seoul National Univ. of Science and Tech.,
Seoul, Korea
[2] MSDE Progam, Seoul National Univ. of Science and Tech., Seoul, Korea
[3] HaesungOptics Co., Ltd, Hwasung, Korea
[4] Dept. of Strategy and Info., AnySmart Co., Seoul, Korea
dwarfxx@gmail.com

Abstract. As one of the attempt to energy saving, selective LED lighting control is considered to have many effects. It is possible to save energy through the on/off switching of lighting depending on someone needs or the focusing the lighting where the people is crowed. But, domestic LED lighting have many problem to use as individual lighting because most of the domestic LED lighting did not support individual control and variety lighting is only connected to one switch so it is need to additional wiring work. In this paper, we proposed the method of the individual lighting control system using VLC technique that easy to install and easy to usage. So it is expected to implement the system of individual lighting control and to avoid the difficulty of wiring.

Keywords: LED light, VLC(Visual Light Communication), Smart-Phone, MCU(Micro-Control Unit).

1 Introduction

As a result of that energy saving became the focus of public attention, incandescent or fluorescent lamps are being replaced to the LED lighting and all the lights connected to one switch are being changed to separated switch. In addition, it is accelerated that various activity to save energy such as automatic on/off switching control system[1][2]. According to those reason, the LED lighting control system using human detection sensor is recently researched actively[3]. But this system sometime operates abnormally when sensor detects the human incorrectly. So individual lighting control need to prevent incorrect detect. To solve this matter, individual lighting control must be connected to each wiring but it bring to accompany many cost and workload. Wireless solution such as RF resource can help to relief cost and workload, but RF resource is almost used at another system and a large amount of RF resource make harmful effect to the human body in the indoor environment.

---

* Corresponding author.

T.-h. Kim et al. (Eds.): MulGraB/BSBT/IUrC 2012, CCIS 353, pp. 152–155, 2012.
© Springer-Verlag Berlin Heidelberg 2012

So, instead of the previous RF resource, we propose the VLC wireless solution to prevent incorrect human detection through the simple implementation of the hardware.

2   A Summary of VLC and Lighting Control Technique

The RF communication and VLC technique is considered for the indoor wireless communication solution. Although the RF communication is already developed enough, it is not a good solution because of the expansive development cost and saturation of RF frequency allocation. On the other hand, VLC technique is not harmful to human body and it can be constituted as the simple hardware implementation. So it is a profitable indoor wireless communication solution. VLC technique is digital data transmission method with on/off switching of the visual light and it is not harmful to human's eye because they did not recognize the 30 Hz on/off switching speed of visual light. In addition, it is possible to high-speed data transmission because the wavelength size is very short. Recently, Human detection sensors that are IR sensor and Ultrasonic sensor have attracted a lot of attention. It has attracted attention as a useful technique for energy-saving by human detection through the lights on/off. Automatic method by human detection sensor is the convenience and effective for energy savings. However, it is behave differently to the intention of the person. It's the most passive way switches are used in conjunction with but, manually switch are connected the all lights in the space. So it is used to turn on or turn off as a whole. Therefore, it is a reality that does not control for the lighting.

3   VLC Transceiver Implementation

VLC transmitter implementation is very simple to implement. In this paper, we propose two ways. The first method, this method is implemented by using LED and MCU (Micro-Control Unit). The concept is shown in Fig. 1. As you can see in the figure, It is a simple on / off control of LED using the MCU's GPIO (General Purpose I / O) and for LED Driving Tr. Therefore, the digital data can be transmitted.

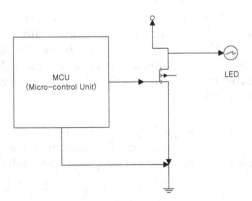

Fig. 1. Implementation example using MCU and LED Transmitter

The second method, it is able to take advantage of the LED flash near camera of smart device. It is possible to simplify the implementation that develops LED Flash Control App (application) on the smart device without implementation of hardware. The concept is shown in Fig. 2(a).

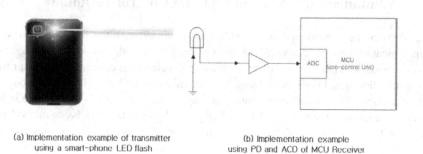

(a) Implementation example of transmitter using a smart-phone LED flash

(b) Implementation example using PD and ACD of MCU Receiver

Fig. 2. Implementation example of transmitter using a smart-phone LED flash and PD/ACD of MCU Receiver

VLC receiver be able to be implemented through PD (Photo diode) and MCU. The voltage of the PD varies depending on the intensity of the light that is visible. This voltage be able to be detected through the ADC port of MCU. Voltage values that read via the ADC port according to the protocol are able to be implemented receiver that converts digital data. Also, it is able to increase recognizes the range and angle when PD covers the lens. The concept is shown in Fig. 2(b).

4   Conclusion

There are a variety of ways to save energy. There are a variety of ways to save energy. Among them, substantial research on the lighting control is able to be most easily, and the effect is greater. The purpose of this paper, we were implemented visible light wireless communication utilizing individual lighting controls. As a result, we are able to propose effective ways to reduce energy. Hardware and software method of VLC that is able to be implemented more easily than RF communications is presented. We proposed lighting control method using smart device without additional hardware. Therefore, it is expected to have a large effect on reducing energy through product development.

Acknowledgment. This work was partially supported by the regional economic spoting Research Institute ("Packaging module development combined with UWB and the ultra wide angle lens for the endoscopic equipment", No. A0043 00013) from 2012.

References

1. Zeng, L., O'Brien: Improvement of Date Rate by using Equalization in an Indoor Visible Light Communication System. In: ICCSC 2008, pp. 678–682 (May 2008)
2. Basic study on indoor location estimation using Visible Light Communication platform. In: 2009 IEEE 20th International Symposium on Personal, pp. 1893–1897 (2009)
3. Saari, R.: A passive infrared sensor for combustion efficiency and process control. University of Toronto, Canada (2007) MR27365

The Study of Video Based Monitoring
for PCB Assembly Line

Jaesang Cha and Hyung-O Kim[*]

Dept. of Electronic & IT Media Eng., Seoul National Univ. of Science and Tech.,
Seoul, Korea
hokim76@gmail.com

Abstract. Rework costs can occur because workers don't perform the right unit process in specialization PCB assembly process. It is an important issue of assembly line management. This paper proposes an image processing method to decide a right working of unit process. And We implemented a video based monitoring system with our experimental system in labaratory and obtained reliable its results.

Keywords: Image Processing, PCB Assembly line, Surveillance.

1   Introduction

Since Toyota Motor Corp. announced JIT(Just In Time) system, Manufacture industries changed from mass production of a few selected items to diversified small-quantity production[1]. There is also a growing trend towards the use of PCBs in all of industries. Most important of all to reduce of rework is to prevent workers' misoperation. We propose a system to detect workers' misoperation and to notify it.

1.1   Related Work

S.J. Nam, S.W. Lee proposed a monitoring system design that composed two systems: a DAS(Data Acquisition System) getting status of manufacture equipments and a monitoring system based on android mobile device[2]. Quanfu Fan et.al. proposed a generative framework for detecting repetitive sequential events with strong temporal dependencies and potential overlaps. they further demonstrated its effectiveness in a retail example where the predominant activity of the cashier has been analyzed [3].

1.2   Our Approach

As explained in the introduction, To prevent workers' misoperation is important to reduce of rework. And we propose a monitoring system based on CCTV camera. It is essential to decide a position of camera in image processing applications. In this

---

[*] Corresponding author.

T.-h. Kim et al. (Eds.): MulGraB/BSBT/IUrC 2012, CCIS 353, pp. 156–158, 2012.

paper, we choose a dome camera to mount it in ceiling. Ceiling mounted camera has biggest advantage to simply measure a size of PCB.

This paper is organized as follows. In Section 2 of this paper describes design for the rule to detect workers' misoperations. Section 3 explains how to implement rules by image processing, section 4 describes the experimental results and discusses future research plans.   •

2   Monitoring Rule Design

As shown on Figure 1 (a), A conveyor belt looks like a rectangle from the top view. PCB flows from (A) area to (B) area. And worker picks up PCB first and then he put out an assembled PCB. The table below presents a detail work scenario for assembly line.

```
(a) PCB enters (A) area.
(b) Worker shift PCB from conveyor to workbench.
(c) Worker put out an operated PCB.
(d) An operated PCB moves to next process through (B)
area
```

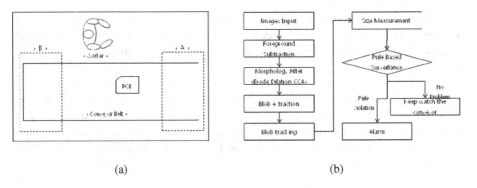

(a)   (b)

Fig. 1. (a) Concept diagram - assembly line, (b) Flowchart

3   Processing Flow

Fig. 1(b) depicts a flowchart for our proposed procedure to extract a PCB and tracking it. We choose AGMM(Adaptive Gaussian Mixture) algorithm for extracting a foreground in input video[4]. To remove of noise in foreground, we used a morphology method as erode, dilation and CCA[5].

It needs a criteria to choose some PCB in blobs. This paper proposes to use a size of blob and moving direction for classification criteria.

4   Experimental

We prepared experimental sets in laboratory. Fig. 3(a) is a captured image by ceiling mounted camera. We can know that the image includes a workers' motion. Fig 3(b). shows the result of AGMM with morphology filters. Fig 3(c). shows the qualitative results of our method on several PCBs. Extracting PCB are marked with a green rectangle in figure.

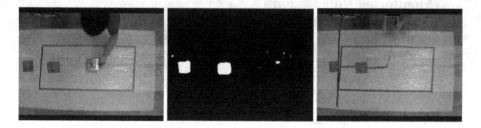

Fig. 2. (a) Input image (b) Foreground image (c) Object moving history

5   Conclusions

We describe a system that is able to monitor PCB line based on CCTV, to detect workers' misoperations. We further demonstrated its effectiveness in a experimental sets. Our current work focuses on monitoring unattended buildings with CCTV and sensor network.

Acknowledgments. This work was partially supported by The Research Institute funded Korea Small and Medium Business Administration as part of Business for The Technology Development with a small & medium Business Convergence ("Integrated monitoring system for the observation of unmanned environment", No. S2023602) from 2012.

References

1. Seong, D.-H.: A Study on the implementation of JIT in Korean manufacturing companies. International Business Review 5, 111–128 (2001)
2. Nam, S.J., Lee, S.W., Lee, J.K.: Design of Android-based Monitoring System for Product Facilities on Shop-floor. In: KSPE Autumn Conference, pp. 277–278 (2011)
3. Fan, Q., Bobbitt, R., Zhai, Y., Yanagawa, A., Pankanti, S., Hampapur, A.: Recognition of Repetitive Sequential Human Activity. In: CVPR, pp. 943–950 (2009)
4. Chris Stauffer, W., Grimson, E.L.: Adaptive background mixture models for real-time tracking. In: CVPR, pp. 2246–2252 (1999)
5. Pratt, W.K.: Digital Image Processing, 4th edn., pp. 453–455. Wiley (2007)

A Study about Implementation of BcN
Using WiFi/ZigBee in Smart Water Grid

Jaesang Cha[1], Jintae Kim[2], and Yongsik Kang[1,*]

[1] Dept. of Electronic & IT Media Eng., Seoul National Univ. of Science and Tech.,
Seoul, Korea
[2] Graduates school of Info. & Comm, Konkuk Univ., Seoul, and Fivetek Co., Sungnam, Korea
yongsikgun@gmail.com

Abstract. In this paper, we propose the design and construction of Broadband Convergence Network(BcN) with WiFi and ZigBee combination to transmit sensor data in smart water grid. We collected sensor data to a broadband modem using ZigBee communication for integrated management server to transmit the sensor data values used in the wastewater treatment plant. And then, we were built the system that transmitted collected sensor data real-time to the integration management server through WiFi communication. BcN with broadband modem improves the control capabilities the existing wastewater treatment plant. It is an efficient energy management is possible. Therefore, contribute to improve the energy efficiency of wastewater treatment plant is expected.

Keywords: WiFi, ZigBee, Broadband Convergence Network, Wastewater Treatment Plant, Smart Water Grid.

1   Introduction

In the wastewater treatment facilities, monitoring system is importance one of the smart-gird components for the energy saving and protection of the environment, which automatically monitors and measures consecutive water states[1]. Also the existing environmental monitoring system is reliant on the imported products and it has many problem of the setting and maintenance[2][3]. Therefore, for the improvement of domestic technique and technical development of wastewater process control, integrated management of water resources and energy is required, which is possible to effectively maintain and control waste water treatment processing[4][5].

For the implementation of integrated wide band network and efficient energy management in smart water-grid, this paper design the wide band modem operated with Zigbee and Wifi. Also we demonstrate the usefulness of proposed system through the experiment.

In this paper, we explain the broadband modem system structure for building broadband convergence network at Section 2. In the next section, design the proposed

---

* Corresponding author.

T.-h. Kim et al. (Eds.): MulGraB/BSBT/IUrC 2012, CCIS 353, pp. 159–162, 2012.

broadband modem. Then we were built the BcN. at Section 4. Finally, we make the conclusion of this paper.

2   Summary of Broadband Modem for BcN Construction

There are monitoring data values through sensors at all times in wastewater treatment plant. The data values are transferred to the integrated management server by BcN configuration. The system is configured as shown in Fig. 1.

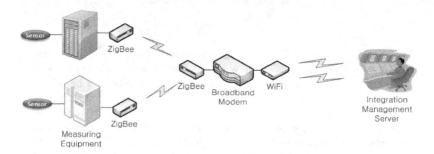

Fig. 1. BcN Architecture

The sensor data is collected to each measuring device in wastewater treatment plant. And then, the collected data is sent to a broadband modem through the ZigBee module. Sensor data that collected to the broadband modem is sent to the integrated management server through the WiFi module. Therefore, integrated management server is possible to verify the sensor data in real time. The existing data to the server to send and receive wire was used. However, It was restricted space and environmental. Therefore, ZigBee, such as low-power wireless communication and WiFi interworking BcN was built, efficient energy management and control system to operate smoothly.

3   Design of System for BcN Construction

We proposed the BcN that to send the sensor data to the integrated management server. The following flow chart as shown in Figure 3 was designed.

Looking block access to BcN in Fig. 3, Each of the collected sensor data values are encapsulated by the ZigBee protocol. And It integrated network modem is collected by the ZigBee communication. to check have been correctly ZigBee receiving. It has been properly delivered and received by the ZigBee module. Sensor data serialization of data through decapsulation.And then, It is transmitted via WiFi through WiFi encapsulation. Therefore, sensor data output is possible.

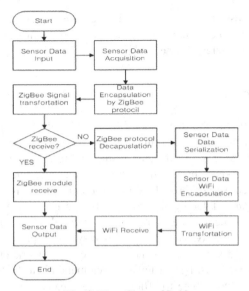

Fig. 2. Flow Chart of BcN

4   Implementation Example of BcN System

Fig. 4 shows the configuration is an example of a broadband modem for BcN in wastewater treatment plant.

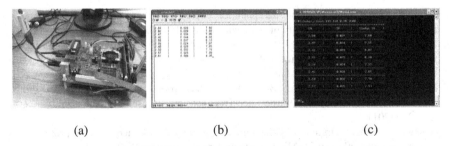

(a)   (b)   (c)

Fig. 3. Broadband modem example

We develop the software that is WiFi and ZigBee module installation to collect sensor data and to transmit real-time integrated management server on board to use as a broadband modem. sensor data sent to the broadband modem by ZigBee module. and then, it displayed on integration management server in real-time. (a) for the broadband modem board. (b) sends the sensor data from the broadband modem. (c) the integration on the management server is displayed.

The system collected various sensor data using a low-power ZigBee communication to broadband modem, because this system will enable efficient energy management. It is compared to the wired space is not limited. , And its utilization is high, so the installation of the sensors it is possible. Also It transmit integrated management server by WiFi communication in real-time. Therefore, we were able to confirm its usefulness by the implementation of a new integrated network.

5   Conclusion

In this paper, we configure the BcN using ZigBee and WiFi for efficient management of wastewater treatment facilities within the Smart Water Grid. Sensor data that use in wastewater treatment process is collected to the measuring device. And then, It is sent to a broadband modem through the ZigBee communication and It is sent to the integrated management server through WiFi communication in real time. The control of a wastewater treatment facility improvements and energy-efficient management performance improvement was confirmed through the proposed system implementation based on BcN. Thus, the proposed system is proved the usefulness.

So We were to build a new broadband convergence network in order to improve the environment of the existing wastewater treatment plant In the future, we are expected to be able to contribute to efficient energy management in the wastewater treatment plant through the proposed system.

Acknowledgments. This subject is supported by Korea Ministry of Environment as "Global Top Project"(Project No.:GT-11-B-02-014-3).

References

1. Ministry of environment, National plan for energy saving and production in sewage treatment plant, pp.4–8. Ministry of environment, Seoul (2010)
2. Kim, W.W., Jang, S.D., Park, J.H., Jang, E.J.: Development of a Remote Monitoring and Management System for Sewage and Waste Water. In: KIISE Fall Conference, vol. 31(2), pp. 397–399 (October 2004)
3. Kim, J.-T., Hwang, H., Hong, B., Byun, H.: The Background and Direction of R&D Project for Advanced Technology of Wastewater Treatment and Reuse. Membrane Journal 21(3), 277–289 (2011)
4. Korea environment corporation,The report on the propriety of energy saving project in the sewage treatment plant, p.51. Ministry of environment, Seoul (2008)
5. The National Energy Technology Laboratory (NETL), A Vision for the Smart Grid (2009)

A Design for Sensibility Factor of Digital Sound and LED Sensibility Illumination Color

Jaesang Cha[1], Choenil Park[1], Seungyoun Yang[2], and Juyoung Lee[1,*]

[1] Dept. of Media Engineering, Seoul National, University of Technology, Seoul, Korea
[2] Dept. R&D Center, Fivetek Co., Sungnam, Korea
dacoup@naver.com

Abstract. In this paper, we analyzed the characteristic of the visible lighting spectrum in LED emotional lighting and audible frequency of digital sound. And we proposed effective and intelligent emotional system better than existing matching system, it is based on matching scheme of similar factor in sound and LED lighting color. Also we demonstrated the usefulness of proposed system through the simulation and implementation, fabrication of SW/HW.

Keywords: Sensibility Factor, Digital Sound, LED Sensibility Illumination.

1 Introduction

Recently, lighting systems using audio signal of audible frequency and frequency spectrum of visible lighting are studied. And various related products are being sold and released commercially. Also demands of emotional matching algorithm and system which includes effective and methodical designs are being increased. And the importance related with this scheme has increased. Therefore, this paper proposed the emotional matching algorithm using emotional factors of digital sound and color matching of LED emotional lighting. This paper is organized as follows. In Section 2, this paper describes the structure and flow of emotional matching. Section 3 explains how to analyze the digital sound, and section 4 describes the simulations results using LabView.

2 Emotional Matching System

In Fig. 1(a), we show a flowchart of the emotional matching system. A source of sound can have many different frequencies mixed. The frequency spectrum can be generated via a Fourier transform of the signal with DSP board. Fig. 1(b) shows the process of digital signal processing. Our proposed matching system is done by emotional pattern matching between previous resulting values and LED emotional color values. Finally, Matched LED emotional color value display various color based a digital sound with DMX LED driver controller.

---

* Corresponding author.

T.-h. Kim et al. (Eds.): MulGraB/BSBT/IUrC 2012, CCIS 353, pp. 163–165, 2012.
© Springer-Verlag Berlin Heidelberg 2012

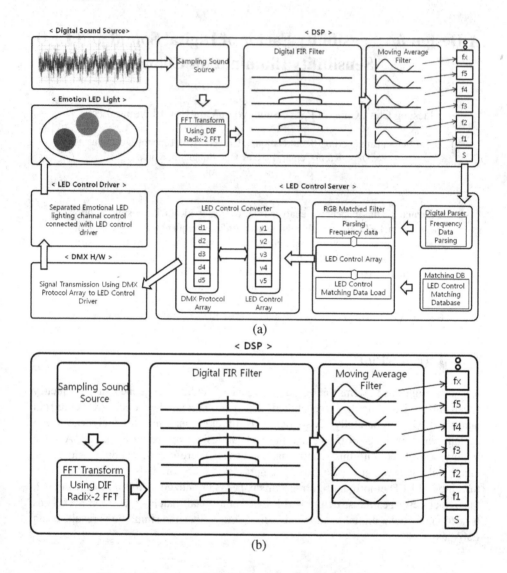

Fig. 1. (a) Flowchart (b) DSP Frequency analysis of digital sound

3   Sound Analysis Using DSP Board

Using DSP board is proper method to analyze digital sound and extract emotional factors. It is also a good solution to control various LED devices. The resulting spectrum values should match with emotional factors of LED lights to control LED.

4   LabView Simulation to Control H/W

In order to evaluate the performance of our system, we prepared a simulation environment with LabView HW and SW. The Extracting an emotional factor of sound method method described above has been implemented and tested in a simulation environment as shown in Fig. 3(a)(b).

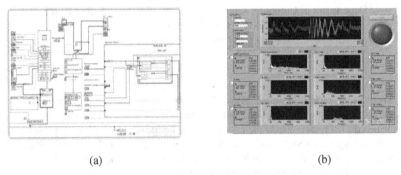

(a)   (b)

Fig. 2. (a) LabView Block diagram (b) LED control simulation GUI

5   Conclusions

This paper proposed the emotional matching algorithm using emotional factors of digital sound and color matching of LED emotional lighting, it includes characteristic analysis for emotional matching of audio signal of audible frequency and frequency spectrum of visible lighting. The proposed algorithm used moving average method for matching LED color. Also we demonstrated the function of the proposed algorithm which is possible to effectively deliver the emotional information through simulation and analysis of the algorithm.

Acknowledgments. This research was supported by a grant(C-12-5) from Gyeonggi Technology Development Program funded by Gyeonggi Province.

References

1. IESNA: A The IESNA Lighting handbook: IESNA, 9th edn., pp. 1–3 (2000)
2. Ohno, Y.: Color Rendering and luminous efficacy of white LED spectra. In: Proc. of SPIE, vol. 5530, p. 88 (2004)
3. Oi, N.: Preferred Combinations between Illuminance and Color Temperature in Several Settings for Daily Living Activities. In: Proceedings of the 2nd International Symposium on Design of Artificial Environments, pp. 214–215 (2007)
4. Mark, S.: A new approach to understanding the impact of circadian disruption on human health. J. Circadian Rhythms 6(1) (2008)

Head Selection Scheme to Apply Location Information for Distributed Cluster Routing

Jin-Han Kim[1], Young-Min Kim[2], and Ryum-Duck Oh[1,*]

[1] Department of Software
[2] Department of Computer science and Information Engineering Korea
National University of Transportation, Korea
{jhkim,rdoh}@ut.ac.kr

Abstract. In recent, Wireless Sensor Network related technologies are widely applied for various applications but efficient use of limited resources is still unsolved. Its typical study is a cluster-based routing protocol which forms clusters targeting sensor nodes, selects cluster heads and reduces the energy needed to communicate in order to maximize the network lifetime. But the existing cluster-based routing protocols such as LEACH, LEACH-C, HEED have a few problems like inequality of energy consumption due to a biased distribution of cluster heads, unnecessary energy consumption due to additional data transfer, and overhead problem due to remaining energy calculation and transfer. Therefore, this study proposes techniques for selecting the cluster head with use of the distance between the cluster components.

Keywords: Clustering, Energy, Partitioning, Head selection scheme.

1 Introduction

In the wireless sensor network, it must efficiently use such resources as battery, memory, processors, etc because of the limited energy and hardware performance unlike the traditional infrastructure-based network. Therefore the associated routing protocols are being developed to consume less energy [1].

General sensor network routing protocol can be classified, depending on the structure, into three categories: Flat based routing protocol, Location based routing protocol, and Hierarchical based routing protocol. Among these, Cluster-based hierarchical based routing protocol that considers the data aggregation of sensor nodes has been studied a lot in terms of energy efficiency [2]. However, cluster formation algorithms used for the existing routing protocols in maximizing the energy efficiency of sensor networks, for example, in case of LEACH, it selects cluster heads in probabilistic methods, from which there occurred a problem of inequality of energy consumption due to disproportionate distribution of cluster heads, thus shortening life

---

* Corresponding author.

T.-h. Kim et al. (Eds.): MulGraB/BSBT/IUrC 2012, CCIS 353, pp. 166–171, 2012.

expectancy of USN. In case of LEACH-C, it is involved in the Base Station in the process of selection of cluster heads each round, and so unnecessary energy consumption may occur because of transfer of data that does not exist in LEACH. In addition, in case of HEED, it does not consider the difference between the distance between nodes and distance to BS in the selection process of cluster head and so cluster heads are distributed biased and overheads occur due to residual energy calculation and transfer, thus causing extra energy consumption. Therefore cluster head selection scheme is required so that such existing routing protocols compensate the problems of energy inefficiency that occurs in the selection process of cluster heads and prolong the network lifetime by maximizing energy efficiency of USN.

This study proposes Efficient Cluster Head Selection Mechanism (E2CS) that partitions sensor node-distributed area based on the location values of each node at the beginning of cluster in order to solve the problem of biased selection of cluster heads and the energy inefficiency of each node that occurs from the cluster formation of existing routing protocols and selects cluster head between sensor node locally in each segmented region.

2   Related Research

LEACH(Low-Energy Adaptive Clustering Hierarchy) is a cluster-based routing technique that equalize the energy consumption of all the sensor nodes in the network and selects cluster head in the unit of time i.e. round by chance in order maximize the lifetime of network, and transfers to the sink node by collecting the data from the cluster in the cluster head in order to reduce the overall communication costs [3]. Each round consists of set-up stage that consists of cluster head and cluster and steady-state stage that data transfers according to the TDMA schedule, and the cluster head is determined by formula of probability equation [4].

LEACH selects cluster head in probability and gives opportunity of cluster head to all the node in the cluster but, as it does not consider energy reserves and it is simply selected as cluster head in probability, inequality of energy consumption and biased distribution of cluster head may occur. LEACH-C(LEACH-Centralized) may be able to configure efficient cluster as BS is involved in selecting the optimal cluster head which minimizes energy consumption when member nodes constituting cluster transmits data to cluster head[5]. In LEACH-C, BS receives, in the Set-up stage, energy information and location information of all nodes to calculate the average energy of all nodes.

Once cluster head selection process is completed, BS broadcasts the messages that cluster head ID is written to all the nodes and nodes are selected as cluster head if a cluster head ID that is in the message that one receives is identical to one's ID. If cluster head ID is not identical, it is configured as cluster member, and when TDMA schedule is written, Set-up stage ends. Thereafter the Steady-state stage operates in the same way as the existing LEACH [6].

LEACH-C possibly configures energy-efficient cluster by selecting the optimal cluster head but, it has shortcomings that it has considerably bigger overheads due to additional exchange of information for the best configuration of cluster.

3   Non-uniform Static Grid-Based E2CS Technique

The cluster-based routing protocol techniques such as LEACH, LEACH-C, HEED may cause energy efficiency problems as described in the relevant studies and biased distribution of cluster head due to cluster head selection by probability formula as in Fig. 1 [7]. In order solve such problems, this paper proposes energy efficient cluster head selection mechanism based on Non-uniform Static Grid. E2CS technique is used in the Set-up stage forming clusters.

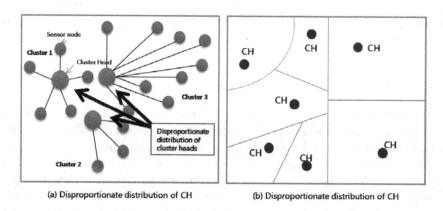

(a) Disproportionate distribution of CH   (b) Disproportionate distribution of CH

Fig. 1. Distribution of cluster heads of the exiting scheme

E2CS technique that is proposed in this paper assumes that all the sensor nodes are evenly distributed without being biased to any particular area, the distributed node is fixed, the initial energy value of the fixed nodes is identical, and all the fixed nodes know their own location information.

E2CS technique partitions areas based on the location information of sensor nodes and calculates the difference of distance between nodes in the area and in order to compensate problems of biased distribution and overhead, cluster formation process is classified into three stages.

In the first stage of initialization, all the sensor nodes to be located in the sensor field may be evenly distributed in any particular area not to be biased and transmits its own location information to BS. In the second stage of Static Grid-based Segmentation, it partitions unevenly sensor fields based on the location information of each node that BS receives. And in the partitioned area, distance between nodes, distance to the center value of region, distance to BS, and each node's energy consumption are compared and proceeds to the stage of cluster head selection. The operation process is shown in Fig. 2.

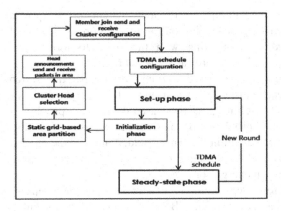

Fig. 2. E2CS technique during the operation

The cluster head selected through the three stages creates head announcement packet, flooding into the area. The head announcement packet is a packet that cluster head itself announces that itself is a head, and so includes head location and zone identifier, head announcement packet creation time, duration of head, and the duration of head is determined by sensor node that holds the amount of battery more than the boundary value based on its own amount of value by measuring the consumed amount of energy. The node that received head announcement packet within the area sends Member Join Packet to cluster head and is consisted of cluster member node. The cluster head that received Member Join Packet uses information of member node, configures TDMA scheduling, and then if it sends again to the member node, Set-up stage is completed and the Steady-state stage works in the same way as the existing LEACH.

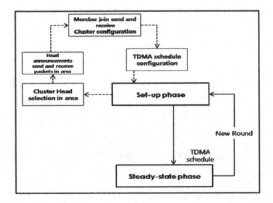

Fig. 3. Regional cluster head selection

In E2CS technique, all the sensor nodes calculates its own amount of energy consumption fluctuating depending on the time before the end of the existing round for flooding, and by comparing with the fixed location information it selects circulatory cluster head in the area as shown in Fig. 3.

In the existing cluster-based routing protocols, the difference of energy consumption of each cluster may occur due to the changes of the number of member node in the cluster resulting from the biased distribution problem of cluster head. In order to prevent such problems, BS partitions area based on the location information of sensor nodes located within the sensor field, compares the number of sensor nodes, and proposes Unequal Partitioning Algorithm that prevents biased distribution of cluster head and equal energy consumption.

In the Non-uniform Segmentation, if we call a rectangular sensor field including all the sensor nodes as A(x-y plane), BS that receives location information of sensor nodes equalizes the number of sensor node that two areas have if the number of sensor node in the area that partitions the sensor field is even-numbered, and if it is odd-numbered, it moves to the criteria axis where there are more sensor nodes among the two partitioned areas and inclines to make the number of sensor node even-numbered in the area where there are more sensor nodes. The sensor node in the sensor field are not biased but evenly distributed and the number of sensor node is distributed equally or is made different by one at the maximum and each area gives Grid ID code to be distinguished from the other area. Grid ID code adds bit 0 if the partitioned area is in the left side or in the bottom when partitioning the area, and adds bit 1 if it is in the right side or in the top. Unequal Partitioning Algorithm is as follows.

```
1:      Begin
2:          RegionNum <- ClusterNum
3:          RegionCounter = 1;
4:          M <- TotalArea;
5:          While(1)
6:            If(RegionCounter mod 2 == 1) then
7:               xAxis Split(M);
8:               newXAxis = SensorNum/2;
9:               GridID[i++] = RegionSP(M, newXAxis);
10:            else
11:               yAxis Split(M);
12:               newYAxis = SensorNum/2;
13:               GridID[i++] = RegionSP(M, newYAxis);
14:            end if
15:            update GridIDcode(GridID[i]);
16:            if(RegionNum == RegionCounter) then
17:               break;
18:            end if
19:            RegionCounter++;
20:          end while
21:      End
```

Fig. 4. Configuration of non-equal segmentation algorithm

In Fig. 4 Unequal Partitioning Algorithm, it sets the optimal number of cluster to the RegionNum to be partitioned and sets the RegionCounter to be compared with the RegionNum, the area to be partitioned.

4   Future Works and Conclusions

This paper proposes cluster formation method that ensures uniform head distribution by partitioning the placement area based on the location of sensor nodes. The cluster configuration of the proposed technique uses locational information of sensor nodes distributed in the first stage of cluster formation, partitions areas so that BS is possible to equally distribute sensor nodes, thus making the number of nodes in a cluster being equal or different by one. And it gives identifier to the partitioned area and selects cluster head between the nodes in the same area. It selects the optimal cluster heads, considering the distance to the center value of each area, distance difference between nodes, distance to BS as cluster head selection factors, thus reducing energy consumption.

Acknowledgement. The research was supported by a grant from the Academic Research Program of Korea National University of Transportation in 2012.

References

1. Kahn, J.M., Katz, R.H., Pister, K.S.J.: Next Century Challenges: Mobile Networking for "Smart Dust". In: Proc. of the 5th Annual ACM/IEEE International Conference on Mobile Computing and Networking, Seattle, WA, pp. 271–278 (1999)
2. Lee, S.H., Kim, D.H., Yoo, J.J.: Ubiquitous Sensor Network Technology Development Trends. Korea Society for Internet Information 5(3), 58–67 (2004)
3. Heinzelman, W.R., Chandrakasan, A., Balakrishnam, H.: Energy - Efficient Communication Protocol for Wireless Microsensor Networks. In: Proc. Hawaii International Conference on System Sciences, vol. 8, pp. 1–10 (2000)
4. Ibriq, J., Mahgoub, I.: Cluster-Based Routing in Wireless Sensor Networks: Issues and Challenges. In: Proceeding of the 2004 Symposium on Performance Evaluation of Computer Telecommunication Systems, pp. 759–766 (2004)
5. Heinzelman, W.B., Chandrakasan, A.P., Balakrishnan, H.: An application-specific protocol architecture for wireless microsensor networks. Wireless Comm. IEEE 1(4), 660–670 (2002)
6. Bandyopadhyay, S., et al.: An Energy - Efficient Hierarchical Clustering Algorithm for Wireless Sensor Networks. In: IEEE INFOCOM, vol. 3, pp. 1713–1723 (2003)
7. Bouhafs, F., Merabti, M., Mokhtar, H.: A Semantic Clustering Routing Protocol for Wireless Sensor Networks. In: Proceeding of CCNC, vol. 1, pp. 351–355 (2006)

Vehicle Detection Using Running Gaussian Average and Laplacian of Gaussian in the Nighttime

Hyuntae Kim[1], Jingyu Do[1], Gyuyeong Kim[2], Jangsik Park[3], and Yunsik Yu[2]

[1] Department of Multimedia Engineering, Dongeui University, Gaya-dong,
San 24, Busanjin-ku, Busan, 614-714, Korea
`htaekim@deu.ac.kr, mhilt767@naver.com`
[2] Convergence of IT Devices Institute Busan, Gaya-dong, San 24, Busanjin-ku,
Busan, 614-714, Korea
`{nz90nz,ysyu}@deu.ac.kr`
[3] Department of Electronics Engineering, Kyungsung University, Daeyeon3-dong,
110-1, Nam-gu, Busan, 608-736, Korea
`jsipark@ks.ac.kr`

Abstract. In this paper, we propose a nighttime vehicle detection algorithm using RGA (Gunning Gaussian Average) and LoG (Laplacian of Gaussian). At the first stage, background could be estimated using RGA from CCTV input image. At the next stage, 2-D LoG function applied to input image. And then "AND" operator could be applied between each other. Finally, threshold of headlight brightness could be supported to the output of AND operation. As the results of simulations using recoded real video signal, it is shown that proposed algorithm is useful for detection vehicles in the nighttime.

Keywords: RGA (Running Gaussian Average), LoG (Laplacian of Gaussian), Nighttime Vehicle Detection.

1 Introduction

Vision-based traffic surveillance systems extract useful and accurate traffic information for traffic flow control, such as vehicle count, vehicle speed, and vehicle classification. The basic techniques for traffic surveillance include vehicle detection and tracking [1]–[4], surveillance camera calibration, etc. However, most of the state-of-the-art methods concentrate on traffic monitoring in the daytime, and few works address the issue of nighttime traffic monitoring.

In daytime traffic monitoring systems, vehicles are commonly detected and analyzed by exploiting the grayscale, color, and motion information. However, under the nighttime traffic environment, the foregoing information becomes invalid, and the vehicle can only be observed by its headlight and rear light. Furthermore, there are strong reflections on the road surface, which further complicate the problem. In this paper, we concentrate on nighttime vehicle headlight detection and tracking in grayscale image.

T.-h. Kim et al. (Eds.): MulGraB/BSBT/IUrC 2012, CCIS 353, pp. 172–177, 2012.

2   RGA(Running Gaussian Average)

Wren et al [5], propose to model the background by analyzing each pixel (i, j) of the image. The background model consists in the probabilistic modeling of each pixel value via Gaussian probability function (p.d.f.), characterized by its mean μ and variance σ^2.

Mean and variance for each frame t (μ_t, σ_t^2) are updated as follows:

$$\mu_t = \rho I_t + (1 - \rho)\mu_{t-1} \tag{1}$$

$$\sigma_t^2 = \rho(I_t - \mu_t)^2 + (1 - \rho)\sigma_{t-1}^2 \tag{2}$$

Where is the value of the pixel under analysis in the current frame; μ_t, σ_t^2 are, respectively, the mean and variance of the Gaussian distribution, ρ is a weight that defines the updating velocity (commonly $\rho = 0.01$).

This updating step allows a background model evolution, making it robust to soft illumination changes, a common situation in outdoor scenarios.

For each frame, the pixel value I_t is classified as foreground according to equation (3):

$$|I_t - \mu_t| > k\sigma_t \tag{3}$$

Where is the threshold parameter (usually 2.5).

When the inequality is satisfied, the pixel I_t is considered foreground. Otherwise, it is considered background. Koller et al. [6] emphasize that the updating process has to be done only if the pixel is considered background, replacing Equation 3 by Equation 4.

$$\mu_t = M\mu_{t-1} + (1 - M)(\alpha I_t + (1 - \alpha)\mu_{t-1}) \tag{4}$$

Where M=1 if I_t is considered as foreground, and M=0 otherwise.

This method presents the main advantages of less memory and computational cost requirements: only two parameters per pixel are stored (mean and variance (μ_t, σ_t^2)).

3   LoG (Laplacian of Gaussian)

Laplacian of Gaussian (LoG) operator or Marr-Hildreth operator was first proposed by Marr and Hildreth in 1980 based on their investigation of the human visual system [7].

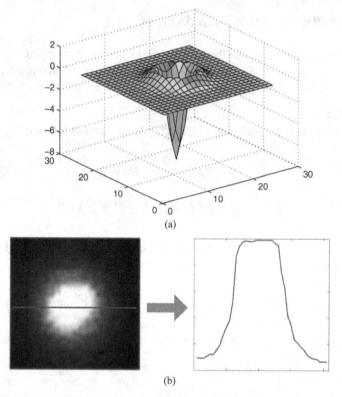

(a)

(b)

Fig. 1. (a) LoG filter, (b) Exponential attenuation property of light source

The LoG filter is illustrated in Fig. 1(a). According to the atmospheric scattering model in [11], the intensity of the light source decreases in an exponential manner, which is depicted in Fig. 1(b) by the intensity along the diameter of the light source. When the LoG filter is applied on the image, a high value can be obtained in the exponentially decreasing regions around the headlight, whereas a negative value can be obtained in the light source region because of the negative value in the center of the LoG filter. The 2-D LoG function centered on zero and with Gaussian standard deviation σ has the form:

$$LoG\ (i,j) = -\frac{1}{\pi\sigma^2}[1 - \frac{i^2 + j^2}{2\sigma^2}]\frac{e^{i^2+j^2}}{2\sigma^2} \tag{5}$$

A discrete kernel that approximates this function (for a Gaussian $\sigma = 1.4$) is shown in Figure 2.

0	1	1	2	2	2	1	1	0
1	2	4	5	5	5	4	2	1
1	4	5	3	0	3	5	4	1
2	5	3	-12	-24	-12	3	5	2
2	5	0	-24	-40	-24	0	5	2
2	5	3	-12	-24	-12	3	5	2
1	4	5	3	0	3	5	4	1
1	2	4	5	5	5	4	2	1
0	1	1	2	2	2	1	1	0

Fig. 2. Discrete approximation to LoG function with Gaussian $\sigma = 1.4$

We normalize LoG to obtain a unity maximum value, and let the results be $\overline{LoG} = LoG \ / \ Max \ (LoG)$.

4   Experimental Results

The proposed algorithm is implemented in Visual Studio 2010 tool and open source library OpenCV on Intel(R) Core(TM) 3.3 GHz PC with 4 GB of RAM. We have applied the proposed method on various traffic sequences to evaluate its effectiveness, and all the image sequences are sampled to a size of 1280 x 720 at the frame rate 24 f/s.

In the proposed method, a headlight of the vehicle was detected (Fig. 3). The nomination of image was post-processing.

(a)Situation I   (b)Situation II

Fig. 3. The experimental results in the night image

Each frame is classified as foreground according to equation 4 (Fig. 4).

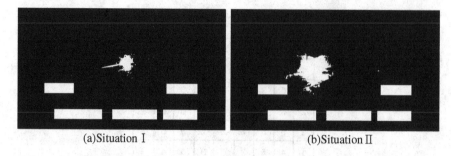

(a)Situation Ⅰ   (b)Situation Ⅱ

Fig. 4. Foreground (Background Subtraction by RGA)

The results for applying the LoG operator to vehicle image in nighttime are shown in Fig. 5.

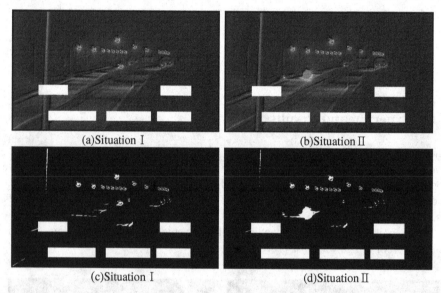

(a)Situation Ⅰ   (b)Situation Ⅱ

(c)Situation Ⅰ   (d)Situation Ⅱ

Fig. 5. (a) and (b) is image by LoG (Laplacian of Gaussian) filter. (c) and (d) is candidate image of vehicle on LoG.

The results of operator AND for LoG and foreground are shown in fig. 6.

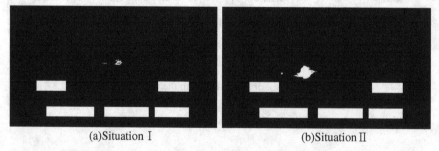

(a)Situation Ⅰ   (b)Situation Ⅱ

Fig. 6. The results of AND operation for LoG and foreground image

The detection results for morphology and skeletonization are shown in fig. 7.

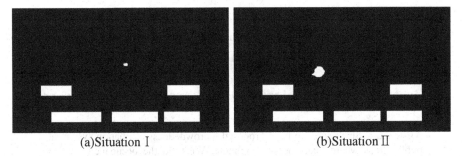

(a)Situation I   (b)Situation II

Fig. 7. The results for using morphology and skeletonization

5   Conclusions

In this paper, the vehicles were detected and tracked by RGA and LoG filter in the video frames. RGA has the advantages of less memory usage and computational cost: only two parameters per pixel are stored. In addition, RGA is one of the fastest among the background subtraction methods. The LoG filtered image highlights the regions of rapid intensity change. Thus, vehicles were detected using the LoG filter. The experimental results showed relatively fast run time and accurate detection.

Acknologement. This work was supported in part by MKE (NIPA), Busan Metropolitan City and Dong-Eui University.(B1100-1101-0010, Convergence of IT Devices Institute Busan).

References

1. Pang, C.C.C., Lam, W.W.L., Yung, N.H.C.: A method for vehicle count in the presence of multiple-vehicle occlusions in traffic images. IEEE Trans. Intell. Transp. Syst. 8(3), 441–459 (2007)
2. Zhang, W., Wu, Q.M.J., Yang, X., Fang, X.: Multilevel framework to detect and handle vehicle occlusion. IEEE Trans. Intell. Transp. Syst. 9(1), 161–174 (2008)
3. Kato, J., Watanabe, T., Joga, S., Liu, Y., Hase, H.: HMM/MRF-based stochastic framework for robust vehicle tracking. IEEE Trans. Intell. Transp. Syst. 5(3), 142–154 (2004)
4. Morris, B.T., Trivedi, M.M.: Learning, modeling, and classification of vehicle track patterns from live video. IEEE Trans. Intell. Transp. Syst. 9(3), 425–437 (2008)
5. Wren, C.R., Azarbayejani, A., Darrell, T., Pentland, A.P.: Real-Time Tracking of the Human Body. IEEE Transactions on Pattern Analysis and Machine Intelligence (1997)
6. Koller, D., Weber, J., Huang, T., Malik, J., Ogasawara, G., Rao, B., Russell, S.: Towards robust automatic traffic scene analysis in real-time. In: Proceedings of the 12th IAPR International Conference on Pattern Recognition Conference A: Computer Vision & Image Processing, vol. 1 (1994)
7. Marr, D., Hildreth, H.: Theory of edge detection. Proc. Roy. Soc. London B207, 187–217 (1980)

Real Time Crowdedness Estimation System

Cheoljun Jeong[1], Kwangyoung Park[2], and Gooman Park[2]

[1] Hitron Systems Inc.
[2] Seoul National University of Science and Technology
{jeongcj,youngman}@hitron.co.kr, gmpark@seoultech.ac.kr

Abstract. In this paper we have proposed a crowdedness estimation system at public areas where many people commute. We used the occupancy time to estimate the crowdedness per specific time duration. The estimated information is accumulated on database and will be used as statistical information.

Keywords: We would like to encourage you to list your keywords in this section.

1   Introduction

The automated surveillance system saves the human resources and covers large area with the help of network cameras that employ the video analytics algorithms. One of the important analytic functions is people counting or estimating the crowdedness at a place. There are some previous works in crowdedness estimation. In order to estimate the number of people in a crowd, a fractal dimension method is suggested after edge detection and morphological operation and shadow removal[1]. The extracted features are used as the input for classifier and the crowdedness is estimated by neural network training procedure[2]. MRF(Markov Random Field is used for density estimation of passenger at the platform of subway station[3]. Optical flow and feature extraction method are used for counting the people[4]. Velastin verified that there is the linear relationship between foreground edge and the number of people[5]. Perspective transform calibrated the image coordinate with regard to the real world[6] and the linearity between the amount of foreground pixel the number of people[7]. This paper is organized as follows. Section 2 introduces proposed people counting method. In section 3, we discussed the performance of our method through the experiment. Finally, we concluded in section 4.

2   Proposed Counting Method

2.1   Overall System

The first step for the input image is background subtraction by Gaussian mixture model. In order to remove the shadow removal, morphological operation, edge detector and edge normalization was employed. We extracted normalized feature by Minkowski Fractal Dimension method which use the edge information and resultantly estimated the crowdedness.

T.-h. Kim et al. (Eds.): MulGraB/BSBT/IUrC 2012, CCIS 353, pp. 178–182, 2012.

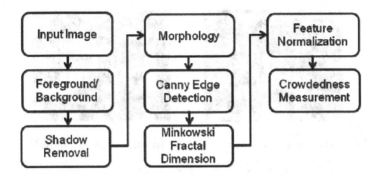

Fig. 1. Block diagram of proposed crowdedness estimator

2.2 Feature Extraction

In order to subtract the background, basically we used the Gaussian mixture model with some modification for the case in which objects stay for a long time. Figure1 shows the block diagram of proposed estimator. Figure2 shows the edge extraction result.

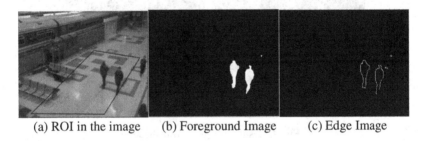

(a) ROI in the image   (b) Foreground Image   (c) Edge Image

Fig. 2. Original image and detected objects with edge information

2.3 Shadow Removal

The shadow in the foreground bothers the accurate object detection. We used the intensity distortion and color distortion information to remove the shadow noise.

$$\begin{aligned}
BD &= \mathrm{argmin}(\bar{F}ore - \alpha \bar{B}ack)^2 \\
BD &= \bar{F}ore - \alpha \bar{B}ack / \bar{B}ack^2 \\
CD &= \|\bar{F}ore - \alpha \bar{B}ack\|
\end{aligned} \tag{1}$$

Figure3 shows the shadow removal result.

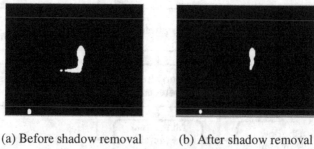

(a) Before shadow removal   (b) After shadow removal

Fig. 3. Result of shadow removal

2.4   Feature Normalization

Each pixel has different size depending on the position in a picture. As shown in Figure 4(a), the pixel size is different in the designated region. In order to make an objects size same wherever it is, the normalization process is applied. Fig 4(b) shows the density map used in our method.

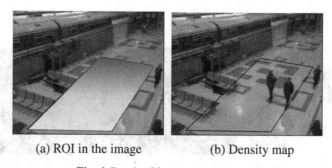

(a) ROI in the image   (b) Density map

Fig. 4. Result of feature normalization

2.5   Density Estimation

The same objects in an image show different sizes depending on its position in the scene and camera tilt angles. We estimate the crowd density with the consideration of position factors.

$$Crowd_t = \frac{\sum_{x \in ROI} w_d(x) \cdot MFD(x)}{\sum_{x \in ROI} w_d(x)} \tag{2}$$

$Crowd_t$ means the density of ith crowdedness and $w_d(x)$ means relative weight at position x. $MFD(x)$ is the Minkowski fractal dimension variable.

3   Experimental Results

In our experiment, we distinguished the crowdedness in five levels; very low, low, moderate, high, and very high. Figure5 shows the estimation results.

Fig. 5. Crowd Estimation Result

Figure6 shows the comparative results between true crowd density and estimated density.

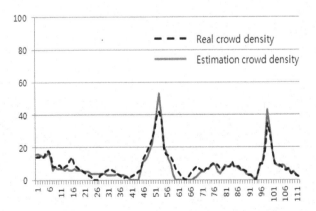

Fig. 6. Comparison of crowd estimation result

4   Conclusion

In this paper we estimated the crowdedness to apply at public area such as airport, subway train stations.

References

1. Marana, A.N.: Estimating Crowd Density with Minkowski Fractal Dimension. In: Acoustic, Speech, and Signal Processing, pp. 3521–3524 (1999)
2. Cho, S.Y., Chow, T.W.S., Leung, C.T.: A Neural-Based Crowd Estimation by Hybrid Global Learning Algorithm. IEEE Trans. on System, Man, and Cybernetics 29(4) (August 1999)
3. Paragios, N., Ramesh, V.: A MRF based approach for real-time subway monitoring. In: IEEE Computer Society Conference on Computer Vision and Pattern Recognition, vol. 1, pp. 1034–1040 (2001)
4. Li, W.: Crowd Density Estimation: An Improved Approach. In: 2010 IEEE 10th International Conference on Signal Processing, pp. 1213–1216 (2010)
5. Velastin, S.A., Yin, J.H., Davies, A.C., Vicencio-Silva, M.A., Allsop, R.E., Penn, A.: Automated Measurement of Crowd Density and Motion using Image Processing. In: Proc. of IEEE International Conference on Road Traffic Monitoring and Control, pp. 127–132 (April 1994)
6. Lin, S.-F.: Estimation of Number of People in Crowded Scenes Using Perspective Trasnformation. IEEE Transactions on System, Man, Cybernetics 31(6) (November 2001)
7. Celik, H., Hanjalic, A., Hendriks, E.A.: Towards a Robust Solution to People Counting. In: Proc. of International Conference of Image Processing, pp. 2401–2404 (October 2006)

Developing Ultrasonic Wave Oscillators Using Low Speed Analog to Digital Converter

Jeong-Jin Kang[1], Keehong Um[2,*], SooyeupYoo[3], Jong-Jin Park[4], and Sang-Bong Park[5]

[1] Department of Information and Communication,
Dong Seoul University, Sungnam-city, Kyunggi-do, Korea
[2] Department of Information Technology, Hansei University,
Gunpo-city, Kyunggi-do, Korea
um@hansei.ac.kr
[3] Dept. of R&D, Taesung Eco. Tech. Ltd.,
Gunpo-city, Kyunggi-do, Korea
[4] Department of Internet,
Chungwoon University, Hongseong, Chungnam, Korea
[5] Department of Computer & Information Science,
Semyung University, Jecheon, Chungbuk, Korea
jjkang@du.ac.kr, um@hansei.ac.kr,
syoo01@paran.com,jjpark@chungwoon.ac.kr, psbcom@semyung.ac.kr

Abstract. The ultrasonic wave converter, digitally controlled, is designed by sampling the high frequency ultrasonic waves. The conventional ultrasonic circuit is composed of oscillation circuits in analog mode. The oscillation circuits can be categorized into two groups i.e., (1) the that generates the fixed frequency regardless of the change of the loads, (2) and the other that controls power and the frequency by changing the voltage and current following the oscillating conditions of oscillators. These circuits are used to fix the frequency of PLL (phase locked loop).The circuit that produces the fixed frequency should select the proper frequency and the power circuit to supply the operating currents. The circuit supplies the frequency with the range of resonance frequency (about the frequency of parallel resonance frequency or the frequency of minimum impedance) and the antiresonance frequency (parallel resonance frequency of maximum impedance).

Keywords: Ultrasonic wave oscillator, analog-to-digital converter (ADC), direct digital synthesizer (DDS), selective harmonic elimination (SHE), field programmable gate array (FPGA),digital signal oscillator(DOS).

1 Introduction

Ultrasound is a cyclic wave of sound pressure with a frequency greater than the upper limit of humanhearing. Thus it is not separated from "normal" (audible) sound based on differences in physical properties [1].

---

* Corresponding author.

T.-h. Kim et al. (Eds.): MulGraB/BSBT/IUrC 2012, CCIS 353, pp. 183–188, 2012.
© Springer-Verlag Berlin Heidelberg 2012

In this paper, we propose a digitally–controlled ultrasonic oscillation driver circuit operating independent of change of loads or oscillations by processing and sampling the high-frequency ultrasonic waves using the low-speed analog to digital converter. An analog-to-digital converter (abbreviated ADC, A/D or A to D) is a device that uses sampling to convert a continuous quantity to a discrete time representation in digital form. The reverse operation is performed by a digital-to-analog converter (DAC) [2].

Our oscillation circuit is composed of oscillator, digital signal generator, power supply, digital signal converter, phase generator, and controller part. Expensive ADC is used to obtain digital signal by sampling high-frequency ultrasonic waves. To manage these problems, we propose to design ultrasonic oscillation driving circuits that show stable operations regardless of the changing values of loads and oscillations. By adopting digital signal processing using digital circuit and microcontroller, we propose the ultrasonic oscillation circuits. It can sample the high-frequency ultrasonic waves by low-speed analog digital converter. Furthermore, all of these circuits are designed in digital fashion with a single integrated chip.

2   System Configurations

2.1   Overall Configuration of the System

The goal of this paper is to present ultrasonic wave oscillator system supporting the stable operation in the situation of changing loads or oscillation conditions. Fig. 1 shows the oscillator system composed of several subsystems.

1. The oscillator is operating to the selective harmonic elimination pulse width modulation (SHE PWM).It is a device resonating with a fixed frequency according to the applied high-frequency alternating power signal.

2.The digital signal oscillator is a function generator producing the digital data corresponding to the same phase and frequency of sine and cosine signals as the same phase and frequency of SHE PWM. As a digital signal oscillator the direct digital synthesizer (DDS) is used. Combined with microprocessor and the digital signal oscillator, the controller can manage the frequency of the high-resolution alternating signals. DDS is a type of frequency synthesizer used for creating arbitrary waveforms from a single, fixed-frequency reference clock.

Applications of DDS include: signal generation, local oscillators in communication systems, function generators, mixers, modulators,sound synthesizers and as part of a digital phase-locked loop [3].

Direct digital synthesis, together with a DAC and a high-performance digital phase detector, overcome several fundamental drawbacks in analog PLLs, such as asymmetry in the phase detector or bandwidth limitations and phase noise in the voltage-controlled oscillator (VCO) [3].

3. The power supply inputs the driving power to the oscillator according to the PWM signal from the Digital signal oscillator.

4. Digital signal converter samples the delayed phase of current delivered to the oscillator.

5. The phase comparator calculates the phase difference of two signals (one from the Digital signal oscillator and the other from the Digital signal converter).

6. The controller controls the SHE PWM from the digital signal oscillator according to the output signal, with the phase difference, from the phase comparator can process alternating output frequency with the high-resolution of unit of mHz.

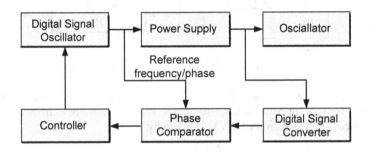

Fig. 1. OverallConfiguration of the ultrasonic oscillator system

2.2   Configuration of Digital Signal Oscillator

In Fig. 2, the detailed configuration of digital signal oscillator is shown. It is composed of the SHE PWM, the sine wave table, and the cosine wave table.

(1) The SHE PWM signal generator, produces the PWM signal to be sent oscillator, according to the controlling output signal of controller system.

(2) The sine wave table produces numerical data corresponding to the digital value of sine waves which have the same phase and frequency as those of SHE PWM, and

(3) The cosine wave table, produces numerical data corresponding to the digital value of cosine waves which have the same phase and frequency as those of SHE PWM.

The digital signal oscillator is implemented by digital logic circuits using the integrated circuit such as the field programmable gate array (FPGA), as an integrated circuit designed to be configured by a customer or a designer after manufacturing, generally specified using a hardware description language (HDL).

    In most FPGAs, the logic blocks also include memory elements, which may be simple flip-flops or more complete blocks of memory [4-6]. The frequency of output signal shows the maximum speed of operation determined by the speed of operation of adder of the system.

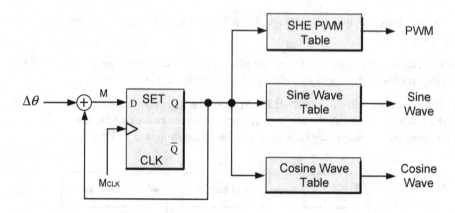

Fig. 2. Detailed configuration of digital signal oscillator

The frequency resolution of the DDS circuit depends on the number of bits of adder. In most of measurements, frequency resolution of few μHz can be well implemented. The resolution of PWM is given by

$$R = 2^{-b} \times f, \tag{1}$$

where b is the number of bits in adder device and f is the operating frequency of digital signal oscillator (DOS). SHE PWM signal generator produces SHE PWM signal with the harmonics removed.

For example, suppose the operating frequency is 40 Mhz, and the internal adder has the 32bits. Using the Eq.(1), the resolution is obtained by

$$40 \times 10^6 \times 2^{-32} = 40 \text{mhz.}$$

In Fig. 3, we show the procedures a particular harmonics (included in the PWM signal which is controlled by the status defined by ON/OFF) are selectively removed. As shown in the Fig. 3 (a), the PWM signal of ON/OFF by the controller shows lots of harmonics. Therefore, harmonics contained in the PWM signals can be removed by adjusting the ON/OFF status of PWM, and the strengths of the remaining pulses are easily adjusted. Fig. 3 (b), shows the PWM signal after the unwanted harmonics (3rd and 5th harmonics) were eliminated from the PWM signal.

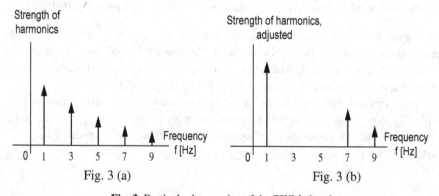

Fig. 3. Particular harmonics of the PWM signal

In Fig. 4, the circuit diagram of digital signal converter is shown. Depending on the signals from the circuit of driving pulse, the "sample and hold circuit" of digital signal converter take in and hold the samples from the current signal , a circuit is an analog device that samples (captures or grabs) the voltage of a continuously varying analog signal and holds (locks or freezes) its value at a constant level for a specified minimal period of time [7]. The "driving pulse input" circuit applies the driving pulse to the "sample and hold circuit" samples the phase value at the delayed time at every period.

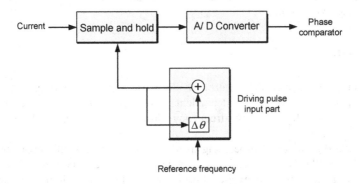

Fig. 4. Circuit of digital signal converter

The "analog to digital converter (A/D converter)" takes the output signal from the "sample and hold circuit" and convert the signal into the digital signal. The "sample and hold circuit", according the driving pulse from the "driving pulse input" part, takes the samples of phase value of current signal, and hold the constant phase until the next pulses are applied. The driving pulse, applied to the "sample and hold circuit", is generated from the "driving pulse input part".

The "driving pulse input part" applies the pulse train, at the time instant of phase shift by $\Delta\theta$ at every period, to the "sample and hold circuit" so that the "sample and hold circuit" can take measurements at the time of shifted phase. As shown in the figure, the "driving pulse input part" sends the impulses to the "sample and hold circuit", for every period, the output pulses are sent to the feedback adder, and the adder shifts the feedbacked signal by $\Delta\theta$ and sends the signal to the "sample and hold circuit". Therefore the driving pulses from the "driving pulse input part" is applied, with the phase shift of $\Delta\theta$, to the "sample and hold circuit", and the "sample and hold circuit", depending on the driving pulses, samples and hold the current signal in order to sent to analog to digital converter.

3   Results and Discussion

The ultrasonic wave oscillators, during the operations of oscillators which varies depending on the load conditions, shows the advantages of shifting the operating frequency to another frequency and measuring the performance of oscillator, which is compared with the best conditions of the operating point. Therefore the best operating frequency can be selected and the output power is easily controlled.

Moreover, the ultrasonic wave oscillator circuits sample the phase value with the constant delay of phase difference at one cycle of the phase of the current from the driving power delivered to the oscillator. The ultrasonic oscillator driver circuit generates the digital signal from the sampled signal so that sampled signal is transformed into in the digital type. In that way it is the advantageous to process the ultrasonic signals into digital signals, by way of adopting the low speed analog digital converter. The series of all of the circuits can be designed to be integrated into one-chip of SOC (system on a chip). It is also possible to implement the SOC with a cheaper cost and to stabilize the quality of product in case of a mass production.

4   Conclusions

We have proposed a digitally–controlled ultrasonic oscillation driver circuit. The oscillator system was working independent of change of loads or oscillations by processing and sampling the high-frequency ultrasonic waves using the low-speed analog digital converter.

By adopting digital signal processing using digital circuit and microcontroller, we proposed the oscillation circuits. It can sample the high-frequency ultrasonic waves by low-speed analog digital converter. Furthermore, all of these circuits are designed in digital fashion with a single integrated chip.

Remark 1. This work is the modified and revised versions of the presentations in the conference; ENGE 2102 (Sep. 16-19, 2012, Jeju, Korea) and the 2012 MulGrab Int'l (Dec. 16-19, 2012, Gangneung, Korea).

Remark 2. This work was supported by Hansei University.

References

1. Corso, J.F.: Bone-conduction Thresholds for Sonic and Ultrasonic Frequencies. J. Acou. Society of America 35(11), 1738–1743 (1963)
2. Walden, R.H.: Analog-to-Digital Converter Survey and Analysis. IEEE J. Selected Areas in Comm. 17(4), 539–550 (1999)
3. Paul, K.: Direct Digital Synthesis Enables Digital PLLs (2007)
4. Dept. of ECE at the University of Toronto : FPGA Architecture for the Challenge, http://www.eecg.toronto.edu/~vaughn/challenge/fpga_arch.html
5. Kuon, I., Rose, J.: Measuring the Gap Between FPGAs and ASICs. In: Proc. of the International Symposium on Field Programmable Gate Arrays – FPGA 2006, p. 21 (2006)
6. Sadrozinski, H.F.-W., Jinyuan, W.: Applications of Field-Programmable Gate Arrays in Scientific Research. Taylor & Francis (2010) ISBN 978-1-4398-4133-4
7. Paul, H., Winfield, H.: The Art of Electronics. Cambridge University Press (2001) ISBN 0-521-37095-7

Tour and Charging Scheduler Development Based on Simulated Annealing for Electric Vehicles*

Byung-Jun Lee, Seulbi Lee, Dae-Yong Im, Hye-Jin Kim,
Gyung-Leen Park, and Junghoon Lee**

Dept. of Computer Science and Statistics
Jeju National University
Jeju-Do, Republic of Korea
{eothsk,gwregx,dlaeodyd123,hjkim82,glpark,jhlee}@jejunu.ac.kr

Abstract. For a rent-a-car business employing electric vehicles which will penetrate into our transportation system in the near future, this paper designs a tour and charging scheduler and develops its search engine based on simulated annealing techniques. The main focus is put on the reduction of driving distance and waiting time taking advantage of sophisticated computer algorithms, to cope with the problem of current battery capacity. Cooling process runs 15,000 times while heating process is inserted every 1,000-th iteration step, permitting an evolution to an adjacent neighbor having higher cost. The performance measurement result obtained from a prototype implementation finds out that we can achieve about 87 % of accuracy when the number of destinations is less than 10 and 70 % of error points lie in the range from 0 to 20 %.

Keywords: electric vehicle, tour and charging schedule, simulated annealing, telematics application, waiting time reduction.

1 Introduction

Electric vehicles, or EVs in short, are one of the most important components in future transport systems which pursue energy efficiency and low greenhouse gas emissions [1]. However, they are suffering from short driving distance and long charging time, so drivers are not willing to replace their vehicles with EVs yet [2]. While the ongoing improvement of battery technologies is expected to solve this problem, intelligent computer applications can also alleviate the user inconvenience until the complete commercialization of advanced batteries [3]. The application can run in in-vehicle computer devices or in remote telematics servers. Moreover, they can be hosted by prevalent personal mobile devices such

---

* This work (Grants No. C0026912) was supported by Business for Cooperative R&D between Industry, Academy, and Research Institute funded by Korea Small and Medium Business Administration in 2012.
** Corresponding author.

T.-h. Kim et al. (Eds.): MulGraB/BSBT/IUrC 2012, CCIS 353, pp. 189–194, 2012.

as smart phones and tablet computers, as those devices usually install geographic maps and location-based utilities.

Long charging time gets more serious especially when the tour distance is long and the EV needs to be charged en-route once or more. If an EV visits more than one destination as in rent-a-cars and home delivery services, the visiting order affects the total driving distance and the waiting time. Basically, backtracking-based exhaustive search can find the optimal visit sequence for the given cost criteria [4]. However, each case must consider additional requirements specific to the application. For example, in an EV-based tour, some destinations can be recommended or added to the original tour plan to avoid wasteful waiting time. On the contrary, some can be dropped if they make the waiting time too much. In addition, a tour plan is highly likely to include restaurant options [5]. After all, such complexity extends the scheduling time, making it necessary to develop a pseudo-optimal scheduler, sacrificing the optimality.

In the mean time, simulated annealing is a classic global optimization method to find an acceptable solution in a large search space which may have several local minima. Basically, it begins with a random solution and keeps improving its quality by replacing the current solution with an adjacent one if the latter is better or has low cost. Particularly, inspired by the physical process of metal cooling, this scheme probabilistically accepts a new one even if it is not better than the current best. Such heating process can overcome the problem that pure cooling process can be stuck at a local optimum. To employ this algorithm, it is necessary to define an appropriate cost function which evaluates the quality of a feasible solution. For example, in TSP (Traveling Salesman Problem), a solution is a tour schedule consisting of destinations to visit. The cost function calculates the sum of all distances between each pair along the visit sequence.

In this regard, this paper designs and develops a tour and charging scheduler based on simulated annealing techniques for electric vehicles. It focuses on the search engine that can further take into account additional complex constraints given from each EV application. Moreover, with the controllable execution time, other search methods can be combined to build a multi-version scheduler.

2   Background

Figure 1 depicts our system model. To begin with, the road network for Jeju City is represented, just covering intersections and links between them. Charging stations and tourist places are embedded on the road map. A driver selects destinations he or she wants to visit through this interface. Currently, the client program is separated from the server program which carries out the time-intensive computation. A new service or a new version of a service is continuously augmented in this telematics server. This client-server architecture requires vehicle networks and they are usually available these days. Moreover, their bandwidth keeps increasing with the penetration of WiFi, cellular networks, and other promising communication technologies. According to the performance upgrade of mobile terminals, essential functions will be migrated to the terminal, making applications independent of network connectivity.

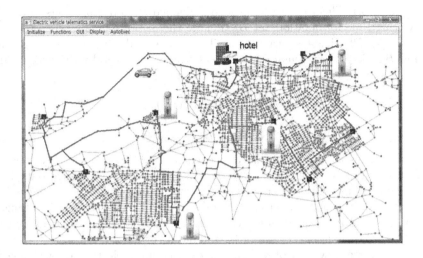

Fig. 1. Tour and charging scheduler interface

As shown in Figure 1, charging stations are installed over the Jeju City area. A tour plan must consider where to charge during the trip. Some tourist places install charging stations, allowing passengers to enjoy the tour while their EVs are charged. To begin with, it is necessary to charge in the tourist spot equipped with charging facilities as much as possible, as both EV charging and tour taking overlap. On the contrary, some stations force drivers to wait without doing anything. If the EV should be charged in those station somewhere in the schedule, how much to charge is also an important factor to reduce the waiting time. Even though this schedule is generated, without a reservation mechanism, the charging station can be already taken by another EV when the EV arrives at the station. Finally, the tour root recommended by the server is displayed on the client interface.

3   Tour and Charging Scheduler

To develop a search engine based on simulated annealing schemes, it is necessary to define a cost function according to the given criteria. For the legacy TSP, its cost function just takes into account the driving distance, and the total cost for a visit sequence, $F(V_1, V_2, ..., V_n)$, can be calculated as shown in Eq. (1).

$$F(V_1, V_2, ..., V_n) = \sum D(V_i \cdot V_{i+1}) + D(V_{i+1} \cdot V_1) \qquad (1)$$

, where V_i denotes a destination and $D(V_i, V_j)$ is the driving distance between V_i and V_j.

In our tour schedule model, an EV is fully charged when tourists start their trip, as it is charged generally overnight. We assume that average stay time is known in priori. Then, the cost function is defined as in our previous work [4]. For waiting time formulation, let B_{in}^i denote the distance credit, when the EV arrives at V_i. B_{av}^i denotes currently available battery. W_i is the waiting time at V_i, and B_{out}^i is battery remaining on its departure. The total waiting time will be $\sum W_i$ and W_i can be obtained as described in Eq. (2).

$$
\begin{aligned}
B_{av}^i &= min(B_{max}, B_{in}^i + T(V_i)) \\
W_i &= W^{i-1} - min(0, B_{av}^i - D(V_i \cdot V_{i+1})) \\
B_{out}^i &= max(0, B_{av}^i - D(V_i \cdot V_{i+1}))
\end{aligned}
\tag{2}
$$

, where B_{max} is the maximum battery capacity and $T(V_i)$ is the stay time at V_i. For more details, refer to [4]. Additionally, for a station installed outside a tourist spot, $T(V_i)$ will be 0, so charging at this station makes W_i get longer.

For the n destination, we select randomly m feasible visit sequences. m ranges from 1 to 5, and it depends on the computation capacity of the execution platform. Each of them is the current order and has its own evolution thread. During the evolution step, two out of n elements are randomly selected and exchanged. Here, every element has equal probability to be selected. These two sequences are taken as adjacent. If a new sequence is better than the current one, the new sequence becomes the current order. Otherwise, the current order is not changed. This cooling process repeats for 15,000 times. Every 1,000-th step, the current order will be replaced even if it a new sequence is not better, as long as the trip length is not larger than the permissible bound. For this heating process, our design experimentally selects the permissible bound to 10 % for the first half and 5 % for the second half.

4   Performance Measurement

This section evaluates the performance of the proposed scheme through a prototype implementation, mainly in terms of trip length, accuracy, and optimality according to the number of destinations. Focusing on the core search engine, our experiment distributes the distance between two stations randomly from 1 km to 10 km. For each number of destinations, 10 sets are generated and their trip distances are averaged. To assess the efficiency of the proposed schedule, the experiment compares with the backtracking-based exhaustive search by modifying the program code developed in our previous work [5].

The first experiment measures the trip length according to the iteration steps to check the operation of simulated annealing. The results are shown in Figure 2 for 10 destination case and in Figure 3 for 11 destination case, respectively. Each figure also plots the optimal trip length obtained by the exhaustive search and the trip length changes from three different seeds, or initial sequences. The trip length increases from time to time due to heating process, but for the almost part of iterations steps, the cooling process gradually reduces the trip length. 1 execution thread for 10 destination case and 2 threads for 11 destination case reach the optimal solution. The others cannot lead to the optimal schedule, as they are stuck at local maxima.

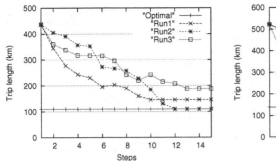

Fig. 2. Trip length for 10 destinations   **Fig. 3.** Trip length for 11 destinations

Next, we measure the effect of the number of seeds, from 1 to 5, to trip length, and the result it shown in Figure 4. Actually, the performance greatly depends on which sequence is selected as first seed. Even though the 11 destination case reaches almost the optimal schedule from the first seed, the 10 destination case shows the advantage of more seeds. As shown in Figure 4, with 5 seeds, we can further reduce the trip length by 22.3 % from the single seed search. Figure 5 plots the optimality of our search engine. We define the optimality as the probability that a scheduling scheme can find the optimal schedule for a given task set, regardless of the difference from the optimal one. As shown in the figure, when the number of destinations gets larger, the optimality deteriorates.

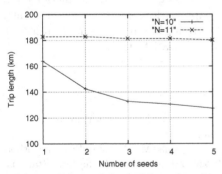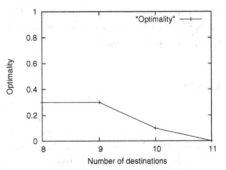

Fig. 4. Effect of the number of seeds   **Fig. 5.** Optimality measurement

Figure 6 demonstrates the accuracy of the developed scheduler, by plotting the error size. The average error gets larger according to the increase in the number of destinations. For 10 and 11 destination cases, the average errors are 12.7 % and 23.0 %, respectively. The gain in the controllable execution time is obtained by this accuracy loss. Finally, Figure 7 plots the error for the entire 40 destination sets. 70 % of error points lie in the range of 0 to 0.2. In Figure 5, 6, and 7, we make the engine run with a single seed. With more seeds and

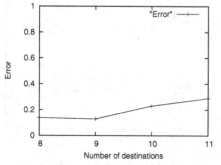
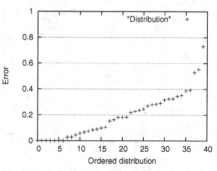

Fig. 6. Accuracy measurement   **Fig. 7.** Error distribution

subsequent execution threads, accuracy and optimality can be much improved. In addition, as their executions are independent, the simulated annealing engine can benefit from threaded computing on a multi-core CPU.

5   Conclusions

In this paper, we have designed and developed a tour and charging scheduler for electric vehicles to alleviate their long charging time based on computational intelligence. The implementation test finds out that we can achieve about 87 % of accuracy when the number of destinations is less than 10 and 70 % of error points lie in the range from 0 to 20 %. It can integrate any cost functions and constraints processing issued from different applications and their requirements. As future work, we are planning to develop a tour place recommendation service to further reduce waiting time and enhance user satisfaction.

References

1. Morrow, K., Karner, D., Francfort, J.: Plug-in Hybrid Electric Vehicle Charging Infrastructure Review. Battelle Energy Alliance (2008)
2. Kobayashi, Y., Kiyama, N., Aoshima, H., Kashiyama, M.: A Route Search Method for Electric Vehicles in Consideration of Range and Locations of Charging Stations. In: IEEE Intelligent Vehicles Symposium, pp. 920–925 (2011)
3. Hermans, Y., Le Cun, B., Bui, A.: Individual Decisions and Schedule Planner in a Vehicle-to-Grid Context. In: International Electric Vehicle Conference (2012)
4. Lee, J., Kim, H., Park, G.: Integration of Battery Charging to Tour Schedule Generation for an EV-Based Rent-a-Car Business. In: Tan, Y., Shi, Y., Ji, Z. (eds.) ICSI 2012, Part II. LNCS, vol. 7332, pp. 399–406. Springer, Heidelberg (2012)
5. Lee, J., Kim, H., Park, G., Lee, B., Lee, S., Im, D.: Tour Schedule Generation Integrating Restaurant Options for Electric Vehicles. To appear at International Conference on Ubiquitous Information Technologies and Applications (2012)

Comparative Performance Analysis of Relocation Policies for Electric Vehicle Sharing Systems*

Junghoon Lee, Gyung-Leen Park**, and Dongwook Lee

Dept. of Computer Science and Statistics,
Jeju National University, 690-756, Jeju Do, Republic of Korea
{jhlee,glpark,seakove}@jejunu.ac.kr

Abstract. This paper selects possible relocation scenarios for electric vehicle sharing systems and measures the service ratio through our analysis framework. The experiment exploits the actual trip records collected in a taxi telematics system in Jeju city area as future sharing demand. Its goals include testing the validity of the analysis framework for a sharing system design as well as discovering the behavioral characteristics in basic relocation policies to take into account when designing a new sophisticated relocation scheme. The sharing performance is measured for even, utilization-based, and morning-focused schemes based on the assumption that the relocation is carried out during the non-operation hours. The performance analysis results find out that it is useful to focus on the pick-up requests during the first few hours after the operation starts and that it is necessary to develop a prediction-based proactive relocation scheme to cope with request fluctuation in the airport area.

Keywords: Smart transportation, electric vehicles, sharing stations, vehicle relocation, service ratio.

1 Introduction

The future power system called the smart grid is empowered by computational intelligence from information and communication technologies to achieve smart energy consumption [1]. Particularly, it can benefit from sophisticated computing algorithms for complex system optimization, real-time communication protocols, large-volume data management, and diverse sensor devices. Smart power consumption can be pursued also in transportation area, while this smart transportation is essentially based on electric vehicles, or EVs, in short. Even though their energies are still obtained by burning fossil fuels, the energy efficiency of EVs is much better than gasoline-powered vehicles and the air pollution is much

---

* This research was supported by the MKE (The Ministry of Knowledge Economy), Republic of Korea, under IT/SW Creative research program supervised by the NIPA (National IT Industry Promotion Agency) (NIPA-2012-(H0502-12-1002)).

** Corresponding author.

T.-h. Kim et al. (Eds.): MulGraB/BSBT/IUrC 2012, CCIS 353, pp. 195–201, 2012.

less. Moreover, the steady improvement of battery capacity can lead to the broad employment of renewable energies for smart transportation.

However, it is not easy for an individual to own an EV due to high cost. Thus, EV sharing is a reasonable business model, which relieves users of the economic burden on vehicle ownership, maintenance, and insurance. Carsharing systems are originally considered to be an alternative to private vehicle ownership. Especially in megacities having high population density, carsharing can improve mobility, lower carbon emissions, and reduce traffic congestion [2]. Persons access a fleet of shared-use vehicles in the sharing stations on a short-term and on-demand basis. For better convenience, EV sharing systems facilitate one-way rentals, that is, a customer can return an EV to a different station where it was picked up. Essentially, a customer can take a car only when the station has at least one EV. However, the one-way rental makes the number of EVs in each station uneven and some stations may have no EV. Thus, the relocation of vehicle is one of the most critical issues for serviceability of EV sharing systems.

The EV relocation policy must consider such factors as relocation time, the number of service men, and relocation goal. One of the most fundamental and manageable ways is to relocate EVs at non-operational hours. Until the beginning of next operation hours, quite much time is available for relocation. Then, the relocation problem becomes to decide the number of EVs to assign to each station. This paper considers 3 strategies and evaluates their performance using the sharing system analysis framework implemented in our previous work [3]. The first strategy, named *even* relocation, evenly distributes EVs to each station. The second strategy, named *utilization-based* relocation, calculates the number of pick-ups during a sufficiently large interval and assigns EVs according to the observed ratio for each station. Next, the third strategy, named *morning-focused* relocation, just focuses on the pick-ups during the morning time, namely, just the first a few hours in the operation time.

2   Background and Related Work

The Republic of Korea was designated as one of the two smart grid initiative countries together with Italy during the expanded G8 Summit in 2009 [4]. The Korean national government launched the Jeju smart grid test-bed, aiming at testing leading-edge technologies and developing business models in 5 major areas consisting of smart power grid, smart place, smart transportation, smart renewables, and smart electricity services. Among these, smart transportation first builds an area-wide charging infrastructure for the large deployment of EVs. In addition, several consortiums participating in this enterprise are planning to test diverse business models on EV sharing, EV rent-a-cars, and integration of wind energies to EV charging [5]. This part embraces the battery technology to overcome the problem of long charging time and short driving distance in EVs.

As for related work on EV relocation, in the PICAV (Personal Intelligent City Accessible Vehicles) system, in operation in Genoa, Italy, a vehicle is electrically powered and for a single driver [2]. Vehicles are networked and can communicate each other as well as with city infrastructure, making it possible to exploit centralized coordination. PICAV can be characterized by an open-ended reservation system and one-way trips over multiple sharing stations. Due to uneven demand, the number of vehicles at each station soon becomes disproportionally distributed. To cope with this problem, PICAV develops a fully user-based relocation strategy in which a system supervisor recommends or assigns a station a customer returns vehicles to. Here, in deciding fleet relocation, a cost function is defined. As the search space is extremely large, a simulated annealing scheme is adopted for minimization problem solving. In addition, they implement a microscopic simulator to track the second-by-second activity of each user and vehicle.

[6] attempts to solve vehicle stock imbalance in one-way car sharing systems by selecting optimal station locations. To begin with, this approach assumes that vehicles are relocated to the original positions by service persons at the end of the day. Then, 3 trip selection scenarios are investigated. First, the controlled service assigns a vehicle only to a trip which is advantageous to the system profit, for example, balance level, irrespective of whether there are vehicles in the pick-up station. Second, the full service will accept all trips as long as they begin and end at existing stations. Third, the conditional service accepts a trip only if a vehicle is available at the pick-up station. For those scenarios, the authors develop mathematical optimization models to find the best depot locations out of the given candidate location set. This model also finds the number of vehicles to satisfy the requirement for each service mode. Then, this optimization model was applied to the trip matrix collected by a geo-coded survey in Lisbon, Portugal, in 1990s.

[7] designs a three-phase decision support system to determine manpower and operating parameters for vehicle relocation, testing on a set of commercially operational data from the Honda carsharing system in Singapore. The first phase, *Optimizer*, allocates staff resources and activities to minimize the relocation cost, considering customer pick-up and return patterns, number of parking stalls, inter-station relocation cost, and the like. After formulating a mixed integer linear programming model based on the definition of an objective function and necessary constraints, the problem is solved by the branch-and-bound technique. Then, phase 2, *Trend Filter*, filters the optimized results exploiting a series of heuristics to complete a recommendation set of operating parameters, mainly focusing on shift hours, relocation techniques, station threshold values, and so on. Finally, in phase 3, its simulator part evaluates the effectiveness of recommended parameters in terms of zero-vehicle-time, full-port-time, and number of relocations.

Our previous work has built a serviceability analysis framework for EV sharing systems to help to decide the sharing station locations and assess relocation strategies [4]. This framework can accurately trace the number of available EVs in each station based on the actual trip data consisting of pick-up and drop-off locations collected from the taxi telematics system in Jeju City, Republic of Korea. Each point is mapped to a specific sharing station. For the given parameters including the number of EVs and access distance to the stations virtually placed on the city map, we can conduct experiments to measure the service ratio, moving distance, per-station EV distribution at relocation time. It is also possible to model EV sharing demand and the number of available EVs for each station. Neural networks can efficiently build a non-linear model for those time series to predict the future demand and develop proactive relocation strategies [8].

3   Service Scenarios

Jeju city has a well maintained road network consisting of about 18,000 intersections and 27,000 road segments. Now, this city is building charging stations all over the province and the number of EVs keeps growing. After the analysis of the pick-up point distribution and easiness-to-install, we have selected 5 candidate places for sharing stations. They are the Jeju international airport, a shopping mall in residential area, Jeju city hall, Jeju national university, and a shopping mall in the tourist hotel area. They are numbered from Station 1 to Station 5 sequentially, namely, S_1 to S_5. Above-mentioned 5 locations are ordered by the traffic load, availability of charging facility, manageability, and many other factors.

Airplanes are the major transportation methods to connect Jeju city to other towns, as Jeju city is located in an island. Many vehicle trips begin and end at the international airport for both residents and tourists. Jeju area hosts several million visitors every year. Second, the shopping mall in the residential area is appropriate for a sharing station. Shoppers from various city area visit here due to large parking space and easy reachability. Third, Jeju city hall area includes many public institutions such as the city hall, the bus terminal, governmental offices, and the like. Fourth, in Jeju national university, many students, faculty members, and visitors want to use EVs in addition to the public transportation such as buses. Fifth, another shopping mall in a seaside area gathers a lot of traffic not just for shoppers but tourists, as this area has many restaurants and tourist accommodations.

Actually, taxi pick-up and drop-off locations are scattered over the wide area, our analysis framework defines access distance. For a trip record starting within a given access distance from a station, this request can be covered by the sharing system. In addition, if there is at least one EV at the station, the request can be served. The service ratio is the main performance criteria for the assessment of EV sharing infrastructures. We assume that the operation hour begins at 7 AM and ends at 1 AM next day. The relocation procedure is performed during the non-operation time, namely, from 1 AM to 7 AM. The number of service men is sufficient to relocate EVs during this interval.

Let N denote the total number of EVs in the sharing system and V_i the number of EVs for S_i. Additionally, N_s is the number of stations. Then, the even relocation scheme decides V_i as shown in Eq. (1).

$$V_i = \lfloor \frac{N}{N_s} \rfloor \tag{1}$$

, while $N - \lfloor \frac{N}{N_S} \rfloor$ will be assigned randomly. Next, the utilization-based relocation scheme allocates EVs as shown in Eq. (2).

$$V_i = N \times \frac{P_i}{\sum P_i} \tag{2}$$

, where P_i denotes the number of pick-ups during the whole observation interval. Here again, the remnants will be assigned randomly. Finally, the morning-focuses relocation scheme replaces P_i in Eq. (2) by M_i. Namely,

$$V_i = N \times \frac{M_i}{\sum M_i} \tag{3}$$

, where M_i is the number of pick-ups during the morning time of the observation interval.

4 Experiment Result

The first experiment measures the success ratio, or interchangeably serviceability, for each relocation scheme according to the number of EVs. Success ratio is the probability that an EV is available when a pick-up request arrives at a station. Figure 1 plots the success ratio for two difference access distances of 300 m and 500 m, respectively, while the number of EVs ranges from 5 to 50. The smaller access distance corresponds to a more exact demand for sharing. According to Figure 1(a), the morning-focused relocation scheme shows the best service ratio, while the utilization-based scheme is the worst. Fir the sharing demand in Jeju area, the service ratio increases slowly beyond the point of 30 EVs. The performance gap between morning-focuses and even relocation schemes reaches 2.3 % when for 15 EVs, while the gap gets smaller, and the service ratio for each case is almost the same for the sufficiently large number of EVs.

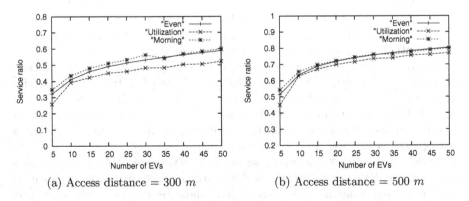

(a) Access distance = 300 m (b) Access distance = 500 m

Fig. 1. Service ratio analysis according to the number of EVs

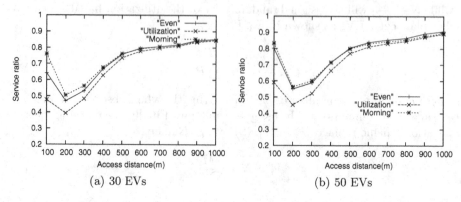

Fig. 2. Service ratio analysis according to access distance

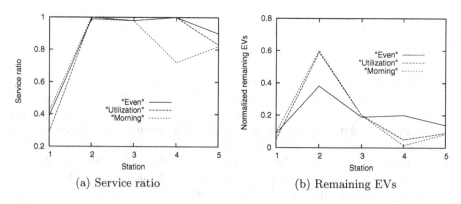

Fig. 3. Per-station statistics

Next experiment measures the success ratio according to the access distance for 30 EVs and 50 EVs, respectively. When the access distance is 100 m, very small number of pick-up records can be included in the simulation, so the service ratio at this point is not consistent with other distance values. Morning-based scheme largely has the best service ratio, but the access distance is 1,000 m, the service ratio is not affected by the relocation strategy.

Finally, Figure 3 shows per-station statistics. Figure 3(a) plots the station-by-station service ratio, discovering the airport area has the poorest service ratio. The pick-up and return at this area is extremely skewed in a day and unpredictable, affected by day-of-week and weather conditions. It indicates that how to improve the service ratio in the airport is the key issue to design a new relocation scheme. As the number of pick-ups in Jeju university is not so significant, its impact on the overall service ratio is not critical. Figure 3(b) shows the remaining EVs at relocation time. Interestingly, even relocation scheme ends with most even remaining EV distribution. Many returns are concentrated on the city hall area.

5 Conclusions

In this paper, we have first tested the validity of the analysis framework for the sharing system design. Next, the behavioral characteristics of service ratio have been investigated for the given relocation policies. The analysis framework allows us to virtually place sharing stations, trace the number of available EVs, and measure the service ratio in each station, assuming that the taxi pick-up and drop-off patterns will be similar to EV sharing request patterns. The experiments are conducted for even, utilization-based, and morning-focused schemes based on the assumption that the relocation is carried out during the non-operation time. The performance analysis results find out that it is useful to focus on the pick-up requests during the first few hours after the operation starts and that it is necessary to develop a prediction-based proactive relocation scheme to cope with request fluctuation in the airport area. These results will be fed into the design of a new sophisticated relocation scheme in Jeju city, which is now hosting many EV-related business models.

References

1. Ipakchi, A., Albuyeh, F.: Grid of the Future. IEEE Power & Energy Magazine, 52–62 (2009)
2. Cepolina, E., Farina, A.: A New Shared Vehicle System for Urban Areas. Transportation Research Part C, 230–243 (2012)
3. Lee, J., Kim, H., Park, G., Kwak, H., Lee, M.: Analysis Framework for Electric Vehicle Sharing Systems Using Vehicle Movement Data Stream. In: Wang, H., Zou, L., Huang, G., He, J., Pang, C., Zhang, H.L., Zhao, D., Yi, Z. (eds.) APWeb 2012 Workshops. LNCS, vol. 7234, pp. 89–94. Springer, Heidelberg (2012)
4. Lee, J., Kim, H., Park, G., Kang, M.: Energy Consumption Scheduler for Demand Response Systems in the Smart Grid. To appear in Journal of Information Science and Engineering (2012)
5. Lee, J., Kim, H., Park, G.: Renewable Energy and Power Management in Smart Transportation. In: Pan, J.-S., Chen, S.-M., Nguyen, N.T. (eds.) ACIIDS 2012, Part III. LNCS, vol. 7198, pp. 247–255. Springer, Heidelberg (2012)
6. Correia, G., Antunes, A.: Optimization Approach to Depot Location and Trip Selection in One-Way Carshring Systems. Transportation Research Part E, 233–247 (2012)
7. Kek, A., Cheu, R., Meng, Q., Fung, C.: A Decision Support System for Vehicle Relocation Operations in Carsharing Systems. Transportation Research Part E, 149–158 (2009)
8. Silva, D., Yu, X., Alahakoon, D., Holmes, G.: Semi-Supervised Classification of Characterized Patterns for Demand Forecasting using Smart Electricity Meters. In: International Conference on Electrical Machines and Systems, pp. 1–6 (2011)

Use-Case Driven Requirements Analysis
for Context-Aware Systems

Jongmyung Choi and Youngho Lee

Department of Computer Engineering, Mokpo National University, Jeonnam, Korea
{jmchoi,youngho}@mokpo.ac.kr

Abstract. Context-awareness and context-aware systems have been getting popular but there have been only a few of researches on requirements analysis method for context-aware systems. In this paper, we propose a requirement elicitation method for context-aware systems. We contend that analysts should consider system platform, target users, and service intelligence as context related issues, and we also argue that they should gather and document context related issues during use case gathering process because context related information is very important in context-aware systems. Our work contributes to context-aware system field because we consider context information as first citizen of software engineering, so that users, analysts, and designers have some agreement on context-aware services.

Keywords: Context-aware, Requirement Elicitation, Use Case, Decision Table.

1 Introduction

Context-awareness and context-aware system have been getting attention from both academia and the industry, and there have been various research topics such as experimental context-aware systems, context modeling, context inference method, and software engineering. Even though there have been some researches on software engineering for context-aware systems, we still do not enough researches on requirement analysis for the systems. As it is well-kwon, wrong or not enough requirements cause huge costs in the system development or even project failure, so that requirement analysis for context-aware systems is very important.

In this paper, we extend our previous work [1], and propose a requirement gathering method for context-aware systems. We first consider system platform, target users, and the intelligence level of smart services as context related information because these issues are closely related to context-aware services. We also try to consider contexts as major information in gathering use cases and service scenarios, so that we argue that analysts have to find out context related information, document it, and communicate with other stakeholders to get agreement on contexts and context-aware services. We believe that this process will raise context's position in software engineering to first citizen from second or third citizen.

For gathering context information and functional requirements, we utilize use case technique. Use case has been used for getting functional requirements, but it has not

T.-h. Kim et al. (Eds.): MulGraB/BSBT/IUrC 2012, CCIS 353, pp. 202–209, 2012.
© Springer-Verlag Berlin Heidelberg 2012

been used to gather or describe context information. Therefore, the stakeholders of the system have troubles in understanding context and context-aware services, or having agreement about the systems. The context related requirements should be gathered explicitly from users and the stakeholders and documented explicitly. In this paper, we propose a method for gathering and documenting context requirements. We also introduce decision table techniques to understand contexts and context-aware services.

We contribute three fold to context-aware systems and software engineering fields. First, our proposal gives stakeholders a chance to understand contexts as major requirements in context-aware system development. Because context-aware services lead to huge efforts and costs, they have to understand the difficulties and complexities. Second, our proposal provides the integrated requirement analysis method for context requirements and functional requirements because we argue that context requirements should be gathered and documented. Third, our proposal will reduce stakeholders' efforts in development of context-aware services because clear understanding of the requirement will show solutions clearly.

This paper consists of five sections. In section 2, we summarize the related works and compare our work with them. In section 3, we propose how to elicit requirements, and we show an example case of tour guide system in section 4. After that, we reveal our conclusions in section 5.

2   Related Work

Our work is about requirement elicitation for context-aware systems, and there have been some researches on this topic. In our previous work [1], we proposed context-driven requirements elicitation techniques. In the work, we argued that contexts are very important in requirements elicitation and analysts had to consider contexts in their work. We also proposed variations of UML diagrams including use case diagram and context transition diagram.

Dan Hong [3] classified contexts into three groups (computing, user, and physical context), and proposed a meta-model for requirements elicitation. He also proposed some guideline and procedure for requirements gathering of context-aware systems. Naoyasu [4] divided context-aware systems into two parts (system and context), and formalized the system with VDM, in which contexts were represented as Aspects. The approach of separation of system and contexts is similar to our previous work [1]. Hannes [5] proposed a method to find context driven use cases. The work introduced how to use context matrix which connects context information to sub-goal. Anthony [6] proposed a reflection-based requirements framework. The interesting feature of the work is that the requirements should be changed when the contexts are changed in execution time. Therefore the requirements elicitation framework should support reflection mechanism. It is very meaningful because it applied reflection mechanism to requirements elicitation.

3   Use-Case Driven Context Analysis

3.1   Use Case Driven Requirement Analysis

Use case approach has been widely used for gathering functional requirements from stakeholders. It includes actor(s), title, main scenario, and extension(s). The extension part describes some exceptional scenarios different from the main scenario. Use case diagram, the visual notation of use case, includes some notations for "include", "extend", and actor extension. These notations allow requirement analysts to describe the main successful scenarios and some variances of the scenarios for the functional requirements. According to Cockburn [2], there is a main success scenario for a use case. It is the case in which everything goes right. However, there can be something wrong, and the main scenario cannot work well. Then we can add *extension* part in the use case. For the extension, we have to describe some conditions for the exceptional situation. Then we describe the alternative scenario path for the exceptional situation. Fig. 1 shows an example of extension and extension point. Extension and extension point provide analysts with some mechanism to describe alternative scenarios and alternative paths for the basic task.

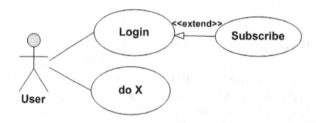

Fig. 1. Use Case Extension and Extension Point

Use case is very popular, but it has some limitation because it does not have enough features to describe contexts and context dependent service scenarios. It has extension and extension point mechanism to describe some exception cases and the exceptional cases can be considered context dependent. In use case, extension is used to describe some alternative scenarios or exceptional scenario. It means that the extension is considered as exceptional or even some kind of error conditions. However, the real world is so complicated that even a use case may have a lot of service scenarios and a lot of cases to be considered but they are not considered as any error conditions.

3.2   Context-Aware System's Features

Context-aware systems have distinguishing features compared to the traditional systems, and these features make analysts and developers hard to analyze and develop context-aware systems. The first feature is unclear system scope. The traditional systems have rather explicit and concrete system scope to develop. However, context-aware systems have unclear system scope because the scope can be extended easily according to contexts or other context related issues such as service intelligence.

The second feature is about system end users, or target users. Context-aware systems have various types of target users compared to the traditional systems, and the different users may require similar but different service implementation. Therefore, the service developers should develop different version of services for each different users.

The third feature is about use case realization. In the traditional system, a use case is realized as a service, but in context-aware system, use case may be realized as several services because each service may be different according to context. This will require more time and effort in realization of use cases.

The fourth feature is that context-aware systems are heterogeneous, so that the systems are very complicated compared to the traditional systems. It may also influence on determining system platform.

The fifth feature is that context-aware systems require intelligence in their services, but we do not have clear cut technologies for the intelligence. The intelligence level can cause huge confusing in the system definition and determining system scope.

The sixth feature is that we do not have clear requirements or concept about context-aware services or smart services that are considering contexts or user's situation. Therefore, we need some mechanism to describe contexts and context-aware services.

The seventh feature is that contexts and context-aware services are related to culture and sociology because contexts are basically understood by people. Therefore, stakeholders should have agreement on contexts and context-aware services. If they do not agree on them, the system cannot be successful.

3.3   Methods for Requirements Elicitation

In this section, we introduce four techniques for requirement elicitation of context-aware systems. Three of them are the existing techniques for gathering requirements from users and stakeholders. However, requirements analysts have to pay attention to context and context-aware services during requirement gathering process.

Defining Scope of Systems

System's scope is very important in system development. In defining system scope, stakeholders have been used to define functional features. However, in the context-aware systems, there are other important features such as system platforms, target users, and intelligence level of the system.

In the defining system's scope, stakeholders have to define system platforms because context-aware systems are heterogeneous and the system can be implemented in various other platforms. Therefore, stakeholders have to clearly define the system platforms that the system supports. The system can contain desktop application, smart phone app, web application, or even in embedded system application. We have various choices for some services and they all require different technologies, advantage, and disadvantage.

The second important issue is about target users. The traditional systems have unified target users or limited number of users according to their roles or privileges. However, in context-aware systems, there are various target users and they receive similar services but the services are all different and are implemented in different presentation or different algorithms.

The third important issue is about intelligence for the services. Context-aware services have some intelligence in their services, but the level of intelligence is all different according to systems' goals. Some researches aim so high that the system will be able to read user's mind and do some things without user's explicit requests. But others have simple intelligence that the systems operate according to predefined condition or rules. The problem is that according to the system's goal, the system development may have difficulties or not. The worse thing is that the current technology cannot support fully smart services.

Service Identification

Requirement analysts usually conduct interview with users and stakeholders in order to gather requirements and understand the business logic. In the traditional requirements analysis process, they focus on functional requirements and business logic. However, in context-aware system analysis, analysts have to pay attention to contexts and possible context-aware services because these can be big source of costs and efforts for the system implementation. This is based on a reason that a context-aware service may require several version of service implementation according to contexts. For example, for calling service, in normal context, the phone will ring, in meeting context, it will vibrate, and in driving, it will connect to car audio system automatically. Some of the service implementation may similar, but others are totally different.

Stakeholders should have discussion or brainstorming over the use cases, and have agreement on determining context-aware services. They have to choose possible context-aware services from the use cases which are gathered from the interview and literature survey. And they also have to make documents on contexts and context-aware services. They have to put the context condition on the beginning of the use cases, and they also have to make a document about all the possible contexts in the system.

Decision Table or Tree

From the use case gathering process, stakeholders have all possible context-aware services. And they also figure out the all possible contexts in the system and services. However, they do not know yet how to determine the contexts and how to sense the context information from the real world.

For determining context, we propose decision table or tree. Decision table describes context information and services. Analysts have to get context information and possible context-aware services for the context from the users and stakeholders because this is very important to understand the user's intention. Table 1 shows an example of decision table for heater and air conditioner controller system at home. In "Empty" context, the system does not operate, but "In use" context, it operates according to the temperature.

Table 1. An Example of Decision Table

Temperature	Over 28°C	5°C – 28°C	Under 5°C
In use	Activate the air conditioner	X	Activate the heater
Empty	X	X	X

4   Case Study

In this section, we will show how to apply our proposal to context-aware services. We choose a tour guide system for the example system because many tour guide systems have been proposed as context-aware systems.

4.1   Context-Aware System Scope

Our tour guide system has two main functional features: to propose tour route, and to provide information about relic and exhibitions in the museum. Defining the functional scope of the system is similar to the traditional approach.

In section 3, we argued that we have to consider the service platform for context-aware systems. The tour guide system can be implemented as a smartphone application, museum property system such as specific PDA or wall attached panel system, text message (known as SMS) based system, or even desktop application. In this case, we choose smartphone application for the system platform because the number of smartphone users will increase rapidly.

For determining target users, we have to consider two things: languages and disabled users. For foreign tourists, the system has to support different language services, and we have to limit the number of languages because the system cannot support all different languages with limited budgets. Furthermore, for disabled users, the system has to have different presentation mechanisms. For example, for hearing-impaired users, the system should support text based information presentation services. And for visually-impaired users, the system should support voice and touch based services.

For smart intelligence, we have to make it clear because it can be a big source of confusing in the communication and requirements. In the tour guide system, we can think all the possible intelligence levels. For tour route suggestion service, the system may provide smart services that it considers user's preference by analyzing his/her past tour information and analyzing his/her mental or psychological status. Or it may suggest the most popular places according to other tourists' evaluation or recommendations. The first one has different level of intelligence and technologies compared to the second one. If we choose the first one approach, we have to pay a lot of efforts to the research on the intelligence. However, if we choose the second approach, we will not pay much effort for the implementation.

4.2   Service Identification

Requirement analysts conduct interview with users and stakeholders in order to gather requirements for the system. From the interview, they find out two simple but important two use cases: tour rout suggestion and explanation of relic or the exhibitions in the museum. Fig. 2 shows the use case diagram for the system. It only shows the traditional actor and use cases.

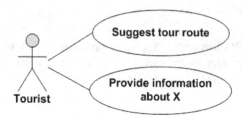

Fig. 2. Use Case Diagram for Tour Guide System

Fig. 3 shows the context-aware use case diagram for the tour guide system. It has two more target users compared to the traditional use case diagram in Fig. 2. It also has different context-aware services for each use case. It has context-aware services for "Suggest tour route" use case, and two more services for "Provide information about X" use case. These context-aware services show that there are context requirements for each use case and the necessity of multiple versions of service implementation.

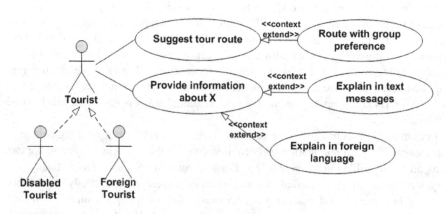

Fig. 3. Context-aware Use Case Diagram

In the use case diagram, we have to describe context related information in order to understand the system and communicate explicitly with other stakeholders especially designers and programmers.

4.3   Decision Table or Tree

Decision table make the relation of contexts and context-aware services clear. For the tout guide system, we can make decision table as shown in table 2. In the table, the stakeholders understand what context-aware services are used when some contexts happen.

Table 2. Decision Table for Tout Guide System

	Suggest tour route	Provide information
Group preference	Route according to group preference	
Disabled		Provide information to overcome the impaired senses
Foreigner		Provide information with foreigners, but the default language is English.

5   Conclusions

Context-aware services have been getting attentions, but we still have some limitations for the real world services. In this paper, we proposed a method for requirements gathering for context-aware systems. The method is not so new for requirement elicitation process, but we contend that during the process, analysts and stakeholders should pay attentions to context related issues such as system platform, target users, intelligence, possible context-aware services and agreement with other stakeholders, and understanding contexts with decision tables and trees. We also raise the context as major issue in requirement analysis, and we call it context requirements.

References

1. Choi, J.: Context-Driven Requirements Analysis. In: Gervasi, O., Gavrilova, M.L. (eds.) ICCSA 2007, Part III. LNCS, vol. 4707, pp. 739–748. Springer, Heidelberg (2007)
2. Cockburn, A.: Writing Effective Use Cases. Addison-Wesley (2000)
3. Hong, D., Chiu, D.K.W., Shen, V.Y.: Requirements Elicitation for the Design of Context-aware Applications in a Ubiquitous Environment. In: Proc. of ICEC (August 2005)
4. Ubayashi, N., Nakajima, S.: Context-aware Feature-Oriented Modeling with an Aspect Extension of VDM. In: Proc. of SAC (March 2007)
5. Omasreister, H., Metzker, E.: A Context-Driven Use Case Creation Process for Specifying Automotive Driver Assistance Systems. In: Proc. of Int'l Requirements Engineering Conf. (2004)
6. Finkelstein, A., Savigni, A.: A Framework for Requirements Engineering for Context-Aware Services. In: Proc. of International Workshop From Software Requirements to Architectures (2001)

Utilization of Local Cultural Resources Based on the Concept of Ecomuseum: Focused on Cheorwon, Gangwon Province

Jin Young Kim and Jae Yeong Lee

Hankuk University of Foreign Studies, 107 Imun-ro, Dongdaemun-gu,
130-791, Seoul, Korea
staci21@naver.com, jylee@hufs.ac.kr

Abstract. Cheorwon is a field of our history where military cultural relics as well as historical cultural assets are located as the capital of Taebong that took the world by storm. The DMZ near the city shows the possibility of the city as a good ecotourism site encompassing the historicity and clean image. Nevertheless, it cannot dispel the negative image resulted from the tension of armistice frontier, severely cold winter weather and the poverty of rural community. Accordingly, this study proposes a method to improve the image of the region by utilizing the cultural resources of Cheorwon based on the concept of eco-museum. Eco-museum which becomes theoretical base of the study is a new form of museum to make a whole area as a museum unlike conventional museums attracting audiences to the collections exhibited in the limited space. The ecomuseum will contribute to the activation of sustainable local economy.

Keywords: The DMZ, cultural asset, local cultural resources, ecomuseum, ecotourisim, sustainable development.

1   Preface

1.1   Background and Purpose of Study

Industrialization accelerates escape from agricultural communities and urban concentration and the sense of relative deprivation causes vacantization and impoverishment of agricultural villages. Accordingly, eradication of economic gap between cities and rural villages becomes the goal of major policies of local governments as well as the central government. Consequently, various divisions have performed a wide variety of farming economy activation policies under different titles such as green tourism, beautiful village-making, eco-village making and traditional theme villages. They may be positive in a way of encouraging visitors to experience rural life, yet locals did not have enough chances to take part in [1]. From this context, these programs may be degenerated into profit pursuing one-time program responding to the interest of tourists rather than improving the understanding on the region or preserving sustainable local cultural assets.

Thus, this study suggests to utilize cultural assets of Cheorwon and to promote local economy through sustainable development by introducing the concept of

T.-h. Kim et al. (Eds.): MulGraB/BSBT/IUrC 2012, CCIS 353, pp. 210–216, 2012.
© Springer-Verlag Berlin Heidelberg 2012

ecomuseum which comprises with functions of the museum such as the preservation of local assets, exhibition and education and local residents' participation.

1.2   Scope and Methods of Study

The study selected historical and cultural resources dispersed in Cheorwon area as the subjects of ecomuseum and tried to propose a sustainable utilization method by identifying the current status of those assets. It also tried to identify the method to preserve the ecology and cultural resources in the region efficiently and to connect them to eco-museum. For the purpose of this, it was tried to understand the concept of eco-museum first and to propose practical and applicable methods. This study is composed of three times' site visit, visit to Cheorwon Office and Cheorwon Cultural Museum and literature review.

1.3   Definition of Ecomuseum

Georges Henri Riviere, founder of ecomuseum, defined ecomuseum as "the museum to historically explore the life of local residents, and the development process of natural environments and social environments, and to contribute to local community development through preservation, cultivation and exhibition of natural and cultural assets in the field." Ecomuseum contributes to the development of local community by preserving the dispersed relics and assets in the field intact and utilizing local legacies with local governments, allowing the residents to participate in actively unlike conventional museums which attract audiences passively in a building [2]. There is another definition by European Network of Eco-museum. It defines eco-museum as 'a dynamic way to preserve, interpret and manage the inheritance of local community for the sustainable development of the community.' In other words, the participation of local residents is very important in eco-museum, as it prevents the vacantization of agricultural communities by enhancing the pride in the region and improving the love for the community and promotes local economy. Additionally, ecomuseum is the strategy to let other people than the local residents evaluate the value of the region by enabling the local residents to understand the local history, culture and life of the region and to have attachment and pride in the region, and the field to understand the traces of ancestors in the time flow from pre-history to the present and to prospect the future [3].

2   Current Status and Utilization of Cultural Resources in Cheorwon

2.1   Current Status of Cultural Resources

Cheorwon in Gangwon Province was selected as the subject of ecomuseum for the study. It is because Cheorwon has military cultural assets such as Labor Party

Headquarter[1] and infiltration tunnels of North Korea as the field of 'Security Education' and various cultural remains such as Gungye's Castle and Dopiansa or Dopiansa Temple, as the old capital of Taebong[2] as well as potentiality of ecotourism with beautiful natural environment including the Hantan River. As of December 2012, Cheorwon in Gangwon Province is composed of 4 eups(counties) and 7 myeons(districts) and has the population of 48,084. It records 2.41 people per household ranked at the 9th place among 18 cities and rural counties. It is the second largest rural county in Gangwon Province after Hongcheon. It is equipped with favorable conditions to make an ecomuseum utilizing the human resources of the region.

Geographically, Cheorwon shares the boundary with Hwacheon and Yanggu in the east, Yeoncheon in Gyeonggi Province in the west, Pocheon in the south and Pyeonggang in the north. It includes 43.6 miles of armistice line of 155 miles (28%). Considering the historical and ecological meaning of DMZ[3] although it can be fluctuated with political environment, Cheorwon can be said to have highly meaningful ecological cultural assets. As the access of general public has been controlled and regulated since Korean War, DMZ can have previous ecological resources by restoring natural ecology in northern area of the Civil Control Line. Conclusively, borderlands including Cheorwon are evaluated as the region with high ecological values so as to be called as 'Rich Repository of Natural Ecology' not only domestically but also internationally. Additionally, it attracted worldly attention because of it is the symbol of cold war as the one and only remaining division in the world. Considering the coming unification, it emerges as the land of opportunity that can be utilized as frontier base of South-North Unification, Repository of Ecology and Site for Tourism and History Education. To increase the in-flow of tourists, transportation and convenience facilities are also important. From this perspective, Cheorwon has good conditions of location as it is at most 90km's radius from Seoul. It is highly probable to develop the area as a place for leisure activities of capital area population.

In Cheorwon, there are various modern cultural assets such as Woljeong Station, Labor Party Headquarter and Iron Triangle War Remains as well as 21 cultural assets including national cultural assets, provincial cultural assets and registered cultural asset. Additionally, it has the most optimal conditions as an experiential and ecological tourists' attraction utilizing its beautiful nature such as the Hantan River, Togyo Reserve, Jiktang Waterfalls, and Sundam Valley. The followings are the cultural properties of Cheorwon.

---

[1] The three-story building located at Cheorwon-eup is constructed in 1946. Used as The House of Labor Party until the break of the Korean War, it is now one of the tourist attractions that keep the vestiges of the Korean War. This place was designated as a Cultural Property on February, 2001.

[2] Taebong or Later Goguryeo was a country established by Gung Ye on the Korean peninsula in 901 during the Later Three Kingdoms period.

[3] According to the official DMZ site, DMZ is a buffer zone to prevent an armed conflict after the armistice agreement. DMZ of Korea is established on 27 July, 1953 in accordance with 'The Armistice Agreement about military truce of Korea'. It is 248km long and 2km width on each side, south and north.

Table 1. Status of Major Cultural Assets in Cheorwon

Status	Name of property
National Treasure No.63	Dopiansa Cheoljobirojana Buddha Sitting Statue
Treasure No.223	Dopiansa Three-story Stone Tower
Natural Monument No.245	Habitat for Migratory
Natural Monument No.436	The Hantan River Daegyo-cheon Basalt Canyon
Gangwon-do Tangible Cultural Asset No.105	General Kim Eung-ha's epitaph
Gangwon-do Intangible Cultural Asset No.9	Sangnori Jigyeong Dajigi
Gangwon-do Monument No.8	Gosekjeong and Sundam
Gangwon-do Monument No.22	
Gangwon-do Monument No.72	Cheorwon Jiseok Tomb Group
	Chungryeolsa Site Municipal and Provincial
Gangwon-do Monument No.24	Monument
Gangwon-do Monument No.78	Cheolson Earthen Ramparts and Stone Structures
Gangwon-do Monument No.87	Seongsan Castle
Cultural Heritage Material No.33	Cheorwon Hyanggyo Site
Registered Cultural Asset No.22	Dongsong Mae Buddha Statue
Registered Cultural Asset No.23	Labor Party Headquarter
Registered Cultural Asset No.24	Methodist Church
Registered Cultural Asset No.25	Ice Warehouse
Registered Cultural Asset No.26	Agricultural Products Inspection Office
Registered Cultural Asset No.112	Seungil Bridge
Registered Cultural Asset No.137-2	Geumgang Mountain Electric Rail Bridge
Registered Cultural Asset No.160	Site of Financial Institutes' Association Office
	Water Supply Tower in the Waterworks Bureau

Cheorwon Office

When classifying these cultural assets, we have historical cultural assets such as Dopiansa and Cheorwon Hyanggyo[4] site that encompass hundreds of history and modern cultural assets such as Labor Party Headquarter, Seungil Bridge, Methodist Church and Agricultural Product Investigation Office. Basalt Canyon, Habitat for Migratory, and Goseokjeong[5] can be natural cultural assets representing the beautiful scenery of Cheorwon. Cultural assets dispersed in the area can be essential elements to compose an ecomuseum and we need to develop a program with diverse combinations considering the characteristics, movement lines, preference and taste of tourists.

---

[4] The Hyanggyo were state-run provincial schools established separately during the Goryeo Dynasty (AD918-1392) and Joseon Dynasty (AD1392-1910). They served primarily the children of the yangban, or ruling elite upper-class.

[5] Goseokjeong designated as nation tourist attraction in 1977 is one of Cheorwon 8 wonderful sceneries located on midstream of the Hantan River, which is famous for a huge curious rock dominating in the middle of the river.

2.2   Utilization and Improvements of Cultural Assets in Cheorwon

Cheorwon has been performing three programs for tourism. First, there is a security tourism program utilizing its geographical characteristics linking Iron Triangle War Remains, the second tunnel, Cheorwon Peace Observatory, Woljeong Station, Cheorwon Crane Observatory and Labor Party's Headquarters. The second course is the theme course mixing cultural assets and ecological attractions together including Sambuyeon Falls, Sundam Valley, Seungil Bridge, Goseokjeong, Jiktang Falls and Dopiansa, and the last is experiential course where tourists can experience and enjoy rafting, bungee jump, trekking, survival game, 4 wheel biking, cart riding and Haneoul path trekking.

However, these programs are not organically linked but performed independently. Therefore they are insufficient to solidify 'unification of local community and residents', the basic ideology of eco-museum. Tourists who participate in various tourism programs including security spots do not get good guidance. If educational program explaining history of the region and military cultural assets linking with military experience events such as survival games or simple military exercises is introduced rather than finishing the course as simple visits, it will improve the effects of security education and can be developed as tourism contents improving historical and geographical identity of Cheorwon located in the front line. If a program including visits of security places and military experiences targeting foreigners who are nearly impossible to get military training unlike Koreans with conscription system is introduced, it will give foreigners interesting and exotic experiences. Additionally, we can publicize our potential energy that developed democracy overcoming the ruins of war and achieved economic prosperity.

In case of ecological tourism, it is recommended to develop a 'Rice Farming Experience' program linking with Odae Rice, the main crop of Cheorwon. It will extend the stay of tourists and can be developed into the experiential program providing constant visits by season or by terms escaping from the one-time tour. During this process, local residents will actively participate in the delivery of their accumulated farming experiences. Ecological tourism and rice farming experiential program can be linked with local festival such as Taebong Festival in September and promote the festival by enjoying the delight of harvest together with local residents and tourists. Considering the zeal for educational in Korea, rice farming experience will gain popularity as natural ecology learning field of children who are born and brought up in cities.

To attract participation of local residents, culture interpretation programs should be expanded which is available to some security tourists only at the moment. For this, it is recommended to open local culture education program such as 'Introduction of Cheorwon' for local residents to improve their pride as residents and to provide them with opportunities to actively participate in tourism programs in the area. Considering that most of local economy improvement policies are being operated based on the experts' opinions rather than local residents' opinions regardless of their positive intentions, it is needed to organize a local committee responsible for education of community members and sharing roles in order to build a practical eco-museum. Such committee should select cultural assets of the area, recruit human resources and operate eco-museum letting the residents the subjects of the operation in order to make the sustainable development the area. Additionally, it is necessary to provide concrete assistance to the residents such as tax cut and subsidization by Cheorwon authority.

Cheorwon is one of the coldest places in Korea. If introducing efficient weather marketing, the severely cold weather can be another attraction of eco-museum. For example, it can hold a sports festival such as ski, skate and sledge, or snow or ice festival. Considering the big success of Hwacheon's 'Landlocked Salmon Festival', Cheorwon can be a tourists' attraction throughout the year if utilizing winter weather marketing on ecomuseum components.

Paradigm shift is required for military facility protection area which occupies 95% of Cheorwon area. Ironically, it is the power to protect the beautiful ecology by preventing reckless development. As a result, Cheorwon can preserve its clean nature as it does not have factories that contaminate the local environment. As the aforementioned, if we can transit the severely cold winter weather to positive element and make it a brand such as 'Mecca of Winter Sports', it will maximize the positive image of nature-friendly agricultural village preserved by military protection area.

Considering the present situation that smartphone users are increasing geometrically, it is needed to develop an app more actively. Such apps should be able to provide tangible and intangible information inclusively such as introduction and contact number of culture interpreter who can guide the tour, transportation and accommodation as well as basic tourism information such as location, history, things to do and things to eat. It is needed to pay delicate attentions to post services for tourists so that it may not be limited to one-time tour only. The provision of information on local festivals and events will enforce the communications between residents and tourists and naturally induce revisits of the tourists.

3   Conclusion

Once, security was perceived as negative mechanism coercing democracy under the name of 'anti-communism' in the tragic history of Korea. However, national security cannot be ignored even after the reunification because the geopolitical factors of the Korean Peninsula. Therefore, the location and history of Cheorwon are big assets. DMZ which represents painful history of Korea is a natural paradise with its dramatic story-telling and the well-preserved nature. Accordingly, ecomuseum of Cheorwon mixed with ecology, culture and Korean history will be the foundation of reunified Korea to transit its stiffened image to history education field as an advance guard of national security.

References

1. Bang, H.Y., Choi, H.S.: The Activation Guideline of Rural District and Eco-museum whole Area are Museu. The Journal of Korean Rural Architecture 4(3), 39–52 (2002)
2. Han, J.H., Park, K.B.: A Study on Preservation of Regional Inheritances and Utilization Method Based on the Concept of Eco-Museum - Focusing on Cheonan. Journal of Korean Architecture 11(1), 67–74 (2009)
3. Kang, H.K.: Discussing the Rural Area: Values and Utilization of Rural Resources Korea Rural Economy Institute and Korea Culture & Tourism Institute Joint Symposium, pp.3–14 (2010)
4. Davis, P.: Ecomuseums: A Sense of Place, Continuum, 2nd edn., pp. 3–49 (2011)

Internet Website

Korea Tourism Organization   www.asiaenglish.visitkorea.or.kr
Gangwon Province Office   www.provin.gangwon.kr
Cheorwon Office   www.cwg.go.kr

The International Sculpture Symposium in Icheon as Local Cultural Values and a Possibility of Ecomuseum

Eun Sok Bae and Sung Young Lee

Hankuk University of Foreign Studies, 107 Imun-ro, Dongdaemun-gu,
130-791, Seoul, Korea
best-96@hanmail.net, hlamb@hufs.ac.kr

Abstract. The present study aims to investigate the local-cultural values of International Sculpture Symposium Icheon (ISSI) which is one of the cultural and art resources of the city and its suitability for an eco museum. Started in 1998, ISSI was annually hosted until 2012, for 15 years where popular sculptors have participated and left outstanding art works. However, the international event has not been systematically managed or even properly promoted. To address these problems, spreading recognition that the art works left by world-class artists who participated in the ISSI are the culture and resources of Icheon city was necessary. Also, city officials, citizens, local artists and experts should discuss improving the brand value of the city. The present study suggests diverse methods for managing cultural contents and discussed how to develop and implement a cultural contents-oriented ecomuseum. The present study is meaningful in that it contributes to the sustainable development of Ichoen city.

Keywords: Ichoen, International Sculpture Symposium Icheon, Ecomuseum, Cultural contents, Sustainable Development.

1   Introduction

Icheon city, an urban-rural integrated city in Korea, where the annual artist festival, ISSI was hosted 15times, has been a part of the urban landscape and locality. The present study aims to discuss what the art works imply for the citizens and how the implications should be developed in the future. Icheon city has a unique culture of ceramics that has been traditionally handed down. Based on the unique culture, the city became the first city in Korea to be designated as a UNESCO Creative Cities in the category of crafts and folk arts, in July 2010.

The entry into the UNESCO Creative Cities Network has a lot to do with the cultural and artistic atmosphere of the city and the volunteering citizens. Besides the ceramics, ISSI is another cultural and art resources of Icheon. It was interesting that high renowned artists from all over the world complete their art works based on the inspiration they acquired while staying in Icheon. The sculptures created from the international events were installed throughout the city bringing about an atmosphere of public arts throughout the city. However the art works have neither been properly promoted nor systematically managed requiring the need for research in this field. In this regard, the present study makes a practical attempt to apply the concept of

T.-h. Kim et al. (Eds.): MulGraB/BSBT/IUrC 2012, CCIS 353, pp. 217–223, 2012.
© Springer-Verlag Berlin Heidelberg 2012

'Ecomuseum' to the city so that the local cultural and art resources can be utilized by constructing their network while being systematically collected, recorded and conserved.

2   Value and Potential of ISSI

2.1   What's ISSI

ISSI is an international artistic & cultural event aimed at; encouraging international exchange in the field of sculpture art; inheriting the historical value of international culture of sculpture; promoting the public's appreciation of sculptures; and forming an image of a cultural city for Icheon. The annual festival that has reached its 15th year in 2012 has represented monumental arts and crafts since 1998. The sculptures installed around Sulbong park and Oncheon Park have provided the visitors of Icheon with an opportunity to enjoy culture and arts of living and have contributed to the image of a creative city of Icheon.

Table 1. History of ISSI

	Period	Participants (nations)	Participant Artists (persons)	Art Works (ea)
1st	1998.7.10 - 7.24	22	23	23
2nd	1999.8.12 - 8.29	17	24	24
3rd	2000.8.17 - 9.3	13	15	15
4th	2001.9.1 - 9.18	14	15	15
5th	2002.9.1 - 9.18	8	14	14
6th	2003.9.18 - 10.2	12	13	20
7th	2004.9.1 - 9.24	8	8	8
8th	2005.8.26 - 9.12	12	14	14
9th	2006.9.1 - 9.18	10	14	14
10th	2007.11.1 - 11.19	8	8	9
11th	2008.8.22 - 9.11	6	10	10
12th	2009.3.13 - 4.3	4	10	10
13th	2010.8.26 - 9.16	5	10	10
14th	2011.9.20 - 10.10	6	10	10
15th	2012.7.9 - 7.31	6	10	10
Total		**50**	**188**	**206**

ISSI has so far presented 206 art crafts and 188 participants from 50 countries.

2.2 ISSI 2012

The present study investigated ISSI 2012 to figure out the characteristics of ISSI. The event was held from 9th through 30th July 2012 at Sulbong park in Icheon. 10 sculptors from China, Hungary, Spain, Malaysia as well as Korea created their works of art for 21 days on the theme "Sculpture, Embraces the light." The theme of the international art festival was selected by the committee based on the following reasoning.

Light is a decisive factor for the recognition of things.

In the beginning, from chaos, vacant darkness, a brilliant light sparks like a sudden explosion. Blue water soared up to the air to create a sky. Water under the sky created an ocean, and run to a place to reveal grounds. Out of the ground, wild herb, greens with seeds and trees with fruits grew up to finally create a law of beauty.

Now sculptures are yearning for transcendental investigation beyond perfection by calling in the aid of God. Sculptures turn shapes out of the mass and the lights shapes the extension of sculptures.

Physical beings will be born again with transcendental beauty by their creators' hands of artistry.

The arts and their creators were judged based on the above reasoning also made based on the artistic career and portfolios of the artists with their sketches for reflection of the theme. Preferred, are the artists who have vigorously worked in domestic and world stages, who can put endeavors to their art works during the festival, and who can create an art craft based on the theme of the symposium. Art crafts that fit to the theme of the symposium and that can be installed in public spaces such as an agricultural theme park in the city and that can be harmonized with the surrounding environment were selected. Based on this context, the symposium provide an opportunity to help people get closer to art by disclosing the process of the art crafts' creation. ISSI also aims at the exchange of opinions between the artists. The following table shows artists and their art works in ISSI 2012.

Table 2. Participant Artists & Art Works in ISSI 2012

Artist	Nationality	Art Work
Myung Keun Koh	Korea	The thing to watch
Seung Young Kim	Korea	Everyone has a garden in his heart.
Kuk Tak Chung	Korea	Pivotman
Ikk Hoon Eom	Korea	Propagation
Jae Choul Jeoung	Korea	Picture of Taoist
Isrvan Eross	Hungary	Untitled
Leandro Seixas	Spain	Butterflies
Lin Gang	China	The hosts of heaven
Rumen Dimitrov	Bulgaria	Shining Wave Project
Ramlan Abdullah	Malaysia	Minaret -Connections

As represented in the above table, artists from Hungary, Spain, China, Bulgaria and Malaysia with Korean artists created their art works in cooperation for 20 days during ISSI 2012.

2.3   Regional/Cultural Values of ISSI

(1) Temporality

Temporality refers to all the process a sculpture is made and takes its place in the lives of people. Temporality is an important feature of ISSI, signifying participation in the creation of art works, starting from nothing. All artists start with a sketch they created and work to make a complete shape. Icheon supports each artists with materials they need and provide staffs to support and assist the artists. During the 20 days, the participating artists create their art works and build friendship with each other by exchanging opinions. All the process of creation is open to the public so that people can watch and understand how an art work is created. The completed projects are installed throughout the city and will be a part of the landscape of the city and of the citizens' life. Now we discuss the process of creation of art work with a specific case. The following figures are art works created by Seung Young Kim during ISSI 2012.

Fig. 1. Everyone has a garden in his heart

As shown in Figure 1, Kim selected a spot and built a wall using bricks. The name of Kim's art work is 'Everyone has a garden in his heart', which is created based on the subject 'Memory.' Each red brick in his work lists a name of a person who resides in the memory of Kim. On a side of the wall stacked in a circle, we can see a steel door decorated with leaf-like shapes which people can walk through. Inside the wall, a tree is planted next to a lighting stand. When becomes dark outside, a yellowish-light shines on the wall. The difference of this art work is that it is created on the spot, not installed after being created. The creator described his expectation that the tree will grow as time goes by and thus complete the art work.

(2) Spatiality

Spatiality refers to the fact that art crafts created during the annual event contributes to the art and culture of the local public becoming cultural art resources of the city. Art crafting is carried out mainly in Sulbong Park, and the art works are moved to public places throughout the city. These works of art become a part of the daily lives of the citizens and visitors which can be easily accessed and appreciated.

Fig. 2. Creation to Installation of Art Work

In the left picture of Figure 2 Yincia Feng, a Chinese artist is working on his work 'Revised MoMo Doll No.6'in 2011, while the right picture shows an installed creation in a park in a harmony with the surrounding nature. The art work provides an artistic view on the public facility environment creating further energetic scenes. The annual festival that reached its 15th year in 2012, has represented monumental art crafts since 1998. The sculptures installed around Sulbong park and Oncheon Park have provided visitors of Icheon with an opportunity to enjoy culture and arts of living and have contributed to the image of the creative city of Icheon. ISSI has so far presented around 200 art crafts and 188 participants from 50 countries. However the art works have not been systematically managed and thus have become superannuated. Now, systematically managing and arranging the art works, participating artists and countries is necessary to conserve the culture and art resources of Icheon. To do so, the present study investigates methods to apply the concept of 'Ecomuseum' to the city so that the cultural art resources can be collected, recorded, conserved and utilized.

2.4   ISSI's Possibility to Be An Ecomuseum

The word 'Ecomuseum' was formed from the words 'eco' referring to ecology and residential environment and 'museum.' However, the word is muddled by similar words including ecology museum, environment museum, local museum, folks museum, écomusée and community museum. Ecomuseum is a new type of museum that inherits the local tradition and cultural/natural heritage, and descended customs and lifestyles. In the process of excavation, conservation, investigation and research of the customs and traditions, the residents can find their identity while visitors can experience the life in the city and can be informed of the local life. [1]

Peter Davis regarded the Ecomuseum as clasp to connect the pearls. He said one essential feature of any necklace is the clasp; without it such jewellery is useless. [2] Ecomuseum also functions as threads in a limited region to organically connect the local landscape, location, region, memory, nature, heritage and the community with each other. This also applies an organic function of connected sites in the city. In other words, the system connecting the core museum, peripheral museum and other useful sites has everything to do with being an Ecomuseum.[3] Ohara describes Ecomuseum with 3 core factors. According to Ohara, an Ecomuseum is formed by the interactions of three factors; heritage of the region, residents' participation and activities of museum based on the territory. Heritage refers to conservation of the natural environment, cultural heritage, industrial heritage and collected memories in the region. Participation of residents underlines voluntary participation of residents while being aware of their identities. Museum activities means typical, activities of museums such as excavation, exhibition, conservation, investigation and research.[4] Ecomuseum has its basis on the idea that the heritage in a community must be conserved in the very region and thus can be realized in the process of networking between the local communities for the contributions to the local communities development and sustainability. For Icheon, 15 year-old ISSI and cultural and art resources including the sculptures deployed in Sulbong and Hot Spring Parks are heritages of the region as well as museum activities. Also, the workshops in the region falls under cultural art resources. Nevertheless, Icheon has a relatively low level of resident participation in the conservation and investigation of the resources.

There are several ways to encourage the interest and participation of the residents. First, a smart application can help increase the interest in Icheon's cultural art resources. Using the app, information of the regional culture and art can be provided and distributed. Also the app can be used for notice on created arts from ISSI or guidelines helping citizens and visitors enjoy the event and the art. Using the apps, we can expect positive effects by connecting sightseeing and administration information.

Secondly, documentary film and promotion activities can address the problem. Documentary film showing and implying art and life, friendship, communication between volunteers and citizens can be made and used for exposures on Youtube and blogs.

Third is a publication based on sophisticated stories. The interviews of participating artists on their episodes and stories regarding their art, process and so forth can be introduced to further understanding of the arts and crafts itself. Also episodes regarding the art works and the citizens of   Icheon can also be acknowledged.

Fourth is a Photo/UCC competition and online exhibition. When based on this strategy, the public art awareness of ISSI can be improved and thus the ecomuseum in Icheon can be developed by integrated recognition.

If these measures are taken, it is possible to improve the public awareness and recognition of ISSI and its continuous activities for the past 15 years while also developing an ecomuseum which can integrate sculptures, ceramics craft culture, workshops and museums.

3   Conclusion

Icheon has developed diverse contents such as festival and rural theme park using local productions including rice, peach and corni. However content development efforts have not been actively made with consideration to the cultural art resources in the region. If using the suggestions provided in the present study, it is possible to realize sustainable development through building network of cultural art resources and rural resources. Ecomuseum which initiated in France, has spread all over the world in the form of a cultural movement for residents' community. Ecomuseum has especially influenced Japan where it thrived by combining with the concept of building up a community. If we adopt the concept of ecomuseum to Icheon, and develop an ecomuseum using cultural contents, it will expectantly improve the residents sense of ownership of the cultural art resources and their pride as well. This will also make contributions in making Icheon a better place, and the city's sustainable development in the future by fostering citizens' spirit of culture and art so that they can even enjoy them in their daily lives.

References

1. Bae, E.S.: Rural Ecomuseum Model Studies for Sustainable Development - Focus on Bu-raemi Community in Yulmyeon, HUFS, doctoral dissertation (2012)
2. Davis, P.: Ecomuseums A SENCE OF PLACE, Continuum (2011)
3. Ohara, K.: The community is full of treasures, Translated by Hyun Jeong Kim, Arche (2008)

A Cultural Environment Analysis and Use Proposal of HongDae Streets

Focused on Book Cafes

Jun-Ran Choi and Dae-Geun Lim

Department of Global Culture and Contents,
Graduate School Hankuk University of Foeign Studies, Korea
chran71@hanmail.net, rooot@hufs.ac.kr

Abstract. This study reviews the cultural characteristics of book cafés and suggests some methods to efficiently use city spaces such as book cafés. Why do publishing companies run book cafés of its own?: To meet with authors and readers as well as to promote their books. In other words, book cafés originally opened as a marketing strategy. But book cafés can be further developed to as a space with various cultural functions. Book cafés can offer more services for citizens and this study suggests that they should evolve to become a place for education and communication, as well as a place of multiple cultures.

Keywords: HongDae Streets, book cafés, Hongik University area, book festival, Cultural space, multi-culture.

1 Introduction

1.1 Background and Objective of Study

Hong-ik University (HongDae) district has become a very hot place in Korea. Young painters and artists come in groups to HongDae streets, offering their own unique items and sensitivity. Clubs in which many young people enjoy dance and song in are in full bloom. Novelty shops characterized by idea and specialty and cafés with diverse themes attract people. Troops of foreigners and young people who live in the country come and explore streets of HongDae.

As HongDae streets became famous, competition became tougher: shops with no particular competitive edge had hard time just to get by or to survive. The rise in rent made even the most popular stores to shut down and move to other areas: on the other hand, this also caused HongDae commercial district to widen further.

HongDae originally indicated Hong-ik University but it became a term which covers 200-meter radius from the gate of the university to Yang-Hwa riverside road. HongDae streets are widely divided into Wa-Woo Mountain Road, Picasso Streets and a parking lot alley. Wa-Woo Mountain Road starts from the gate of Hong-ik University to Sanwoolim Theater and on both sides of this road, there are art institutes, galleries and painting shops. This road best represents the image of the university as

T.-h. Kim et al. (Eds.): MulGraB/BSBT/IUrC 2012, CCIS 353, pp. 224–229, 2012.

the second largest art school in the world. Around Picasso street and parking lot alley, there are many restaurants, performance theater and cultural space like Sangsang-madang.

According to Jung-Ran Shin and Chang-Gyu Choi (2010)[1], Hongik University neighborhood has a complex culture based on painting, arts and club culture. This area has special human base like artists, professionals and specialists in cultural business and foreigners.

HongDae streets are crowded with foreigners, university students and tourists who have free and open mind., which mad Hongdae area the Mecca of street arts and club culture.

So-called book cafés in Korea were created amid this cultural phenomenon. This study will review the cultural characteristics of book cafés in this area, together with methods to efficiently use them as the city's cultural space.

1.2 Book Cafés: Cultural Characteristics and Current Status

HongDae area has special atmosphere with many artists and specialists engaged in music, design, advertisement, publishing and many other businesses.

Hongik University Station of airport railway opened lately to induce more foreign tourists, who use guest houses near HongDae area.[2] Between 1990 and 2000, guest houses were usually built in Jong-ro and Myeong-dong which are close to tourist attractions. But now, owing to convenience of traffic and HongDae street culture, many guest houses are built near HongDae.

The area is also packed with leading publishing companies, which also made the commercial district around HongDae even bigger. Then there came book cafés in large numbers.

Let's take a look at several book cafés around HongDae area.

Munhakdongne runs a book café called Café Comma. Here, publishers meet authors; and authors meet readers. Various companies hold events related to literature in this café . Inside, one wall is decorated with high bookshelves, adding class to the overall atmosphere. This café was used as the winter Olympian Yuna Kim shoot a commercial for a coffee brand and is often used as an interview venue for magazines and newspapers.

In Café Comma, customers can buy and have coffee, reading for free books published by Munhakdongne. They can also buy these books at 50% discount. Café Comma opened its second store lately, which has some library space so that customers can study and work here.

Another publisher, Chang-Bi, has opened Humanities Café Chang-Bi and holds events more than twice a week, with the books it has published. Average 80 people are invited at one event and drinks are free on these occasions. The café is virtually not for profit – it aims to serve the publisher's readers.

---

[1] Jung-Ran Shin, Chang-Gyu Choi:Impacts of Human Factors on the Placeness in the Hongik University Area, Journal of Urban Planning "Land planning" 45(2010), p. 6.

[2] http://www.hani.co.kr/arti/society/society_general/490786.html

Moonju Publishing Company has KAMA, an interdisciplinary art[3] space that has a book café at one corner. In KAMA, the publisher exhibits various artists' works, 50 pieces of performance materials and around 1,000 books it has published. The publisher also holds interdisciplinary art events or exhibitions with novelists, critics, painters, about five or six times a year.

There is a unique place run by Humanitas, which is famous for having the publishing company inside the café. You walk into the café and see the employees of the publisher working inside. The café announces on its website its reading meetings before a new book is published. When a new book comes out, Humanitas often offers reading events and meetings with authors.

To sum up, publishing companies open book cafés: first, to promote new books; second, to attract loyal readers; third, to give readers an opportunity to meet the publisher's employees or authors. Often the customers find the famous author sitting at the table next to them. Customers also can buy returned books at a specially reduced price. Besides, the readers and customers have an opportunity to participate in author's reading and book concert.

2   Main Analysis

2.1   Book Café's Function as a Cultural Space

A book café originally meant a place where customers could have coffee or tea and read books for free–books that were placed in the space as decorations. That is, at first book cafés were not connected with publishing company.

However, HongDae area as a publishing district enabled book cafés to sell books: now a book café means bookstore as well. A book café is a special cultural space where a publishing company can promote its new books, connecting books to readers, readers to authors.

However, this is not something new under the sun. In the early 2000s, there were publisher's book cafes although they closed soon after. Sigongsa opened Café Libro, located around the playground at the front of Hongik University

But why so many book cafés by publishers? Why now? The answer is that a book café has is not merely a place that sells coffee but a space with diverse multi-cultural functions.

Its first function is to offer a space where the publishers can sell new books and returned books[4] at discount.

Second function is to offer a venue for meetings with authors to and for the promotion of new books. Publishing companies do not depend only on traditional media or bookstores for promotion these days. There are new PR marketing strategy that

---

[3] Interdisciplinary art combines various genres such as music, arts and literature.

[4] Returned books: Stocks returned by the bookstore to the publishing company, after an extended period on bookshelves.

includes book concerts and readings, to freely communicate with readers and secure potential readers.

2.2 Cultural Events and Spaces Related to HongDae Book Cafés

1) Seoul Wa-Woo Book Festival
This festival is a multi-art, wide-range book festival that enables publishers, authors, public institutions and general citizens meet through books.

Book-play programs, meeting with authors, recitation nights, forums, lectures and symposium are offered in this festival.

2) Thanks-Books Bookstore
Thanks-Books opened near Sangsang Madang. It is a bookstore that best represents the characteristics and needs of the inhabitants around HongDae through the books on its bookshelves.

The bookstore looks like an art gallery with books from outside and it also has an atmosphere of a book café. Thanks-Books holds many events where artists-authors and inhabitants around HongDae district can gather together.

3) Integrated Cultural Space
There are so many integrated cultural spaces that offers exhibitions, performances and other events in HongDae district. Eri café is one of them: it is a book caféspecializing in arts and it offers books on design, photography and fine arts that cannot be easily found in Korea. It also offers various events including plays, performances and exhibitions.

Anyung Bada calls itself an "Indie Café." It is favored by the general public as a place to enjoy the indie-culture, whose distinctive aspects have been neutralized so much as the district is becoming more and more commercial. On weekends, the book café offers free indie band performances and arts exhibitions by indie artists.

2.3 Proposal to Use Book Café as a Cultural Space

Cultural characteristics around HongDae district is in full bloom. However, if they are driven purely by commercialism, the place will turn into a place of simple entertainment–people will come here only in pursuit of eat, play and spend. Yet many are striving to protect and advance the area even further, with its unique cultural characteristics intact. For this purpose, book cafés can be of much use, and this study offers some proposals in this regard.

A cultural space is recognized as a space or facility that can directly produce and educate some cultural products in life or where citizens can come and appreciate arts and culture. In this study, a cultural space generally includes: a place lawfully classified as a "cultural facility"[5]; and a "potential space"[6] that has not been designated as a cultural facility by law but that can accommodate cultural activities.

---

[5] According to the law of culture art(2008), the cultural facilities are classified as performance facilities, exhibition facilities, city facilities and so on.

A book café is a potential space in this regard and hence can be further developed by public institutions and specialists in community culture in this district. The proposal here is that book cafés run by publishing companies be expanded further to take charge of cultural training in the community as well.

First, these book cafés can offer citizens a wider range of services. For example, publishers can make joint efforts, including book outlets or used book bazaars or discussion forum for reading in general.

Second, publishers can work together with public institutions and make education programs in which tourists can participate. A tourist's guide for book cafés might be useful, as well as HongDae street guide, in as many language as possible. Book cafés can function as a medium that communicates cultural characteristics of this area.

Another suggestion is a multi-culture book café for foreign residents in Korea. The first multi-culture book café has been opened by Su-won Foreigner's Welfare Center[7] in March of 2011. It can work as a center for education and communication for foreign residents, offering some Korean language programs. If properly operated, it can go beyond a book café and become a community space.

3   Conclusion

This study reviews the cultural characteristics of book cafés and suggests some methods to efficiently use city spaces such as book cafés.

HongDae area is crowded with painters, artists and musicians–it is virtually a Mecca of club culture. Since the 2000s, publishers gathered around this district and opened many book cafés: Café Comma, Humaniies Café Chang-bi, KAMA and so on.

Why do they run book cafés of its own?: To meet with authors and readers as well as to promote their books. In other words, book cafés originally opened as a PR marketing strategy.

But book cafés can be further developed to as a space with various cultural functions. They can offer more services for citizens and this study suggests that they should evolve to become a place for education and communication, as well as a place of multi-culture. They should act as an open cultural space, offering joint book outlets or used book bazaars and so on.

They can also work with public institutions, creating education programs for foreign tourists and attracting them to the book cafés to experience the cultural characteristics of the area. A multi-culture center created together with a community center will be very useful.

A cultural space must change according to the needs of the times. There should be more studies in this regard, to explore various methods to use cultural spaces in our society.

---

[6] Potential space means parks, squares, public spaces in commercial districts, cafés or clubs, where performances can be done. It means commercial spaces in the city that are closely related to the production and consumption of culture.

[7] http://www.anewsa.com/print_paper.php?news_article=news_article&number=196410

References

1. Kim, H.-J.: Building Culture Complex Belt of Innovation City through Mixture of Cultural, Educational and Public Space. Journal of the Korea Contents Association Book 10(9) (2010)
2. Park, N.-J., Han, B.-S.: Discourses on the Meaning of Consumption in Cultural Space: Case Study of "Free Admission". Policy, Korea Tourism Society Tourism Research Book 33(4) (2009)
3. Seo, B.-K., Lee, J.-W., Ha, J.-M.: A Basic Study on Types of Cultural Space Formation in Downtown. Architectural Institute of Korea 24 (2008)
4. Kwon, D.-Y., Kim, K.-H.: A Study on the Changes in Urban Architectures and its Implications:Focused on Hong-dae area. Seoul, Architectural Institute of Korea Book 29(1) (2009)
5. Shin, J.-R., Choi, C.-G.: Impacts of Human Factors on the Placeness in the Hongik University Area. Land Planning: A Journal of Urban Planning Book 45(7) (2010)
6. Oh, D.-H.: A Comparative Study on Successful Cases of the Advanced Urban Regeneration "Granville Island, Vancouver vs. KulturBrauerei, Berlin. Korean Society for city administration Urban Public Administration Book 23(1) (2009)
7. HANkyoreh Information, http://www.hani.co.kr
8. Asia News Agency, http://www.anewsa.com

Contextual Environments of DMZ Docs

Na Yun Kim, Jae Yeong Lee, and Sangheon Kim

Hankuk University of Foreign Studies, 107 Imun-ro, Seoul, Korea
luce728@naver.com, jylee@hufs.ac.kr, shkim@gcrc.kr

Abstract. The DMZ Korean International Documentary Film Festival is a film festival held in Paju which is the only demilitarized zone of a divided country in the world and at the same time a book city. DMZ is the only Demilitarized Zone in the world, where the reality of national division into North and South can be known. Cultural resources and context of DMZ are considered which is foundation of DMZ DOCS contents. The value of DMZ and the context of DMZ Docs presented in this study will contribute to discovery of diverse subject matters and values as well as planning and development of contents suitable for the ecological environment of the area.

Keywords: DMZ Docs, DMZ, DMZ cultural resources, DMZ context.

1   Introduction

DMZ is the only Demilitarized Zone in the world, where the reality of national division into North and South can be known. It is a symbol of life and communication space of peace and ecological environment, and is a tourist attraction in Korea most preferred by foreign tourists.

The DMZ Korean International Documentary Film Festival is a film festival held in Paju which is the only demilitarized zone of a divided country in the world and at the same time a book city. This is the 4th year the place of harmonization of the world people is held under the slogan of peace, life and communication of DMZ. It is not too much to say that the growth of the DMZ Korean International Documentary Film Festival has been influenced by the peculiarity of the space, DMZ.

The objective of this study is to analyze the temporal and spatial context as well as social context of such DMZ Korean International Documentary Film Festival (hereinafter called "DMZ Docs"). This paper is comprised as follows: In Chapter 2, the basic content of the DMZ Docs is introduced; in Chapter 3, the political, social and cultural background of the DMZ is explained; in Chapter 4, the content of the DMZ Docs event is analyzed around the 2012 program; and, in Chapter 5, a conclusion is made.

2   Explanation of DMZ Docs

The DMZ Korean International Documentary Film Festival is a festival held since 2009 in Paju which is the only demilitarized zone of a divided country in the world

T.-h. Kim et al. (Eds.): MulGraB/BSBT/IUrC 2012, CCIS 353, pp. 230–237, 2012.

and at the same time a book city. The characteristics of the DMZ Korean International Documentary Film Festival held under the slogan of peace, life and communication, though it is paradoxical in DMZ which is a space of division, confrontation and tension, are as follows:

First, it is a film festival held with a spatial background of DMZ, the only demilitarized zone in the world. An international documentary film festival held in a DMZ where numerous species of animals and plants are distributed and the natural ecology system is well preserved can be said to have properly reflected the spatial context of DMZ. Opening a film festival under the theme "Peace, Life and Communication" in the only zone which symbolizes military confrontation and division contributes to conversion of the image of DMZ to a positive aspect. Also, harmonization of DMZ, a space where nature and ecology, sorrows of life in a troubled region, peace and diverse communications coexist, with documentary genre makes the most of the characteristics of DMZ space and creates a synergy effect.

Second, it is a film festival characterized by documentary genre. In this era of fusion when Internet, communication and broadcasting have been fused and communication with public originators such as UCC has become important since 2000s, an international documentary film festival becomes a place where we can communicate with world people under the diverse themes such as politics, economy, society, history, culture and nature, in the aspect that documentary is the field where participation of public has been achieved first of all.

Third, it contributes to securement of popularity and industrialization/ advancement of film festival through programs and diverse planned events connected with the film festival. Project Market-Crossing Borders held for the first time in Korea in 2012 contributes to advancement of domestic film industry by fostering domestic documentary producers equipped with international competitiveness, and it is a productive film festival which contributes to establishment of a global network wherein domestic and overseas documentaries exchange with each other, by arranging a chance for domestic documentaries to enter into overseas market and for foreigners to make an investment in Korea. Moreover, it is a chance to experience the meaning and nature of the DMZ Korean International Documentary Film Festival in person not only by wishing for successful opening of the film festival through planned events such as the DMZ Peaceful Bicycle March or the Sangsangdonghwa Parade but also by experiencing the meaning of peace, life and communication the DMZ has.

Fourth, it is a film festival designed for diverse classes of public through production of the related programs such as documentaries for teenagers. Diverse classes of audience from teenagers to the aged together deliver the DMZ's spirit of peace, life and communication through diverse subsidiary events such as the Teenager Documentary Discussion Contest, and Documentary Essay Contest, and contribute to expansion of the base of documentary. Finally, DMZ Korean International Documentary Film Festival is a film festival held in the film production center located in the northwestern Gyeonggi area, and, at the same time, is taking off as the biggest international documentary film festival in Asia utilizing DMZ.

3   DMZ and Cultural Resources

DMZ is a military buffer zone between South Korea and North made as a result of the Korean War, and is a demilitarized zone where arming is prohibited by an international convention or agreement. Though it is difficult to analytically list the roles/functions of DMZ and the elements of resources which provide such roles/functions as they are mutual connected, the locational/spatial, historic/cultural, ecological/environmental and war/security related resources of the whole area of DMZ can be stereotyped in spatial, temporal and social contexts as follows:

1) Spatial Context of the Whole Area of DMZ

The whole area of DMZ which refers to the demilitarized zone in a wide meaning includes DMZ, the controlled and protected area pursuant to the Protection of Military Bases and Installations Act (Civilian Control Line: CCL), and the boarder area pursuant to Border Area Support Act. At present, the area of DMZ is about 907 km², and, though there is no barrier like a barbed wire fence on the MDL (Military Demarcation Line) itself and the 4 km space between the barbed wire fences on the southern and the northern limit lines installed 2 km away from the MDL respectively is physically closed, it is an open space ecologically, culturally and historically. At present, as the area to the south of the MDL is under the control of the Military Armistice Commission (MAC) of UN, entry into the DMZ is not possible without getting a permit from the MAC and the total number of persons allowed to enter the area at one time cannot exceed 1,000.

The CCZ (Civilian Control Zone) is a control and protection area established within 10 km to the south of the MDL wherein general activities of civilians such as entry are restricted, and the designated area within 25 km to the south of MDL (about 4,904 km²) is classified as a Military Installations Protection Zone.

The Border Area, at present, lies over 15 cities and guns of Gyeonggi-do, Gangwon-do and Incheon Metropolitan City, and is largely classified into DMZ, and the northern and southern areas of CCL, and the whole northern area of CCL and a part of the southern area of CCL are managed being designated as a Military Installations Protection Zone.

2) Temporal Context of DMZ (Formation History)

DMZ was installed by the provision of Paragraph 1, Article 1 of the Armistice Agreement concluded on July 27, 1953 after the Korean War was stopped, which reads "Occurrence of accidents which may cause recurrence of hostile actions shall be prevented by setting a MDL and by both parties retreating 2 km from the MDL respectively to establish a DMZ between the hostile countries as a buffer zone." The Korean DMZ means the buffer zone of about 300 million pyeong established between the southern and northern limit lines 2 km away to the south and north from the MDL which extends over 155 miles (about 248 km) from the estuary of Imjin River to the west to Myeongho-ri, Goseong of the East Coast (Unification Observatory).

3) Social Context of DMZ

① Residents of DMZ

The CCL villages in the whole area of DMZ belong to Paju-si, and Yeoncheon-gun of Gyeonggi-do, and Cheolwon-gun of Gangwon-do under the administrative district system, and total 1,049 households and 2,651 persons are residing in 10 places including the Village of Freedom (Daeseong-dong Village) located in the DMZ, and most of the residents are engaged in farming.

② Ecological/environmental Resources of DMZ

The ecological system of the DMZ is evaluated to be a global ecological area as a space which symbolizes the recuperative power of nature, and the government, Gyeonggi-do and Gangwon-do are currently striving for designation of the DMZ as a UNESCO Biosphere Reserve. Total 1,930 species of diverse living things and endangered rare species including 151 families/2,451 species of plants, 16 families/45 species of mammals, 29 families/260 species of birds, 12 families/31 species of amphibians and reptiles, and 35 families/143 species of fishes are inhibiting in this area. Moreover, as there are 12 natural monuments, 3 natural reserves of 287,741,346 ㎡ size, and there is a place designated as an Ecological and Scenery Conservation Area, it is also a superior ecological area selected by the Ministry of Environment. As it has been almost free of artificial influence because there has been no human approach for a long period of time since the armistice in 1953, it has an important function for academic research on ecology or in the aspect of education, tourism and environment.

③ Historic and Cultural Resources of DMZ

There are numerous cultural resources such as remains and records related to the stream of times from the epoch of three kingdoms to Joseon Dynasty, and 43 state designated cultural assets, and 21 city/province designated and non-designated cultural assets are distributed over the area. Historic and cultural resources are evenly distributed over Paju-si and Yeoncheon-gun of Gyeonggi-do, and Cheolwon-gun, Hwacheon-gun, Yanggu-dun and Goseong-gun of Gangwon-do, and, as we can say the history of Korea starts from the basins of Imjin River and Hantan River which are CCZs, it is utilized as an element of education and tourism.

④ War/Security related Resources of DMZ

The resources are divided into the remains and traces generated during the Korean War (6.25), the underground tunnels and infiltration routes, and observation decks/observation posts made under the divided situation after the war, and the symbolic icons built praying for peace. The observation decks/observation posts made after the war are used for military purpose and as observatories for tourists. Among those, Dorasan Station, a symbol of peace, is the northernmost station of railroad located at Dorasan-ri, Gunnae-myeon, Paju-si, Gyeonggi-do, within the CCL, which connects Seoul and Sinuiju. It is a place which became a representative symbol of peace after George W. Bush, the US president, who visited Korea in 2002 had an event of signing on a railway sleeper, and a symbol of longing for unification of Han Peninsular after the visit of the late president Kim Dae-jung.

Table 1. Cultural Resources of DMZ

Type of Resources		Resource Elements	Summary	Resource Examples
Ecological·Environment Resources	Level of Number of Species of Living Things	Biological Diversity	Total 2,930 species of living things comprised of ▪ 2,451 species of plants, ▪ 45 species of mammals, ▪ 260 species of birds, ▪ 31 species of amphibians and reptiles, ▪ 143 species of fishes, are inhibiting.	All species of living things in the DMZ, Red-crowned cranes, Spoonbills, goats, etc.
		Endangered Species	Total 82 endangered species comprised of ▪ 14 species of plants, 11 species of mammals, 41 species of birds, 5 species of amphibians and reptiles, 11 species of fishes, are inhibiting. ▪ Natural monuments of 6 species of mammals, 31 species of birds and 2 species of fishes are inhibiting.	
		Rare Species	▪ 95 rare species of plants and 2 rare species of fishes are inhibiting.	
	Level of Ecological System	Specific Habitats	▪ 12 natural monuments (including 3 natural reserves), 7 forest genetic resource reserve, 1 wetland protection area and 2 ecology and scenery conservation areas.	Forest, soil and river basins in the DMZ, etc.
		Forest/Soil	▪ Forest and soil environment in the whole area of DMZ	
		Wetlands	▪ 31 wetlands	
	Level of Scenery	Habitats Connectivity	▪ DMZ space which forms the east-west ecological axis	Water surface scenery, columnar joints and forest scenery in the whole DMZ
		Peculiar Scenes/ Geographical Features	▪ Watersides, wetlands, forest scenery and columnar joints	
Historic/Cultural Resources		Historic/ cultural Resources	▪ 43 state designated cultural assets ▪ 21 city/gun designated and non-designated cultural assets	Historical sites such as Prehistoric remains, Royal tombs, and Mountain fortress, and cultural assets, ferries
		Culture of Divided Society	▪ 10 CCL villages/2,651 residents ▪ Military culture, military facilities, etc.	Villages and military facilities

Table 1. (*continued*)

War/Security related Resources	War Remains and Traces	• Panjunjeom, Bridge of Death, Bridge of freedom, Gyeongui Line locomotive, angle of intersection of Gyeongui Line Bridge, Jangdan-myeon Office, Old Jangdan Station site, Freedom House, bridge of electric railroad in Geumgang mountain, Station building in Sintan-ri, Janggun ferry, Bridge of No Return, etc.	War sites and records, Panmungeom, Gyeongui Line locomotive, End point of railroad, Bridge of Freedom, and DMZ itself
	Symbolic Icons of Division	• Underground tunnels/infiltration route, observation decks/observation ports, monuments, symbols of peace in the whole area of Imjingak, etc.	DMZ itself, Observatories, Underground tunnels, and **Dorasan Station**

Though DMZ is a site of confrontation and conflict historically remembered together with the war, it is paradoxically a place having a potential of communication and coexistence. The intangible value elements of the residents and soldiers who create unique life culture within the topography, scenery and living things in the DMZ, numerous historic remains and stories they contain, and controls and restrictions, mutually and complexly influence each other under the spatial, temporal and social contexts.

4   2012 DMZ Docs Contents

A film festival is a place of festival communicating with the audience through films. A film festival can be largely divided into various subsidiary events such as programs, opening ceremony and closing ceremony, special exhibition, and programs connected to the film festival such as market. The main contents of the DMZ Korean International Documentary Film Festival held for 7 days from Sep. 21 to 27, 2012, were as follows:

First, the most basic and representative factor of a film festival is the program, and diverse films of the countries all over the world strictly selected are shown. For the fourth DMZ Korean International Documentary Film Festival, 665 movies from 80 countries have entered, among which 115 movies from 37 countries strictly selected reflecting the identity of the film festival have been shown. The film festival program in this year consisted of diverse sections such as 'Global Vision' which introduced the competitive sector (international competition, competition of Korean movies, and competition among movies produced by teenagers), superior works of masters, and the latest controversial works, 'Gaze of Asia' which showed the present address of Asian documentaries which bound forward recently, and 'Special Showing of Polish Documentaries' which shows a collection of documentaries of Poland, a traditional strong producer of documentaries. In the aspect of the themes of the program as well, while there were many movies focused on the conflicts and disputes of DMZ in the past, the width and subject matters were widened to environment, poverty, discrimination and corrupted judicial system in this year. This means that the film festival is making efforts to become a film festival which widely covers the documentary genre breaking away from the political and social ideologies, and to closely breath with public through documentary films.

The next things which show the nature of a film festival are opening ceremony, closing ceremony and various planned events. The opening ceremony of the fourth DMZ Korean International Documentary Film Festival was held in Dorasan Station Building. The Dorasan Station located in the CCL is the northernmost railroad station and is currently a historic and cultural space represented as a place symbolizing peace, and adds to the meaning of the DMZ film festival together with the temporal/spatial context and social context of DMZ.

In addition, the DMZ People Photo Exhibition of Kim Joong-man photographer is a special exhibition of the pictures of the landscape in the DMZ of the only divided area in the world and the people who have been living there, taken with the 60th anniversary of armistice ahead, and is shedding new light on the value of DMZ which has been the symbol of the cold war and division.

'Sansangdonghwa' of Lee Yong-baek producer: For the planned performance of 'Angel Solider & Flower Tank' parade, a flower tank with a message of peace was built by decorating a tank with flowers, and about 100 persons comprised of a drum and fife band, general citizens, north Korean defectors, movie directors, and actors marched along the street together with the tank wearing military uniforms. Sangsangdonghwa is an ambiguous title bearing the meaning of the reality of division, and, though it looks like coexistence of war and peace which are mutually different, it contains the theme consciousness behind it that they are after all one.

In addition, the DMZ Korean International Documentary Film Festival is making efforts to take off as the key Asian film festival through conversation with movie directors and audience, and support for teenagers' production.

5   Conclusion

DMZ is an area formed as a result of Korean War. The unique historic, cultural and eco-environmental background this area has gives it a special value as a cultural resource. The DMZ Docs is a documentary film festival which has the environment of DMZ as the background. In addition to the intrinsic events of film festival, it is contributing to re-discovery of the value of DMZ through diverse programs which uses the DMZ as the motive. The value of DMZ and the context of DMZ Docs presented in this study will contribute to discovery of diverse subject matters and values as well as planning and development of contents suitable for the ecological environment of the area.

References

1. Choi, S.-R., Park, E.-J.: Conservation Values of Major Resources in the Korean DMZ and its Vicinity, RIG·GRI (2010)
2. Sung, H.-C., et al.: A Study on the Conservation of Natural Environment & Ecotourism on DMZ, GRI (2007)
3. Kim, D.-H., et al.: Report on Performance Analysis of The First DMZ Korean International Documentary Film Festival, Gyeonggi-do, Gyeonggi Film Commission (2010)
4. Kim, D.-H., et al.: Report on Performance Analysis of The Second DMZ Korean International Documentary Film Festival, Gyeonggi-do, Gyeonggi Film Commission (2011)

The Korean Wave: A Decade of Ups and Downs

Jin Young Kim and Jong Oh Lee

Hankuk University of Foreign Studies, 107 Imun-ro, Dongdaemun-gu,
130-791, Seoul, Korea
staci21@naver.com, santon@hanmail.net

Abstract. The Korean wave or Hallyu refers to the phenomenon of Korean entertainment and popular culture causing a great sensation in the world with pop music, TV dramas, and movies. Over the last decade, Korea has emerged as a new center for the production of transnational pop culture. However, an anti-hallyu movement is often rising in some parts of the world. In this regard, this study suggests that we should look back on the decade by analyzing the backlashes and achievement of Hallyu to develop concrete ideas on how to consistently develop it. In order to do so, it is essential for the government to contribute to the progress of cultural exchange with countries where Korean pop culture is making inroads.

Keywords: the Korean wave, Hallyu, anti-Hallyu, entertainment business, K-pop, Korean drama.

1   Introduction

Numerous popular culture contents have been introduced to international market since *'Winter Sonata'* which brought sensational popularity of Korean dramas in early 2000s. However, there are some problems behind the glory of Hallyu or so-called the Korean wave, which has astronomical economic value, has made the unprecedented diplomatic achievements in history and has lifted the national brand of Korea. As seen in conflicts between JYJ and SM Entertainment, crooked profit sharing structure between stars and entertainment companies and the issue of unequal contract so to speak slave contract often make legal disputes as more and more stars go overseas and the profit scale of related fields is growing enormously. Additionally, poor production environments in broadcasting and movie industry cause criticisms such as the mass production of fragment script dramas or poor remakes.

In music industry, similar looking new groups boasting of well-made group dancing with dance music have been being introduced nearly every day, as many idol groups get popular among youths. Of course, there can be some idol singers equipped with talents and gifts but most of young singers are being forgotten after a few years' popularity in spite of such years of severe training.

In addition to somewhat backward production system and problems in related personnel nurturing system in Korea, external problems are not a few. There is a new trend of resistance such as hatred and disgust against Korea. When looking into

T.-h. Kim et al. (Eds.): MulGraB/BSBT/IUrC 2012, CCIS 353, pp. 238–243, 2012.
© Springer-Verlag Berlin Heidelberg 2012

Hallyu from the positive perspectives, we can self-praise it as Asia Continent centered culture phenomenon. On the other hand, we need to examine if Korean pop culture is peppered throughout the world based on the respect of the local cultures. It has already been 10 years since the new terminology 'Hallyu' emerged in early 2000. As it is said that 10 years changes everything, Hallyu has been changed many times and is entering its maturity. Therefore, it is time to establish prospective cooperation with other cultures and to prepare grounds to leap into culturally advanced countries. To do this, this study reviewed the achievements and the future tasks of Hallyu and tried to propose a method for the sustainable development.

2   Achievement of the Korean Wave

Hallyu can be divided into many stages such as development stage from late 1990s to early 2000s, growth stage from early 2000s to mid 2000s and maturity after mid 2000s to present. Since the late 1990s, the Korean Wave has spread in Asian countries including China, Taiwan, Vietnam, Singapore, and Japan. A Korean drama, titled *What is Love All About?* broadcast through Chinese TV in 1997, became the first hit Korean drama while Autumn Tale gained popularity on Taiwanese television. Gradually, in Vietnam, 60 Korean dramas were broadcast between 1997 and 2000 alone. In Japan, Korean actors Yong-Jun Bae and Yong-Ha Park, heroes on *Winter Sonata*, became the most popular celebrities in 2004. According to a report from a Japanese institute, this unbelievably popular drama has helped create more than $2 billion effect in exports that includes tourism to Korea in the mid-2000's.

Hallyu has been growing up to be a motive power of trading thanks to cultural contents since mid 2000s. In 2000s, Hallyu has moved its horizon to culture contents business which is welcomed as highly value-added futuristic industry including games, shows, dramas and movies. As cultural contents industry grows more than 6.3% in average between 2004 and 2008, the full scale growth stage has been announced. Additionally, culture contents overseas marketing has made its first step in mid 2000s by grafting Hallyu with exporting business. In particular, it is significant that the grafting of Hallyu and export marketing was very successful in China, one of the biggest exporting counterparts of Korea.

Not only in Asian countries but also in Europe, the Korean Wave reached France, which is a core of European culture. In 2011, Korean pop music industry held a large scale concert in Paris for the first time in Korean pop music history mainly by entertainers in SM Town. It was a big success with long queue of ticket-buyers and the emergence of black market. It was an event showing Hallyu's success beyond Asia. The love on K-pop of Hallyu fans naturally lead them to the favorable feelings on Korean products and travel sites. According to the survey by Paris Branch Office of Korea Tourism Organization through its overseas PR site (www.visitkorea.or.kr), this trend becomes more conspicuous. In particular, more than 90% of Hallyu fans in France answered that they would like to visit Korea, while 72.1% answered 'Came to know Korea for the first time' and 66.3% answered that 'Came to have interest in Korean culture' after listening to K-pop. Generally speaking, Hallyu fans came to have integrated motivation to learn Korean culture after contacting Korean cultural contents such as K-pop or dramas. It seems very positive for the continuous culture exchange and expansion of the base.

As the Korean Wave has clearly become a major trend in pan-Asian pop culture, it has inspired high domestic expectations for both commercial profit and promotion of national brand. The Korean government and corporations have been eager to promote its essence and develop necessary strategies to sustain it. The Korean government introduced the Basic Law for Cultural Industry Promotion in 1999 and launched the Culture and Content Agency under the purview of the Ministry of Culture and Tourism in 2001. In 2002, Online Digital Contents Industry Development Act was enacted to contribute to enhancement of quality of life and sound development of national economics by fixing necessary items for the promotion of contents industry to compose the base of contents industry and enforce competitiveness. In 2010, basic plans regarding contents industry promotion were established to secure government driven contents industry development system, and Online Digital Contents Industry Development Act was amended in full scale and renamed as 'Contents Industry Promotion Act' to secure various administrative and financial supporting grounds necessary for the development of contents industry. In 2012, Ministry of Culture, Sports and Tourism officially established 'Hallyu Culture Promotion Organization' to promulgate Korean traditional culture grafting with its pop culture. Additionally, Korea foundation for International Culture Exchange is the organization established to continue and develop Hallyu, in which Korea Cultural Contents Promotion Corporation, Game Industry Development Corporation, Broadcasting Media Industry Promotion Corporation, Independent Production Association, and the Federation of Korean Industries are participating as board members.

In spite of the concerns of bureaucracy depending on the success of Hallyu, it is evident that public policies and institutions acted favorably on Korean Contents' entering international market. According to the international income and expenditure statistics by Bank of Korea, the revenue of Hallyu related contents from overseas broke the record of 150 billion won in the first half of 2012, and foreign currency income related to K-Pop and media contents reached 150 billion won in the first half. It is 11% increase from the first half of last year. From this context, Hallyu naturally contributed to export increase of Korean products by expanding Korean culture, and brought visible economic effects such as enhancement of the national brand image in a relatively short time.

What are the backgrounds of the success of Hallyu to become a mainstream of Asian culture? The first cause can be found in the commonality that Asian people share. Popular culture is delivered to the accommodators who have similar culture and emotion in the region. In other words, nostalgia to the virtues that are forgotten in industrial communities such as respect to the old and filial love between parents and children and similar racial characteristics in the contents made Hallyu delivered beyond the physical national boundaries in Asia.

From the perspective of external aspects such as laws, institutions, technologies and environments necessary for the expansion of contents, the change of mediascape and the development of digital media played important roles. It is the same context of the mega hit of Psy's 'Gangnam Style' without special PRs recording over 300 million downloads in YouTube at the end of September 2012. Large entertainment companies in Korea usually upload music video on YouTube when artists release new numbers to share it with fans. Additionally, they usually communicate with fans through their homepages or Facebook pages when they select a new song for media exposure and fix concert schedule, and make efforts to reflect requirements of fans whenever they can. While culture was transmitted through direct contacts in the past, the emergence of new media made it possible to expand a culture without direct contacts.

3   Anti-Hallyu

As Hallyu became popular in pan-Asia area, there became a new motion of 'Anti-Hallyu' which means resistance to Korean popular culture and Korea itself because of the added economic and cultural values of Hallyu. Nevertheless, the analysis of anti-Hallyu is not sufficient comparing to the studies on its achievements and policy supports, and is limited to protective and temporary resolutions rather than fundamental solutions based on the mutual sympathy. If the success of Hallyu is based on the commonality that can encompass pan-Asia, anti-Hallyu may be resulted from the overlook on differences between Korean culture and local cultures shown at encounters. It does not end with the reduced export of Korean dramas but may cause multi-faceted conflicts in politics, social matters and economics with the counterpart countries.

Anti-Hallyu is spewed whenever there are politically sensitive issues such as history or territory issues in Hallyu core countries such as Japan and China. For example, 'Manga Anti-Hallyu' published in 2006 in Japan sold more than 300,000 copies in a month in spite of hostile and crooked descriptions. There are trials to make use of anti-Hallyu to consulate communities in Japan after earthquake in 2011, and in 2010 an actress who was appointed as an Ambassador of Dokdo had to quit her activities because of demonstrations of right-wing organizations. In July, 2011, Takaoka Soske, a Japanese actor starred in Japanese movie 'Bakchigi' describing the sorrows of Korean-Japanese in Japan posted a text in his twitter that jobs for Japanese entertainers were reduced as Korean dramas and songs became the main subjects of Japanese mass media, which fueled the controversy of Anti-Hallyu. Recently, with the visit of Dokdo by President Lee Myung-bak, anti-Korea fever has been raised and some of Hallyu stars were refused to enter Japan. As such Hallyu in Japan is the scale showing the political dynamics of two countries. Anti-Hallyu opinions are distributed through non-official paths such as internet sites like 2ch, personal blogs, and bulletin board of right-wing organizations rather than official and trust-worthy media such as newspapers and broadcast.

China was very favorable to Korean pop culture in early times, as it first used the pronoun of 'Hallyu' in 1999. However, when the popularity triggered by dramas became so high as to change the tastes of youths with K-pop, it raised criticism on the occlusive characteristics of Korean culture industry and history distortion through patriotic historical dramas through mass media. China made it a policy to regulate Hallyu concretely since mid 2000s. As a result, in golden hours of 7 to 10 pm foreign contents cannot be broadcasted in 2012. The Chinese government also limited total on air time of foreign dramas and regulated Hallyu. China expressed uncomfortable feelings for the strong pride of Korean culture, and considered the excessively ethnic colors as cultural chauvinism. Most of Chinese mass media criticized the quality of cultural products and personal problems of stars such as same monotonous stories in dramas, too expensive guarantees, or insincere attitude of some stars. As in Japan, anti-Hallyu in China is mostly from misunderstanding and hostility because of political situations between Korean and China rather than the criticism against the popular culture itself. Especially, after the establishment of Lee Myung-bak administration, the relationship has become distant and negative feelings against Korea in China has been increasing because of default or overdue wages of Korean companies in China. Accordingly, Korean producers are looking for alternatives to overcome anti-Hallyu in China such as starring Korean stars in Chinese dramas or producing programs with Chinese productions.

In Thailand, the popularity of Hallyu started with the fever of '*Daejanggeum*' in mid 2000s, and the interest in Korean culture including cosmetics, food and language became very high. However, the dramas on air in Thailand TV reduced to 26 from 43 in 2009, and the share of Korean online games became reduced because of Chinese games. There is pessimistic prospect that Hallyu is in its period of decline. In 2012, there was anti-Korea spirit for a while because of an idol group named 'Block B' ignored and despised local people in an interview with a Thailand media during the promotion. Although they shaved their heads and uploaded an apology video and apology letters, the anti-Korea feelings persisted. In Thailand, discourses to enforce their own competitiveness to tighten vigilance against Hallyu are being composed rather than criticizing Hallyu directly. They tend to worry about economic and social influences of Hallyu. Consequently, they tried to cut down the influence of Hallyu or to define it as temporary phenomenon.

Up to now, western countries did not have many opportunities to contact Korean pop culture so there have not been an atmosphere called anti-Hallyu. However, when SM Entertainment held Hallyu Concert successfully in Paris, France in 2011, major European newspapers and media including BBC and Le Monde commented infringement of human rights of minor trainees such as severe training and long-term unequal contract. Those media analyzed that the success of K-pop was the result of tyranny of large entertainment companies and interests of government emphasizing economic value only. Behind such negative articles, there may be curiosity about the unique star nurturing system including language and manners training and psychology of check and control against Hallyu which became the core culture of Asia.

4   Conclusion

Korean cultural contents were introduced to international stage through global phenomenon called Hallyu in a decade. Numerous contents appear and disappear from '*Winter Sonata*' to Psy's '*Gangnam Style*', and visited culture consumers alternating success and failure. At present when Hallyu fandom and anti-Hallyu coexist although there is some difference in extent, it is difficult to expand influence in the market only with Hallyu the consumer of which is limited to youths only. To encompass core consumers enjoying Korean culture and values, it is necessary to develop diverse contents. In other words, while Hallyu used to be a product refining western pop culture up to now, the next ten years should be the period to search for the originality of Korea. We have infinite subjects introducing beautiful traditional culture, original technology and story-telling.

As Hallyu is considered as a product using Korean culture as a medium, it is the window through which other Asian countries look at Korea. In this context, Hallyu should shift its paradigm from the darling of culture industry to an overall phenomenon encompassing politics, economics and social matters. However, Korean government tends to see Hallyu as a strategic industry to improve exports. As there were the supports of USA, the ultra super power country behind the phenomenon that American culture became a universal culture in the world, the government's role is very important. However, considering fluctuation of culture, institutional supports should be provided to produce high quality cultural contents through continuous study and analysis of local consumers. Culture planners in Korea should have prospective strategies not only to create economic profits but also to support long-term sustainable overseas expansion. To do this, we need to develop programs supplement the backward system, systemize related personnel training, compose committee with related institutions in order to respond to anti-Hallyu proactively and to compose new image of 'Koreans who share their talents and wealth' escaping from the old image of 'Koreans who scrape money' through donation, know-how transfer and establishment of Youth Cultural Educational Institutions.

Half century ago, M. McLuhan forecasted the current media environments that make influences on local communities to globe beyond the personal dimension through his famous phrase of 'The medium is the message.' New media such as SNS, Facebook, and YouTube based on Internet technology has been developed to distribute contents all over the world beyond the physical boundaries of nations in near real time. As Psy's 'Gangnam Style' made a sensational success and became the best pop culture product in 2012, it is the time that the consumers find the contents that they want borrowing the power of new media. From this perspective, we need to provide Korean culture product consumers with opportunities to contact diverse cultures in the world using new media as well as explore good cultural contents and introduce them to the other parts of the world.

References

1. Cho, Y.: Desperately Seeking East Asia Amidst the Popularity of South Korean Pop Culture in Asia. Cultural Studies 25(3), 383–404 (2011)
2. Shin, H.J.: Have you ever seen the Rain? And who will stop the Rain?: the globalizing project of Korean pop. Inter-Asian Cultural Studies 10(4), 507–523 (2009)
3. Sung, S.Y.: Constructing a New Image, Hallyu in Taiwan. European Journal of East Asian Studies 9(1), 25–45 (2010)
4. Jang, G.S.: Study of the Korean Wave's origin and Its Usage. Korea Contents 11(9), 166–173 (2011)
5. Kim, H.Y.: Study on the Diffusion of Korean Movie Focusing on the Korean Wave. Kogito 11, 276–303 (2011)
6. Report on the Second Half of the year of 2012, Korea Creative Contents Agency (2012)

Memory as Content and Context – Testimonial Literature

O-Sik Shin and Hyoun-Jin Ju

Chungnam National University, 220 Gung-dong, Yuseong-gu,
305-764, Daejeon, Korea
shinosik@cnu.ac.kr, charmante91@gmail.com

Abstract. This study would like to present memory as a new cultural content through the definition of testimonial literature. In particular, by composing the already established catalogue of testimonial literature, this discussion presents the new concept that memory can serve as new content. This study also pursues an in-depth study on "testimony in literature" that has not been covered in Korean literary circles until now. Actually, "testimonial literature", unfamiliar to Korean academic circles, is not a subject that is briskly addressed by French humanities as well as by scholars in the other countries. A theme of "testimony and literature" just recently appeared in some global websites of humanities like "H-net". Accordingly, we have a great ambition to lead a new trend of humanities in the world through the project.

Keywords: memory, testimonial literature, historical context, poems.

1 Introduction: Memory as Content Based on Historical Context

History has continuously provided contents to literature since a beginning that can't even be fathomed. The transformation of history as literary content has been made possible through testimonials based on memory. 20th century history in particular has been interspersed with incidents that need to be remembered. The first and second world wars and the times before and after both wars dominated the human memory with genocide and massive destruction, and inevitably led to desires of direct and/or indirect testimonials. This desire for testimonials continues even today and has expressed itself in the form of historical records as well as in the form of literature. There are even literatures based on this testimonial desires that have come to establish itself as a proposition within the field. For example, France's 'participatory poems' started as literature that opposes German Nazism and Fascism before and during World War II. Similarly, Korea's 'oppositional poems' are examples of testimonial literature becoming a valid proposition within the field. That is, poets such as Paul Eluard, Louis Aragon, Yuksa Lee, Yongun Han, and Dongju Yun and their historical context of content are unanimously accepted as poetry trends within literature. These poets actively and dutifully responded to the injustices of their social structures and

T.-h. Kim et al. (Eds.): MulGraB/BSBT/IUrC 2012, CCIS 353, pp. 244–249, 2012.

represented the voices of justice of the time. Nevertheless, these testimonials remain as indirect testimonials from those observers of the specific time period. These indirect testimonial pieces that produced a individually respected literary piece have been the topic of numerous researches. However, the direct testimonials of individuals who actually underwent the experiences of the times have not been as actively or carefully studied in comparison to the literary works. This may be because the latters' works are far less in number than the formers' works. Yet, the main reason is because the latter group of testimonials did not adopt a literary approach to recording their testimonials.

Let's discuss literature that have been produced directly from the perspective of those that directly experienced a certain historical incident in order to define the literature created from testimonials of direct observers as an independent category. So, how must one categorize the testimonials of Primo Levi and Robert Antelme who testify Shoah (Jewish holocaust), or those of Varlam Chalamov and Anna Akhmatova who testify Soviet Stalin's concentration camps and social suppression, or those of Jean Hatzfeld who testify Rwanda's genocide? Within our own frontier, how must one categorize those literary pieces that have been created to testify the true images of the Korean War? Or how must one interpret the poems of poets who were imprisoned for political purposes? Can these all simply be grouped as 'historical literature,' or 'war literature,' or even 'participatory poems?'

These questions are relevant to the fates of all members of the 20th century modern history. Yet, there are too many that are outside the communal circle of 'the tumultuous modern history of the 20th century.' For this reason, there is a need to convert the memory of one that should not be forgotten and forever imprint it into a form that can be shared by all. This means that there is a need to transform a memory based on 'context' into 'content.' This then is testimonial literature. Therefore, this research attempts to classify all creative literature (novels, poems, essays, journals) that is based on an individual experiencing a specific historical incident as testimonial literature. Hence, testimonial literature believes that a specific historical incident is shared by the act of perceiving a particular memory based on 'context' as 'content.' This is because testimonials are completely dependent on memory along. This study would like to present memory as a new cultural content through the definition of testimonial literature. In particular, by composing the already established catalogue of testimonial literature, this discussion presents the new concept that memory can serve as new content.

2   Discussion: Concepts and Contemplation on Testimonial Literature

This study will only refer to those pieces that contain a personal discussion resulting from memory from a direct experience with a certain historical incident. That is those literatures that testify to the experiences from a concentration camp, war, genocide, and imprisonment. Specifically, examples of the literature examined for this study would be Robert Antelme's "L'espece humaine," which recounted his time in concentration camp in 1944, as well as Marguerite Duras' "La Douleur," which records her experience of enduring abysmal pain as she tried to save her husband from the concentration camp, or Primo Levi's testimonial journals "Si C'est Un Homme," and finally the poetry anthology, "La Treve." All these pieces are essential in identifying the characteristics and discussion of testimonial literature. Although Primo Levi is not a French author, he is somewhat of a symbol of those that testify or are authors of testimonial pieces recounting Shoah, and is therefore an individual that must be studied when discussing the topic of testimonial literature. Furthermore, "Requiem, Poème Sans Héros, et Autres Poems" by Akhmatova and "Récits de la Kolyma" by Chalamov, where both pieces opposed Soviet Stalin suppression, as well as "Dans le nu de la vie" and "Une saison de machettes" both works by the reporter Jean Hatzfeld who testified for the Rwanda genocide are also representative works of testimonial literature. Moreover, research into the testimonial pieces from the Korea War should also receive much attention. In particular, there is a need to justify the view of Korean testimonial literature through works by poets that testify to the incidents and perspectives of the time. As such, it can be said that much of the last century was a long journey where an individual's memory was fused with that of the collective history and culture. This therefore entails that testimonial literature is what validates memory as content. Hence, it is necessary to establish a definition of testimonial literature and specify the development of the discussion.

2.1 Establishment of the Concepts of Testimonial Literature

World War I, World War II, Holocaust, Soviet Union's concentration camps, Japanese massacre of the Chinese, Hiroshima and Nagasaki atomic bombs and other political and social catastrophic historical incidents dominate the memory of the 20th century human history. These memories have been recounted in both the creative and the falsified fields of literature. There were no precedence to the complete destruction (of particular groups of peoples) and dramatic human action as seen in the 20th century modern history and for this reason the shock that humanity responded to this violent history was indescribable. The recounting of the incidents has prevailed over long periods of time and those testimonials still continue today. From literary pieces that testify to the 'current' circumstances of these historical incidents, to those literary pieces that testify to the 'current' of what remains in the memory of the narrator have been diligently presented as testimonial literature. Now then, the critical interpretation of the past testimonial literature productions remain as the responsibility of the 'current' days. That is, the unification of 'testimonial' and 'literature' is a topic that the past 20th century has thrown upon us and is the content that the 21st century must now learn to insert into its literature.

The first testimonial literature, which is the meeting of the periodical reality with literature, first occurred in France following World War I and the emergence of various war novels. Soon after the popularity of the war novels were the 'voices' that opposed suppression. These voices were related not only to France but to Korea and eventually to the whole world. The voices of poets and other authors testified to the periodical reality of the inter-war period as well as World War II and came to represent the sentiments of the peoples of the time. The periodical reality in France was Fascism (a general meaning of Fascism) and the participatory poems that emerged as voices against this social structure. On the other hand, the periodical reality in Korea was the Japanese invasion and the voices against this suppression through the oppositional poems. Both forms of poetry are inseparable to the historical (periodical) circumstances and therefore are globally classified as testimonial literature. The first testimonial literary poems that denounced the periodical reality of French society during the 1930s were mainly produced by Eluard and Aragon. Both poets act as the testifiers to the historical period of the time after World War II until both propose a new form of participatory poem that encourages Communism. Of course these two poets were not the only individuals who testified to the social circumstances of the time. Rene Char and Robert Desnos and numerous other poets also testified to the social orders and the historical realities of the period. This type of poems however were attributed a more specific and direct proposition as participatory poems before they were classified as testimonial literature. Also, participatory poems that testify to the realities of the time period are not testimonial literature that is comprised of the witness-author that existed as the subject of ordeal. And it is here that one can distinguish the global and regional interpretation of the definition of testimonial literature. The definition put forth by this study is the regional definition of testimonial literature where the recounting is produced by the witness-author where the witness-author directly experiences the event. The emergence of this witness-author was after World War II, that is, after the ordeal has ended. Hence, Robert Antelme who was a French poet and resistance member and his recounting of his time in the concentration camp through "L'espece humaine," which was published in 1947 therefore can be said to be the first witness-author piece. Furthermore, the most prominent Western witness-author Primo Levi also produced his "Si C'est Un Homme" that recounts his experience in Auschwitz concentration camp in 1947. As such pieces that are written by those that directly experience a particular historical incident are only produced mid-20th century. Still, this period was a time where the productions were limited to those people such as Antelme and Levi who had already been producing poems and other writings. And in actuality, the general witnesses only started to reproduce their experiences into written form only after a long period of silence. Furthermore, for the last few decades there have been a continuation of 'events that are worthy of testifying' and just like the reporter Jean Hatzfeld, there have been various testimonials that are both real and fictional from reporters, authors, and the general public. As a result, the emergence of the concept of testimonial literature in France, as well as the treatment of testimonial literature as a research topic has been fairly recent. In particular, it was only through the efforts of a very few such as Claude Mouchard and Cahterine Coquio, that testimonial literature has come to establish itself as a valid and academic research topic in France. The study of testimonial literature does not treat historical literature from a perspective of historical criticism. Rather from a perspective of 'testimonial discussion,' the field of testimonial literature studies the new topics that today's literary researchers should examine.

2.2   Contemplation of Testimonial Literature, Historical Context

'Testimonial' and 'Memory,' which are both ideas that represent the interconnectivity of history and literature, only recently appeared within the field of liberal arts. As a result, there aren't many past research works on the topic of 'testimonial literature.' Furthermore, most of the past studies on testimonial pieces tend to be true to the historical aspect of the pieces. This means that most of the foreign references are related to the socio- and/or politico- philosophical perspectives of the testimonial records. In particular, the research works on Korean culture and history are mainly concentrated on the historical perspective or the nationalistic perspective and therefore are often unable to overcome the conceptual conflict within the work of study. Thus, the general tendency of studying these testimonial pieces has been to understand the specific intentions of the writings as a result of focusing on the historical context of these writings. For example, in the "Responsorial Between the Korean War and the Korean Poem," Jaehong Kim does not analyze the perspective of the 'testimonials' provided by those that participated in the war. Instead, Kim intercepts the literary articles produced by the participants of the war with Korea's political theories and in doing so tries to define the identity of Korean poems that have been regenerated through the historical hardship. On the other hand, through the "Korean War and the Correspondent Author," Youngduk Shin does weakly establish the position of the witness-author. Still, Shin's analysis continues to be bound by the discussion of theoretical conflict and fails to move beyond this contemplation. The 'group of correspondent authors' that are emphasized in Shin's discussion was a group with a specific goal of encouraging the fighting spirit during the wartime. As a result, it can be somewhat expected and natural for Shin's analysis to be insular in regards to examining this 'group.' Regardless, Shin's book still simply organizes the recountings that have specific intentions from the writer. In other words, although correspondent authors depict a specific intention through their writing, there are still a few pieces that testify to the harsh realities of the war and a direct experience of specific incidents and for this reason, there is a need to study and contemplate on the perspective of the 'testimonial.'

As a result, this discussion will move beyond the study of the '-ism' that biases the analysis of the testimonial writings. Instead, it will examine the witness-author's writings from the perspective of the 'testimonial discussion.' Hence, this study will emphasize the restructuring of the 'memory' as a cultural content. Within this direction, it is expected that this research will provide a new interpretation of the relationship between history and literature from the perspective of the testimonial. Also through the comparison between various international testimonial pieces and Korean testimonial pieces, this study is expected to provide the characteristics of testimonial literatures. In this process, there is a need to study the goal of a testimonial, the methodology of a testimonial, as well as the discussion of a testimonial. This means, answering questions such as, what does the French poet who experienced the Jewish concentration camp intend to testify to?; or what do the poets who acted as the correspondent authors of the Korean War or a specific individual such as Suyong Kim who survived the Gujedo prison camp intend to express through their testimonials? Through seeking the answers to questions such as those listed above, this discussion will be able to provide a direction towards the methodology in which to change 'memory' into 'contents' in the future.

3   Conclusion

As identified earlier, the testimonial writings by authors such as Primo Levi, Robert Antelme, Varlam Chalamov, Anna Akhmatova, and Jean Hatzfeld who all underwent the ordeals thrown upon them by history, take up a significant portion of the 20th century literary heritage. In particular, the Shoah related writings as well as the writings that oppose Stalin's Soviet government take up most of the mid-20th century testimonial literature. This is a result of the unimaginable genocide and destruction brought out by socially structured political theories and the misuse of technology that has never seen precedence and the countless victims that were at the mercy of such violence. This great tragedy was not only limited to a specific group of people. 'Memorable historical incidents' occurred simultaneously throughout the world and is still going on, and the recountings of such events continue to be produced. For example, the Vietnamese War and the Iraq War as well as the Rwanda genocide are the most recent historical tragedies whose testimonial products still continue. Korea also has her own collection of testimonial literature as a result of undergoing social travesties such as the Korea War and the Gwangju Revolution that are all referred to as 'massacre and destruction.' Also, the historical events that occurred in 20th century Korea can be argued to be the most tragedies that one civilization can undergo in one century. As a result, history has been a prevailing topic within modern Korean literature. The first application was of course the oppositional poems that publicized the atrocities of the Japanese invasion. This phenomenon is similar in context to French participatory poems that married modern poems with history. Strictly speaking, the participatory poems and oppositional poems are in essence an angry and emotional outcry towards destruction and suppression imposed upon humanity. As such, testimonial writings pieces have been studied over time and have been classified as 'participatory poems' or 'oppositional poems.' Yet, the discussion of these testimonial articles written by those witness-authors have never been completely isolated into a new classification and has always revolved within other literary forms. Hence this research aims to totally isolate those pieces that have been produced by authors that have personally experienced extreme violence such as through concentration camps or genocide, and provide a regional definition to testimonial literature. Furthermore, the study intends to classify these literary pieces within the category of '21st century cultural contents that remembers the past.' First of all, the process of making 'content' out of a group's memory is necessary. But with the expansion of the perception of 'content-ifying of memory,' it is possible to establish a background where an individuals' memory can be converted into 'content.' Therefore, to categorize a group's memory into content will be a very meaningful process that will aid the development of the human history.

Development of Value Oriented Customized Contents

Sung Young Lee, Eun Sok Bae, and Bo Eun Jung[*]

Hankuk University of Foreign Studies, 107 Imun-ro, Dongdaemun-gu,
130-791, Seoul, Korea
hlamb@hufs.ac.kr, best-96@hanmail.net, qingtian88@naver.com

Abstract. Consumption values vary according to contexts. However, these values become ultimately the utopic value at the moment of decision whatever it will be because decisions are made to get maximum profit. In the era of scarcity and post-scarcity, the values most wanted are the utopic values in this sense. In the era of scarcity, consuming is caused by practical reasons such as survival necessities. On the contrary, in the era of post-scarcity, there is a great tendency of consuming values out of contents instead of contents themselves. This article goes to explain the different consuming patterns observed with Chinese tourists visiting Korea in two different eras, scarcity and post-scarcity, based on the consumption value theory and value shifting theory.

Keywords: consumption values, utopic value, value shifting, post-scarcity, self-consuming value.

1 Introduction

When we are asked for choose one among many other products that have no difference in terms of quality and price, the crucial elements that enter into the decision-making process are located place outside of products. Particularly, this is definitive with low-involvement products that are accessible to everyone and have no difference between them. This is not only observed with physical products but also with non-physical ones such as cultural contents.

Korea and China have lots in common in historical and cultural aspects. In particular they are geographically very close. Around China, Korea is the only advanced and westernized country where Chinese is not spoken, except Japan. For cultural and geographical reasons, Korea is very preferable country for Chinese whose holidays are very short. However, Korean traditional cultural contents are not so different from those of China. In fact, there are no great differences between them at least in physical aspect.

If there is no difference between contents, the properties and values outside of the contents are crucial for choices. This study goes to explain the consuming pattern and its changes of Chinese tourists visiting Korea whose cultural contents are not so different in terms of consumption value theory and value shifting theory. And this

---

[*] Corresponding author (Hankuk University of Foreign Studies).

T.-h. Kim et al. (Eds.): MulGraB/BSBT/IUrC 2012, CCIS 353, pp. 250–257, 2012.
© Springer-Verlag Berlin Heidelberg 2012

goes also to suggest what kind of values we should take into consideration to keep and increase continuous consuming of Chinese tourist in Korea.

2   Utopic Value and Change of Consuming Paradigm

2.1   Utopic Value

Decision-making is always done for the maximum profit whatever the context is. But it is not easy to say what the maximum profit is. It can be money, quality or something quantitative. However, it is still difficult to say what the maximum profit with respect to emotions is. Because the profits we looks for in emotional domains are subjective and relative. But I believe that, whatever it will be, it is the utopic value. Lee (2012) defines that all the values that we pursue for maximum profit are utopic values regardless of given contexts. Maximizing profit in any context is what we do in decision-making process and this becomes the utopic value.

It is now possible to say pursuing utopic value and consuming contents are the same thing. As it was mentioned earlier, the utopic values in question vary according to environmental conditions or domains, namely contexts. Contents are consuming objects. So consuming contents to satisfy human desires is consuming utopic values for each one. Everyone has different and his own desires. So the utopic values are not always same depending upon contents and contexts. It can be different for personal reasons or for contextual reasons.

2.2   Change of Consuming Paradigm

In the world, there are poor and rich countries and the poor and the wealthy. Some countries are already at the fully industrialized level having entered in post-scarcity era. Some others are still in the era of scarcity. But there is no doubt that the world goes gradually from the era of scarcity to the post-scarcity.

Consuming is basically the behavior to solve the necessities. When the necessities cause consumption, economic condition and purchasing power are crucial in decision-making process. These conditions are closely related to personal or national income. With increased income and purchasing power, consumption patterns change. Entering in the post-scarcity era, abstract values out of contents are getting more weight and play crucial role in decision-making process. The value-oriented values are getting more importance than the object-oriented values such as practical and critical ones. Therefore increasing income triggers naturally consumption patterns changes .The main consumption pattern in scarcity era is material and physical consumption. In post-scarcity era, consumption focuses on the values out of contents, namely emotion oriented consumption.

The values out of contents are additional values whose representative example is brand reputation. Consuming a particular content without special reason or paying much more than the others are the very case of consuming the satisfactory feeling instead of content itself. In the era of post-scarcity, consumers tend to consume not only content itself but also consumers themselves. Now consuming is not for necessity and survival but to satisfy emotional values. Now the consumption pattern is in post-scarcity era is, in a word, value-oriented consumption.

Table 1.

Scarcity Era	Post-scarcity Era
Critical value Practical value	Ludic value Utopic value

Table 2.

Scarcity Era	Post-scarcity Era
Content internal value> Content external value Quantitative value > Qualitative value	Content internal value < Content external value Quantitative value < Qualitative value

The values considered most desirable in the era of scarcity do not maintain no longer same weight in the era of post-scarcity. On the contrary, some values that had not been taken into consideration now can become ideal ones as utopic values in the post-scarcity era. So raising income level changes consumption paradigm and in turn, this causes changes of contents, object of consumption.

One of the most prominent examples that show the changes of consumption patterns is a computer related product. At the mid of 80s, computers were high-involvement products. They were expensive in terms of quality/price. But nowadays, everyone use computers at work places and at home. Computers are one of the must independent from its basic purpose and limited functions. They are now low-involvement products, which are accessible to almost everyone. If they are belonging to low-involvement product category, it is expected that the values outside product take great role to persuade consumers or to consuming the content in question, namely here computers.

At first look, above advertising seems nothing special. But I think the copy emphasizing "quad core" shows well the consuming pattern changes according to time. Except some professional users in particular IT area, the majority of computer users buy computers for the purpose of simple works such as word processing, calculating and so on. If only for these reasons, it may not necessary to buy such strong and high formative computers. Especially quad core processor is meaningless

Fig. 1.

for most end users at home. To take advantage of quad core processor, the operation system and applications should be designed to use and support 4 processors at the same time. Actually the programs that most end-users use run under single processor. In fact, there is no great difference between dual and quad core for ordinary users.

In spite of this, the reason why above advertising successfully arrives to persuade clients is that it puts weight on external values rather than computer itself. At some point, it needs to have high performance computers in order to get seamless working speed. But between high performance computers, consumers want to consume some images and values related to consumers themselves buying them. For example, they want to put weight on maximizing their satisfaction of being belonged to a high level class who consumes cutting-edge technological culture buying highly advanced products. One of the similar cases is that of buying luxury items.

Buying those items or their copies, they delude themselves as high society members. This is because of projection effect. In this context, the content to be consumed is "self-value"

In the course of going from the scarcity and to the post-scarcity era, consumption patterns change from object oriented consuming into value-oriented consuming highlighting on emotional values. But the change of eras is not the necessary condition for causing consumption pattern changes. In case of selective consuming of same level products in equivalent contexts, consumption patterns put more weight on emotional values, namely utopic values than physical ones.

Even in the era of post-scarcity, critical and practical value consumptions do not disappear. Only the volume of utopic value consumption increases. Those who live in this era show a great tendency to focus on self-consuming. Then it is matter of how supply self-consuming value to keep continuous consumption in this environment. Contents, as objects of consuming, must contain self-consuming values whatever they are because they are the utopic values satisfying human desires.

3 Change of Consumption Paradigm and Development of Customized Contents: A Case Study

3.1 Change of Consumption Paradigm of Chinese Tourists Visiting Korea

China occupies second position in the world economy. But due to the great gap between the wealthy and the poor, the number of those who have purchasing power is about 40-50 million. Chinese began to accumulate capital and to go foreign countries for sightseeing just after reform and opening. This means that consumption patterns before and after reform and opening are different. Especially there is great difference in consumption pattern between those who undergone the change and those who didn't.

Table 3.

Generations	1950-1970	1980-1989	1990-
Characters	Compensational	Practical	Emotional

The generation of 50-70 who underwent reform and opening can be characterized in terms of compensational consumption. Those who are over 50 years old experienced the period of shortage and lack of all kind of materials to survive and now entered into the post-scarcity era. So they have tendency to consume what they wanted but couldn't in the past. They consume for the purpose of satisfying compensational value. And this type of consuming shows object-oriented and self-ostentation characters. This meets also self-satisfaction and can be considered as a utopic value for them. But it is not in fact self-consuming. Because it is different from the real utopic values because they are aware of the way other people are looking at them. Self-consuming is basically egocentric.

The next generation of 1980-1989 who are around 30-40 years old did not experience reform and opening contrary to their parents. Even though they did not undergo scarcity, they observed the life of their parents. So this generation shows mixed consuming patterns. They are practical and rational for themselves. But they show self-ostentation consumption pattern with their children.

The generation of after 1990 lives in the post-scarcity era with their parents who did not undergo or experience the shortage too. In the affluent society, they enjoy themselves consuming value-oriented contents to satisfy their emotional needs. In other words, they are looking for their identities over simple consumption of content itself.

3.2 Value-Oriented Customized Contents for Chinese Tourist Visiting Korea

The main purposes of Chinese tourists visiting Korea are sightseeing and shopping. Tourism is principally designed with visiting places. So it is natural that sightseeing is one of the main purposes. By the way, it seems that shopping is closely related the classification of generations above mentioned.

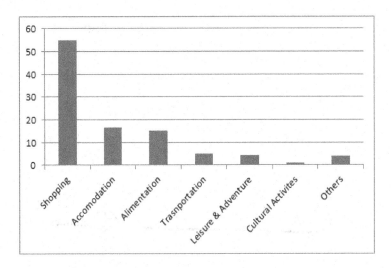

Fig. 2.

The majority of Chinese tourists visiting Korea is the generation of 1950-1970 for whom compensational value is more important than any others. To satisfy this value, they sink into shopping. For them, offering purchasing chances and showing material products are useful to catch their attention because they want prove physically who they are.

Today, however, it is not possible to catch their attention with those contents only emphasizing object-oriented values. For the generation after 90s, object-oriented values are no more attractive because they already have what they need and what they want in material aspect. Until now, Korean contents are not well prepared to catch up with this kind of change. The number of Chinese tourists visiting Korea does not pass 3 % of the total number of Chinese tourist visiting foreign countries.

This estimation is not limited only to the Chinese case. It is common phenomena that appears in all the societies under way to the post-scarcity era overcoming shortage and lack.

As I told earlier, there is no big intuitive difference between Korean and Chinese traditional cultural contents. The reason why they choose Korea in spite of no difference in contents is the geographical accessibility. Chinese who have no enough long holidays, the accessibility condition is crucial to choose a foreign country to go. Furthermore, there is no emotional conflict and high quality of products can satisfy the compensational needs with reasonable expenses. Therefore it is essential to develop new contents with value-oriented consumption values rather than traditional cultural values to satisfy self-consuming needs. These contents contains following properties.

For the Chinese tourists in question entering in post-scarcity era, medical contents can be a good example because of their great concern about health and poor quality of medical service in their homeland.

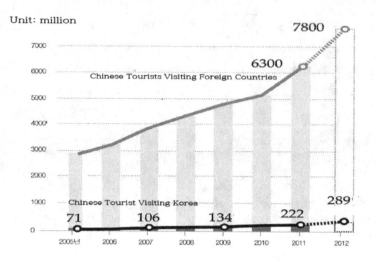

Fig. 3.

Table 4.

Scarcity	■ Materialism ■ Self-ostentation ■ Others' Estimation	✓ Purchasing material products ✓ Purchasing new items ✓ Over consuming ✓ Luxury goods
Post-scarcity	■ Value Orientation ■ Self-centeredness	✓ Identity ✓ Curiosity ✓ Aberration ✓ Adventure ✓ Self-contentment

4   Conclusion

This study has focused on the reason that makes changes of consumption pattern in the course of moving from the scarcity to the post-scarcity era. In the era of scarcity, consumption is the behavior to satisfy the needs consuming material products or object-oriented values. But in the post-scarcity era, what is consumed is the value-oriented values, principally self-consuming values. I explained these changes in terms of the consumption value theory and the value shifting theory. I used Chinese tourists visiting Korea to testify the theories but I am very sure that the approach done in this work is also valuable to many other cases.

References

1. Hofstede, G.: Culture's Consquences, 2nd edn. Sage Publications (2011)
2. Floch, J.M.: Sémiotique, Marketing et Communication, PUF (1990)
3. Lee, S.Y.: A Comparative Case-study of Orientation Types and Interpretations of Value Indicators for the Utopic Value. Advanced Science and Technology Letters 12, 55–67 (2012)
4. Lee, S.Y.: Defining Utopic Value Based on Orientation Types in Different Context. Advanced Science and Technology Letters 12, 55–67 (2012)

Cultural Context Indicator of Fermented Food

Focused on Types and Classification of Asian Fermented Fish Food Products

Jong Oh Lee and Jin Young Kim

Hankuk University of Foreign Studies, 107 Imun-ro, Dongdaemun-gu,
130-791, Seoul, Korea
santon@hanmail.net, staci21@naver.com

Abstract. Fermented fish food products have been extensively studied in Asia's fermented food culture. We have attempted to categorize the different types of fermented fish products seen in some of the Asian countries as part of a cultural context indicator analysis. Categorization is available through two cultural context indicators: the macro cultural context indicator and micro cultural context indicator. The categorization of fermented fish products for this study is according to the macro cultural context indicator. Types and nomenclature of different fermented fish products found in different countries have been compared to ones found in Korea and categorized accordingly. East Asian countries' fermented fish food, fermented with salt, is categorized into *jeot*, *jeotgal*, paste, sauce, and *sikhae* in terms of form and ingredients. Two essential ingredients involved in the fermentation process are salt and rice. In other words, fermented fish food products were first introduced in cultures where rice is the staple cuisine. Salt is also used for preservation. The comparison and categorization of Asian fermented fish food as part of a cultural context indicator analysis provides an opportunity to understand its unique characteristics and qualities. It can eventually establish a fundamental frame of inherent properties of Asia's fermented food culture and provide cultural indicators that can measure them. The study can be utilized to understand the identity of the fermented food culture in East Asia.

Keywords: Jeot(gal), Shrimp Paste, Fish Paste, Fish Sauce, Shrimp Sauce, Sikhae, East Asian Countries.

1   Introduction

It is not an overstatement that living culture in the modern society has been perceived as part of the food culture, or more specifically fermented food culture. The importance of fermented food culture is assured by the fact that Asia's traditional fermented fish food products are fundamentally linked to the local environment and the everyday life of its people. An investigation into the environment and development of fermented food and how it is closely related to our everyday life provides an understanding of not only the characteristics and properties of different

T.-h. Kim et al. (Eds.): MulGraB/BSBT/IUrC 2012, CCIS 353, pp. 258–265, 2012.
© Springer-Verlag Berlin Heidelberg 2012

local environments, but also the context indicators that lie in the cultural identity such as emotions, wisdom, and ways of life. Therefore, fermented food is deeply related to the produce, ways of life, local environment, and eating habits of different regions.

As Steinkraus (1996) put it, studying fermented food is studying the close relationship among the people, microorganism, and the food; since the fermentation process involves biological and cultural phenomena that simultaneously progress.

A country's food culture, which also represents unique fermented food culture, has been cultivated through producing different yet unique fermented food products such as fermented soybean, fermented fish[1], alcoholic drink made from grains, and fermented cabbage or other vegetables. There are different kinds of fermented food in each country, and the superiority of the unique products has been recognized in terms of nutrition. Particularly, fermented soybean and vegetable products have been actively commercialized due to their popularity. Studies have been conducted regarding their microorganism, nutritional contents, and production process.

However, previous studies of fermented fish mainly focused on soybean and vegetable products. The current state of fermented fish products according to the macro cultural context indicator has not been the focus of most previous studies. In order to understand the identity of the dietary culture of fermented fish food products, this study aims to compare and categorize the scope of the fermented fish food culture that is deeply rooted in the dietary culture of everyday life in East Asia. We also hope to discuss types and nomenclature of fermented fish food products of Asia according to each country.

2   The Cultural Context Indicator for Fermented Food

The foremost precondition for survival is to secure food. To assure food security, we rely on resources that are close by and available for preservation. Preserved food helps us overcome the uncertainty and capriciousness of the nature and enables consistent consumption. Historically, by improving storability, preservation of food has played an important role in solving problems of food shortage. Therefore, the most important concept with fermented food is storage, or preservation. Fermentation microorganisms such as amylase, protease, lipase, etc. hydrolyze carbohydrates, protein and fat and make such food that has unique flavors and texture available to us.

Fermented food of a certain ethnic group is closely linked to the region's produce, ways of life, weather, soil, eating habits, etc. Those properties help develop unique traditional fermented food. The development of East Asia's fermented fish food products started from the usual diet available in a traditional agrarian society. The development especially circled around rice and stems from the need of protein in the rice-based diet. In other words, they were in need of a dietary supplement or a condiment that could season bland rice and give it added flavors and smells.

---

[1] Steinkraus (1996) classified fermented fishes as high salt/savory meat-flavored/amino acid/peptide sauce and paste fermentations: (a) fish sauces: Vietnamese nuocmam, Philippine patis, Malaysian budu ; (b) fish pastes: Philippine bagoong, Malaysian belachan, Vietnamese mam, Cambodian prahoc, Indonesian trassi and Korean jeotgal, etc.

Responding to this need, different side dishes must have been introduced which included salted fish. Salting and fermentation techniques for preservation contributed to the uniqueness of the fermented fish food products of each country. Fermented fish food products have established an important status in discussing the foundation of Asian cuisine.

Fermented food that combines salt, rice culture, and fish is a great gift of mother nature and represents the wisdom and hope of mankind. Fermented fish can be researched in two different ways in terms of culture: the macro context and the micro context. The macro context of the fermented fish culture deals with the current state of fermented food, ecocultural approaches to the fermented food of a certain region, the local way of life, etc. The micro context concerns its production process, ideological views of the world observed through fermented food, a country's production and consumption of fermented food, etc. Prior to the discussion of the types and categorization of fermented fish food, the cultural context indicators can be classified as follows:

Research process and classification			Research target
Macro context analysis	1	current state of fermented food	types of fermented fish in each country of the world
	2	geography and terroir	an ecological approach to fermented food of a certain region
	3	-local way of life -cultural elements of fermented food (technical aspect)	fermented food found in nomadic cultures
			fermented food found in settler cultures
Micro context analysis	4	-cultural elements of fermented food (ideological aspect)	production process of fermented food (ceramics, tableware, utensils, cooking tools, fermentation techniques, ingredients)
	5	cultural elements of fermented food (organizational aspect)	ideological world views observed through fermented food(language, religious rituals(taboos), symbolic representation (Yin, Yang, and the Five Elements, mythologies)
	6	investigation into the current state of fermented food	fermented food found in each country: production and consumption patterns of fermented food

Based on the macro cultural context indicators, we attempted to classify and categorize types and nomenclature of fermented fish food found in the East Asia region including Korea and Japan. Such categorization gives us an opportunity to compare and investigate the properties and characteristics that differentiate one region from another.

3   The Scope of Fermented Fish Food Culture in East Asia

Fermented food refers to a condiment that brings flavors out of food. In a narrow sense, it refers to soy sauce. In a broader sense, it also refers to soybean paste, *cheonggukjang* or fast-fermented soybean paste, chili paste, fish sauce, etc. Generally, fermented fish developed in Asia is classified into fermented soybean products, fermented fish products, fermented meat products and others in terms of ingredients.[2]

The most well-known and developed fermented foods in East Asia are fermented fish[3] and fermented soybean. Jeot or *aekjeot* (fish sauce) made from shrimps or fish in all areas of the region is preserved food that goes through the fermentation process. Soybean paste and similar products are produced through the fermentation process and it is also the most well-known preserved food in East Asia. Such jeot or jeotgal contains various kinds of amino acids, especially with a high glutamic acid content. Soybean products also contain amino acids and are used as a rich condiment that is rich in glutamic acid. Reflecting the fact that the regions where fermented food was developed consume rice as a main part of their diet, fermentation culture and rice can be considered to have progressed together. Containing a high amount of sugar, rice in the diet can be balanced with fermented food, which uses salt, in terms of finding a balance between nutrition and flavor.

Jeotgal is a typical salting food in East Asia where rice is a main diet. It has fermented fish and it is guts preserved in salt. Salting the fish increases its storability, which accounts for its unique flavor caused by the disintegration of the meat. It is known that the more jeotgal is aged, the more nutritious it becomes. Besides salting the fish, there are different ways of fermenting seafood such as simply using salt, mixing salt and malt, or fermenting fish with cooked grains. While varied according to region, jeotgal is a preserved food that uses salt, and it can be found across the world.

Among the East Asian countries, both fermented fish food and fermented soybean food are easily found in Korea and Japan due to the climate and geography. Fermented soybean food products have also developed in China. In Southeast Asian countries, such as Indonesia, Thailand, and Vietnam, fermented soybean food products that use malt are rarely developed, except in alcoholic beverages. Most of their fermented foods present fermented fish products due to the natural environment. Accordingly, fermented soybean food products have developed within East Asian countries, such as China, Korea and Japan. On the other hand, Southeast Asian countries like Thailand, Vietnam, Indonesia, Laos, etc. have enjoyed fermented fish food products more variously. Fermented fish food products like anchovy sauce can also be found in some parts of Europe. Rakfisk[4] is enjoyed in Norway, and háar[5] in

---

[2] The most popular fermented soybean foods in East Asia include tempe and ontjon from Indonesia, idli from India, soy sauce, soybean paste, chili paste and *cheonggukjang*, fast-fermented soybean paste from Korea. It also includes sufu, soya sauce, susi, *doubanjiang* (chili bean paste), yellow bean sauce, and *myunjang* from China and also shoyu, miso, natto, etc from Japan.

[3] Jeotgal can be translated in many different ways: salted-fermented fish products, salted fish guts, fermented sea food, etc. In this study, jeotgal refers to the collective term, fermented fish.

[4] Trout or catfish fermented in salt for two to three months.

[5] Fermented shark meat.

Iceland. Sweden also has a fermented fish food called surströming[6], and the Netherlands enjoys haring[7] as well.

4   Types and Classification of Fermented Fish

Fermented fish culture areas are closely linked to regions which contain salt production, rice farming areas, monsoon climates which have a clear distinction of a dry season and a rainy season, and of course a fishing season. Fish fermentation in Asia is believed to have first appeared near the Mekong River area and spread to Korea and Japan during China's Han Dynasty (BC.200-AD.200).

Fermented fish food products are acquired by lactic acid fermentation of fish and shellfish with some level of salt content. Although jeot or jeotgal[8]'s origin is unknown, it is a typical salt-fermented fish food product that originated from the ancient Greek and Roman eras. It has mostly developed in East Asian countries, especially in areas with a predominant rice culture. Therefore, the origin of fermented fish food products nearly coincides with the origin of rice farming. On the other hand, in Shandong Province of China, a fermented fish food product called *yānyú* is made by salting fish with the addition of steamed rice and *shajiang*, shrimp paste made from small shrimp. The most typical fermented fish food products in Korea include *myeolchi-jeotguk*, anchovy sauce and *hwangseokeo-jeotguk*, yellow corvina sauce. Generally, fish sauce and fish paste is filtered out from jeot, and they are the original forms of jeotgal.

The following is types and nomenclature of fermented fish food[9] found in each of the East Asian countries according to its production process.

Country	Types and Classification					
	Jeot(gal)	Shrimp Paste	Fish Paste	Fish Sauce	Shrimp Sauce	Shikhe
Korea	jeot	saewoojeotgal		myeolchi-jeotguk, hwangseokeo-jeotguk		shikhe
Japan	shiokara			shiotsuru ishiri ikanago-shoyu		narezushi funazushi dozozushi

---

[6] Canned herring that is fermented in salt for two months. Surströming in Swedish means sour herring.
[7] Herring fermented in salt.
[8] Jeot or Jeotgal is a salted fermented food in Korean cuisine. It is made with various seafood, for example, shrimp, oysters, shellfish, fish, fish eggs, and fish intestines.
[9] Cf. Kenneth Ruddle and Naomichi Ishige(2010).

China	yujiang	shajiang				y nyú
Vietnam	ca mam	mam ruoc mam tom	mam mem	nuoc mam	mam tom tom chat	mam chua
Myanmar	Ngapigaung	ngapi seinsa, buzunnag api	Ngapitaungtha	Ngagampyaye	Pazunggampyaye	nga(+)ng api, ngaching
Laos	Padaek (padak)		Padaek (padak)	nam paa(nam padek)		som paasom padek
Cambodia	prahoc	kapi	padek	tuk trey	nam tom	phaak
Philippines		paris	pagoong	patis		burongisda
Indonesia	bakasam	kecapikan *trasi	terasi ikan	kecapikan		wadi
Thailand	pla ra	kapi		Nam Pla budu thai pla	nam kapi	pla ra pla som

As shown in the table, considering the form of fish after the fermentation process, some are crushed before the process takes place. The fished product can be in the form of either paste or sauce. It can also be categorized according to its raw material.

Country	Fermented Food	Raw material
Korea	jeot(gal) sikhae	squid, hwangseokeo, hairtail halibut, pollack, squid, trout
Japan	shiokara dozozushi funazushi Narezushi	squid, shioka mudfish carp mackerel
Thailand	pla ra, nam pla	carp anchovy
Cambodia	prahoc	catfish, riel
Philippines	pagoong	anchovy
Laos	nam paa padaek(padak)	anchovy freshwater fish
Vietnam	nuoc mam	anchovy
Myanmar	ngapi	shrimp, freshwater fish

Fish sauce that comes with jeot is made through lactic acid fermentation. Its origin is known to be the Indochinese peninsula as well as Mekong basin areas like Eastern Thailand and Laos. During the monsoon seasons when seasonal winds blow from the Indian Ocean, farmlands become flooded and freshwater fish flock to breed and lay eggs. As the floodwaters recede, the farming area transforms into a fishery, and young fish are trapped and caught for preservation. This area became the center of fisheries, and therefore, the origin of fishery coincides with the origin of rice farming. For preservation, anchovies and hairtail are most used in China. Fish sauce made from anchovies and squid is found in Korea. *Shiotsuru* in Japan uses fish, rice bran and yuzu peels. *Nuoc mam*[10] is commonly used in both Vietnam and Thailand. Also made from shrimp, nouc mam, clear red or brown fish sauce that smells somewhat fishy, is made through a hydrolysis process. In Malaysia, they make it with anchovies, and it is called *budu*. In addition, after paste is fermented for a longer period of time, sauce can be filtered out from the fermented paste. Paste can be made by fermenting fish or shrimp for a long period of time or salting the fish after pounding it hard.

Sikhae is rather a modified version of Jeot. It is made by mixing ingredients such as fish, rice or millet, salt, etc. Its origin is closely related to the distribution of rice. The origin of rice is located in the triangle area of the Ganges River in India. The area is rich with both seawater and freshwater fish, yet with less sunlight. Malt, which is used exclusively in Korea for preservation, is an important ingredient to produce *gazami shikhae,* made with halibut. Myanmar, Thailand, Laos, etc., which are located far from the ocean, lack salt and do not make salted fish. Since drying fish is not an option during a dry season, the countries have developed a way of preserving fish by adding salt and steamed rice to them, which creates lactic acid and prevents decomposition. This is the original form of sikhae. It disappeared from China after the 18th century.[11] In Korea, in order to make sikhae, especially halibut sikhae, malt and chili powder are used. However, in Japan, the two ingredients are not necessary to make narezushi [12] (matured sushi, especially mackerel narezushi with a long fermentation period is called *hon-nare*, and one with a shorter period is called *haya-nare*). Today, sikhae barely survives in Korea while nigiri sushi becomes popular in Japan. There is also funazushi made from carp in Japan. It is less popular with people due to its pungent odor.

5   Conclusion

Fermentation of fish has a close relation with salt, rice, and fish farming areas. It represents the history and culture of preservation that shows the wisdom and hope of mankind. The fish fermentation process is the development of food culture in order to guarantee a healthy way of life. Fermented fish food products, which are found in nearly 10 East Asian countries where fish is a major part of their diet, have been classified into different categories including Jeot, shrimp paste, fish paste, fish sauce, shrimp sauce, sikhae. Categorized in terms of form and raw material, fermented fish food in each country has been differently designated in their own terms and compared with one another according to their properties and characteristics.

The distinction among different types of fermented fish food products is obscure in terms of country, production process, raw material, and purpose. However, they share some common production properties such as the use of salt, boiling or steaming of rice or vegetables, comminution process, and the amount of liquid. Through these steps, paste, sauce, or sikhae can be produced. There were also a few remarkable

---

[10] A type of fish sauce that can accompany rice, stir fried vegetables, steamed fish, rice cake, etc for dipping or seasoning.

[11] LEE Sung-Woo, *Korea Food and Cultural History*, Kyomunsa, 1984, pp. 135.

[12] Narezushi uses vegetables and rice.

points that need to be addressed from the macro culture context perspective. First of all, fermented fish food products in Asia take up a significant part of the diet while fermented food developed in nomadic western cultures do not. Second, geography and terroir play a crucial role in the development of fermented fish food. In both eastern and western cultures, the areas where fermented fish food flourished are hot and humid coastal areas. These areas also have rice as their main diet. These facts leave room for an ecocultural approach to fermented food. However, it is clear that fermented fish food is not particularly demanded in other parts of the world except in Asia.

References

1. Chun, K.-S.: Culture of Fermentation and its Function of Preservation and Communion. Asian Comparative Folklore 41, 223–252 (2008)
2. Ishige, N.: Narezushi in Asia: A Study of Fermented Aquatic Products (2). Bulletin of the National Museum of Ethnology 11(3), 603–668 (1986)
3. Ruddle, K., Ishige, N.: On the Origins, Diffusion and Cultural Context of Fermented Fish Products in Southeast Asia. In: Farrer, J. (ed.) lobalization, Food and Social Identities in the Asia Pacific Region. Sophia University Institute of Comparative Culture, Tokyo (2010)
4. Kim, Y.-M., Kim, D.-S.: Korean Jeotgal. Korean Food Research Institue (1990)
5. Lee, S.-W.: Korea Food and Cultural History. Kyomunsa (1984)
6. Steinkraus, K.: Comparison of Femented Foods of East and West. In: Lee, C.H., Steinkraus, K.H., Reilly, P.J.A. (eds.) Fish Fermentation Technology, pp. 1–10. United Nations University Press, Tokyo (1993)
7. Steinkraus, K.: Handbook of Indigenous Fermented Foods, 2nd edn Edition Revised and Enlarged., 776 p. Marcel Dekker, New York (1996)
8. Steinkraus, K.: Bio-enrichment: production of vitamins in fermented foods. In: Wood, B.J.B. (ed.) Microbiology of Fermented Foods, 2nd edn., vol. 2, pp. 603–621. Blackie Academic, London (1998)

A Hierarchy of Spatial Context for Urban Computing

Sangheon Kim[1] and Heui-Hak Ahn[2]

[1] Hankuk University of Foreign Studies, 107 Imun-ro, Seoul, Korea
[2] Kwandong University, 579 Bumil-ro, G angreung, Korea
shkim@gcrc.kr, hhahn@kd.ac.kr

Abstract. Context which consists of user experience can be described by hierarchy of time context, spatial context, social context and global context, local context, personal context. We Proposed context hierarchy for content strategy. Proposed context hierarchy takes time and spatial index and relations makes formal representation. Spatial Context is presented by spatial elements for spatial information including point, line and region which have explicit values.

Keywords: Context, Spatial Context, Context Hierarchy, Knowledge, Content service design.

1   Introduction

It is difficult to define the term "context'. In general, context is defined as "The surroundings, circumstances, environment, background of settings that determine, specify or clarify the meaning and event or other occurrence." In Linguistics, "The text in which a word or passage appears and which helps ascertain its meaning."[1]

In an Urban computing Service environment, users typically access contents using mobile devices. Since the context of a user is highly dynamic, we should considering the user's context. In terms of context awareness the context information referenced in design can be different from that specified in query on execution time. As a result, it seems that the service cannot properly prepared when the context hierarchy is not properly considered.

Then, for what reason Context study are crucial for content strategy? Contents strategy goals for delivering user optimal experience. Optimal experience means user experience in flow state, by means of information design and experience design in perspective of Contents Design. Experiences are provided by context made of information and knowledge hierarchy. Context which consists of user experience can be described by hierarchy of time context, spatial context, social context and global context, local context, personal context.

In this paper, context hierarchy for content strategy is proposed. Proposed context hierarchy takes time and spatial index and relations makes formal representation. The subsequent sections of this paper are organized as follows. In section 2, the preliminaries relevant to contents and spatial context are explained. In Section 3, a summary of related work in the area of context hierarchy is discussed. In section 4, the hierarchy of spatial context is described and explained. In Section 5 concludes this paper.

T.-h. Kim et al. (Eds.): MulGraB/BSBT/IUrC 2012, CCIS 353, pp. 266–272, 2012.
© Springer-Verlag Berlin Heidelberg 2012

2   Content and Context

Definition of Contents is usually understood in two aspects. First, the knowledge and information in specific domain. It is to define the content of traditional media such as books. Second, it is a concept that includes any of these knowledge or information and the services up to publish. The previous one is the concept of content focused on media, the latter is the concept of content in the digital age, taking into account the format of distribution and user services to be out the dependencies of a particular media. In this paper, We will described on the basis of the concept of the latter, contents are considered with the concept of network and platforms which can be found in OSMU(One Source Multi Use) or COPE(Create Once Publish Everywhere).

The goal of content design is to provide the optimal experiences. Csikszentmihalyi defined optimal experience can be acquired in flow channel that is a status in proper skills and appropriate concentration is maintained. Good experience is an experience keep in or induce to flow channel. Good content service is providing some knowledge or information what user requested in flow channel to have optimal experiences.

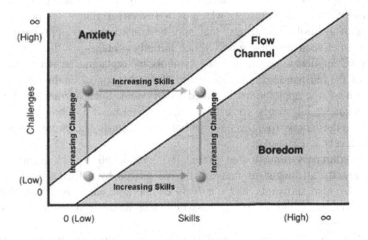

Fig. 1. Flow Channel

Shrendoff defined the knowledge hierarchy as a maturity process of information to knowledge which is initiated by combining context.[2] Knowledge is deliverables of understanding by global and local context, and with personal context configures experiences. In other words, Content made by information though experiences and best experiences are optimal experiences provided by in the process of combining optimal content and proper context.

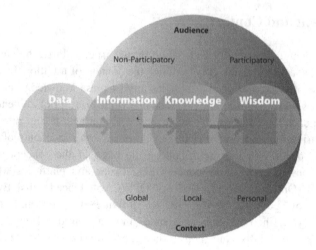

Fig. 2. Data, information, Knowledge and Wisdom

Chomsky Hierarchy is a containment hierarchy of classes of formal grammars. This hierarchy of grammar was described in 1956.[3] A formal grammar defines (or generates) a formal language, which is a (usually infinite) set of finite-length sequences of symbols (i.e. strings) that may be constructed by applying production rules to another sequence of symbols which initially contains just the start symbol. A rule may be applied to a sequence of symbols by replacing an occurrence of the symbols on the left-hand side of the rule with those that appear on the right-hand side. A sequence of rule applications is called a derivation. Such a grammar defines the formal language: all words consisting solely of terminal symbols which can be reached by a derivation from the start symbol. The Chomsky hierarchy consists of the following levels:

Type-0 grammars (unrestricted grammars) include all formal grammars. They generate exactly all languages that can be recognized by a Turing machine. These languages are also known as the recursively enumerable languages. Note that this is different from the recursive languages which can be decided by an always-halting Turing machine.

Type-1 grammars (context-sensitive grammars) generate the context-sensitive languages. These grammars have rules of the form $\alpha A\beta \rightarrow \alpha\gamma\beta$ with A a nonterminal and α, β and γ strings of terminals and nonterminals. The strings α and β may be empty, but γ must be nonempty. The rule $S \rightarrow \varepsilon$ is allowed if S does not appear on the right side of any rule. The languages described by these grammars are exactly all languages that can be recognized by a linear bounded automaton (a nondeterministic Turing machine whose tape is bounded by a constant times the length of the input.)

Type-2 grammars (context-free grammars) generate the context-free languages. These are defined by rules of the form $A \rightarrow \gamma$ with A a nonterminal and γ a string of terminals and nonterminals. These languages are exactly all languages that can be recognized by a non-deterministic pushdown automaton. Context-free languages are the theoretical basis for the syntax of most programming languages.

Type-3 grammars (regular grammars) generate the regular languages. Such a grammar restricts its rules to a single nonterminal on the left-hand side and a right-hand side consisting of a single terminal, possibly followed (or preceded, but not both in the same grammar) by a single nonterminal. The rule $S \rightarrow \varepsilon$ is also allowed here if S does not appear on the right side of any rule. These languages are exactly all languages that can be decided by a finite state automaton. Additionally, this family of formal languages can be obtained by regular expressions. Regular languages are commonly used to define search patterns and the lexical structure of programming languages.

Note that the set of grammars corresponding to recursive languages is not a member of this hierarchy. Every regular language is context-free, every context-free language, not containing the empty string, is context-sensitive and every context-sensitive language is recursive and every recursive language is recursively enumerable. These are all proper inclusions, meaning that there exist recursively enumerable languages which are not context-sensitive, context-sensitive languages which are not context-free and context-free languages which are not regular.

Most of Computer/Programming Languages are context free language to reduce the computation complexity, and in few cases are context-sensitive. By so far Computer languages are not properly reflect context described above.

Table 1. High Context and Low Context

High Context Culture	Low Context Culture
information implicit	information explicit
intuit meaning	clear meaning
rules clear	rules must be negotiated
talking is suspect	talking is trusted
premium on harmony	premium on personal innovation
Japan, Korea, India, Indonesia	England, USA, Germany, Australia

Context is crucial for culture understanding and content development. High context culture and the contrasting low context culture are terms presented by the anthropologist Edward T. Hall in his 1976 book Beyond Culture.[4] It refers to a culture's tendency to use high context messages over low context messages in routine communication. This choice of communication styles translates into a culture that will cater to in-groups, an in-group being a group that has similar experiences and expectations, from which inferences are drawn. In a high context culture, many things are left unsaid, letting the culture explain. Words and word choice become very important in higher context communication, since a few words can communicate a complex message very effectively to an in-group (but less effectively outside that group), while in a lower context culture, the communicator needs to be much more explicit and the value of a single word is less important.

These features of high context communication also appears in content industry. Web services have context features and hyperlinks and hypertext are representing context and flexibility of contents. Users can get a wealth of information from a number of pages containing pictures, videos, multimedia contents and application on the internet provides a rich Context. The context forms useful information only when the best experiences are provided to enable flexibility in the structure of various types and services that reflect the characteristics of the user.

3   Spatial Context Hierarchy

In Human Computer Interaction studies, User Contexts are classified as Table 2.[5] In HCI, Context is classified as physical, social and cultural context and each of which have time, location and other elements.

The Concept of Context in Urban Computing or context-awareness research is as follow. Environmental information or context covers information that is part of an application's operating environment and that can be sensed by the application. This typically includes the location, identity, activity and state of people, groups and objects. The three important aspects of context are where you are, who you are with, and what resources are nearby.[6] This aspect is good for design service models not enough for information priority modeling for content service. So we need hierarchical approach for spatial context.

Table 2. Hierarchy of User Context

	Physical context	Social context	Cultural context
Time	Use time Use day Use season	Work time Time pressure	Time cognition Time emphasis
Location	coordinates Altitude Space plan Dynamic space division Spatial structure Congestion degree	Home/Work Interaction with Others Privacy Source of information	Power distance Individualism/ Collectivism Feminism
other	Lighting Temperature Noise, dust	Hierarchy Duty Division Powers standard	Uncertainty Avoidance Explicit/Implicit culture Dominate tendency

4   Representation of Spatial Context

Spatial context can be represented by a line-region relation. According to the dimension of spatial objects in a space, six types of spatial configurations can be distinguished, which includes point-point, point–line, point-region, line-line, line–region, and region-region.

As the configurations involving point objects are straight forward, the corresponding relations are also simple. As a consequence, attentions have been paid mainly to the cases involving lines or regions. Spatial Context is presented by spatial elements for spatial information including point, line and region which have explicit values. Spatial elements and its representations are as follows.

Table 3. Elements of Spatial Context

Spatial Element	presentation
Point	A point (longitude, latitude, altitude)
Line, path, route	A line (point, point)
Polygon, region	A polygon (set of point lline)

To present a spatial information which have implicit context or uncertain information, some relations with explicit spatial information are required. These relations are presented by registry. Spatial registry has following elements: ID, Type, Topic, Space Limit, Description, Objects, (Relation, Entity). With spatial registry, implicit spatial context are identified, cultural resources and contexts are defined, and relations in cultural objects are clarified.

Table 4. Elements of Spatial Registry

ID	type	topic	Space limit	description	objects	Relation, entity

5   Conclusion

In this paper, We have considered the various aspects of context including areas of culture study, linguistics and ubiquitous computing. Spatial context must be presented with temporal context and social context, also considered with physical context. Some presentations for social contexts are also required.

In this paper we show a spatial context hierarchy and spatial registry model for spatial context representation. This study expected to be the beginning of context representation that can be utilized to present the content of such a hierarchy of context.

References

1. Csikszentmihalyi, M.: Flow: The Psychology of Optimal Experience, Harper Perennial Modern Classics (2008)
2. Shrendroff, N.: Experience Design. Wait Group Press (2009)
3. Chomsky, N.: Three models for the description of language. IRE Transaction on Information Theory 2(3), 11–124 (1956)
4. Hall, E.: Beyond Culture. Anchor Books (1976)
5. Kim, J.W.: Introduction to Human Computer Interaction. Ahn Graphics (2012)
6. Abowd, G.D., Dey, A.K., Brown, P.J., Davies, N., Smith, M., Steggles, P.: Towards a Better Understanding of Context and Context-Awareness. In: Gellersen, H.-W. (ed.) HUC 1999. LNCS, vol. 1707, pp. 304–307. Springer, Heidelberg (1999)
7. Freksa, C., Klippel, A., Winter, S.: A cognitive perspective on spatial context. In: Spatial Cognition: Specialization and Integration, Dagstuhl Seminar Proceedings, vol. (05491) (2007)
8. Deng, M.: A Hierarchical Representation of Line-Region Topological Relations. In: The International Archives of the Photogrammetry, Remote sensing and Spatial Information Sciences, vol. 37 (2008)
9. Ko, H.J., Kang, W.: Enhanced Access Control with Semantic Context Hierarchy Tree for Ubiquitous Computing. International Journal of Computer Science and Network Security 8(10) (2008)
10. GIO, The New New Media : Global lessons on the future of media, content and messaging, IBM (2007)

Mixed Reality in Museum Exhibition Design

Hee-soo Choi[1] and Dong-suk Yi[2]

[1] Department of History, Sangmyung University, 7 Hongji-dong, Jongno-gu, Seoul, Korea
[2] M&C Maru Co., LTD, 239-20 Younghwa Bldg. 2nd Floor Seongsan-dong,
Mapo-gu, Seoul, Korea
choice@smu.ac.kr, yidongsuk@mncmaru.com

Abstract. In the age of digital convergence, examples of digital convergence are often witnessed in all aspects of society. Particularly worthy of note among them is the development of a technology called mixed reality (MR), which are aimed at pushing the limits of human experience. This has laid the foundation for new cultural conditions by manipulating the existing conditions of human experience. Mixed reality (MR) technology has a wide range of applications, and can be effectively applied to museum exhibit environments, should the need arise for information on the uses and functions of artifacts, information on the restoration of damaged artifacts, the spatial characteristics of artifacts, or objects that require the modernization of artifacts. Utilizing mixed reality (MR) technology via mobile applications can be implemented with no additional need for hardware and system. Mixed reality (MR) technology can provide a variety of solutions to help museums fulfill their role and goals.

Keywords: Digital convergence, mixed reality, museum, exhibition content, experience (experiential elements).

1   Development of Cultural Technology in the Age of Digital Convergence

Today's society has entered the age of digital convergence. In other words, digital convergence has become the driving force behind social development. Digital convergence is now the backbone of our society, and their development has lately been remarkably successful. The technology has allowed people to reconstruct reality to push the limits of perceived human experience. Mixed reality (MR) has helped reach beyond the limits of people's perceived natural environment by breaking down the boundaries between the virtual and real worlds.

Such digital technologies represent a radical change in the conditions under which human experience is created. The conditions of human experience that are created and developed are cultural. The change in the conditions of human experience caused by digital technologies is simultaneously a cultural one as well. The argument is therefore convincing that, once these technologies blur the boundaries between virtual

T.-h. Kim et al. (Eds.): MulGraB/BSBT/IUrC 2012, CCIS 353, pp. 273–279, 2012.
© Springer-Verlag Berlin Heidelberg 2012

and real, the new reality created by the collapse of the virtual-real boundaries changes the patterns of human behavior, thereby giving rise to new cultural conditions.[1]

Of the digital convergence technologies, it is mixed reality (MR) that has fundamentally changed the environment of human experience.[2] Meaning the merging of real and virtual worlds, it enables virtual experience that feels more realistic than virtual reality or augmented reality. Since it merges two separate virtual and real worlds to augment the environment of human experience, mixed reality has gradually undermined the spatiotemporal boundaries of reality and made a substantial contribution to improving human abilities in the medical, educational, and media areas.

This presentation discusses the applications of mixed reality in museum[3] exhibit environments. Since museum exhibitions are under greater spatiotemporal constraints than any other environment, they urgently need digital technologies that allow the augmentation of visitors' experiences. This presentation examines how mixed reality can overcome the spatiotemporal limits of museum exhibit settings and bridge the gap in cultural perception that spectators may have while appreciating artifacts of different time periods.

2   Functions of Museums and the Need for Advanced Technology

In the conventional sense of the word, 'museum' means a building devoted to the collection and exhibition of objects of inquiry, research, and appreciation. The key focus here lies on 'exhibition'. 'Exhibition' is the act of appraising and evaluating collected objects, making them accessible to visitors, and drawing interest among researchers and investigators. The criteria of a good museum is its exhibition method. Museums, therefore, adopt a variety of exhibition techniques to provide good exhibitions. In the past, museums merely arranged the objects they deemed important in showcases. However, they started using dioramas to help understand the cultural contexts of artifacts, for example, by recreating their historical settings; with the advancement of digital technologies, museums have also begun to apply IT to their exhibitions.

---

[1] Lee Jong-gwan, Park Seung-eok, Kim Jong-gyu, Im Hyeong-taek: Philosophical Reflections on Convergence Technology in the Digital Cultural Industry. Research on Future Platforms for Digital Convergence II. Korea Information Society Development Institute(2010.12).

[2] There are three types of digital technology that provide the environments of human experience— virtual reality, augmented reality, and mixed reality. The differences among these three are as follows: Virtual reality refers to a computer-simulated environment, which can simulate a physical existence in the real or virtual world. The virtual reality environment can be expressed on a computer screen or a three-dimensional display. Augmented reality is an environment augmented by computer-generated sensory input on a video image of the real world, such as graphics, sounds, and GPS data, and allows an observed reality to be computer-modified or augmented. Lastly, mixed reality encompasses all augmented environments on the reality-virtuality continuum between the real and virtual worlds. The reality-virtuality continuum exists in all variations of augmented reality and augmented virtuality.

[3] The museums here refer to historical museums that display historical artifacts.

According to Carl Liner, among others there are 10 must-dos for successful museum exhibit design. 4 The elements which can be addressed by the use of technology include: motivating and intriguing the visitors, implementing focus contents, engaging the viewers by mutual interaction, immersing them within exhibition spaces. Most popular example is the audio-guide system that provides the visitors with recorded spoken commentaries through the headsets or smartphones. However, they serve a limited role as substitutes for docents and do not fully satisfy the aforementioned 10 elements of successful exhibition.

The previous studies have been focusing on how to immerse the visitors, because we have thought that the level of immersion is the most important factor that determines their perception of exhibited artifacts. However, the implementation of such exhibition technology seems to rather defeat the purpose by distracting the viewers' attention from the artifacts to the visual aspects of technology. The museum technology should serve the purpose of its exhibition, that is to help the viewers to perceive the historical and cultural value of presented artifacts.

In addition, while many studies have taken a general approach to the subject of utilization of technology in museum exhibition space, there are only few that propose an approach more specific as to the types of technology to be employed for different types of presented artifacts.

As shown above, the key must-dos of museum exhibition design include motivating visitors, creating focus content, encouraging the engagement of visitors, sparking their curiosity, interaction, and technology integration. The digital technologies to be applied to museum exhibitions, therefore, have to meet these requirements. Museums have to reach their ultimate goals by helping visitors understand the historical, cultural values of exhibits and sparking their curiosity through motivation, immersion, and interaction.

Once again, museums should aim at overcoming the temporal limitations of artifacts, namely, the objects of exhibitions, the spatial restrictions resulting from the spatial characteristics of exhibitions, and cultural differences that visitors will perceive. This explains the tendency of museums to utilize digital technologies to incorporate all sorts of experiential elements in order to overcome those spatiotemporal limits.

---

4 WHAT MUSEUMS MUST DO - The following are 10 ingredients for successful museum exhibit design: 1. Motivate Visitors: Target an audience—the general public and/or specific communities, 2. Focus Content: Filter content so visitors are not bombarded with information overload, 3. Immersion: Engage visitors with in a "story", 4. Modularity: Present smaller themes instead of one larger complex topic, 5. Skimmability: Information should be easy to take in because visitors are often standing and/or have different levels of education, 6. Patterns: Incorporate traffic/circulation patterns, exhibit sequence patterns and pre-existing framework patterns (architectural elements), 7. Capture Curiosity: Use storytelling techniques to engage visitors, 8. Interaction: Give visitors a "fun" experience by tapping into their emotion, 9. Integrate Technology: Technology should enhance visitor's experience, not distract from it, 10. Layer Content: Present information in a hierarchical manner(Carliner, Saul: Modeling Information for Three-Dimensional Space- Lessons Learned from Museum Exhibit Design. Models, Processes, and Techniques of Information Design, 2000).

To push the spatiotemporal limits of museums is to change the conditions of experience of visitors. In other words, one of the most pressing tasks facing museums today is to overcome the spatial restrictions of museums and the temporal limitations of the artifacts displayed irrespective of their purposes and return artifacts to their original time periods and spaces. That is where mixed reality comes in: mixed reality tears down the barrier between the real and virtual worlds and let visitors experience the real temporal and spatial settings where artifacts originate. The varying features of mixed reality can be applied to a range of exhibits in museums. What follows are a few examples of mixed reality at a level where visitors can easily understand the uses and functions of artifacts, and those of mixed reality that allow a comparison of then and now.

3   How to Apply Mixed Reality to Museum Exhibitions

There are a few types of information that visitors can verify by looking at exhibits in museums. Depending on the context of exhibits, namely, the kind of content that visitors are supposed to understand and experience, these types of information can be summarized as follows: If 1. An artefact has certain uses and functions; 2. The artefact has artistry in itself; 3. The artefact reflects the zeitgeist of a certain time period; 4. The artefact is incomplete (needs to be restored); 5. The original spatial configuration of an artefact is important; and 6. The details of the artefact need to be modernized. Of these six cases, mixed reality can be applied to 1, 4, 5, and 6. Let us take a look at each of them.

First, an artefact has certain uses and functions. Examples are artefacts of the Stone Age, including stone axes, stone knives, stone arrowheads, stone finishing net sinkers, and pottery. Since these artefacts are usually placed in showcases, they require explanations about how to make and use them. Most museums only provide additional explanations or brief descriptions for visitors to check the uses and functions of artefacts. While such methods help visitors understand the uses and functions of artefacts to a certain extent, visitors fail to get further details.

The left image shows pottery exhibited in Shaanxi History Museum in Xi'an, China, and its description. The pottery alone would not be able to grab visitors' attention. The graphic panel that illustrates pumping water offers visitors a clear understanding of the use of the pottery. Furthermore, the mobile application allows visitors to display the pumping image on their smartphones by pointing their phones at the panel. Visitors can enjoy a whole new experience beyond the spatiotemporal limits of the pottery as a museum exhibit when this mixed reality enables the experience of actually watching someone pump water from a river in prehistoric times.

Second, the artefact is incomplete. There are important artefacts whose shapes have been so damaged over time that they are hardly recognizable. Those artefacts are displayed either as they are or along with graphic panels that display their original forms. Visitors find it difficult to accurately identify the actual shapes of those artefacts because they have to move their eyes between the actual artefact and the graphic image of it restored version. Mixed reality should be used to project a restored image of an artefact onto the actual one.

The left image shows Goseonsaji Three-Storey Pagoda standing on the backyard of Gyeongju National Museum in Korea. Though renowned as one of the two stone masterpieces of Silla, along with Gameunsaji Pagoda in Gampo, the pagoda is partially damaged. Worse yet, its original shape of the entire tower from the third storey up is unrecognizable altogether. However, if a smartphone application is developed to project a restored image of Goseonsaji Pagoda onto the actual pagoda, visitors will be able to get an accurate image of the artefact. In fact, a large number of artefacts would benefit from this technology. Aside from historical museums, this technology can be applied to dinosaur bones displayed at museums of natural history.

Third, the original spatial configuration of an artefact is important. In other words, an artefact exists in a certain part of a larger structure, either as an ornament or as a tomb artefact. Such objects are exhibited together with a graphic panel that gives an image of the entire structure, a description of parts where the artefact in question was used, and, if a tomb artefact, a model of the tomb to provide details. However, such exhibit design poses a costly challenge and spatial limitations, especially if models are to be developed. The right picture is a graphic image that describes the used part of the Cheonmado jangni (pad or blanket) at the Gyeongju National Museum and its uses. Next to the exhibit is a restored model of the actual jangni (a device mounted under a saddle to prevent mud splatter) with Cheonmado painted on it. When visitors look at Cheonmado, they would have no idea

where the device was used, or where it was supposed to be during horseback riding. Now, the graphic panel mounted on the showcase. By applying mixed reality, spectators can access the details of Cheonmado right away.

Fourth, the details of an artefact need to be modernized. The crux of the matter here is to bridge cultural differences. Most artefacts that fall under this category are in ancient writing and therefore need to be modernized to help contemporary spectators understand. Examples include ancient books, ancient documents, and artefacts containing ancient scripts. Such exhibits come with additional descriptions for visitors' convenience. The left image represents the dice excavated from Anapji and now displayed at the Gyeongju National Museum. The dice was supposedly made by Silla aristocrats for entertainment purposes, and contains the inscribed rules of punishment on each side of it. The rules are, however, all in Chinese characters and hard for visitors to easily comprehend. There is only a brief description of them next to the dice. A smartphone application using mixed reality will be able to recreate the rules engraved on the sides of the dice in modern writing. Using the smartphone technology to create a mixed-reality dice game in a realistic setting will add experimental elements and help bridge the cultural differences between Silla and contemporary people.

4   Prospects of Merging Museum Exhibition and Digital Technology

Digital technology is most effective for visual presentation. To go beyond the image of an artefact, providing multimedia presentation featuring the historical and human environments in which the artefact was used - hence giving the artefact its context - makes imprints on the memory of the viewers more powerful than when the presentation was with audio text only.

Making the best use of digital technology is the latest trend among museum. In particular, high-tech media has become a popular approach, including 3-D hologram and interactive exhibit content using media tables, markers, and sensors, which provide a variety of experiential elements.

The use of high-tech media, however, requires hardware elements, namely, the medium itself and its enabling system. Museums are forced to make room for hardware installations in their exhibition space, adding further spatial constraints. Another drawback of hard-ware oriented technology is that it is short-lived, quick to be outdated due to rapid development in the IT field.

On the other hand, as discussed in this presentation, mixed reality technology can be realized using digital devices that individual museums retain, without having to procure software and additional devices for artefacts. The exhibition content created through mixed reality not only enables visitors to freely move around but also facilitates one-source multi-use. The content produced for each artefact can be used as it is when creating an interactive exhibition content system like a cyber museum or media table. Now, exhibition content can be viewed from places other than inside the museum with mobile applications. In conclusion, mixed reality is an ideal combination of museum exhibition and digital technology that meets the needs of this 'ubiquitous age'.

References

1. Lee, J.-G., Park, S.-E., Kim, J.-G., Im, H.-T.: Philosophical Reflections on Convergence Technology in the Digital Cultural Industry. Research on Future Platforms for Digital Convergence II. Korea Information Society Development Institute (December 2010)
2. Carliner, S.: Modeling Information for Three-Dimensional Space- Lessons Learned from Museum Exhibit Design. Models, Processes, and Techniques of Information Design (2000)
3. Han, J.-Y., Ahn, J.-K.: Study on the Characteristics of Media Environment of MRS. The Journal of The Korea Contents Society 10(11) (2010)
4. You, G.-S.: Smart-learning Technology Based on Mixed Reality. Journal of Advanced Information Technology and Convergence (JAITC) 9(3) (2011)
5. Kim, T.-E., Kim, B.-C.: A Study of Multimedia Exhibition based on Augmented. The Journal of The Korea Institute of Electronic Communication Sciences 7(3) (2012)
6. Eo, I.-S.: Digital Media Application in Museum. The Journal of The Korea Contents Society 10(9) (2010)

The Locality of Jeju Island
and Planning Visual-Image Contents

Jeong-Hee Kim

SunMoon University, GalSanRi 100, TangJungMyun, Asan, Korea
saviel1@sunmoon.ac.kr

Abstract. A policy for developing local culture has been magnified these days. has served as the backdrop for a number of visual-image content thus far by utilizing its own characteristics, such as its natural environment, its myths, and its living culture. This study attempted to discuss Jeju's strategy, which plans to integrate visual-image content with its local culture. *My Mother the Mermaid* used the strategy of adding its thematic meaning based on a good understanding of the symbolic spatial representation of Jeju. It is important to find any connection with the story from the spatial materials used in the film and apply special meanings to them

Keywords: Local Culture, Visual-image Content, OSMU, Space, Jeju Island, *My Mother the Mermaid.*

1 Production of Visual-Image Content and Regional Revitalization

The economic and social influence of culture is very powerful in the era of the creative economy. Even from the community's perspective, culture is an important element used to create the community's identity and image. The quality of the local residents' cultural life could also be enhanced through the active development of such a community culture.[1] For that reason, a political strategy, which aims to develop the community's culture, has been magnified these days. Visual-image Content especially plays a central role in developing OSMU in Korea, and so local governments actively support this field.

In this regard, Nami Island could be the benchmark model, for it became a famous tourist attraction for foreign tourists due to the influence of Korean drama. Individual local governments actively utilize the filming of local TV dramas as a means of promoting their own communities, or they plan for continuous profits by developing drama location sets as part of their tourism package. Lately, each local government also performs various activities by organizing its own film commission. They try to attract filmmakers by providing the environment and the tools that are

---

[1] Jong-Youl Hong, "Cultural industry and local culture policy in a creative economy era", Seoul: *Journal of Korea Culture Industry*, Vol.13 No.2, 2012, p.70.

T.-h. Kim et al. (Eds.): MulGraB/BSBT/IUrC 2012, CCIS 353, pp. 280–284, 2012.
© Springer-Verlag Berlin Heidelberg 2012

required in order to shoot the visual-image content and they also hold screenwriting contests based on their own communities. As for cities, several, including Seoul, Busan, Jeonju, Bucheon, Gwangju, and Jecheon, hold international film festivals.

Jeju has also actively attracted filmmaking by supporting locations and equipment through the Jeju Film Commission in 2010. The Commission made an effort to establish Jeju as the optimum place, using the slogan: "Island of Film Industry".[2] Jeju has served as the backdrop for a number of visual-image contents thus far by utilizing its own characteristics, such as its natural environment, its myths, and its living culture. This study attempted to discuss Jeju's strategy, which plans to integrate visual-image content with its local culture. For this paper, the film, *My Mother the Mermaid*[3] was selected. In most cases, it is regrettable that Jeju has been utilized as merely a spatial backdrop and a visual element. This movie used the strategy of adding its thematic meaning based on a good understanding of the symbolic spatial representation of Jeju. As such, this study attempted to examine the most effective method to incorporate regional characteristics into the planning of visual-image content.

2   Symbolic Representation of the Sea

Above all else, Jeju's meaning as the backdrop for a visual-image content results from the island's geographical condition. That is, the island is totally surrounded by the natural environment of the sea. Nature is the space where archetypal motifs directly reveal their forms in the common myths shared by all people, no matter their age. For example, symbolic representations of water myths could easily be expressed as sea, river, or lake. Such natural 'backdrops' are less noticeable than characters or incidents and, therefore, they tend to be accepted unconsciously in many cases. However, it could be said that this 'unconsciousness' is intended by the writer.

Bachelard studied materialistic imagination using the following four elements: water, fire, air, and earth. He regards that objects provide us with images as ' materials', not merely as 'forms'. That is, images are not created by external forms but by the substances' own attributes. The materiality of the image has a universality that transcends ages and cultures due to its attributes. According to Bachelard, visual images could change with age but the materialistic images of individual substances are mental images that never change.[4] Therefore, the materialistic imagination could be caused not only by the natural components of the four elements expressed into direct form, but also by various metaphorical materials. Archetypal images of natural backdrops are connected with other images that have similar meanings and that further differentiate their symbolic representations.

---

[2]   Jeju Film Commission official homepage, http://www.jejufc.or.kr/Default.aspx

[3]   This film was produced by Now Film in 2004. Its running time is 110 minutes. It was written by Park Hong-shik and Song Hye-jin and directed by Park Hong-shik. The film starred Jeon Do-yeon, Park Hae-il, and Go Du-shim. This fantasy melodrama genre film is set against the backdrop of Jeju and tells the story of a heroine who returns to the innocent and romantic period of her parents. The film earned directing and acting awards from various film festivals.

[4]   Myeong-Hee Hong, *Imagination and Gaston Bachelard* , Seoul: Salim, 2005, pp. 30-34.

Water symbolizes the most universal maternal instinct or regeneration, which simultaneously includes life and death. In *My Mother the Mermaid*, the reason why Jeju's blue sea has more significant meaning is due to the character's job as a *haenyeo* (female diver). The job of *haenyeo* exists only in Korea and Japan. In the boundless sea, they swim and fish for seafood, using no supporting fishing implements. So, *haenyeos* are mentally very strong and have a strong ability to maintain their livelihood. In the case of Mara-do, where most *haenyeos* live, females are ranked higher than males.[5] This movie utilizes the symbolism of water as its spatial backdrop and it uses the *haenyeo* as its material.

Yeon-sun (the film's heroine) has lived as a *haenyeo* since she was a teenager and she has the strong ability to maintain her livelihood. Now she is middle-aged and earns a living as a professional scrubber in the public bath. Water connects these two jobs. Yeon-sun swam and fished for seafood in the vast sea when she was young, but now she swims in the public bath. In spite of her difficult job, water is the material that provides her with vitality. Therefore, the small public bath is described as a mysterious space. Water simultaneously symbolizes death and life's amniotic fluid. So, the mysterious combination of contradictory materials exists. This movie is representative of the fantasy genre with its story of a daughter who is transported back to 1975, to the time when her mother and her father had first met and fell in love. It could be said that such narration becomes possible through the mysterious characteristics of Jeju's watery environment.

In the movie's present time, the relationship between Yeon-sun and her husband is chilly and quite different from the pure days of their first love. Yeon-sun is full of life and energy but he is calm and timid. There is a financial problem as well. Due to his gentle nature, he lost his money by guaranteeing his friend's debt. Yeon-sun gets angry at everything concerning him and he hides his head whenever she expresses her anger. Finally, he dies of cancer and Yeon-sun is obliged to maintain her livelihood. Her tough character is revealed through her outspoken Jeju dialect and by the behaviors she spits at the public bath. But, this is also a representation of the strong ability to maintain her livelihood and meet her maternal obligation to raise her children. The sea, which is used as the backdrop of the movie, reveals its symbolic representation in this type of maternity.

3   Island, Utopian Space

What kinds of images are used to describe Jeju Island in the visual-image content? First, Jeju is located away from the land. Between the mainland and the island, water is placed, which symbolizes the mystery. That is, Jeju Island is definitely an outer and unknown space. So, new images could be shown to the viewers that differentiate this place from the more familiar space of the mainland. Rothmann focused on the possibility that 'space' might model nonspatial elements, which are semantic or

---

[5] Young-don Kim, *Jeju Residents' Life and Culture*, Jeju: Jeju's Culture, 1993, p. 157.

axiological systems in the artistic text. He defined literary works as semiotic texts that are available to be understood based on their meanings, and he suggested that the world suggested in creative work should have clear objectives and meanings.[6]   First, every story has its own spatial conflicts in terms of its structure. One of the most universal subjects in oral literature is the contrast between 'dom' and 'antidom'.   The separation of the main character's world and from the external environment is basically in antithesis. The implicit meaning between a penthouse and a basement room is definitely different, and this is frequently used in the movie. Likewise, the same differentiation of meaning can be made between a city's forest of buildings and the quiet countryside.

Land reflects our daily lives, which are routine and familiar. In general, land is shown as a realistic and desolate image. In this way, the conflicting image of Jeju tends to be suggested as a very utopian space. The backdrop of the story is shown not as a physical space but as the space that is added with special values. In *My Mother the Mermaid,* Jeju is the pure space of first love. This contrasts with the current life, which is reflected in the backdrop of Seoul. Na-young leaves Seoul for Jeju to look for her father who ran away from home. Through the amazing sorcery of Jeju's space, she moves into the period in which her parents were young. This helps her understand her parents in a new way. Through Na-young's persuasion, Yeon-sun also comes to talk with her husband in Jeju, thereby tearing down the walls that separate them. That is, Jeju is the space where the value of pure love is recovered and the family's reconciliation is possible as a utopian space.

In *Architecture 101*, Jeju is also expressed as the space for first love. This film tells the story of a man who builds a house for his first love who appears unexpectedly 15 years later. Through the process to restore her old house in Jeju, they recall the memory of their first love. They understand the past when they parted from each other due to a certain misunderstanding. When the house is completed, their first love becomes beautiful memory. In the film, *A Love Story*, the love of a couple (the main characters) is nurtured under the backdrop of a house called 'Il Mare (the sea)'. In this film, the sea is used as the spatial material that simultaneously isolates humans and helps open their minds to realize love.[7] That is, it is the symbolic element that embodies both death and reproduction. That movie was remade in US in 2006 as *The Lake House*, and, based on that title we can understand that the material of nature, called water, plays an important role. In *A Love Story,* depicting Jeju as the heroine's hometown has something to do with this as well. The man builds a house for his woman by the sea and names it as 'transcendental love over time'. In this way, Jeju is described as a place that is remote and unfamiliar from the mainland, and suggests a utopian image for love and reconciliation.

---

[6] Yurij M. Lotman, "The Composition of the Verbal Work of Art", *The Structure of The Artistic Text,* Tr. by Gail Lenhoff and Ronald Vroon, Ann Arbor: The University of Michigan, 1977.

[7] Jeong-Hee Kim, *Contents Plan through Storytelling*, Seoul: HUFS Press, 2010, pp.68-70.

4   Conclusion

To reproduce historical facts as they are or to display tourist attractions by enumerating them with visual elements form the foundation of the planning stages of visual-image content. So, it is important to find any connection with the story from the spatial materials used in the film and apply special meanings to them. That is, the space is naturally melded into the story as an important element, and it is closely connected with the other elements in the story. This is the only way that empathy is successfully achieved through storytelling and the way that the film's content becomes memorable to the audience.

My Mother the Mermaid successfully utilizes materials, such as Jeju's *haenyeos*, dialectic language, and living culture and expresses the symbolic meanings of Jeju in a very effective way. As a result, a filmmaking location in Udo became one of the most popular tourist attractions. Tourists visit the place because they can reproduce the story in the film by themselves. The petite Chinese restaurant that the couple in the film visits frequently has now become a famous restaurant on the island. In the inn where the couple in the film stayed while the film was being shot, a special room named for the main characters was built, and the place where they fished was made into one of the tourist attractions. This suggests and implies that the connection of the story with cultural content and regional spaces could have an influence on regional development.

References

1. Hong, J.-Y.: Cultural industry and local culture policy in a creative economy era. Journal of Korea Culture Industry 13(2) (2012)
2. Hong, M.-H.: Imagination and Gaston Bachelard, Salim, Seoul (2005)
3. Kim, J.-H.: Contents Plan through Storytelling. HUFS Press, Seoul (2010)
4. Kim, Y.-D.: Jeju Residents' Life and Culture. Jeju's Culture, Jeju (1993)
5. Lotman, Y.M.: The Composition of the Verbal Work of Art. The Structure of The Artistic Text, Tr. by Gail Lenhoff and Ronald Vroon. The University of Michigan, Ann Arbor (1977)
6. Jeju Film Commission official homepage, http://www.jejufc.or.kr/Default.aspx

A Study on Exhibition Design of the Playing Environment Based Science Museum for Preschoolers

Nak-hyun Jung and Jeong-Ah Choi

Department of Multiplex Contents, Graduate School of Creative Industry,
Andong Univ., 137 Kyoungdong-ro, Andong, Korea
122015@hanmail.net, dalkisjunga@naver.com

Abstract. This study is focused on the research of exhibition design for science museum, dedicated to preschoolers aged from 3 to 5 in their crucial developmental phase for wholesome development to help them explore intellectual curiosity through scientific play and experience. In this process, I propose exhibition design types or structures tailored to preschoolers' science material and development features suitable for their each age group along with preferable play environment plan, and attempted to verify the direction for differentiated new hands-on education against average science museums. Based on the direction mapped out in this study, preschoolers' science museum for their scientific thinking and wholesome human development are expected to be established.

Keywords: Preschoolers' Science museum, Exhibition Design, Holistic Development, Playing Environment, Hands-on Activity.

1 Introduction

Toddlers aged 3 to 5 have inexhaustible energy and presents the crucial and intensive development window through active movement and physical development. Science education for toddlers is referred to the far reaching everyday activities endlessly exploring to find answers to their curiosities, thus it is critically necessary for the growth of toddlers' wholesome development capability and to resolve their intellectual desires.

Despite the recent growth of children museum and playing facilities in Korea, standalone science museum models for toddlers aged 3 to 5 are few and far between. Toddlers need to be exposed to customized environment for science education activities to explore answers to fulfill their innate intellectual curiosity in everyday life and to grow physical development capability through hands-on playing-cum-learning activities.

Therefore, this study suggests the direction of science museums dedicated to toddlers and reviews the possibilities of building such facilities—drawn as preschoolers' science museum exhibition design—based on preschoolers' science resources stemming from hands-on experiences of objects and phenomenon in everyday life.

T.-h. Kim et al. (Eds.): MulGraB/BSBT/IUrC 2012, CCIS 353, pp. 285–291, 2012.

2   Unique Characteristics of Preschoolers' Science Resource

2.1   Direction of Preschoolers' Science Resource

Preschoolers—fervent explorers armed with intellectual curiosity and interests on objects (Duckworth, 1987)—have inseparable relationship with science as all the interactive activities and the concept between natural phenomenon and material in everyday life, which falls into the category of broader definition of science (Ryu Jin-hee, 1985). Also the science concept for those preschoolers is merely the explanation system to describe their experience rather than the rules of science discovered from the nature. In short, the science concept should be suggested to trigger cognitive paradox in kids and awaken them to better understanding of science. For this reason, when dealing with preschoolers' science as resources for education and hands-on exhibition design, suitable classification system should be in place applying science concept conceived by kids and the children's developmental features and levels based on their intellectual curiosity and interest on the basic scientific phenomenon in everyday objects.

2.2   Resource Classification and Features of Preschoolers' Science Museum

The resource of preschoolers' science museum model that this study proposes is classified into natural phenomenon, biology, objects, and material in basic scientific areas or rather in daily life experience.

Natural phenomenon includes the sun, the moon, stars, and shadow with which we deal with everyday. Shadow is a typical experience that even a toddler aged 3 can experience in daily life and draw the link between objects and their shadows (Piaget, 1966). On the other hand, five year olds can further gain the scientific knowledge in complex representation process, enabling them to understand the subject in video images.

Biology encompasses various animals and plants easily found in kids' everyday life and share interactive responses. Children understands that the biggest features of living organisms are movements (Piget, 1929), and develops intense interest and curiosity toward animals prompting fast understanding. As they get older, kids can comprehend the other features of organisms such as growth, death, respiration, and nutrition (Yoon Bok-hee, 1985), and tends to understand organisms in animal and human centered perspective (Park Ah-cheong, Kwon So-young, 1995)

It is not important for kids to grasp the academic concept of Objects and Material, rather children should be able to enjoy consistent exploration process with interests and curiosity toward various activities involved. They tend to interpret the everyday experiences entirely on the circumstances and their cognitive levels. Therefore, it is important to plan exploratory activities of objects and material at their level.

3   Preschoolers' Science Museum Exhibition Design Plan

3.1   Exhibition Direction for Preschoolers' Science Museum

Preschoolers' science museum model is not the exhibition covering the textbook science material. Rather, it is critical for the museum to have customized educational exhibition space offering a variety of active hands-on experiences for children at all developmental stages to answer to scientific questions and curiosities for themselves. Especially the overall theme and design should reflect preschoolers' developmental features, preference and desires, and playing features. Therefore, the friendliness and familiarity of the theme and the environment should come before rest of the others to attract kids to voluntarily participate in the activities.

3.2   Theme Setting and Hands-On Experience of Preschoolers' Science Museum

The theme of preschoolers' science museum was chosen as "Burr Burr Vroom Science World," the adventure based on fairy tales. The main motif from selective fairy tales should be felt close to home for children, not as a distant story so that it can bring about the creativity out of their imagination. Children have the representational ability to make a lot of stories out of one small object, highlighting the need to have selective experience composition for more active and easier management.

The storyline should be planned out based on this. The main theme and smaller theme should be classified and the resources and hands-on play plan can be summarized as below.

Main Theme	Small Theme	Contents	Resources	Experiences
For a Bigger World	Rowdy Animal Farm	Info desk and farm animal play experience	Organisms (animals)	Hands-on, models /block and mobile play
Looking for Master Key	Spin-Spin Curiosity Tunnel	Forest village connecting tunnels become a playing space for everyday curiosity, Master Key purse is issued	Life science, Overall phenomenon	Interactive, Play type video /Games
Forest Village	Hurly Burly Underground Ant's Nest	The birthday party for ants and other insects in underground spaces and ground surfaces between trees	Organism (plants, insects), objects and material	Hands-on, Model/ Block and Mobile, Plaything, and Role- Playing
	Winding Tree Maze	Maze in nature to get the leads to save duck princess	Organism (Animal), Natural Phenomenon	Hands-on, Models
	Yum-yum Poo-Poo Digestive Tunnel	Air bounce tunnel in human body as food is digested	Organism (human)	Hands-on, Special Planning
	Sweet Cavity Snack House	Kids understand the importance of teeth brushing and health at the snack house where the cavity goblin lives	Organism(human), objects and material	Hands-on,Interactive, Experimental, Model, Diorama, Video/Quiz, Game

	Building New Nest	Make a new nest for homeless cat family	Object and material	Hands-on, Interactive, Participatory, Experimental/Role-playing
Conversion of the Road	Fresh Green Town	Nature's Lounge with an Overpass	Organism, Natural Phenomenon	Model
Underwater Town	Freezing Icy Arctic Village	Understanding the risks of the Arctic area melting down by meeting with Arctic animals	Natural Phenomenon, Organism	Field Sensory Type, Videos/Physical activities
	Hubble Bubble Underwater Town	Video game in air bounce space where you experience the life in deep sea water	Objects and Material	Hands-on, Interactive, Dynamic Video/Physical Activities Game
	Sparkly Desert Oasis	Playing experience space for hologram oasis lotus pond	Objects and Material	Hands-on, Interactive, Game
Treasure Hunt	Stealthily Treasure Hunt	Treasure hunt in a shell type cave wearing blue cloak and fighting pilots with magical power	Objects and Material	Hands-on, Interactive, Model, Special Video/Physical Activities
See You Next Time (or Farewell)	Jumpy Giant Elephant	Reading a large pop-up book reminiscent of adventures in a lounge space where kids can lean against a giant elephant stuffed animal	Organism (Animal)	Hands-on, Physical activities

4   Exhibition Design Type for Preschoolers' Science Museum Model

4.1   Exhibition Design Type for Preschoolers' Science Museum

The factors for aforementioned exhibition design types were planned out considering the developmental features and preferred designs for each age group of children aged 3 to 5 to emphasize and reflect changes on exhibition media and spaces, operation services, and science hands-on experience education. It will help preschoolers to find answers to their curiosities and imagination actively utilizing their developmental capabilities and sensory factors and fuel the wholesome development for children as a guide to reasonable problem solving methods and knowledge acquisition. The types are as below.

Category	Exhibition Media and Space		
Preschoolers	Developmental Features	Body	The scale of the space and media considering the body size
		Cognition	Playing activities for assembly, structure, and layout
		Sociability	Role-playing and imaginative playing environment open to other kids' participation
	Preferred Design	Color	Colorful design with rich primary colors
		Texture	Smooth and sleek surface texture for easier hygienic management and safety
		Shape	Easy to look friendly cervical curvaceous shape
Science Experience Education	Exploration		Role-playing environment leading children to explore media for themselves
	Thinking		The environment that encourages children to create second play through block and creative game
	Observation		The makeup of various media including the real nature which facilitates kids' curiosity and observation
	Physical Capability		It should be organized to help kids to enjoy hands-on experience activities using their bodies with media and space
	Cooperation		Choose the space and media where kids naturally cooperate
Playing Environment	Movement		Utilize motion activated video game and motion control art experience
	Convenient		Media provision for cozy and convenient space
	Self-respect		Materialize the dream and imaginative experience one can create or figure out through step-by-step experience
	Privacy		Media provision for the preschooler to create the space for one's own
	Order		Represent everyday life situation for disciplines like keeping order and straightening things
	Health		Exterior and interior space plan that interfaces with the nature, and offering healthy snacks reminding of the theme
	Smoothness		Offers texture hands-on experience with safety guaranteed various materials
	Challenge		Playing facility posing step-by-step challenges to all age groups
	Safety		All four glass walls ensure open view, and parents' lounge spaces along with safe media are added. All the space design is finalized as curve lines.

4.2   Direction toward Space Structure for Age Groups

For better effects of concrete educational hands-on experience, the classification of developmental features on each age group of preschoolers should be accounted for. Although preschoolers at age 3, 4, and 5 demonstrate the intensive developmental capability growth, they still show differences in terms of their understanding, behavior, and interests of science experience, space, experience, and play. Three-year-olds prefer direct multi-sensible experiences through movement, exploration, and discovery but their self-centeredness helps them distinctively claim their objects and their spaces. For the same reason, they prefer to have one on one activity with other individuals, parents, or teachers than other preschoolers. Four to five year olds, however, prefer indirect experiences along with direct experiences. They are also able to enjoy physical activities and to cooperate with and respect others engaging in cooperative plays.

Based on this premise, there should be selective space management plan for both collective experience spaces for kids aged 3 to 5, and the other separate spaces for children aged 3 and another group of kids aged 4 to 5 for. It should be followed up with more systematic plans such as different admission time schedule, booking system, and occupancy limits.

4.3   Exhibition Designs for Final Model Type

The final floor plan for Preschoolers' Science Museum is seen as a sketch as below, which can be divided in to three types as for the exhibition space for 3 year old(①,②), and for 4 to 5 year olds(③④⑤), and the space for 3 to 5 year olds (⑥~⑪).

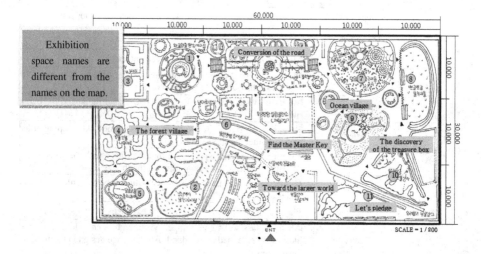

5   Conclusion

This study tried to verify the direction for new hands-on education space which differentiates itself from the average science museum and preschoolers' facilities with all the smaller age groups taken accounted for. The preschoolers' science museum model presents experiences through children's self driven voluntary capabilities, which not only delivers positive fun and thinking but also promotes the wholesome development. Also, as it encourages sociability enhancement with peer group activity and it is expected to establish itself as a family oriented educational cultural space.

References

1. Dattner, R.: Children Playing Environment Design, Gimundang (2005)
2. Ministry of Education & Human Resources Development, Resources for Preschoolers Science Educational Activity through Play, Ministry of Education & Human Resources Development (2003)
3. Kim, H.-K.: Thesis on Theme Park-like Planning and Architecture of Children's Science Museum Korea University of Foreign Studies Thesis, Ph.D (2009)
4. Kim, H.-R.: Research on Children's Science Museum Design Based on Preschoolers' Playing Type Features, Hansei University Thesis, Master's Degree (2010)
5. Kim, K.-H.: The Effects of Science Education Activities through Play on Toddlers' Scientific Attitude and Problem Solving Capability, Incheon University Thesis, Master's Degree (2005)
6. Cho, H.-S., Park, H.-S., Kim, M.-J.: Research on Scientific Questions by 3·4·5 Year Olds, Korean Association for Learner-centered Curriculum and Instruction (2005)
7. Choi, M.-O., Kim, M.-D.: Research on Children's Science Museum Exhibition Space Planning Approached with Playing Concept, Korean Institute of Interior Design (2005)

The Current Situations and the Tasks of Korean Studies Database Construction

Tae Hwan Oh[1,2] and Sangheon Kim[1]

[1] Hankuk University of Foreign Studies, 107 Imun-ro, Seoul, Korea
[2] The Academy of Korean Studies, 323 Haogae-ro, SeongNam, Korea
fanyoh@gmail.com, shkim@gcrc.kr

Abstract. The Korean Wave goes beyond the Asian countries and the world has paid attention to politics, economy, society and culture of Korea. This phenomenon is continuous so that the number of people who learn Korean studies all over the world is increasing. This study researches the current situations of Korean studies database accumulated so far to boost and develop it and examines what needs to be proper contents to the consumers and whether it can be industrialized. Additionally, it suggests the methods that the users can easily access to the data and the private provider can make and spread it. In the past, we put our focuses on building the data, but now we need to make it as a global content, promote to use the data and encourage the spread of information. In case that the privates use, develop the database of Korean studies, and then improves its values both in industry and in studies, these phenomena will last long.

Keywords: Korean Studies, Korea Studies DB, Support of History and Culture, Korean Knowledge Portal.

1 Introduction

'Gangnam Style of Psy' over 0.2 billion clicks on YouTube, Pororo broadcasting in about 120 countries, Galaxy S3 sold 20 million internationally, 5th place in London Olympics. These are the great remarks of Korea in the world that we can be proud of. Since the late 1990s, the Korean Waves started to spread among the Asian countries now become not just an interest in short time but global trends. Thus the government keeps making relevant policies and setting strategies to maintain the Korean Waves. The public and the private cooperate and lead that wave. The academies also support it by studying and developing contents. Due to these efforts, the Korean waves that are the center of pop culture make the world pay attention to Korea itself. The increasing number of natives wants to get a job in the Korean companies in their country. The departments of Korean Studies in the major universities increase. The number of universities that have the department of Korean Studies increased to 810 in 82 countries as of 2012 from 152 in 32 countries in 1992 according to Korean Foundation under Ministry of Foreign Affairs and Trade.[1] The department of Korean

---

[1] Korea Foundation, Resources on Korean Studies Overseas,
http://www.kf.or.kr/kor/06_res/res_gki.asp

T.-h. Kim et al. (Eds.): MulGraB/BSBT/IUrC 2012, CCIS 353, pp. 292–297, 2012.
© Springer-Verlag Berlin Heidelberg 2012

Studies is famous in East Asia, Central Asia and Middle East Countries where the Korean companies are actively entering. In the past, they are just interested in Korea, but currently they learn Korean and apply for positions in the Korean companies. In case of the US, the increasing number of colleges selects and includes the Korean class in their formal curriculum. Moreover, the president Obama mentioned the Korean Education System in the last New Year's Address so that the world focused on that. The status of Korea is getting enhanced. The foundation of Korean Studies Overseas is the resource of history and culture in Korea. Given that the geographical characteristics of Korean studies overseas, the relevant documents and reference books are hardly delivered to the educators of Korean studies so that the importance of its database has grown. If so, we will closely look at the preparation status and steps of the Korean studies database accumulating in Korea and judge whether it has possibility to grow as global contents.

2   Korean Studies and Its Database

2.1   Concept of Korean Studies

Above all, we need to check the concept of Korean studies. The dictionary definition of Korean studies is the comprehensive study dealing with all kinds of knowledge of Korea. Based on the researches carried out in various areas like humanities, society and nature, we will figure out the intrinsic characteristics that existed in society and culture of Korea and aim at promoting the exchange and mutual understanding in the international society. In addition, all areas can be the object of study such as language, history, culture, politics, economy, society, geography and science. It is based on the local and political divisions so that it is classified as a 'Study of Region' and a comprehensive study dealing with all kinds of knowledge about Korea. In other words, it is a study that finds out our own characteristics based on the common attributes of Korea. In the existing studies, it is defined as a study that researches the pre-modern history of Korea in the basis of Humanities and Social Sciences literature and Philosophy.[2]   The study on the overall data about liberal arts of Korea is the center of Korean studies. The resources on history and culture are spreading as Korean Studies. In the international society, educating Korean Studies abroad is the essential part to encourage the mutual understanding and exchange.

2.2   Current Situations of Korean Studies Construction

The practical concept of Korean studies is the database of Korean studies caused by the development of digital technology. The data of Korean studies as the contents of Koreanology is the results of digitalizing the resources of history and culture that are

---

[2] G. H. Bak, Discussions on Korean Studies and Practical Uses of Korean Studies. Study of Koreanology Vol. 8, p. 372.

the information of Korea. The example of this is the management business of knowledge and information. When we are suffering from IMF, the government started public Work on Informalization to solve the unemployment problems and realized the business by enacting Knowledge Information Resource Management Act in January 2000 and establishing the management plans for knowledge information resource in September 2000. 304.9 billion won were invested in 141 studies from 1999 to 2005 to digitalize the major areas like science technology, history, culture and information & communication. In 2006, database construction works for 43 studies were carried forward, investing 4.3 billion won. Also, to make the foundation of using the knowledge information resources jointly, the government operates Korea Knowledge Portal www.knowledge.go.kr). In particular, the integrated meta database were made and the speed of searching were increased to enhance the convenience of using and improve the Knowledge Portal system in 2005. Since March 2006, the service is provided to the people to use the knowledge information of Korea by having partnership with the private portals.[3] The institutions that linked with the information on Korea Knowledge Portal is 1,389 places and the amounts of information are 143,529,861 cases in 2010. Among this, scientific technology sections are 87,592,558 cases, which takes 50% of the whole parts, the history sections are 30,304,980 cases, and culture ones are 5,998,786 cases. The table below shows that the digitalized data are given through Korea Knowledge Portal.

Table 1. Status of Knowledge Information on Korea Knowledge Portal

Classification	Descriptions	Details
Ancient Writings	Ancient Books	The Seven Chinese Classics the Four Books and the Three Classics, the study of Confucian classic, etc.
	Ancient Maps	Maps in Joseon Dynasty like Daedongyeojido
	Administrative Documents	Family Register, Slave Documents, Court and Royal Documents, etc
	Foreign Documents	Data about independence movement, old book of the western about Korea
	People	Activists of Independence and feminism, etc.
Cultural Heritages	Relics and Remains	National TreasuriesTreasures, Tangible Cultural Properties, Folk Relics
	Living	Folks, Clothes, Food, Beliefs
Culture and Arts	Cultural Assets	Intangible cultural assets, data about pattern, etc
	Video	Korean movie films, scenarios, Korea video archives
	Tourism	Leisure Information in Jeju, Gangwon, Gyeongbuk Province

---

[3] National Archives in National Archives of Korea, Knowledge Information Resource Management Act.

Table 1. (*continued*)

Reports	Researches	Science, IT, National Defense
	Statistics	Chronology of statistic, yearbooks
	Publications	Publications issued by public institutions and government, policy information, etc
Papers	Academic Thesis	Academic journals issued by associations or institutions
	Graduate Thesis	Master's or doctor's thesis
Ecology, Environment	Biological Resources	Data sample of fossil, plants, etc., ecosystem zones
	BT	Dielectrics, proteomes, agro-live stocking bio data
	Ocean	Weather information, schools of fish, video clips
	Geological Resources	Distributions of geological features, mines, minerals
	Astronomy, Universe	Celestial images, astronomical phenomena
	GIS	Aerial/forest photographs that have taken since 1960,
Others	Language, Voice	Korean to Other language translation, Voice recognition data
	Laws	Modern Laws from 1910~1948
	North Korea	Administrative system, natural/Human geographical data

2.3   Current Situations of Korea Knowledge Portal Service

As we seen the functional characteristics on Korea Knowledge Portal, there are integrated search, detailed search and directory. They help the users to find the information easily through the finding system with diverse options based on the existing data. Also, this is provided to others outside by the type of OPEN API, which means that the data on Korea Knowledge Portal can be searched through the other sites. Furthermore, it provides the functions to install the desk bar and search box on personal PC. It also gives the fast deliver services of updated information through RSS and protection service of copyrights and mobile web service (m.knowledge.kr) that can be used on smart phone and pads. In addition, it links to mobile web after reading QR codes. Based on these kinds of basic functions, Korea Knowledge Portal serves the users to find the information about Korea. Data of related institutions of Korean studies is given through this portal.

2.4   Issues and Alternatives of Korea Knowledge Portal Service

Despite of these efforts, the level of awareness is not that high. Alliance with private portals makes it bigger and the two of affiliated sites (Paran, Empas, Nate), which are Paran and Empas, are gone. And the user accessibility is relatively low because of development of mobile environment. These days, many people try to build the integrated management system through Shared Data Portal (www.data.go.kr), but if the users do not know that site, the data cannot be used. Thus, the alternatives have to be made to enhance the accessibility of users actively. It can be a good method accessed by mobile searching through the mobile web of Korea Knowledge Portal. Partnership with Yahoo and Google that have lots of internet users abroad can be made to make the historical and cultural resources of Korea Knowledge Portal as global contents. It will help the people in foreign countries consume the information of Korean studies easily. For instance, the Heritage Channel use YouTube to provide the high-quality videos about cultural assets in English. These kinds efforts make the reliable public contents outstanding the most among the trillions of contents.

Now, Korea Knowledge Portal provides OPEN API to others. OPEN API technology is the representative of web 2.0 tech realizing the 'Web' as a platform. And it aims at the spread of information and the vitalization of use. Korea Knowledge Portal set the limits to searching. However, OPEN API is applied to the DB lists, each institution has, the detailed information will be spread faster. For example, if information about the cultural assets of Cultural Heritage Administration, tour information of Korea Tourism Organization and geographical information of National Geographic Information Institute are combined, the package of information may be completed. In case that fusion and combination of information are utilized in the industries, the ripple effect will be great. If the users or the private can use it easily, the knowledge will be distributed effectively.

Moreover, the standardization of basic information about metadata needs to be solved quickly. At first, each institution built their information in different forms so that Korea Knowledge Portal had difficult in establishing the database. Management numbers of each data were able to be integrated through UCI.

In case of utilizing, the mutual relationship between data and the reference have to be activated. Most of the digitalized contents about Korean studies are served respectively on Portal. The relevant information has to be linked systematically. For instance, Korea Local Culture Electric Books contain cultural heritage information of Cultural Heritage Administration, Dongyeodo of Korea Information Portal, the Korean classic DB of Institute for the Translation of Korean Classics according to the local contents and show in one place. These contents have to be combined in one package and delivered to the user to make them understand the information better. That is, various data has to be distributed in different types of platforms following the concept of MSMU (Multi Source Multi Use).

3   Conclusions

Now the world has not acknowledged Korea as the country of dispute and separated nation. It means that our traditional culture and pop culture are getting focused. We put our focuses on constructing database so far, but now we need to pay attention to utilize and spread it. When using it, we set the strategies considering the consumers firmly to have positive effects on sharing and spreads of contents. We need to establish the organized systems to make the Korean and international users utilize the contents developed by the private providers.

References

1. Mo, J.R., et al.: The diagnosis of the Korean Waves and Various Studies to expand continuously – related to the improvement of Korean studies. Study on Policy Issues of Ministry of Education and Human Resources 2005-contest-23 (2005)
2. Lee, W.B., et al.: The Current Status of Korean Studies Overseas and the Researches on
   the development in the medium and long term. Report of the Results on Policy Issues
   2009, Ministry of Education and Human Resources (2009)
3. Choi, J.H.: A Case Study on the MLA as an Example for the National-Level Cooperation
   Cultural Institutions (2008)
4. Jeong, Y.K.: Design Element Analysis for DID (Digital Information Display) Management
   Interface. Korea Design Knowledge Society (2011)
5. Ham, H.H., Bak, S.C.: Digital Archives of Cultural Archetype Contents. Its Problems and
   Direction (2006)
6. Kim, J.I.: Design of Metedata and Development of System for Managing Connection Information of Digital Contents (2009)
7. Kim, M.: Digital History; The Signification and Limitations of Construction Korean Studies Online Database Focused on the Database Search System of Western Books on Korea
   (2011)
8. Yoo, D.H.: The current situation the task of developing the national cultural heritage contents (2008)
9. Jeong, S.W.: The conception of Korean study and its ways of globalization (2010)
10. Korea Culture Information Service Agency. Study on Private Provision Methods of Public
    Culture Information (2010)
11. National Information Society Agency. 2012 Korea Information White Paper (2012)
12. Korea Knowledge Portal, http://www.knowledge.go.kr
13. Data Resource Portal, http://www.data.go.kr
14. Cultural Heritage Administration of Korea, http://www.heritagechannel.tv
15. Encyclopedia of Local Korean Culture, http://www.grandculture.net
16. Korea Foundation, http://www.kf.or.kr

Context of Visual Archive for Cultural Heritage

Byung-eun Park and Dae-kun Lim

Hankuk University of Foreign Studies, 107 Imun-ro, Seoul, Korea
laramagic@naver.com, rooot@hufs.ac.kr

Abstract. This article described context of visual archive for cultural heritage. Cultural heritage becomes the core record of a nation's identity and cultural identity and proves to have sufficient value in itself to be stored permanently. Efficient method of visual recording can be visual images to create an effective information delivery tool which utilizes audible systems. If we are to more clearly classify data and information, we first need to consider the context of producing and utilizing information. As a result, this paper shows that making this process more appealing serves not only as information in these references but also as a medium for us to further and diversify our experiences in cultural heritage. With the help creation of cultural contents.

Keywords: Context, Visual Archive, Cultural heritage.

1 The Need for a Visual Archive of Cultural Heritage

Cultural heritage is a communal product of an ethnic community and as such is optimal in portraying a nation's mental identity; and is a cultural resource that depicts a nation's historicity, artistry and academia. An archive that records such cultural heritage while pertaining to the aforementioned definition becomes the core record of a nation's identity and cultural identity; and proves to have sufficient value in itself to be stored permanently. The following points are derived from the fact that cultural heritage archives must be differentiated from ordinary records. Firstly, cultural heritage archives are the core of a nation's identity and cultural identity. It is vital in comprehending the historical, traditional, and cultural aspects of a nation, and proves to be valuable in providing a base for future scholars to research. A cultural heritage archive becomes the core resource in identifying unrevealed history, properly understanding a culture, and establishing a cultural community. International divides are ever converging due to the development of information technology and heritage archives are valuable in succeeding and maintain the cultural identity of a nation. Secondly, these archives are vital in the restoration and recreation of cultural treasures, as they are subject to damage by mankind and or natural disasters. It serves as a blueprint in restoring impaired and damaged cultural assets, closest to the original condition as possible. Thirdly, it is a fundamental resource of cultural creativity. For foreigners it serves as a good cultural tourism resource, while for us it becomes a base for the derivation of new knowledge. Heritage archives are not only a source of a nation's competitiveness but also became an intangible asset that determines the wealth of a country. Fourthly, these archives are the core resource for the

T.-h. Kim et al. (Eds.): MulGraB/BSBT/IUrC 2012, CCIS 353, pp. 298–302, 2012.

reconsideration of a nation's image and development of cultural industry. In addition to providing tangible economic profits through the development of culture based products, cultural heritage adds value by ameliorating the perception of a country by other nations. In addition to this, it not only becomes an element to be utilized in commercial tourism but also becomes a resource to be utilized as an applied cultural industry. Fifthly, archives are the core resource for realizing culture welfare. It realizes a service of providing cultural welfare through the enjoyment of cultural heritage in addition to a plethora of other services; and also provides an opportunity of education thus nurturing a strong sense of citizenship. Sixthly, these archives serve as a core resource for the development of green industries and as an engine of growth for future industries. Social networks, smart mobile services, smart TV, big data, are all examples of future industries in a digital age that would utilize cultural heritage archives as a base. Archives that accumulate the cultural heritage of a nation become a great cultural resource. Furthermore, the method in which we record this information as well as the medium we utilize can greatly amplify the benefits of such recordings.

2   Definition of a Visual Archive

Art allows us to live and experience a different reality vicariously and if not for this phenomenon much of our lives and actions would be foreign, and problems that incur in the context of our lives can be connected to us emotionally. When encountering new experiences, we discover ourselves reacting to these new situations and find ourselves renewed in our attitude. In the twenty first century, we find that the visual medium has had the biggest influence in how we expose ourselves to indirect experiences and through this medium we connect the problems of the past and present. Presently, the existence of the visual medium alone captures the viewer's conscience. This is because humans acquire and process information through visual systems such as images, markings, symbols, in addition to audible mediums such as music, natural sounds, and human speech. Acquired information is stored within our memory system, and when new information is entered, the recreation and synthesis of this new and old information creates unique nodes and integrals of information. Visual mediums such as images and audible information such as sounds and speech integrate to influence our memory, and catalyze a clearer synthesis of information. The important factor is how the degree of stimuli these visual or audible systems affect the efficacy of information delivery. Visual recordings can be images stored alongside text reports that together archive cultural heritage. An additional yet efficient method of visual recording can be visual images and BG, combined with narrations and on site recordings; to create an effective information delivery tool which utilizes audible systems. The visual medium is superior in that it is efficient in delivering information and leaving a lasting impression when it comes to archiving cultural heritage and the cultural assets that accompany it. It is necessary to store this information in visual mediums because these visual libraries of information are vital in the restoration of cultural assets and treasures when they become damaged.

3   The Context of a Visual Archive

Records can be classified into content, context, and structures, the fact of action (content) placed into a form (structure1) becomes a unique record; and when integrated with other records in filing systems become the physical structure (structure2) and this in turn becomes able to deliver contextual information in the form of function, action, and evidence. A file is formed through the collection of individual records that had been formed for a specific action or need, and a series is formulated through the collection of similar files collected, and these files together form a record group. Records can be subdivided individually into items, files, series, groups, and these classifications are made based on the content, context, and structure. When producing a visual record, the context becomes important following the content, so we examine the context of creating a visual record. We can define context as elements that can influence or change the meaning of a subject; while surrounding the subject. If we are to more clearly classify data and information, we first need to consider the context of producing and utilizing information. Without context, information fails to exist. Not only does context relate to the environment of data, it also relates to where the data came from, why it must be communicated, how it is arranged, and what kind of demeanor and environment a person accepts it in. Because the value and meaning of information changes based on the subject or situation, how the information is created and used is important contextually. Thus, when producing a visual record, not only is the subject matter important but also the context of the subject matter which can include location, environment, and overall scenery.

Table 1. Context needed when producing a visual record

Subject Matter	Classification of Subject Matter	Context
Object	Artifacts, tools, supplies, artwork, clothing, souvenirs, food, etc.	Location of object, Complete and detailed, important traits of object
Character	Interviews of the character, Character in action	Environment of Character
Remains	Buildings, tombs, ancient tombs, relics site, lots, pagodas, tombstones, literature, etc.	Location of remains, multi-dimensional, important characteristics
Scenery	Village panorama, natural scenery	Entire scenery
Events	Rituals, festivals, ceremonies, athletic competitions, plays, performances, exhibitions, etc.	Depiction of people participating in the event, content of event, theme of the participants

The important subject matters when producing a visual record from cultural heritage are: objects, characters, remains, tools, articles, artwork, clothing, specialty items, and food. When capturing objects it is imperative that one does not leave out the location of the object, holistic and detailed views, and it is important that the important traits of the object are emphasized. In the case of recording personal characters, it is also important to record the surroundings and environment of the character being captured. If the character is an academic, the interview should take place in a study or library, and this is important because it portrays what the character does as his main activity. Cultural remains such as buildings, tombs, ancient tombs, relic site, lots, pagodas, tombstones and literature should be filmed so that the surroundings are sufficiently captured in order to indicate the location of the subject matter and thus portray the context of the subject. This is also true when capturing a panorama of a village or natural scenery. Events can be subdivided into rituals, festivals, ceremonies, athletic competitions, plays, performances, and exhibitions; and it is imperative that the themes and images of the participants not be missed. In order for these recordings to remain as information rather than data, the context of the visual records is very important.

4   Realization of a Visual Archive and Its Context

In order for these records to be considered as information rather than data, how should the context of the visual recordings be realized? If we review the object from the 3rd passage, we must film the object with sharp focus, and without distortion, moving from a standard to telephoto viewpoint; filming a more holistic scene before a more detailed scene. By controlling the focus and zooming in and out of the object being filmed , we can emphasize the important aspects of the subject matter. In the case of filming characters, the filming should be done to incorporate the surroundings and the subject matter as naturally as possible, and by utilizing depth of field focusing on the main character, we can help the character stand out. However, when filming a character and the surroundings, it is important that the environment matches the subject matter and actions of the character. When filming cultural remains, it is important to utilize as table composition so that distortion is not present; and it is also important to capture the subject matter from a variety of angles such as the front, sides, and rear. In addition, it is imperative to include the surroundings of the remains so that the location is portrayed. In the case of a village panorama or its natural scenery, the weather can play a critical role. Therefore, the following should be considered carefully when filming: If the subject matter requires a wider angle in comparison to the filming of cultural remains or events, either wide angle lenses or panoramic shots should be utilized. In the case of festivals or anniversaries, it is important to film the events in chronological order in order to properly portray the content of the event. Because the activities and participants need to be emphasized, images that best capture these scenes should not be missed.

5   Conclusion

Cultural heritage has value and should be preserved permanently as a core resource of national and cultural identity, and is also the fruit of an ethnic and communal entity. These archives as a cultural resource retain a high mental value, and reveal a nations identity in addition to the historicity, artistry, and academia of a nation. This cultural resource stimulates the visual and audio senses to effectively deliver information via images, and these images alongside reports become an important method of recording cultural heritage. The reason these recorded images are so effective in delivering information is because the visual images alongside the sounds, stories, narrations, and explanations create both audible and visible stimuli. We reviewed above the methods in which we can realize the context of the archives, and context follows content in the production of recorded imagery. In the process of viewing the recorded images context becomes the main element in influencing the viewers or users. Finally, we review why the context is important. Firstly, we can recreate the actual environment. If we only record the event, characters, or cultural remains without capturing the environment, sounds, and livelihood of the surrounding area, we can easily miss critical information vital to understanding the subject matter. Secondly, we can emphasize characteristics of the cultural region. In the case of cultural remains, events, or scenery, the holistic view of the area portrays the features of that culture. When we record cultural heritage it is important that we also record the characteristics and distinguishable cultural traits of that area. Thirdly, we can sufficiently record relevant information. It is import that we oversee the succession and preservation of an ever rapidly diminishing cultural heritage. In order to achieve this, it is imperative that we record in a detailed fashion, and detailed information regarding the asset itself as well as the surrounding becomes critical information that can utilized in the restoration of cultural treasures. Fourthly, the context can become utilized as a standard in various ways when producing multimedia. There are many ways we can apply recorded images, and sufficient information in these recordings can serve as a platform for further applications. In addition to the characteristics of an archive in storing information, we need to make recorded images more appealing. Making this process more appealing serves not only as information in these references but also as a medium for us to further and diversify our experiences in cultural heritage.

References

1. Kim, S., Kim, N.-Y.: Knowledge hierarchy for culture contents development. The Korea Contents Association 11(12) (2011)
2. Kim, J.-W.: Human Computer Interaction Ahngrapics (2012)
3. Cultural Heritage Administration of Korea, Guidebook of intangible cultural asset recording. Cultural Heritage Administration of Korea (2010)
4. Cultural Heritage Administration of Korea, Methods to establish of information archive for cultural heritage of public order administration organization. Cultural Heritage Administration of Korea (2012)
5. Oh, B.-K., Kang, S.-J.: Textbook of Information Design, Ahngrapics (2008)
6. Lim, Y.-S., Bang, I.-K.: A study on the Korean community(Koryo-Saram) and visual image, a Visual Archive. Human Contents of Association 4, 122–143 (2005)
7. The Academy of Korean Studies, Multimedia contents production project manual. The Korean local culture grand electronic encyclopedia (2012)

Jumbagi: Korea's Dinosaur 3D and OSMU Strategy

Jong-Youl Hong

HanKuk University of Foreign Studies, ImunRo 107, Seoul, Korea
herr_hong@hufs.ac.kr

Abstract. *Jumbagi: Korea's Dinosaur 3D* is one of the good examples of One Source Multi Use. For this, potentials and possibilities of the material 'dinosaurs' played an important role. At the same time it has a special strategy to be recreated as new content. First, the importance of characters was emphasized. The production crew pioneered the new faction genre by combining documentary with storytelling. Another important matter in the movie is that it is the first Korean 3D animation for theaters. It is very meaningful to show the world vision of the Korean image industry, satisfying world movie trends.

Keywords: *Jumbagi: Korea's Dinosaur 3D,* OSMU, Documentary Film, Original Source, Storytelling, 3D Animaition.

1   Introduction

Jumbagi: Korea's Dinosaur 3D[1] is Korea's first 3D animation for theaters that surpassed the one million-viewer mark. It has produced derivative works and has been actively exported as "killer content"; it is one of the good examples of One Source Multi Use (OSMU). It is also unique because its original work was one of the EBS' documentary programs *Koreanosaurus*, aired in 2008. The director, Han Sang-ho, wrote a novel *Dinosaur Warrior, Biin*, and made an animation based on the novel. It is significant to analyze the production process and strategies of *Jumbagi:* a successful case of the Korean image and content industry.

Two important aspects about the *Jumbagi* series project will be discussed. First of all, it's about the matter of the original source. The success of content depends on the value of subject matter; it is an absolute requirement especially for OSMU. We are going to find the value of a subject about dinosaurs and reflect upon scientific references concerning dinosaurs in the Korean peninsula. Also, we use the original documentary as a primary source. We analyze how *Jumbagi* could establish itself as a source for the massive culture industry from a documentary for broadcasting. Second of all, it's about the matter of *Jumbagi*'s multi-use. We study about what methods recreated this animation based on its original source. It was possible to succeed

---

[1] Co-production: Dream Search C&C/ EBS/ Olive Studio, Distribution: CJ Entertainment, Production Period: 36 months, Production Cost: 7 billion, Release Date: 26 January 2012, *Jumbagi* stands for *Jumbagi: Korea's Dinosaur 3D*.

T.-h. Kim et al. (Eds.): MulGraB/BSBT/IUrC 2012, CCIS 353, pp. 303–307, 2012.
© Springer-Verlag Berlin Heidelberg 2012

because of not only the power of its source, but also the competitiveness of itself. We analyze the project point of *Jumbagi*. Furthermore, we are going to see different types of content that has been produced thanks to the success of the film *Jumbagi*.

2   Practical Use of the Original Source

The original source of *Jumbagi* was an EBS' documentary film, *Koreanosaurus*.[2] EBS had planned to produce high quality documentary films since it launched its own channel, the "Intellectual Channel." It produced *Koreanosaurus* from the idea that a big project could be better for promoting. The production cost of the documentary film was 600 million won. Considering the fact that the production cost of a general documentary film in Korea was 50 million won, it sure was a geometrical scale.

The production crew, which dreamed about creating a new and meaningful work, tried to adopt historical restoration through developed CG skills and decided the subject of the work as dinosaurs. However, BBC documentary, 'Walking with Dinosaurs (1999)', spent 12.8 billion won for the production cost, which was 20 times more than the production cost of *Jumbagi*. On top of that, the director wanted to add a 90 minute-long CG to the documentary film. The maximum length of CG was 10 minutes in Korea at that time. In spite of Korea's low personnel expenses, computer graphic companies estimated that at least 6 billion won would cost to make the documentary. At this moment, one animation company called Olive studio contacted EBS to suggest producing the documentary film.

Although the production went through some crises, the extraordinary project of the Korean broadcasting station had been realized. For this, potentials and possibilities of the material 'dinosaurs' played an important role. The direct source of *Jumbagi* is a documentary but it is based on a dinosaur's story. Children's preference for dinosaurs is universal in the world. The EBS production crew took audience measurement and saw the highest rating from the audience of children aged between four and seven. The film exported to the German broadcasting company, RTL-DISNEY at 150 million won, marking the highest amount of export in the Korean documentary history. The film also saw the highest ratings of 4.2% as it was aired during the prime time slot. The film was sold to broadcasting stations in 14 countries including the Italian national broadcast RAI. Especially in North America, the content related to dinosaurs is sure to be a hit. For example, the children's section in bookstores shows a boom in books whose content is related to dinosaurs. *Koreanosaurus* picture book has sold 800,000 copies. On top of that, it has produced over 20 kinds of books, cartoons, stationary, and puzzles.

Jumbagi is appraised as scientific content. The material about dinosaurs uses scientific facts as its resources. Therefore, it needs the recent study and scientific knowledge about dinosaurs. *Koreanosaurus* was advised by a professor, Min Heo, who is Korea's leading scientist in the dinosaur field. The background of this

---

[2] Plan: Dec. 2007, Broadcast: Nov. 2008, Broadcasting Rating: 2.9% (In EBS, it recorded the highest viewing rate), Refer to Production Notes of Documentary *Koreanosaurus* (by Director Sang-ho Han) and Documentary *Secret of Birth, Koreanosaurus*(EBS, 2008).

documentary is that the Korean peninsula was a paradise for dinosaurs 80 million years ago, during the Cretaceous period. The southern cost of Korea, so-called a ballroom of dinosaurs, has many fossils of dinosaur's foot print. It seemed to be home to many kinds of dinosaurs. They would coexist in the area because of the enormous lake. When the producers selected the dinosaurs which could have lived in the Korean peninsula, they based their decisions on scientific facts.

What is the distinction of *Koreanosaurus* as a source of *Jumbagi*? Generally, the composition of scientific documentaries includes the followings: an introduction of artifacts excavation, interviews with a scientist, scene reproduction based on the interviews. However, *Koreanosaurus* combined a story with documentary. Recently, the effect of storytelling has been very influential; a documentary film cannot be an exception. So to speak, this was a faction documentary. In this process, characters as elements of a story were drawn naturally. Tarbosaurus was the main kind of dinosaurs in Asia at that time. The production crew thought it was very important to choose characters that represented Asia and no other parts of the world. The main character, Tarbosaurus, got a name 'Jumbagi,' which is familiar folksy name. That was the announcement of the birth of *Jumbagi*.

Koreanosaurus's producers made a 10 minute-long 3D image after the success of their documentary. The 3D image was screened as a performance combining images and animatronics.[3] It was a big issue when they opened its own exclusive standing theater at Goseong Dinosaur World EXPO. Moreover, they have held the Dinosaur Expedition in the Korean Peninsula including KINTEX in Ilsan, BEXCO in Busan, and KOTREX in Daejeon. As of 2011, the number of admitted audience was 430,000 and the income from admittance was about 5,500 million won. After reviewing the audiences' response through these events, *Jumbagi* was planned to start production.[4]

3   Aspects of Multi-use

Jumbagi plays a key role in OSMU. Even if it is originally from another documentary, the 3D animation *Jumbagi* has been in the center in the process of being used as OSMU. We have figured that it has many merits and strengths through analysis of its source. However, we know that it would still need a special strategy to be recreated as new content. The important points regarding the production of *Jumbagi* are as follows[5]:

First, the importance of characters was emphasized. It characterized storytelling using the name of the main character 'Jumbagi' as the title. Jumbagi and his family's moving to the earthly paradise against the apocalypse was enough to inspire audiences. Most audiences were families with children, so its theme 'family love' was an appropriate theme for audiences. In addition, the dynamic scene of a fight against

---

[3] Compound word formed from "animation" and "electronics".

[4] In July of 2011, director Sang-ho Han published a novel *Dinosaur Warrior Biin* after he got an idea from *Koreanosaurus*.

[5] Refer to Production Report *Jumbagi: Korea's Dinosaur 3D*(DREAM SEARCH C&C), Documentary *Secret of Birth, Jumbagi: Korea's Dinosaur* (EBS, 2012).

Tyrannosaurus reminded them of blockbuster movies. There were 17 different kinds of dinosaurs and 80 total dinosaurs in the movie, which was much more than the previous documentary. And they added more drama through conflict angle between the main character and the enemy. The name, Jumbagi, could be loutish yet friendly. It is getting more awareness internationally, representing Korea's characters. Animation is a genre that has a low cultural discounted rate. It has high public accessibility and it is accepted easily compared to other genres.[6] This is why the personality of a character is also important. Speckles the dinosaur can be more universal than an actor from a specific country, so it can has strong competitiveness in global markets.

Another important matter in the animation is that it is the first Korean 3D animation for theaters. It became a selling point that whole movie is made of digital actors and composed of actual pictures and animation by 100% Korean technology. Jim Chabin, the president of international 3D association, said Korean 3D technology can stand comparison with world-class. It took 3 years to make the animation with 500 staff members. It also used more than 3D animation technology. Its production process shows that the film has an aspect of "digilog".[7] When filming actual backgrounds of the film in New Zealand, it had to be followed by the work of assumption of the actual size and movements of the dinosaurs. The digitalized actions of the characters were also made by acting of actual actors imitating dinosaurs. When it comes to voices, voice actors acted out the voices of the dinosaurs for each age group and the voices were digitalized. Animatronic filming was done with models of dinosaurs that were moved by machines at the actual set. This was done to compensate for graphic insufficiency so it gave scenes a reality. They also composed OST themselves and the OST was played by Prague Philharmonic with surprising depth and great emotion. It is different from over dubbing which uses many small groups and records over the previous record.

By using differentiated methods, *Jumbagi* has become a big hit worldwide. Also seeing the aspect of OSMU, it has become content with various genres. They have published 30 different kinds of books such as educational cartoon, fairy tale books, and puzzle books. As they sold 1.5 million books, it became a top bestseller in the children's book at Kyobo book center. They are developing mobile games, TCG games, and online games, as well as a smart phone application for learning about dinosaurs. There are also various exhibitions and Korean dinosaurs 4D LIVE SHOW being ready to be held. They are planning to build 'Cretapark' at a theme park. Speckles will also be characterized into furniture, food and beverage, stationary, and mobile phone cases.

4   Conclusion

There used to be a prejudice about dinosaur movies that only major studios with an enormous sum of money and technology could make dinosaur movies such as

---

[6] Ki-Soo Park, Cultural Communication through Media(chapter8), Seoul: Non-Hyung, 2004, p. 254.
[7] Eo-ryeong Lee, Declaration of Digilog, Seoul: Tree of Thought, 2006.

Jurassic Park. Jumbagi is the first 3D movie with Korean technology and it resulted great outcomes. It is very meaningful to show the world vision of the Korean image industry, satisfying world movie trends. It was possible to produce the outcomes thanks to the endeavors of the production crew and their spirit of digilog. It is also meaningful that they pioneered the new faction genre by combining documentary with storytelling. Sympathizing with the audience through drama implicit was an important implement for the success. The global success of *Jumbagi* proves that the level of Korean storytelling, which used to be pointed out as a limit, has improved. The success was not built in a day. It was not only creative ideas and planning but wise investments in the film. It was exceptional that Olive studio suggested joint production and profit share for the production of *Koreanosaurus*. There has been an argument that the investment system of the Korean culture industry is based on extremely short-term investments. To create global killer content, we need accurate judgments and an environment for long-term investments.

References

1. Lee, E.-R.: Declaration of Digilog, Tree of Thought, Seoul (2006)
2. Park, K.-S.: Cultural Communication through Media, ch. 8, NonHyung, Seoul (2004)
3. Production Report Jumbagi: Korea's Dinosaur 3D. DREAM SEARCH C&C, Seoul (2012)
4. Production Notes of Koreanosaurus (by Director Sang-ho Han), Seoul (2008)
5. Documentary Secret of Birth, Jumbagi: Korea's Dinosaur (EBS), Seoul (2012)
6. Documentary Secret of Birth, Koreanosaurus (EBS), Seoul (2008)

A Study about the Space Based Story-Telling for Exhibition of Literature Museum

Dong-hwan Yoo and Hyo-min Kim

Department of Multiplex Contents, Graduate School of Creative Industry,
Andong Univ., 137 Kyoungdong-ro, Andong, Korea
philsm@andong.ac.kr, realme07@naver.com

Abstract. Museums have continuously evolved according to the points to accommodate the needs of each period and created their own identities with the changes within them by shaping various types through spaces and media. Especially the literary museums are in a particular position to exhibit both the work, story itself and a story creator, the storyteller, committed to deliver the very specific meaning and its symbolism of the story. Therefore, the storytelling of literature museum requires both the approach to literature and the three-dimensional storytelling to implement the literacy. This Paper considers and suggests the ways to apply the characteristics the fairy tale-telling might have when they are exhibited and the guideline how to exhibit storytelling.

Keywords: museum, literature museum, storytelling, space based storytelling, fairy tale, exhibition.

1 Introduction

The definition and the concepts of museums have been continuously redefined as time goes by and the exhibition and management methods of museums have been changed according to the spectators ' needs. Museums are functioned as not only exhibition venue but also complex cultural facilities since spectators consider museums as experiential space of leisure life. Storytelling has been introduced by museums as an alternative for an changing exhibition environment and spectators can learn the objectives of exhibition effectively through storytelling.

Especially Literature Museums are in a specific position to reinterpret the conventional storytelling ,that is, literature as a spatial storytelling. However, the problem lies in that currently museums faithfully function as Figures Memorials not as Speciality Museums. This Paper finds out what is a real storytelling in museums and attempts to understand the particularities of the Literary Museum exhibition. Futhermore this Paper tries to set the direction of spatial storytelling for the Literary Museum exhibition by analyzing fairy tale, a genre of literature as a concrete example.

2 Storytelling of Museums

Storytelling is a process turning a story into a telling and it has a form described by the order of the beginning, middle and end; and has elements like events, characters

T.-h. Kim et al. (Eds.): MulGraB/BSBT/IUrC 2012, CCIS 353, pp. 308–312, 2012.

and background. A story is different from a simple information that conveys the experience of the events and W. Benjamin differentiates and defines the two as below in Table 1.

Table 1. The Difference between Story and Infomation

Story	an Interesting Story that happened far away	intended to be remembered by the Listener	maintain the vitality and usefulness of the contents for a long time	conveying not only the events and things but also people ' s experiences
Infor mation	a Verifiable Story that is happening nearby	intended to provoke the Listener	start to lose its vitality and usefulness at the very moment of delivering the contents	conveying the pure reality of events and things

Like this, storytelling is a freely deformable communication tool considering the speaker's intent and the listener, not an meager conveying tool of the objective facts.

Museums are choosing space as a tool to communicate with spectators and designing a story-based exhibition in order to effectively convey the story according to the exhibition purpose. However, since Spatial storytelling is three-dimensional in its nature, it is very different from the text-based conventional storytelling.

Unlike the text-based story described according to a certain logic and conveyed depending on the reader's understanding and imagination, space-based story is conveyed directly through the immediate spatial experience. Therefore the exhibition space must be designed to keep the user experience fully in mind, following the structure of the conventional storytelling. By doing so, museum storytelling tends to create an another story through interaction between spectators, works, objets and connection among objets, exhibition space and the flow of human traffic.

While the three elements of the conventional storytelling are motifs, characters, and plot, the counterparts of the exhibition space might be key objets, objets, and plot.

First, key objets are the essence of the story, that is, the starting point as the most important element that penetrates the results of material analysis and concept extraction. Second, objets are the other important selected objets except key objets and arrangement and connecting points of those objets can divide the space as a sub story unit. Third, plot like that of the conventional story, is an element that help proceed the story in a certain order functioning as the compass to set the direction of the story.

Since space-based storytelling clearly considers objets, space, and spectators in conveying the story, the exhibition form requires to consider space zoning, a storyline of exhibition and medium selection that effectively implement the exhibit. Museums need various storytelling methods that will effectively deliver many stories as the totality of experiences including objets.

3   Particularities of the Literary Museum Exhibition

Literary museums are in a particular position among other sub-museums because they are speciality museums that exhibit story works but also they hqve to include a specific person called the writer as exhibition material.That ' s the reason literature museums are considered as figures memorials to feature the writer ' s life and most of them function like this.

Naturally, the writer ' s relics have an advantage over literary work at the museum exhibition because the problem lies in the uniqueness of literature that the reader cannot fully understand the writer ' s intention and the contents of the story without reading the work that exists as a text in person. If you fail to consider a way to effectively display this exhibition material, you have to make the museum function as relic exhibition that relatively easily show the trace the writer ' s life. That ' s why each lierary museum arrange the so-called writer ' s room, the reproduction of writing room in the main hall of the exhibition space.

However, such an exhibition method as a result works as an element that weakens the power of gathering spectators who only have fragmentary information or curiosity about the work and even brings an negative effect on the general museum management

Literature and literature museums have the medium role that links objects and objects in common. The connection link of objects here go down the list like the reader and the reader, the reader and the message, or the spectator and the objet, the spectator and the message and so on. What is clear is that everything exists as a method for communication. What is different here is the physical dimensions of the properties like text and space. Then all you have to do is to apply modified communication method that is suitable for the medium's property. That's the only way to make the communication between objects and objects possible.

Generally, spectators who want to visit a literature museum actually go there acquiring advance information and curiosity about the literary work. That means that spectators' primary needs are based on the work, in other words, they utilize literature museums as light leisure play and educational space rather than a venue for awe and respect for the writers.

Thanks to this revelation, literature museums recently are making efforts like restoring the writer's house nearby their museums and restoring the background village of the literary work in the form of literature village. Those efforts help fortify place of literature museums and satisfy spectators' expectations at the same time. However, restored writer's houses and background villages look remote from the natural changes of times and thoes restoration works are not exactly restoring as they were in the past, mostly building anew, failing to make spectators feel nostalgia about the literary work.

The real space that is the spatial background of the literary work can be edited according to the writer's intention and can be reborn as a personal space by the reader of the work. This can be translated that there is ,in fact, a huge distance between the real space and the personal, imaginative space the spectators is creating while reading the work.

This is why you need a new exhibition method of literature museums that enables spectators really experience the message of the literature , in which the author dissolved his live and ideas, in a space not in their imagination. On top of that, each literature museum might have differentiation effect if all the literary museums may apply different exhibition and management methods according to their own purpose of the exhibition. Moreover, in order to exhibit each literature genre that has its own different expression method within a comprehensive range called literature, you need to fully consider the singularity of the material.

4   Fairy Tale Analysis as Exhibition Material

Fairy tale is narrative literature written based on innocence of childhood for children as a specific reader group and it has its own specific storytelling elements such as fantastic elements, the simplicity of the configuration, and educational content. However, you need to reinterpret it in the aspect of exhibition material when it is exhibited at the literature museum that works as a three-dimensional medium.

First, fantastic elements
Spectators expect to expand their own experiences through substantialized objets which they can see and touch in person. In this, literature exhibition halls can be seen as an extraordinary space that matches a successful meeting between objets and spectators.

Fantastic elements, which can distinguish between fairy tale and general literature and determine the general atmosphere of the work, can be visualized to spectators at the exhibition space through substantialized time and space. Unified atmosphere of the space design can explain the background of the work that is hard for concrete objets to express and the space design can provide real hands-on experience rather than imaginative experience. Such an spatial experience can be proceeded according to the exhibition curator's story progression and this help spectators accept the theme of the exhibition more naturally.

Second, the simplicity and symbolism of the configuration
Exhibition is based on the premise that it is a work that displays objets in a certain lace and imprints the images on the mind of spectators within a certain space. So, the story of exhibition space must be simple and more intuitive.

Fairy tales not only expand the reader's imagination by utilizing symbols but also progress the events in a simple and clear manner by selecting typical characters and limited and repeated vocabulary. Thank to that, young readers can read clearly the message of ther work without losing interest according to the writer's intention.

The story of the exhibition must be as simple and core as possible in order to maximize the story delivery to spectators within the limited time and space. the story can be expressed in a simple space or by a intense objet.

Third, educational content
One of the bigger goals of the exhibition is in that it can convey associated knowledge about the exhibition through collected and managed objets in a right way and help spectators understand them and objets are cultural assets that reflect their own society's cultural and natural heritage.

Since fairy tale is basically written for growing children, it can play a role of educational material in its nature. That's the reason the tale are often read by their parents and teachers for children, the main reader group and mostly, the educators' choice of work directly link to children's reading. At the writing of fairy tale, the writer must keep this in mind to convey the educational message more effectively and adds fantastic elements and repeated use of simple vocabulary in order to provoke the reader's interest.

Fairy tale has maintained vitality for a long time, evolving from oral to text. The perpetuity fairy tale literature has can be utilized as a strategy of how to activate the Literature Museum by developing as a spatial story. In fact, fairy tale storytelling elements such as fantastic elements, the simplicity and symbolism of the configuration, and educational content can be utilized as exhibition materials and they can function for extraordinary exhibition experiences through spatial and production configuration, intuitive exhibition story that can be modified and expanded and educational purpose by applying real spectators.

5   Conclusion

Literature is a medium that conveys a message between the writer and the reader and the goal of literature museums is that help make the communication that is the property proper of the literature happen in a certain space. To do this, first extract the writer's world view-a story that is based on all of his works- as a concept and systemize all the space and exhibition based on this concept.

Next, Find the contact point that connects the message of the literature and the writer's life and symbolize it and reproduce it as space. All this process must be implemented through concrete methods such as minimized text, symbolized images, reprocessed space and analogic experiences and through those concrete implementations, spectators can read as a hands-on experience a story that controls the whole exhibition hall. Such a metaphorical way of the story will eventually determine the value of the museum because this way will help expand the exhibition territory through emotional experiences, not simply recognizing exhibition space by functional separation.

References

1. Benjamin, W.: Walter Benjamin's Literary theory (1983); Translated by Ban, S-W., Minumsa
2. Choi, B.-S.: The Birth of the New Museums. Dongmunsun (2010)
3. Lee, I.-H., et al.: Digital Storytelling. Golden Bough Publishing (2003)

Urban Media Storytelling Based on Narrative Schema

Jeong-Hee Kim and Jong-Youl Hong

SunMoon University, GalSanRi 100, TangJungMyun, Asan, Korea
HanKuk University of Foreign Studies, ImunRo 107, Seoul, Korea
savie11@sunmoon.ac.kr,
herr_hong@hufs.ac.kr

Abstract. This study sets up an Urban Media Storytelling Model based on "narrative schema". Narrative schema is known as the universal model of story structure and has been widely utilized in the storytelling of cultural content. Individual content, represented through urban media, can also be utilized in the structure of storytelling. Likewise, it can set up storytelling for an entire city. This study attempts to connect the phases within a narrative schema and thus lead to recognition of the city's image as a narrative schema, through people entering the city, being provided with information and entertainment, and exploring the city.

Keywords: Narrative Schema, Storytelling, Urban Media, Greimas, Narrative Semiology.

1 Narrative Schema

In this section, a method to plan Urban Storytelling, based on narrative schema, is investigated. First, the narrative schema, which can be utilized as a useful tool for content storytelling planning, is suggested. In narrative semiology, the narrativity is defined as the "transformation" from the first situation to the final situation. It is formulated as follows:

$$(S \cup O) \rightarrow (S \cap O)$$
(S: Subject, O: Object, U: Disjunction, ∩: Conjunction)

Greimas determined that the integrated unit of a story has three forms of *épreuves*: 1) *épreuves qualifiante* is the phase in which the subject achieves the required competences; 2) *épreuves principale* is the phase in which the subject duels and wins in order to possess the object; and 3) *épreuves glorifiante* is the phase in which the subject is confirmed as the final hero (or heroine). Greimas suggested the relationship between these elements and the narrative grammar through one narrative schema[1].

Contract / manipulation → competence → performance → sanction

First is the phase in which the subject manipulates or makes a certain contract in order to seek the object. The second phase is when the subject achieves the required competences in order to take the object. In the third phase, the subject acquires the

---

[1] A. J. Greimas, *Sémiotique et sciences sociales,* Paris: Seuil, 1976.

T.-h. Kim et al. (Eds.): MulGraB/BSBT/IUrC 2012, CCIS 353, pp. 313–318, 2012.

object while the last phase is when the subject receives a prize or sanction according to his/her performance.

For example, the structure of the story of Cinderella shows Cinderella as the subject of the story. However, she lacks the value called "love" due to the absence of her mother, and this is recovered at the end of the story. That is, the story encompasses the process in which the subject achieves the object called "love," which she seeks. The heroine acquires "competence" in order to tempt the prince through the godmother's "manipulation." She meets the prince at a ball and "performs" so that she can achieve love. She is then rewarded with marriage, i.e., a prize or sanction is executed. This flow of the narrative schema described above can be found not only in folktales but also a number of modern stories.

2   Storytelling Based on Narrative Schema

It is suggested that Greimas' narrative schema comprises the most universal of systems and can be applied to all kinds of narrative texts. This paper therefore seeks to determine whether or not this schema can be applied to a variety of current cultural content storytelling as represented in the image and digital media of today. The most representative plots of all stories are the romantic and heroic plots. [2] *Titanic* falls into the romantic plot category, and it maintained succeeded in breaking records as the world's greatest box office hit for over 10 years. *Harry Potter*, however, falls into the heroic plot category and was produced as a series, which caused a sensation. These two stories could be analyzed through narrative schema as follows:

In *Titanic*, the story begins with Rose's (heroine) suicide attempt due to the pressure brought about by her impending marriage to Cal, a young aristocrat. The heroine's condition, in which she wishes to lead her life according to her own will, indicates a kind of "lacking." This story overcomes the imbalanced phase and returns the heroine to a balanced condition, i.e., Rose comes to lead the life she really wants in the end by denying the false consciousness of high society. This transformation coincides with her process of achieving "love."

When Rose tries to jump into the sea from the bow, Jack (hero) rescues her dramatically. He makes her lead her life without giving up on herself. Although Jack is so poor that he has to travel tourist-class, he is a man with a free spirit. Cal and Jack find themselves in an antagonistic relationship with each other, but the meeting with Jack could be considered as a "manipulation" to make Rose find her true love. Jack is invited to dinner with the aristocrats but tactfully deals with the situation and then takes Rose to a tourist-class party. Once there, Rose dances as much as she likes and has a good time. Furthermore, Jack is an excellent painter and Rose invites him to draw her naked body. This episode provides an opportunity for them to fall in love with each other. In other words, Rose runs away from the normative and hypocritical life of the aristocrats and bravely selects romance with Jack. As a result, she acquires "competence" in order to achieve true love.

---

[2] Patrick Colm Hogan, *The Mind and Its Stories: Narrative Universals and Human Emotion*, Cambridge : Cambridge University Press, 2003.

As the ship, the Titanic, dramatically starts to sink when it hits an iceberg, their love takes a dramatic turn. Rose does not get into a lifeboat like the other first-class passengers. She looks for Jack who is locked in a tourist-class room. They cling to the end of the ship together but ultimately, Jack drowns. Before this, however, Jack finds a piece of floating debris and puts Rose on it. He is dying but asks her not to give up on her life. In order to keep her promise to him, Rose blows a whistle and is rescued. Therefore, although Jack is dead, Rose "performs" by having achieved true love. She transforms herself as a result of finding true love and subsequently acts according to her own will. Rose survives but does not return to Cal, Instead, she lives a fruitful life of her own, as she wants. This could be considered the "prize or sanction" part of the performance.

Harry Potter and the Sorcerer's Stone can also be examined through narrative schema. The main character, Harry Potter, loses his parents when he is young and goes to live with his aunt and her family. The closet under the stairs is his room, and he is ill-treated by his aunt's family (uncle and cousin). This covers the "transformation" in that Harry Potter, who lives a sad life with no sense of who he is, finds his identity as a sorcerer and thereafter lives happily.

Harry has his 11th birthday ahead, and a few days before this, he receives a letter. It is an admission invitation from the legendary Hogwarts School of Witchcraft and Wizardry. A giant called Hagrid, who visits to take Harry there, relays the fact that Harry is a sorcerer with the greatest power. This is considered to be "manipulation" by the principal (Dumbledore). The process of his learning about various mysterious sorceries at Hogwarts School is the phase of "competence" acquisition. Quidditch games and adventures with amazing animals unfold. Meanwhile, Harry comes to know the "sorcerer's stone," which is hidden in the basement of Hogwarts school, but it is also wanted by Voldemort, who had killed Harry's parents. Harry's action to find and protect the stone from Voldemort is the "performance," which is the core point of the story. In doing so, Harry saves Hogwarts from danger and makes it peaceful. Moreover, Harry then happily leads the life of a sorcerer.

Table 1. Narrative schema of Film Storytelling

Narrative Schema	Titanic	Harry Potter
Manipulation	Jack's dramatic saving of Rose.	Dumbledore's invitation for Harry to go to Hogwarts.
Competence	Participation in the free party with the tourist-class people. Jack's drawing of Rose's naked body.	Harry's learning of mysterious sorceries in Hogwarts.
Performance	Jack and Rose's efforts to keep their love alive in spite of the ship's sinking.	Successfully defending the sorcerer's stone from Voldemort.
Prize and Sanction	Rose keeping her promise to Jack by leading her life according to her will until the end.	Peace at Hogwarts.

Narrative schema is shown together with the genres that are applied to storytelling. In the case of a computer game, it has an open storytelling structure based on the characteristics of its interaction with the user. That is, the user plays a role as the hero (or heroine) and intervenes in the storytelling. At the moment when the user understands the game's principles and presses the start button, a "contract" is made. The success of the most important mission in the game is the "performance." Achieving the necessary items and/or powers prior to this is the "competence" phase. The "prize and sanction" are provided according to the game's result. Narrative schema can be applied to offline content, such as theme parks or festivals, as well. Therefore, narrative schema will now be applied to urban media storytelling.

3   Application to Urban Media Storytelling

Urban media is commonly defined as the methodology in which data is transformed for use in urban spaces and represented in a visible way. That is, it primarily aims to deliver urban information to the public in an effective way. For this, the city requires users who are able to travel into the city. They live in the city or travel with the help of urban media. Fundamentally, users come to acquire knowledge of the city or gain a particular impression through these experiences. The series of such processes could be assumed to be storytelling. Hence this paper seeks to analyze urban media storytelling's phases through narrative schema.

At the moment of inflow into the city, regardless of the mechanisms, e.g., house-moving or sightseeing, a "contract" is made. Image promotion about the city plays an important role in this: it could appeal to the inflow into the city through urban advantages, such as natural environments, cultural resources, and cultural programs. Also, it is important in order to draw out initial motivation and curiosity. Urban information and images are imperative as well and are provided at gateways, such as airports, train stations, or terminals. A city "manipulates" people into experiencing it in various ways. It is advantageous for regional development for people to stay in the city for as long as possible, and therefore the city attempts to provide maximum activities for people to pursue. At the same time, in a sense, it establishes a positive image of the city.

If a user comes into the city, it is essential to acquire a level of "competence," which helps them to explore the city and/or live there. For this, various urban media are utilized. In general, urban media visualizes and delivers information about urban spaces. Information is important for the user. Greimas suggested four aspects of competence. [3] They are *pouvoir* (power: able to do), *savoir* (knowledge: knows how to do), *devoir* (obligation: obliged to do), and *vouloir* (will: want to do), respectively. In this context, information about the city refers to knowledge. However, another competence that is important is vouloir (want). That is, besides the delivery of information about the city, entertainment content should be added to the entertaining elements.

---

[3] Anne Hénault, *Nrratologie, Sémiotique générale*, Paris: P.U.F., 1983.

Some people have a different view, which purports that urban media does not convey simple information. A scholar might look at the city as a public space and a media environment in which the public can freely participate and express themselves. [4] In other words, the giant media called a city is not planned by an expert, but it is a space for the public to immerse and enjoy themselves. Urban media is more likely to be developed as entertainment that is enjoyed by the public, over and above the actual information that it delivers. Entertainment content based on storytelling could utilize the storytelling method. It could also be developed as infotainment content, which reflects the shape of games, although its main objective is to deliver information. Therefore, narrative schema could be utilized not only at a macroscopic level but also in individual media content.

If the phase of competence is accomplished effectively, the user's "performance" could be undertaken in a much smoother way. For sightseeing or settling in a city to live, competence could be a great help. In the performance phase, users experience and enjoy both hardware and software elements: hardware elements involve buildings and cultural artifacts while software elements include various cultural programs, such as exhibitions and festivals. As a result, the additional value of the city comes into play. "Prize and sanction" are the evaluation of the performance. It depends on how users recognize the city. In the case of positive evaluation, satisfaction with life and the overall urban experience increases. Furthermore, users establish the intention to revisit the city. Fundamentally, such an effect leads to regional development.

4   Conclusion

Based on discussions in this study, the model of urban media storytelling could be demonstrated as follows:

Table 2. Urban Media Storytelling Model

Narrative Schema	Urban Media Storytelling	Content
Manipulation	Entering the city	Promoting urban images: in advance or at a city's gateways
Competence	Acquiring information about urban spaces	Infotainment: Information element Entertainment: Story element
Performance	Exploring the city (sightseeing/residence)	Hardware: Buildings, cultural artifacts Software: Exhibitions, festivals, cultural programs
Prize and Sanction	Recognizing the urban image	Increase of amenity, intention of re-visit

---

[4] Hyun-Jin Lee, "Expanding Urban Media Screen Experiences: the City as a Big Canvas", *Design Studies* Vol.24, No.1, pp.5-14, Seoul: Korean Society of Design Science, 2011.

From a macroscopic perspective, urban media storytelling could be understood as a narrative schema to assimilate the urban image by entering and exploring city. That is, it could be understood from the perspective that the city itself is an urban media as well as, like games, it has an open narrative structure derived from users' interaction. In general, urban media is closest to the competence phase if you focus on its information delivery function. For this, more effects could be produced if the simple information is developed into game or story content. However, enjoying urban media might be considered as the performance itself from a macroscopic perspective. In any case, the narrative schema could be utilized to represent the universal structure of the story for both individual content and recognition of the urban image overall.

References

1. Greimas, A.J.: Sémiotique et sciences sociales, Seuil, Paris (1976)
2. Hénault, A.: Nrratologie, Sémiotique générale, P.U.F., Paris (1983)
3. Hogan, P.C.: The Mind and Its Stories: Narrative Universals and Human Emotion. Cambridge University Press, Cambridge (2003)
4. Lee, H.-J.: Expanding Urban Media Screen Experiences: the City as a Big Canvas. Design Studies 24(1), 5–14 (2011)

A Story Bank Design for Modern Succession and the Variability of Folk Tale

Dong-hwan Yoo and Dae-jin Jeon

Department of Multiplex Contents, Graduate School of Creative Industry,
Andong Univ., 137 Kyoungdong-ro, Andong, Korea
philsm@andong.ac.kr, cbluesky7@naver.com

Abstract. This paper briefly examined basic characteristics and storytelling of folk tales in order to implement variable particularities according to interactivity and oral tradition of folk tales and designed a fundamental direction of folk tale story bank. Until now, folk tale archiving and folk tale filing has been focusing on fossilization of folk tales, time has come for folk tales to be implemented in a new method of interactive storytelling thanks to the development of digital technology. Moreover, the concept of such a story bank will not end up being a story bank itself, it enables participants to have a new experience through folk tale contents that reflect participatory as well as spatial characteristics of the digital environment.

Keywords: story bank, Folk tale, interactivity, digital storytelling, interactive storytelling.

1   Introduction

The emergence of digital media helped convert information of almost all the fields into online archiving from offline one. This holds true for folk tales. Folk tales that are collected from Speech material Category of <The royal library materials Jangseogak digital archive(Jangseogak)> from 1980 till 1988 are provided in the form of speech and its recording

However, oral literature series of <Jangseogak> has a limit in functioning as a very basic digital archiving. Especially, oral literature series of <Jangseogak> fundamentally chose the system of digital archiving that they overlook the very essential characteristic of folk tales-variability that appears in the process of oral tradition and oral narration environment.

This paper suggests a basic design for a story bank of folk tales for folk tales' modern reproduction that is recently under discussion and folk tales' variability that is the essential characteristic.

2   Suggestions on the Characteristics of Folk Tale

Studies on folk tales are being conducted in the two circles-folk lore academia and literary world. While the former does to gain study materials for reflection of the

T.-h. Kim et al. (Eds.): MulGraB/BSBT/IUrC 2012, CCIS 353, pp. 319–325, 2012.

grassroots culture and for local features and the national consciousness revealed by the co-creation of folk tales, the latter does to gain study materials to find the origin of literature, especially the fundamental form of narrative literature and to establish the development process of folk tales. The two circles roughly coincides about characteristics of folk tales and those characteristics that were extracted from Introduction of Oral Literature, can be summed up as six points as mentioned below.

First, folk tale are fabricated stories with a certain structure(fictiveness).

Second, folk tales are passed on orally(oral tradition).

Third, folk tales are written in prose(prose style).

Forth, the number of oral narration and the eligibility of narrator has no limitation(unlimitedness of oral narration).

Fifth, all narration take place between the speaker and the listener face-to-face(interactivity).

Sixth, folk tales have the highest possibility of being converted into text among many other oral literature genres(text convertibility)

On top of these six characteristics, you can add folk tales' taxonomic characteristics such as material formalism and structural formalism, then you have the very essential eight characteristics.

Especially, out of these eight characteristics, oral tradition and interactivity as well as material formalism and structural formalism are very important in the aspect of storytelling. Because these characteristics make folk tales variable and interactive stories unlike other documented literature.

Folk tales change as passed on orally. More details can be added or omitted depending on who the speaker is and they can be changed following the listener's reaction. The oral narration that takes place within interactivity between the speaker and the listener face to face naturally draws the listener's attention and the speaker in return reacts to the listener's very reaction, making the tale longer or shorter and sometimes changing the viewpoint of the tale. In this process, a new 'rare story', which is completely different from the original storyline, can be born. However, this process doesn't complicate the story and helps make the story easier to remember for both the speaker and the listener thank to the material/ structural formalism. In other words, variations can be born within a certain form of structure and common materials.

While studies on the rprinciples of variability of folk tale and on its original form have been conducted as before-mentioned, the discussion for the succession of that variability in the modern viewpoint hasn't almost been conducted. In the domestic nation there are oral literature series pages of <Jangseogak>set aside as folk tale archive, these pages end up simply recording various variations of folk tale- rare stories- in the form of digital media and classifying them according to their type, materials and the regions where they have been orally passed on.

Thanks to the development of digital technology, however, not only the convenience of recording and classifying but also interactive storytelling that the human race has forgotten for a long time, is possible. This is digital storytelling utilizing digital technology.

3   Folk Tale Narration in the 21st Century ― Digital Storytelling

Digital storytelling to put simply is digital technology -storytelling using digital media. Digital technology here doesn't necessarily mean efficient storing technology or various expression technology of images and voice. According to Janet Murray, environmental characteristics of digital media are four mentioned below.

The first characteristics is reasoning process to infer the process of sending and receiving information, and to respond to the user's actions based on the results, the second one is a participatory characteristic where the user can take part in the story implemented by digital media. The third one is spatial characteristic that the digital environment can guide the user go through the digital space, the forth is an encyclopedia characteristic that allows the user to experience the peripheral stories the writer often omits within the original narrative story readily and in detail through enormous storing function and world-wide networks.

In short, we do not simply record folk tales but listen to the extended folk tale story in width as well as in the depth which allows us experience the story that was from the past and changes according to our inquiry and request and further makes us the hero of the story thanks to digital storytelling.

To this end, we must solve two prerequisites. First, in order to elicit story changes according to the user's participation I mentioned earlier, we need to make folk tales structured suitable for digital storytelling and second, we need to create a new narration venue that allows the listener easily access to, modify and experience for himself the structured folk tale without learning about the structured information in a professional way.

Fortunately, structuring of folk tales is almost completed by the folklore academia and literary circle. All we have to do is that making this structuring suitable for the user to enjoy various experiences and modifying this fit for digital media.

4   Preparation of a New Narration Venue ― Structuring Folk Tale

One of the traditional approaches to analyze the story is to examine the three elements like figures, events, and background and this approach holds true for folk tales.

In particular, a scholar who studied the characters and events with focus on them is Kim,hwa-kyung who I previously mentioned. Kim outlined four structures of Korean folk tales based on the results of Prop's discussion on the magic tales and Dundes' extended discussion of Prop's discussion. The ascending flow that satisfies the lack, the descending flow that is the counter part of the ascending flow, the eclectic flow that shows the complex pattern of up and down flows and the recurrence flow that returns to satisfaction from lack or returns to lack from satisfaction back and forth.

Such structuring types of Korean folk tales have the inevitable connection with the function of characters. That means that structure types of folk tales will determine the order of events.

However, structuring folk tales based on only one element-the flow of events-is unreasonable even if we ignore criticism from many commentators saying diversity is one of the important features of folk tales since there are the other two elements such as 'figures' and 'background'.

First, figures are sometimes controlled by the flow of events and other times they change the flow of events. Especially, in the case of the main figure, this character has a deep-rooted connection with the 'lack' such as the secret of the birth or a very special gift. If you take a closer look at the classification of the type/motif, you can get a clear idea, the most common examples are that the main figures are a superman or a monster or a half-blood. This means that the main figures are innately born with the conditions of lack by their own identity itself and to be persecuted by their natural identity.

Even if a certain main figure is confirmed and follows the certain flow of events, what kind of background place the main figure is in will change the course of events. Here we find the importance of the third element-background.

If you allow me to outline the three elements once again, they will be represented as a variable(V) and a constant(C) as below

	main figure	place	movement	movement	movement
ex.	son of the sea king	seashore village	seashore village	sea	palace of sea kings
	the disable	the woods next to the pond	Hanyang houses	the state exam test place	palace
	genius	mountain village	mountain valley	a tiger's den	heaven on earth
V	main figure	place	movement	movement	movement
C	lack		being dispatched	meeting with a helper	test and trial...

The specific development of each event will be modified initially according to the identity and characteristics of the main character and the course of reaching the final result will be modified according to the places where the hero goes and appears. since the identity and characteristics of the protagonist has a relation with 'lack'-the source of the whole story and places have relations with peripheral characters who are associated with the flow of events.

However, the classification and hierarchy such as data and meta-data between each element is required for better structuring of folk tale elements fit for digital environment. Especially, upper category that classifies detailed elements like places and characters is required and classification like Table 2 is possible because of formalism of folk tales.

main figure > superman	place>transcending place	structure type >ascending
> the great man	> real place	> descending
> the deformed		> eclectic
> the good man		> recurrence
> the evil man		
>a man of talent		
> animal		

The two categories combined with functions create a folk tale work and this folk tale belongs to a certain structural type.

What's important now is how to enable the listener/the participant to change the story with structured folk tale elements, This is possible thanks to a new folk tale narration venue(or a new speaker). the space where folk tale works are accumulated and unlimited rare variations are created by the participants is the very story bank of folk tales.

5   Direction of a New Narration Venue − Folk Tale Story Bank

In order to clearly understand the story bank we must delve into the archives, the original form of story bank. Even though the terminology of Archive include three concepts such as 'actual records to be preserved', 'an institution which is responsible for the collection and management of permanently valuable records', and a place to preserve the historical records, the latter two concepts are usually circulated. In short, Archive means a place as well as an institution where permanently valuable records to be preserved are collected and managed.

Story bank is also a kind of archive. while you place all documentary and records in the common archive, story bank only deals with the 'story' -it is one of the topic-centered archives.

While the general archive functions include collecting and managing the data and providing the data to users as an effective form, story bank has one more function on top of the general functions. Another feature is that it must be the provider of the information of the original story at the same time the producer of the info and must provide services in conjunction with the story and provide community space in order for the story culture to be activated in. . Along with the uniqueness in the aspect of data collection and management by turning stories into database, the core uniqueness of story bank can be found in the function as a 'producer' I mentioned right above. However it doesn't necessarily mean that as institution called archive itself creates a certain story. As Jang, Mi-jin mentioned, story bank as a space that activates the story culture not only provides users with information about the story but also leads users to creates their own variations and reflect the variated stories into the archive. Structuring of folk tales that I mentioned earlier can be a preparation step for this process.

Of course, folk tale story bank cannot be operated only with structuring of folk tales. As the current archive theory puts emphasis on the management role that connects the provider and the user, one step forward from simply providing professional information through categories and keyword search, Story bank of folk tales must be made to provide the information participants want and allow them to enjoy various experiences using the features of digital environment. I would like to outline here briefly the big direction folk tale story bank should take.

The first is participant-led information reading utilizing the encyclopedia characteristic of digital media. It includes providing not only basic information like narrative voice, original dialect and its interpretation, related term dictionary and so on, but also secondary information associated with folk tales or re-fabricated information like secondary information revealed through folk tales or academic classification about folk tales, or classification by materials or interest.

The second is the simplest interactive function that utilizing the participatory characteristic of digital media of story bank. This is story editing function which enables other participant selectively edit structurally accumulated folk tale and store the newly-created work as an associated work of the original, boosting interest in a new content and recreation of the work.

The third function makes the participant the main figure of the folk tale and experience and use the spatial characteristics of digital media. This function allows the participant choose the main figure by utilizing accumulated data of the folk tale and the participant leads the story. What is important here is that this function helps the participant can be immersed in the story itself, without concerning professional knowledge or specific structure of the folk tale unlike the story editing function, making this function participant-centered contents.

6   Conclusion

Until now, this paper briefly examined the fundamental direction of folk tale story bank for modern succession and variability and essentially necessary parts to do this. Story bank can be an alternative plan for us to experience in a modern and efficient way the variability of folk tales that was overlooked in the process of fossilization of voice data and text data.

However there are many tasks to be done such as how to make the structure of folk tales and how to make networks among detailed items as well as what kind of interface should be for a participant who will experience folk tale story bank in person. Especially, the former requires a further study on database and for the latter, you need to review ,in advance, studies on interface and studies on interactive contents that are currently published in many places and then you can draw a concrete picture of a folk tale story bank that is suitable for both the characteristics and the needs of the participant.

References

1. Prop, V.: Folk Tale Morphology (2009); Translated by Lee, G-J., Zman, Z.:
2. Jang, D.-S., et al.: Introduction of Oral Literature, Ilchokak (2006)
3. Kim, H.-G.: Study on the Korean Folk Tales. Yeungnam University Press (1987)
4. Murray, J.: Interactive Storytelling (2001); Translated by Han,Y-H., Byun, J-Y.: Ahn Graphics
5. Miller, C.H.: Digital Media Storytelling (2006); Translated by Lee Y-S., et al.: Communication Books
6. Lee, S.-Y.: Digital Archiving and Standardization of the OAIS Reference Model. Journal of Information Management 33(3), 45–68 (2002)
7. Jang, M.-J., et al.: Story Bank Operation Plan. Korean Culture and Policy Institute (2000)
8. Yakel, E.: Creating an archive, pp. 10–21. Truth Exploration Publishing (2003); Translated by Kang, M-S.:
9. A Study on Folk Tale Story Bank Design Method using Digital Storytelling Andong National University, Graduate School of Korean Culture Industry Master (2012)

Requirements and Design Issues
of Ubiquitous Community Care Systems
for Low-Income Pediatric Asthma Patients

Jongmyung Choi[1] and Rosa I. Arriaga[2]

[1] Department of Computer Engineering, Mokpo National University, Jeonnam, Korea
jmchoi@mokpo.ac.kr
[2] School of Interactive Computing, Georgia Institute of Technology, Atlanta, GA, USA
arriaga@cc.gatech.edu

Abstract. The social support in self-management has shown positive results in chronic condition treatment. In this paper, for low-income children with asthma, we propose ubiquitous community care system, and introduce requirements and some design issues for the system. We elicit sixteen requirements from analyzing interview with seven low-income families and six providers. Based on the requirements, we introduce design issues for the system: being ubiquitous, community care, regimen specific support, easiness of system usage, and privacy concerns. We also propose a centralized architecture for our ubiquitous community care system. We contend that our requirements and design issues for pediatric asthma management can be utilized in building the systems. Furthermore, our work can be applied to other chronic condition management system with minor modification.

Keywords: Chronic Illness, Asthma, Self-management, Social Support System, Requirements, Design Issues.

1 Introduction

Asthma is one of serious illness because of its high morbidity and mortality. The worse thing is that it is a prevalent chronic illness among children in the United States [1]. Chronic illness such as asthma requires long-term treatment and self-management. Self-management includes "understanding of one's disease, effective management of symptoms using a plan of action, medication, and appropriate psychological coping skills" [2]. However, in nature, pediatric asthma patients have difficulties in managing asthma by themselves because 1) they are too young to know how to manage it, 2) they cannot control their desire (for example, playing with their friends) even though they have asthma exacerbation symptoms, and 3) sometimes asthma attack happens so fast that they require the emergency treatment. Therefore they require the support from their family and sometimes community members such as schoolteachers, school nurses, and even neighbors. The support includes "helping the children to avoid asthma triggers", "helping them to medicate regularly", "helping them to manage symptoms properly", and "handling emergency situations".

T.-h. Kim et al. (Eds.): MulGraB/BSBT/IUrC 2012, CCIS 353, pp. 326–333, 2012.
© Springer-Verlag Berlin Heidelberg 2012

After analyzing interview data [3], we found out the necessity of the systems that are ubiquitous and community-based for caring of pediatric asthma patients [4,5]. In this paper, we introduce the requirements for the ubiquitous community care systems and some design issues for the system implementation. We elicited the thirteen functional requirements and three nonfunctional requirements from the interviews. From the all requirements, the most important functional requirements are that the system should be 1) ubiquitous, 2) community-based, 3) able to support communication, and 4) able to be used for analyzing the symptom trends. The most important nonfunctional requirement is cost, because the system is for low-income families. Based on the requirements, we propose SMS-based, social network service communication system, called Asthma411. Cell phone is almost ubiquitous because people always carry with it. Based on cell phone, we design a small community social network service in which the main subjects are related to asthma and the children with asthma. In the cell-phone based social network, they can communicate each other for help the children to manage themselves with the help from others such as family and school-teachers.

This paper consists of five sections. In section 2, we summarize the related works and compare our work with them. In section 3, we describe our findings and requirements that are elicited from the interview. In section 4, we discuss the design issues for asthma management system. After that, we show a centralized architecture for Asthma411 in section 5. Finally, we reveal our conclusions in section 6.

2   Related Work

There have been various research topics on pediatric asthma patients. This paper is related to the research on self-management programs for pediatric asthma (with social support or not) and ICT-based systems for asthma management.

There have been researches on asthma self-management and self-management program. Arvind Kumar [2] suggests general guideline for asthma self-management: 1) knowledge about asthma, 2) accepting the disease, 3) skill of taking medication, 4) keeping a daily routine (such as taking prescription medication), 5) monitoring symptoms, 6) adjusting medication, 7) avoiding triggers, 8) knowing when/how to contact hospital, 9) accessing social support mechanisms, and 10) coping mechanism with psychological sequelae. J M Ignacio-Garcia and P Gonzalez-Santos [6] show that asthma self-management improves morbidity parameters (days lost from work, asthma attacks, and emergency room visits).

There have been researches on ICT-based self-management programs. Victor van der Meer and his colleagues [7] argue that internet-based asthma self-management can utilize electronic monitoring, accessibility to information, e-mail, and an electronic action plan. Victor van der Meer's another work [8] shows that Internet based asthma self-management improves asthma control and lung function, but not exacerbations.

Compared to the existing researches, our work has some uniqueness. First, there has been no try on asthma self-management with ubiquitous technology, even though it does not require high technology. Second, there have been some arguments for community support for asthma self-management, but there has been no ICT-based system for the arguments. As far as we know, our system is the first try in this field. Third, our proposed system can support closed social networks for caring the children with asthma. This is also new try in building a social network with SMS.

3   Requirements for Asthma Care

In order to understand pediatric asthma and their management, we interviewed seven low-income families suffering from pediatric asthma (seven parents and eight children with asthma) and six providers (a pediatric pulmonologist, an allergist, a nurse, a respiratory therapist, a physician assistant, and a certified asthma educator who was a school nurse) in our previous study [3]. By analyzing the interview data, we got some findings and requirements for asthma management systems.

- F1. One important problem in asthma management is that asthma attacks or exacerbations can happen anywhere and at any time. It means that people who are around the child should be able to help him/her. The people can be schoolteachers, school nurses, his/her friend's parents, or even school bus driver. This finding leads two requirements: (R1) being ubiquitous and (R2) ability to get the information required for helping the child.
- F2. Early treatment in time is critical. Asthma exacerbation should be managed in time, or it might cause a serious situation like emergency room or even death. This leads at least two requirements: (R3) knowledge for proper treatment of asthma exacerbation, and (R4) constant monitoring the child with asthma.
- F3. Like many other chronic conditions, the child's asthma condition changes continuously. Therefore, if it is not properly managed, the condition gets worse, and the treatment action called asthma action plan should be changed. This leads this requirement: (R5) keeping updated asthma status information.
- F4. Asthma patients visit clinics to see doctors on the regular basis (every three to four months according to their severity). During the visit, doctors ask patients about their asthma symptom since the last visit, but the answer is not so accurate. This leads two requirements: (R6) recording asthma symptoms and (R7) summarizing the symptoms information for doctors.
- F5. Caregivers (parents, schoolteachers, doctors and nurses, and CHWs) communicate each other with various purpose and various media including face-to-face, phone calls, emails, text messages, sticky notes, and even fax. Phone call is very easy to talk, but sometimes it is hard to connect to the caregivers. (R8) For implementation, the communication media should be limited to a couple of media.
- F6. For asthma management, it is important to keep daily routines including taking medicine every day, and checking lung capacity. Sometimes, family members cooperate to help their child keep the daily routines. This finding leads two requirements: (R9) a mechanism to cooperate each other to keep daily routines, and (R10) reminder mechanism not to miss the daily routines.

- F7. Asthma patients should avoid asthma triggers. Asthma triggers are various, but the well-known triggers include smoking, dust, high or low temperature, high humidity, and pollen. This finding leads to the requirement: (R11) sensing asthma triggers and (R12) providing weather information.
- F8. Parents want to get educated about asthma management. Therefore, (R13) the system should have a mechanism that community members give parents medical information for asthma management.

In addition to findings from interview data, we can also elicit other requirements from general information. These requirements are not related to system's function, but these are also very important. Requirement from 14th through 16th are those non-functional requirements.

- (R14) Cost is a very important feature because it is for low-income families. If the system is expensive, they will not be able to utilize the system.
- (R15) The system should be easy to use. If it is hard to use, they will not use the system, and they cannot help the children with asthma.
- (R16) In medical information, privacy and security are very important issues. Somehow, this requirement is contrast to the requirement R2.

We have sixteen requirements, but some of them are non-functional requirements and some functional requirements are combined into a couple of functions.

4   Design Issues for Ubiquitous Community Care System

4.1   System Usage Scenario

The following usage scenario will reveal how our system works. This is a scenario of monitoring and helping the child with asthma at school:

At school, John (child with asthma) has a bad cough, so his homeroom teacher requests his asthma action plan from the Blackboard and checks his status. According to his asthma action plan, he has to take a specific medication, so she takes him to the school nurse and leaves a message about his status on the system for other caregivers: his parents and his after school basketball coach. And the school nurse gives him the medication, and she also leaves a message to his parents, "Make sure he brings his medication to school tomorrow", because his medication almost runs out.

In this scenario, the schoolteacher is the caregiver. She senses his bad cough, checks his asthma action plan, and cares him by taking him to the school nurse. If she does not sense or does not check his status, she might ignore his cough, and it might cause an emergency situation.

4.2   System Model

From the requirements, we made system model in our previous work: being ubiquitous, blackboard communication, and community care [4,5]. In this section, we will describe the model from the perspective of system design. It is closely related to our system platform and core technology for the system.

Being Ubiquitous

From the requirement R1, the system should be ubiquitous, and it also should be able to monitor the children (R4) and to provide proper information (R2). For being ubiquitous, there are two possible approaches. First approach is for the children to carry a device to everywhere all the time. The device can be a cellphone or other special device such as Smart Asthma Box [9], which is suggested because most of asthma patients keep their asthma box when they go out. Cellphone have been used as an assistant technology for helping the children with asthma [10]. The second approach is to implant sensors everywhere the children go. There have been researches on embedding sensors in home [11] for asthma patients. From the two approaches, we choose the first approach, because the second approach cannot cover all places where the children go.

Blackboard Communication and Community Care

The Blackboard Communication meets many requirements. First, Blackboard Communication is combined with cellphone SMS or data communication such as smartphone app or desktop web. The unified data communication (R8) allows all the data transferred to be processed and stored. The unified communication allows all care givers to communicate more conveniently and more effectively (R9). Second, Blackboard Communication plus an information processing component meet the information processing related requirements: R10 and R12. Blackboard Communication plus information retrieval function can help care givers (including doctors) to care the children with proper information (R3 and R7). They can get the information via cellphones and desktop computers. Blackboard Communication plus storing function meet the requirements R5 and R6. Any care givers can record the children's asthma symptoms and their current status using SMS. The stored data are very helpful when care givers treat emergency situation and when doctors determine the children's asthma severity.

4.3   Regimen Specific Features

The systems that support chronic illness self-management should support regimen specific features because it has been known that regimen specific self-management have positive influence. Therefore, our system also should support asthma specific features: avoiding triggers, performing routine tasks, early treatment, and sensitivity to the weather. These asthma specific features are covered by the requirements, so that our system meets the asthma specific requirements.

4.4   Easy to Use

There have been successful efforts using SMS in healthcare [12], and we extend SMS to a social support platform for chronic illness management. The SMS communication should be easy to use (R15). The communication types are categorized into two: sending "write" messages and "read" (request) messages to the system. This covers getting information about patients, leaving messages about the patients, giving educational messages for caregivers, communicating with each other, and time-specific task reminders.

When a user wants to share information, he/she can use the system following a simple text message format: <command, person, message>.

For example,

```
R John's action plan
W John had a bad cough at school
```

The first message requests (R) John's asthma action plan from Asthma411, and the second one saves John's status to the system (here "W" is writing the John's status).

4.5   Openness and Privacy Issues

Healthcare information is very private and it should be protected (R16). However, in order to get helps from care givers, the access to the information should be open (R2). Therefore, there is contradiction in privacy and openness. In our system, we utilize two approaches. The first one is to build a closed social group consisting of family, schoolteachers, school nurses, coaches, CHWs, and other neighbors. The group members can access the information freely, but others can access only the information for emergency situation. The second approach is to get the grant that allows everyone to access the information at initial stage from the parents. The parents can choose one from the two approaches.

5   System Overview and Architecture

5.1   System Overview

Asthma411 is a system that has four main features: it is asthma-specific, patient-centered, and ubiquitous (accessible from anywhere at any time by anyone) and socially mediated. Its goal is to mitigate asthma symptoms and increase the quality of life for asthma patients and caregivers. This goal will be accomplished by 1) providing communication paths that are available at any time and from anywhere, 2) helping caregivers to send asthma related information on a regular and timely basis.

We classify Asthma411 users into three groups according to their roles: parents and family, schoolteachers and extra-curricular caregivers (for simplicity's sake we will refer to them as "coaches"), and CHWs. Parents are the primary caregivers. They are responsible for monitoring their children's asthma status, making sure their children are taking their medicine and managing communication about the children's asthma with the other caregivers. Schoolteachers and coaches monitor the students and manage the students' activities while the students are in their care. CHWs help parents and children with asthma get educated on how to take medicines, what to be avoided, and how to manage their houses.

5.2   System Architecture

Every message is transferred to the Asthma411 server, it is processed there, and then it is delivered to a specific caregiver or is open to everyone. It follows the centralized client server architecture as shown in Fig. 1.

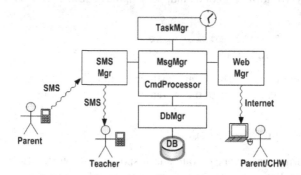

Fig. 1. Asthma411 System Architecture

In Ashtma411, there are two types of clients: web client accessed from desktop and SMS client accessed from cell phones. SmsMgr plays the bridge between cell phones and the information system. It receives SMS and transfers it to MsgMgr, which processes messages according to its meaning. MsgMgr includes CmdProcessor, which interprets commands and process the message. TaskMgr executes time-specific tasks such as reminder jobs. WebMgr makes web pages with accumulated message data for web users.

6   Conclusions

Pediatric asthma is a widely prevalent chronic illness, and it requires management strategies that mediate communication between numbers of care givers. In this paper we proposed a ubiquitous community care system, and introduced sixteen requirements and six design issues for the system. The system requirements were elicited from the interview with seven low-income families suffering from pediatric asthma and six providers. The requirements cover the needs for asthma specific treatment such as sensing asthma triggers and getting weather information. They also cover the needs for general chronic illness management including routine task reminder function.

Based on the requirements, we proposed six design issues: being ubiquitous, blackboard communication, community care, regimen specific support, easiness of system, and privacy concerns. After considering the design issues, we chose SMS-based, centralized system architecture for our ubiquitous community care system.

We contend that our system model can be used to build the ubiquitous community care system. Furthermore, our proposal and design issues can be applied to caring for a variety of populations where communication between varieties of caregivers must be established. This includes the elderly and patients with other chronic illnesses such as diabetes. In the future, we plan to implement Asthma411 system that follows our requirements and our design, and conduct user studies with the system.

References

1. Centers for Disease Control and Prevention, Asthma in the US (2011),
   http://www.cdc.gov/VitalSigns/Asthma/
2. Kumar, A., Eric Gershwin, M.: Self-management in asthma: Empowering the Patient. In: Bronchial Asthma, Current Clinical Practice, pp. 343–356. Springer (2006)
3. Jeong, H.Y., et al.: Act Collectively: Opportunities for Technologies to Support Low-Income Children with Asthma. In: Proc. of British HCI (2011)
4. Choi, J., Arriaga, R.I.: Community-Based Social Media for Low-Income Pediatric Asthma Patients. In: Lee, G., Howard, D., Ślęzak, D., Hong, Y.S. (eds.) ICHIT 2012. CCIS, vol. 310, pp. 203–210. Springer, Heidelberg (2012)
5. Choi, J., Jeong, H.Y., Arriaga, R.I.: A Ubiquitous Community Care Model for Pediatric Asthma Patients. In: Park, J.H(J.), Jin, Q., Yeo, M.S.-s., Hu, B. (eds.) Human Centric Technology and Service in Smart Space. LNEE, vol. 182, pp. 137–144. Springer, Heidelberg (2012)
6. Ignacio-Garcia, J.M., Gonzalez-Santos, P.: Asthma self-management education program by home monitoring of peak expiratory flow. American Journal of Respiratory and Critical Care Medicine 151(2), 353–359 (1995)
7. van der Meer, V., van Stel, H.F., Detmar, S.B., Otten, W., Sterk, P.J., Sont, J.K.: Internet-Based Self-Management Offers an Opportunity To Achieve Better Asthma Control in Adolescents. CHEST 132(1), 112–119 (2007)
8. van der Meer, V., et al.: Internet-Based Self-management Plus Education Compared With Usual Care in Asthma. Annals of Internal Medicine 151(2), 110–120 (2009)
9. Brown, A.S., et al.: Family and Home Asthma Services across the Controlling Asthma in American Cities Project. Journal of Urban Health 88, 100–112 (2011)
10. Yun, T.-J.: Technology design for pediatric asthma management. In: Proc. of CHI EA 2011. ACM (2011)
11. Yun, T.-J., et al.: Assessing asthma management practices through in-home technology probes. In: Proc. of Pervasive Computing Technologies for Healthcare. IEEE (2010)
12. Krishna, S., Boren, S., Balas, E.: Healthcare via cell phones: a systematic review. Telemedicine and e-Health 15(3), 231–240 (2009)

A Cognitively Motivated Vertically Layered Two-Pass Agent Architecture for Realizing Ambient Intelligence in Urban Computing

Youngho Lee and Jongmyung Choi

Department of Computer Engineering, Mokpo National University,
Jeonnam, Korea
{youngho,jmchoi}@mokpo.ac.kr

Abstract. We argue that a cognitively motivated vertically layered two-pass agent architecture with a correspondingly layered knowledge representation formalism is necessary for implementing responsive, reactive, and pro-active behavior into smart objects and smart environments. Being cognitively motivated, our approach aims to respect the cognitive demands of a human being, to deliver an adequate human-computer interface to urban computing environments. The vertically layered two-pass agent architecture allows separating time-critical processes with low computational demands from the computationally more expensive processing needed for intelligent systems. Additionally, representation mechanisms are necessary that correspond in expressive power and processing complexity to the available resources on each layer. We give an outline of a multi-agent system and representation formalism that fulfill these requirements.

Keywords: Layered Architecture, Context Integration, Reasoning, Cognitive Agent.

1 Introduction

The principal question we have to address is the question of what an urban computing system is. The notion of computing systems, in fact, must be conceived of in a wide sense. In urban computing, the range of devices available to the system, its computing power, users, and many other system variables – which are guaranteed to be more or less stable on conventional computing systems during the execution of basic commands – are subject to change or replacement at any time. A large number of different aspects have to be handled, in order to process data retrieved from a device, a sensor, or other applications in an environment to using the information contained in these data within an application.

From the viewpoint of ambient intelligence, it is, for instance, not important which of the involved devices in an urban computing environment actually triggers or executes an application. This question is rather a question of distributed computing, that is, of the underlying urban computing platform. Application frameworks, such as

T.-h. Kim et al. (Eds.): MulGraB/BSBT/IUrC 2012, CCIS 353, pp. 334–341, 2012.

unified context-aware application model [5], the Context Toolkit of Dey [2], or the framework by Henricksen and Indulska [4] allow separating the applications running on a smart device from the necessary infrastructure to connect them. We will thus in the following assume that smart objects but also smart environments, that is, groups of smart objects that are fixed with respect to some parameter of context, are intelligent systems embedded in such an application framework.

Thus, we consider three questions as primarily relevant for the development of ambient intelligence systems: 1) coalition formation: the question how to group smart objects and/or smart environments into smart environments based on a common context, 2)context integration: how to integrate contextual information from different sources, so as to obtain higher level representations of the current situation, and 3) context management: how to react appropriately to an identified situation using contextual information.

In this paper, we suggest a cognitively motivated layered multi-agent system to realize these demands. Agents in our model represent separate cognitive facilities of an intelligent system, which can be a smart object or a smart environment with respect to the underlying urban computing infrastructure. We assume three types of agents, which correspond to layers of representational abstraction found in human cognition. We identify these layers of abstraction with critical time frames of tasks in a dynamic environment.

2   A Cognitively Motivated Agent Architecture

The proposed agent architecture has three layers for continuous responsiveness, immediate reaction, and pro-activity [10]. The layer of continuous responsiveness is bound to the time frame of visual continuity. Sensors should react without any perceivable delay. Likewise the movement of an animation on a screen or of other actuators has to stay within this time frame. A camera tracking a moving object should work within this timeframe. The layer of immediate reaction, on the other hand, is bound by the time frame of well-learned reactions to sudden change. We chose a threshold of one second maximal delay for this layer. In the case of an obstacle appearing suddenly on a road, for instance, a driver would within one second be able to generate a more or less adequate reaction, such as breaking, steering, or a learned sequence of these actions. The third layer is the layer of pro-activity. Intelligent actions in a changing but predictable world require computational processes of higher complexity. When a human being constructs a piece of work, makes a sketch or note, in order not to forget an intermediate step in some advanced task, the time frame depends on the actual complexity and gain expected from the task itself. Accordingly, the time frame is unbounded on the third layer.

Architectures that fulfill the above time requirements have been investigated in research on intelligent agent systems. Wooldridge [8][9] summarizes several advantages of agent-oriented programming in comparison to object-oriented programming, which we consider to be crucial for realizing ambient intelligence:

- Objects have only control over their state, but not over their behavior, as methods are called from the outside, i.e. by other objects. Agents, in contrast, act according to some request, and can thus, for instance, include refined strategies for avoiding security problems.
- Agents in contrast to methods of objects are by default executed concurrently. Each agent in a multi-agent system has its own thread or threads. Multi-agent systems are therefore an ideal programming paradigm for spatially distributed smart objects.
- Agents have higher flexibility and autonomy than objects. Agent behavior is reactive, pro-active, and social. The first two characteristics were already mentioned above, however, we allow for separate reactive and pro-active facilities so that they can be distributed computational entities in smart space. Regarding the metaphor of social strategies, inter-agent communication relations are especially important for solving issues of privacy or potential for deadlocks in ambient intelligence systems.

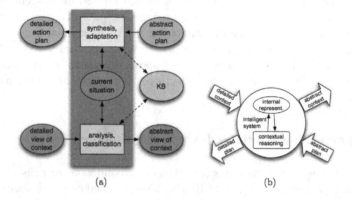

Fig. 1. Primitive agent architecture (b): an agent can receive detailed, contextual information from agents on a layer below it and process this information into more abstract information for agents on the layer above (context integration, lower row in (a)); the processed contextual information is also used to concretize plans received from the higher layer into plan understood on a lower layer (context management, upper row in (a)).

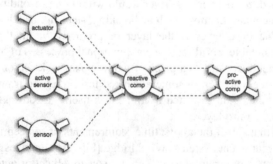

Fig. 2. Simple example for a multi-agent system of five agents configured so as to realize ambient intelligence

Each agent adheres to the primitive structure of an intelligent system, but additionally can communicate with other agents with which it is connected, so as to generate more detailed, concrete plans out of coarse, abstract plans and coarsened, abstract representations from detailed, concrete representations (Fig. 1). Since we leave out all details regarding the establishment and removal of communication links between agents as being solved by the underlying urban computing system, we can consider communication between agents as a flow of information whose update rate is determined by the layer to which the agent is committed to belong. Fig. 2 shows a group of agents connected according to their position in the layer mechanism that are configured so as to form a coalition solving a certain problem.

3   Layers in Agent Architecture

Ambient intelligence, that is, pro-active behavior beyond triggered responses from an urban computing environment, can be achieved by combining and processing contextual information from diverse sensors. One way to achieve this, and the method we will follow below, is to simply consider the pro-active component to be a classical symbolic knowledge representation and reasoning system. The main problem we then encounter with a coalition architecture as shown in Fig. 2 is the well-known symbol grounding problem. The reactive component has to somehow relate between the possibly non-symbolic input from the sensory layer and the symbolic output required for the pro-active layer. We can thus derive a urban computing system for achieving ambient intelligence in our framework as a vertically layered two-pass architecture with three layers, as shown in Fig. 3. The main benefit of using two-pass architecture is that we can get immediate reactions to sensory input while still performing further processing and accumulation of knowledge.

In our layered architecture, context integration, that is the integration of contextual information from various sources, is a step-wise process of abstraction through classification and analysis (shown in the lower row of Fig. 3). Contextual information can be integrated from low-level sensory information, to object-based and situation-based knowledge on the reactive layer, and finally to high-level, situation-independent logic- based knowledge on the pro-active layer:

- On the layer of responsiveness, the intelligence of smart sensors can be implemented: an aggregation component would be able, for instance, to identify positions in successive frames for object tracking, or to aggregate basic coordinate data and sensor values with clustering techniques into object regions.
- On the reactive layer, basic situation and object recognition can be implemented: identification includes recognizing gestures from hand movements, i.e. matching shapes and other sensory input to objects and states of objects stored in the object-oriented knowledge-base or recognizing situations from a particular layout of objects or a particular succession of events.
- On the pro-active layer, facts about the world are extracted from the constant flow of situations and objects detected at the lower layer: reasoning is required, so that an agent can keep track of changes occurring in the world, generate representations of the current state of the world at varying levels of detail, and identify courses of events and their possible outcomes to avert disasters and reach goals.

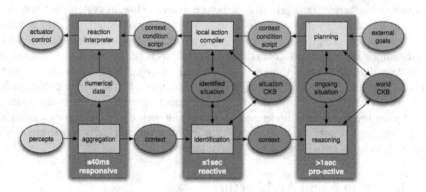

Fig. 3. A vertically layered two-pass agent architecture for realizing ambient intelligence with smart objects and smart spaces

In order to invoke services and actions appropriate in a context with appropriate contextual information, not only the external, sensed context has to be handled but also internal, contextual information, such as the status of the system with respect to fulfilling long-term goals. Accordingly, context management is performed as stepwise refinement and realization of plans through adaptation of current action plans and synthesis of new plans (shown in the upper row of Fig. 3): from generating local action plans in response to a user's overall goals, to generating concrete instantiations of those actions within a local context, to translation of these actions to actuator responses appropriate to a dynamically changing world.

- On the pro-active layer, goals of a user, facts about the world, and rules of causality are employed to generate plans, i.e. short parameterized sequences of commands: planning is required, so that an agent can solve complex problems, and achieve goals involving currently not existing objects, and situations.
- On the reactive layer, condition-based action triggering can be implemented: local action planning means linking parameters in an action plan to objects and situations of a context and triggering the next action in a plan based on identified parameters and preferred behaviors.
- On the layer of responsiveness, the intelligence of smart actuators can be implemented: a reaction interpreter would be able to generate behavior comparable to involuntary response directly from perceptual input, to generate behavior comparable to voluntary response by interpreting a local action, and to interpret the local action with respect to continuously updated information retrieved from perception, such as tracking data.

The representations used on each layer have to differ so as to support the individual tasks within the required time frame and flexibility.

- On the layer of responsiveness, computation is performed directly on the mostly numerical input from sensors. This allows for especially fast processing, as required for algorithms at the sensor interface, which have to handle continuous input streams, e.g., for computer vision algorithms. The result of analysis is on the one hand directly transferred to the reaction interpreter, and on the other hand transformed into an object-oriented representation of the context, which is distributed to recipient agents on the reactive layer.

- On the reactive layer, context is represented in an object-oriented format. Information about parameters of the current context from different sources is integrated into one context object, so as to obtain a precise and complete representation of the current state of the world around an agent. Meaning is given to the context object by relating it to previous contexts, context objects given in application ontologies, and context objects contained in a user profile. This information about the current context can easily be translated into a logic-based format, which can be sent to recipients on the pro-active layer for further analysis. The identified situation can be used for instantiating local action plans as responses to a changed situation. Thus instantiated plans can then be sent to recipients on the layer of responsiveness, i.e. to the smart actuators.

- On the pro-active layer, logic-based knowledge representation systems can be realized. The input from the reactive layer is sufficiently abstract, so as to be accessible to higher-level reasoning. Information about the current context can be decontextualized, in order to receive a more objective and far-reaching representation about ongoing and past processes. Based on this representation, a planning component can generate plans as concrete goals in a succession of contexts based on external goals, as in a conventional belief-desire-intention architecture.

4   Representations of Context on the Reactive Layer

The reactive layer has been a focus of our research for three reasons. First, the time frame of one second demands a specialized fast reasoning mechanism for all domains of parameters of context. Second, the symbol grounding problem has to be handled on this layer, between the sensory input and the logic-based representations on the one hand, and the underspecified logic-based plans and the concrete, contextualized local action plans, on the other hand. The third reason for highlighting the special role of the reactive layer, is that the notion of context is established and dealt with on this layer.

Key to realizing this layer is an appropriate representation of context. The representation of context we aim at needs to have all three properties given by Benerecetti et al. [1]: contexts have to be represented as partial, approximative, and perspectival entities. Contextual reasoning then covers relations between partial and more global views, between fine-grained and coarsened views, and between perspectives. A simple and yet expressive formalism is needed, in order to stay within the permitted time frame of 1s. Following Jang et al. [7], our representation is based on six parameters of context: the context of an interacting coalition of agents in this model is fully described if we know the participants – in particular, the users or their avatars –, the time, place, objects, causes, and the manner of an interaction within this coalition.

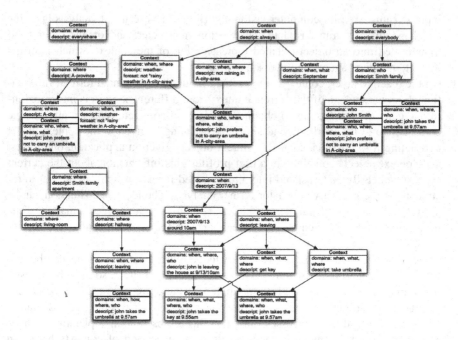

Fig. 4. Three directed acyclic graphs storing preferences and other context information about location, time, and users

In [6], we investigated relations between partial views for four of the six parameters, namely classes of users and objects with respective taxonomic relations and temporal and spatial extents with mereologic relations. The four relations can be axiomatically characterized as partial orders. Consequently, a reasoning system for partial view reasoning over the four parameters of context can be realized as a partial order reasoner, which can be implemented in a very efficient way using directed acyclic graphs. Fig. 4 illustrates how context objects are inserted into four directed acyclic graphs, in order to represent, and reason about the time, location, users, and objects of the current context.

However, the context model and context logic of Hong et al. [5] currently only supports representing the basic relations between partial views and does not address the causal context of an interaction, that is the how and why of context in the model of Jang et al. [7]. These extensions are a focus of ongoing work. A promising candidate for specifying the two domains of how and why are the structures resulting from same time rules and next time rules in the framework of Galton and Augusto[3].

The context logic formalism supports reasoning about taxonomic and spatio-temporal hierarchies. These reasoning capabilities are needed for two distinct purposes. The first purpose was illustrated above (Fig. 4): each agent keeps track of its changing contexts and receives information from other agents, which it can use to react appropriately in a situation and to extend its ontology. The agent builts up contextual information structures, such as shown in Fig. 4 over its lifetime and the duration of tasks. But additionally at any single time t, relations between agents are determined by the positions in the taxonomic and spatio-temporal hierarchy, to which these agents contribute information. In particular, their similarity and proximity with respect to this structure at t are crucial. A user entering a room with a smart phone, for instance, would be represented as being in the location of the room. The smart phone's position at that time would be close to, and similar to the position of the room in the where-hierarchy. Likewise, the position of the room's inbuilt devices with respect to the who-hierarchy would be similar to the position of the smart phone at time t, since the user of the smart phone would be entering the community of users of the devices.

5   Conclusions and Future Work

We presented a cognitively motivated vertically layered two-pass agent architecture. We also discussed context representation to realize ambient intelligence in urban computing environments. In future, we have a plan to design and implement an intelligent system with our approach in urban computing infrastructure.

References

1. Benerecetti, M., Bouquet, P., Ghidini, C.: Contextual reasoning distilled. Journal of Experimental and Theoretical Artificial Intelligence 12(3), 279–305 (2000)
2. Dey, A.K.: Providing Architectural Support for Building Context-Aware Applications. PhD thesis, Georgia Institute of Technology (2000)
3. Galton, A., Augusto, J.C.: Stratified causal theories for reasoning about deterministic devices and protocols. In: TIME, pp. 52–54 (2002)
4. Henricksen, K., Indulska, J.: Developing context-aware pervasive computing applications: Models and approach. Pervasive and Mobile Computing 2, 37–64 (2006)
5. Hong, D., Suh, Y., Choi, A., Rashid, U., Woo, W.: wear-UCAM: A Toolkit for Mobile User Interactions in Smart Environments. In: Sha, E., Han, S.-K., Xu, C.-Z., Kim, M.-H., Yang, L.T., Xiao, B. (eds.) EUC 2006. LNCS, vol. 4096, pp. 1047–1057. Springer, Heidelberg (2006)
6. Hong, D., Schmidtke, H.R., Woo, W.: Linking context modelling and contextual reasoning. In: 4th International Workshop on Modeling and Reasoning in Context (MRC), pp. 37–48 (2007)
7. Jang, S., Ko, E.-J., Woo, W.: Unified user-centric context: Who, where, when, what, how and why. In: Personalized Context Modeling and Management for UbiComp Applications. CEUR-WS, vol. 149, pp. 26–34 (2005)
8. Wooldridge, M.: Intelligent agents, Multiagent Systems. MIT Press (1999)
9. Wooldridge, M.: Intelligent Agents: The Key Concepts. In: Mařík, V., Štěpánková, O., Krautwurmová, H., Luck, M. (eds.) MASA 2001. LNCS (LNAI), vol. 2322, pp. 3–43. Springer, Heidelberg (2002) MASA 2001,
10. Lee, Y., Schmidtke, H.R., Suh, Y., Woo, W.: Realizing Seamless Interaction: a Cognitive Agent Architecture for Virtual and Smart Environments. In: International Symposium on Ubiquitous Virtual Reality, pp. 1–2 (2007)

Implementation of Visual Indicators
for Residential Development

Choong Sik Kim[1] and Eun Joo Yoon[2]

[1] Dept. of Environmental Landscape Architecture, Gangneung-Wonju National University,
South Korea
[2] LH Land and Housing Institute, Research Fellow, South Korea

Abstract. In recent years, residential tower blocks, residential rights such as a right to enjoy sunshine and good view have become socially sensitive matters. The research aimed to establish a methodology to find out the extent of visual damage and households caused by residential development. The research aims to make a quantitative calculation of visual grading and degree of concealment from residential development. Kumho residential apartment development was selected as a case study. Within the case study, 5 blocks were chosen to simulate which is located between Han River and Dalmaji hill. The degree of visual screening is analysed into three different visual exposures; Visual Exposure, Distance-weighed Visual Exposure and Area-weighed Visual Exposure. Then the Visual Exposures were compared with visual damage and landscape simulations. In particular, Area-weighed Visual Exposure has a great potential to be implemented into planning process including disputes, grant and assessment since it does reflect human visual perceptions.

Keywords: Visibility Analysis, 3D Simulation, NURBS, VE3D, Arcview, Visual Exposure.

1   Introduction

Recently, within residential tower blocks, residential rights such as a right to enjoy sunshine and good view have become socially sensitive matters. Since visually valuable natural resources are within urban areas such as river and mountain, local planning authorities are concerned about the social rights and attempt to minimise or avoid any possible dispute. For local planning authority's point of view, the visibility issues become significant in policy making (Kang, 2004).

Visual Density Indicator is used for various statutory legislations for height and density on residential projects. This research develops Visual Indicators which human visual senses were taken into account focusing on small size residential developments. The research also assesses the extent of visual damages caused by the development and therefore, the research finding aims to contribute in planning policy establishments.

T.-h. Kim et al. (Eds.): MulGraB/BSBT/IUrC 2012, CCIS 353, pp. 342–350, 2012.
© Springer-Verlag Berlin Heidelberg 2012

2   Development of Visual Indicator using 3D Visual Exposure

2.1   Developing 3D Visual Exposure

Visual Exposure quantifies visual opportunities and visual frequency from multiple viewpoints[1]. However, raster dataset based Visual Exposure is not suitable for urban areas where built up structures are dominant. Moreover, simple black and white (visible and not visible) analysis does not reflect visible distance and characteristics of the site (Caldwell et al., 2003; Kwon, 2011a; Kwon, 2011b).

If Visual Exposure is carried out based on building elevations, the visibility opportunity, grading, and degree of concealment could be calculated. For this analysis, 3D modelling has to be performed based on vector datasets of terrain and buildings. Vector modelling technique is able to represent landscapes in better reality including mesh and surface. Recently, vector modelling programmes are highly advanced; however, vector modelling techniques for Visibility Exposure has not been developed yet.

The calculation of Visibility Exposure is measured from Lines Of Sight (LOS) and whether the LOSs hitting the objects. Consequently, the length of LOS becomes visibility distance and cumulative LOS makes Visibility Exposure map. In order to visualise this process within vector models, Visual Exposure 3D (VE3D) was developed[2].

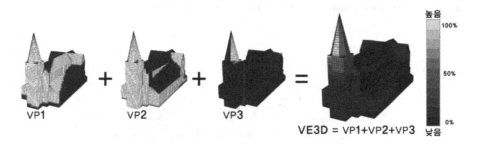

Fig. 1. The Process of VE3D

2.2   Visual Exposure with Human Visual Perception

Traditionally, Visual Exposure and cumulative visibility map are produced without taking distances into account. However, human perceives visual objects based on distances and as a trade-off, visible objects are inverse proportion to squared distance (Gibson, 1950). Therefore, visible distance and object size need to be considered in order to produce more accurate visible exposure results.

---

[1] Visual Exposure means degree of visibility and uses same term with cumulative visibility (Kim et al., 2011).

[2] VE3D was developed using Grasshopper 0.8.0066, plug-in for Rhinoceros 5.0 (http://www.grasshopper3d.com)

Vf: Visual Exposure **Vd: Distance-weighed Visual Exposure** **Va: Area-weighed Visual Exposure**

$$Vf = \sum_{i=1}^{m} \sum_{j=1}^{n} V_{ij} \qquad Vd = \sum_{i=1}^{m} \sum_{j=1}^{n} \frac{V_{ij}}{D_{ij}} \qquad Va = \sum_{i=1}^{m} \sum_{j=1}^{n} \frac{V_{ij}}{D_i^2}$$

i: viewpoints on the building (m number), j: view objectives (n number), Vij: visibility (visible=0, invisible=1), Dij: distance between building (i) and view objects (j)

Fig. 2. Calculation of Visual Exposure

3 Methodology

The research aims to make a quantitative calculation of visual grading and degree of concealment from residential development. Kumho residential apartment development was selected as a case study. Within the case study, 5 blocks were chosen to simulate which is located between Han River and Dalmaji hill.

10 thresholds of visual grading were classified based on Visual Exposure[3]. Single residential block was also divided with 3m grids for use in individual households' Visual Exposure. Total 36 viewpoints were chosen to assess visible and not visible status and size/distance were considered as in 600m, 1000m, and 1800m (Hong, 2010). 36 grids (200m x 200m) were created which include near distance 5, mid distance 11, and long distance 20 from the centre point.

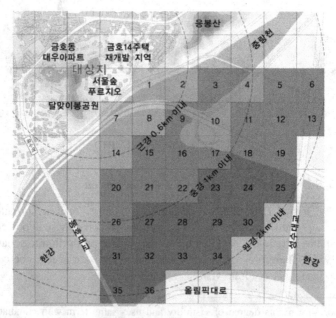

Fig. 3. Grid Methodology

---

[3] In fact, 11 grading were designed including 0 grading (visual exposure = 0).

4   Research Results

4.1   Efficiency on Producing Visibility Analysis

4.1.1   Processing Efficiency

The analysis models were created with Rhinoceros 5.0 in particular, NURBS were used for terrains and surface was implemented for buildings and other built up structures. For Visual Exposure analysis, VE3D were utilised. The system was Windows 7, Intel Core i7 950 3.07GHz CUP, 12GB DDR3 RAM, Nvidia GeForce GTx 460, 7200rpm Sata HDD. For instance, 134463 surfaces were calculated for façade of 7 residential blocks from a single viewpoint and it took 8 minutes 10 seconds. The more invisible surfaces increase, the quicker calculations were made. This result indicates that it could be common practice to carry out 3D Visual Exposure analysis using 3D models in urban landscape.

4.1.2   Visibility Analysis

In order to check accuracy of the process viewpoint no 8 was exemplified for comparison of before, after, simulation, visual areas and VE3D. According to the perspectives, from the viewpoint no 8, lower levels of 113/ 114 blocks and mid levels of 201-203 blocks can be visible. This is the same results with VE3D analysis. After the new residential blocks, only from mid levels of 202 and 203 blocks viewpoint no 8 was visible. The research compared visibility before and after new residential blocks, then mid and lower levels of 7 blocks were visually affected. Meanwhile, VE3D results were matching with computerised landscape simulation; therefore, the results from visibility analysis by VE3D are credible. Moreover, VE3D would be effective for visibility comparisons of visual damage on highly valuable landmarks and assessing the extent of the damage.

Table 1. VE3D Visibility Comparison (Viewpoint No 8)

Landscape Simulation		VE3D Analysis		Visual Damage
Before the New Residential Blocks	After the New Residential Blocks	Before the New Residential Blocks	After the New Residential Blocks	

4.2   Visual Indicator Comparison

4.2.1   Visibility Classification

Visibility maps were produced from 36 viewpoints and then, using the formula (Figure 2), Visual Exposure (Vf), Distance-weighed Visual Exposure (Vd), and Area-weighed Visual Exposure (Va) were made. Each visual exposure was standardised as 10 grading system.

Before the new residential blocks, grade 10 (maximum) was scored in most of block no 113 – no 203 in Vf, high/mid levels of no 203 in Vd and mid/low levels of no 203 in Va.

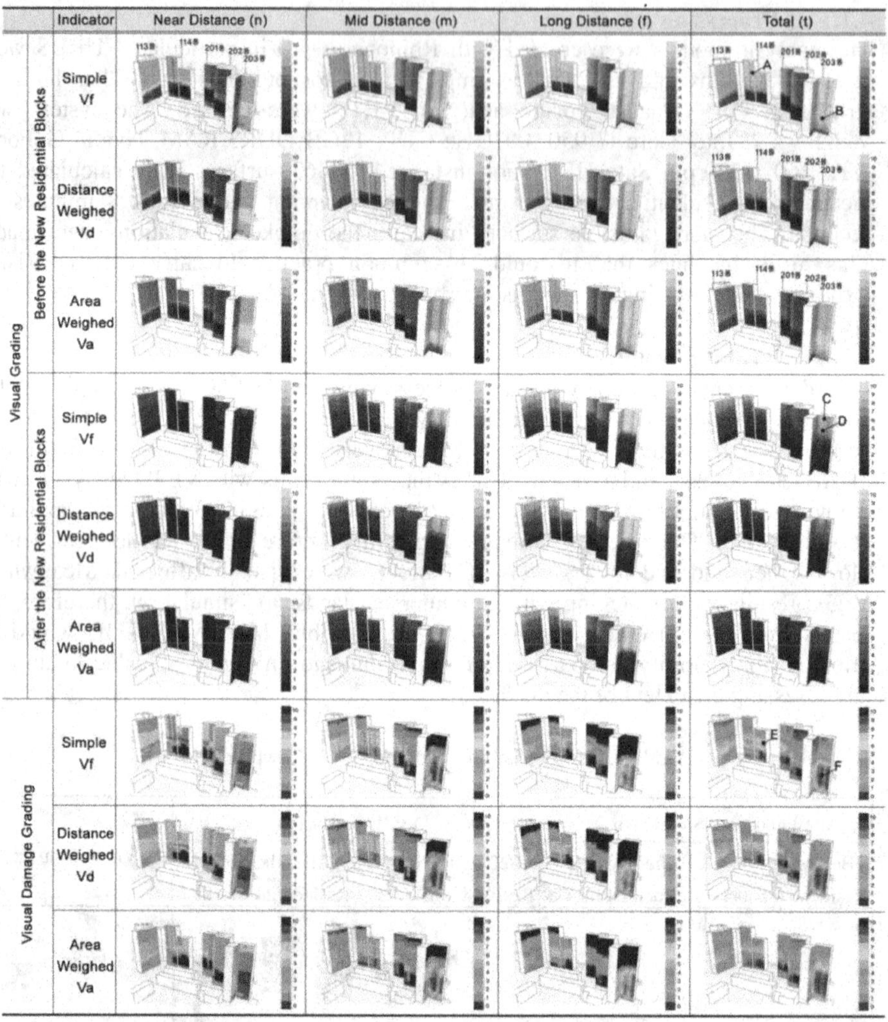

Fig. 4. Visual Exposure Results

4.2.2   Visibility Indication Distinction

The produced visual indicators were cross checked with computerised simulations for accuracy and credibility.

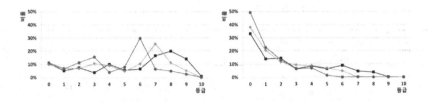

Fig. 5. Visual Indicators before/after the new residential blocks

Based on Figure 6 and 7, there are some discrepancies between Vf and Va due to the area differences. Accordingly, the results illustrated the areas of high value in Va have more visual damages.

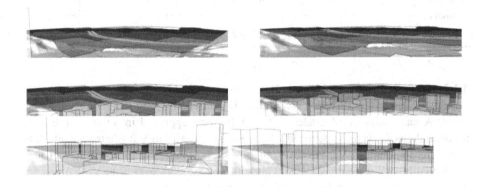

Fig. 6. Locations A, B, C, D, E and F (Green-Near Distance, Red-Mid Distance, Blue-Long Distance)

4.3   Visual Indicator Analysis on Residential Tower Block

4.3.1   Visual Indicator Analysis Based on Area Units
The research introduced 3x3m grid which represents single household within residential tower blocks. Total of 7 tower blocks were applied and 1728 viewpoints were accordingly created. During the process, the majority grids in Vf fell into grade 7-9, in Vd most of grids were grade 7 and grade 6 as well as 2 and 3 were mostly appeared in Va.

After new residential blocks were constructed, grade 9 and 10 would be disappeared in Vf; whereas, grade 1-8 remained same. Moreover, grade 0 was increased from 10.7% to 33.3%, which lead into increase of visual screening as 22.6%. However, grade 0 in Va increased from 11.3% to 49.2% which indicated nearly half of balcony of the households were screened. In addition, view towards Han River was sharply blocked since grade 6 – 10 were disappeared.

Table 2. Visual Indicator (per area, %)

Landscape	Indicator Grade	0	1	2	3	4	5	6	7	8	9	10
Before New Residential Blocks	Vf	10.7	5.2	7.3	3.7	10.0	5.4	6.4	16.4	19.9	14.1	0.8
	Vd	9.9	7.1	6.7	10.6	9.0	4.6	10.3	25.5	11.1	5.2	0.1
	Va	11.3	6.6	11.3	15.5	3.9	7.9	29.8	6.4	4.9	2.5	0.1
After New Residential Blocks	Vf	33.3	14.1	14.5	6.3	8.3	6.3	8.9	4.5	3.7	0.2	-
	Vd	38.1	20.5	11.6	9.3	8.7	6.8	4.7	-	0.2	-	-
	Va	49.2	22.8	13.2	6.2	6.9	1.4	-	0.2	-	-	-

4.3.2   Visual Indicator Analysis Based on Households Units

Residential tower blocks which contained 552 households were included for the case study. A large number of grades 7, 9 and 10 were appeared in Vf in before new. residential blocks were constructed. Grade 8 is in majority in Vd; whereas, grade 4, 6, 7, 9 were dominant in Va. However, there were no grade 6 – 10 in Va in after new residential blocks were constructed. Grade 0 increase 600- 800 % in Vf, Vd and Va which means view to Han River would be screened dramatically.

Table 3. Visual Damage (households)

Landscape		Indicator Grade	0	1	2	3	4	5	6	7	8	9	10
Visual Grading	Before New Residential Blocks	Vf	18	54	20	29	25	54	49	65	40	107	91
		Vd	17	41	38	38	41	70	32	72	121	52	30
		Va	25	38	46	63	88	25	74	104	1	75	13
	After New Residential Blocks	Vf	128	97	57	66	32	59	42	28	29	14	0
		Vd	149	105	83	59	68	33	28	23	4	0	0
		Va	160	164	96	66	34	28	0	4	0	0	0
Visual Damage		Vf	30	140	58	67	56	67	49	34	21	30	0
		Vd	17	93	93	88	78	59	55	25	13	31	0
		Va	22	77	97	88	91	70	43	17	10	37	0

For visual damage, grade 0 increased from 3.3% to 23.2% in Vf, which indicated 19.9% of the households were blocked the view towards Han River. However, according to Va results grade 0 increased from 4.5% to 29% and households which were blocked views from Han River was 24.5%.

5   Conclusion

The research aimed to establish a methodology to find out the extent of visual damage and households caused by residential development. Visual exposure programme which developed in the research can be run in Windows based computers and have large potential to be implemented in common development practice. Moreover, the degree of visual screening is analysed into three different visual exposures; Visual Exposure, Distance-weighed Visual Exposure and Area-weighed Visual Exposure. Then the Visual Exposures were compared with visual damage and landscape simulations.

In particular, Area-weighed Visual Exposure has a great potential to be implemented into planning process including disputes, grant and assessment since it does reflect human visual perceptions.

References

1. Anastasopoulos, P.C., Islam, M.B., Perperidou, D., Karlaftis, M.G.: Hazard-Based Analysis of Travel Distance in Urban Environments: Longitudinal Data Approach. Journal of Urban Planning and Development-Asce 138(1), 53–61 (2012)
2. Zheng, Z., Bohong, Z.: Study on Spatial Structure of Yangtze River Delta Urban Agglomeration and Its Effects on Urban and Rural Regions. Journal of Urban Planning and Development-Asce 138(1), 78–89 (2012)
3. Lee, D., Choe, H.: Estimating the Impacts of Urban Expansion on Landscape Ecology: Forestland Perspective in the Greater Seoul Metropolitan Area. Journal of Urban Planning and Development-Asce 137(4), 425–437 (2011)
4. Oakil, A.T.M., Ettema, D., Arentze, T., Timmermans, H.: Longitudinal Model of Longer-Term Mobility Decisions: Framework and First Empirical Tests. Journal of Urban Planning and Development-Asce 137(3), 220–229 (2011)
5. Hui, E.C.-M., Ng, I.M.-H., Lo, K.-K.: Analysis of the Viability of an Urban Renewal Project under a Risk-Based Option Pricing Framework. Journal of Urban Planning and Development-Asce 137(2), 101–111 (2011)
6. Park, B.-J., Furuya, K., Kasetani, T., Takayama, N., Kagawa, T., Miyazaki, Y.: Relationship between psychological responses and physical environments in forest settings. Landscape and Urban Planning 102(1), 24–32 (2011)
7. Kirkpatrick, J.B., Daniels, G.D., Davison, A.: Temporal and spatial variation in garden and street trees in six eastern Australian cities. Landscape and Urban Planning 1021(3), 244–252 (2011)

8. Domingo-Santos, J.M., de Villarán, R.F., Rapp-Arrarás, Í., de Provens, E.C.-P.: The visual exposure in forest and rural landscapes: An algorithm and a GIS tool. Landscape and Urban Planning 101(1), 52–58 (2011)
9. Domon, G.: Landscape as resource: Consequences, challenges and opportunities for rural development. Landscape and Urban Planning 100(1), 338–340 (2011)
10. Jorgensen, A.: Beyond the view: Future directions in landscape aesthetics research. Landscape and Urban Planning 100(1), 353–355 (2011)

Assessment and Connection Method of Fragmentary Urban Green Space Using Gravity Model

Soo Dong Lee

Department of Landscape Architecture, Jinju National University,
South Korea

Abstract. This research presents the connecting method for the ecological network among the selected areas through the evaluation of the connectivity of the classified urban green space in Seoul. The study was divided into two; 1st stage of the classification of the types of greens and 2nd stage of the evaluation of connectivity. In the stage of classification of the type of the greens, the research evaluated the diversity of the vegetation and the value of the possibility of inhabitation of wild birds and then, classified the greens into a core green, which is a patch, base green, and connecting or stepping stone-type green, which is a corridor, in aspect of the landscape ecology. In the evaluation of connectivity, the research also selected and classified the areas for ecological network and suggested the connecting method by conducting the evaluation based on a gravity model with indexes such as area index, conference index, and fractal index, in order to find the relationship between the greens.

Keywords: Core Green Area, Base Green Area, Linkage or Stepping Stone Green Area, Gravity Model, District Ecological Network, Basin Ecological Network.

1   Introduction

Recently, development flow has been changed from physical development alone to balanced development with environment and restoring equilibrium of ecosystem for new understanding of necessity of new development flow. Based on this new understanding, preservation area and development area are divided through site analysis and new land use plan has been established for the future development area(Ministry of construction & transportation . Korea institute of construction technology, 2002).

The large scale of development may scatter the green spaces. This can block the opportunity of access to green space and increase air pollution because of damaging ecosystem and dropping capability of purification followed by declining green space in urban area (Kim, 1998). In terms of urban ecological geography, there are many wild animals have been exterminated and reduced biological diversity due to scattering green space and decreasing green area(Scott et al., 1993). On this reason, necessity of urban green space connectivity has been increased and greenway, green axis, ecosystem network and other idea have been introduced (MacArthur and Wilson, 1967).

T.-h. Kim et al. (Eds.): MulGraB/BSBT/IUrC 2012, CCIS 353, pp. 351–359, 2012.
© Springer-Verlag Berlin Heidelberg 2012

The biggest possibility of threatening species diversity is frequently occurred isolation of green spaces. This phenomenon, natural habitat fragmentation and isolation, lead to reduce the number of individual. Moreover, this affects the minimizing quality and quantity of habitat spaces or destroys the habitat and isolation through interfering ecosystem (Wilcove et al., 1986; Laurance and Bierregaard, 1997). The purpose of this research proposes ecological network method in ecologically isolated mountainous urban green spaces. The valuation and pattern of horticultural diversity and value of habitat for wild birds are analysed and proposed using research of linking scattered each urban green area.

2   Research Contents and Procedure

This research is divided by 2 phases, green spaces type and rating connectivity, to build ecological network in existing urban area. In the 1stphase, rating items, ecology diversity and valuation of wild birds habitat, are established through theory study for evaluating possibility of life habitat. Evaluating connectivity is proceeded followed by establishing connectivity index, evaluating connectivity, and site selection and modelling in phase 2.

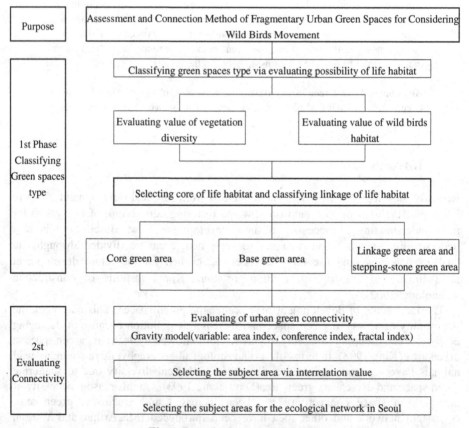

Fig. 1. Research Procedure Concept

In order to select the ecological network site, interrelation value between distance of patch, size, and fractal index are enumerated by matrix method to find out the relation between each patch. To select the site, location which has highest interrelation value between patch is selected and simple relation between core green area or base green area, linkage green area, and stepping-stone green area are excluded. Finally, patch interrelations are established; core green area or base green area~core green area or base green area, core green area or base green area~base green area or linkage green area and stepping-stone green area.

3   Material and Methods

3.1   Study Site

The concept of basin district can be assumed that it was formed early 10th century in Korea dynasty when the concept of Baekdudaegan was a scent of revolution. However, based on Sangyeongpyo which was systemized and for mountains the concept of basin district had been estimated constituted. In general, drainage basin goes around the Marukum like patch in the mountain area. And collected water at the basin is merged with other basin over and over again.

The research site is Seoul surrounded by Naesasan (linked with Bugaksan (Mt.)), Inwangsan (Mt.), Namsan (Mt.), Naksan (Mt.) very natural way like castle walls) and Oesasan (basin formed by Bukhansan (Mt.), Gwanaksan (Mt.), Yongmasan (Mt.), Deoyangsan (Mt.)). Therefore, basin district is established by Oesasan, surrounding outside of Seoul and City limit which is linked with Dobongsan (Mt.), Suraksan(Mt.), Buramsan(Mt.), Yongmasan (Mt.), Iljasan (Mt.), Daemosan (Mt.), Guryongsan (Mt.), Illeungsan (Mt.), Cheonggyesan(Mt.), Bongsan(Mt.), Marukum of Seo-o-reung urban natural park. As a matter of selecting inside of basin district, 5 basin district(boundary of Hangang (River), Jungnangcheon (Stream), Anyangcheon (Stream), Tancheon (Stream)) which are soundly maintain its function are selected by Sanjabunsuryeong in inside of Marukum. Among these selected basin district, ecological network site is established through green space type and connectivity in Gangbuk area.

3.2   Methodology

3.2.1   Study Area Survey and Data Analyses

To estimate fragmentized and patched vegetation diversity inside of urbanized area, it should be considered both current site condition and potential value at the same time (Kleyer, 1994). It is desired that area and current disturbance scale are estimated to maintain vegetation diversity in urban area for estimation of current condition and the age of a tree showing ecological succession stage, constituted multi-layered vegetation structure or not, and forest stabilization is estimated to analyse potential value estimation(Kim and Lee, 1977).

Based on all these results, stability, characteristics of nature, rareness, generation period are estimated. In the point of green vegetation diversity estimation, stability is estimated by minimum area which can keep stable condition without disturbance and irruption from outside (Wilcove *et al.,* 1986). Ogle (1981) and Wittig *et al.*(1983) classified as 3 classes which are over 40ha, stable regardless of outside condition, under 10ha, unstable against the artificial damage and penetration, and in between. To estimate characteristics of nature which has been used to estimate indigene and introduced species ratio, damaged degree of substratum followed by human intervention, it is classified as 3 classes followed Ogle (1981) and Tans' standard (1974) over 70% of natural forest (no change more than 50% in all layers), between 50~70% of natural forest(high ratio of damaging lower layer vegetation) and under 50% of natural forest(high ratio of damaging lower layer). Rareness is showing richness of habitat type and this is used for estimating ecological succession stage and changed degree of vegetation (Woodland *et al.,* 1995).

It is classified as 3 classes; later, primary or middle period of succession, and artificial forest including natural forest. Generation period estimates forest stability following its growth (Witting & Schreiber, 1983). Less than 10 years forest or ecosystem are fairly stabilized because it is generated stage. Therefore it is classified as 3 classes that over 20 years trees are standardized for estimation in terms of preservation and development(Korea Land Corporation, 2001), under 10 year forest or ecosystem and others.

Table 1. Criteria for evaluating the diversity of vegetation in the urban green area

Degree of category	Evaluation criteria
Stability	•High: 40 ha>, Medium: 10~40 ha, Low: 10 ha<
Nature	•High: more than 70% of natural forest, more than 50% of changeless forest in the whole tree layer structure, Medium: natural forest 50~70%, 50% of changeless forest in the whole tree layer structure or more than 70% of natural forest but where is damaged under tree layer structure, Low: less than 50% of natural forest and damage under tree layer structure.
Rareness	•High: the late succession natural forest, Medium: the primary natural forest, the middle period of succession natural forest, Low: the artificial forest or natural forest which including artificial afforestation species
Generation period	•High: more than 50years of climax forest, 20~50years of stably natural forest , Medium: 20~50years of Unstably artificial forest, 10~20years of young age class natural forest, Low: 3~10years of initial stage forest, less than 3years of bare land and grassland

In the result of research about wild birds which inhabit in urban green area, even there are some differences in quality of green spaces, there are very close relation with urban green area and diversity of wild birds (Linehan *et al.,* 1967). In addition to, diversity of green, tree layer structure, rear green space distance and other effects from outside are closely related with wild birds abundant chart (Shibuya et al., 1987; Hayama, 1994; Cho, 1993). Based on these items, stabilization, diversity, isolation and growth of forest are estimated.

Based on the number of community and age of tree, it is classified as 3 classes. The most suitable distance to keep maintaining wild birds population in green area which is separated from back green area is under 500m and the maximum distance is 1500m. Over 1500m, the research presents that it is impossible to move (Miller et al., 1998). In urbanized area, however, the possible distance of exchange for individual and gene is less than 200m and for extermination is 1000m based on including obstruction and intensive land use (Jedicke, 1994). It is classified as 3 grade because there are structures, road and other obstructions in urban green area. Habitat possibility to find out development degree of forest is classified as 3 levels which are considered with diameter at breast height (D.B.H) of upper tree layer and natural characteristics of dominant species (Park, 1994; Choi, 2004).

Bio-Tope map by Seoul metropolitan government has been used for fundamental data to estimate vegetation and diversity of wild bird habitat in urban green area. Stability is calculated from area per green area. The characteristics of nature is calculated from each type of vegetation area. Each category are classified as natural forest, artificial forest, and mixed forest. Rareness is calculated with total area of sere and growth period is calculated and applied using piece of wood from tree.

Each type of area is mapped by each vegetation type green boundary using AutoCAD MAP 6 and measured the area by Arc-View 3.3. To estimate isolation, the distance between green area is measured by Arc-View 3.3 to find out the shortest distance. The distance between green area is measured by the shortest distance between circumscribed circle. Because there are possible errors come from when we measure the distance between each center of circle. To measure diameter at breast height(D.B.H) which is needed to estimate the growth of forest, D.B.H of natural forest, artificial forest and mixed forest, Bio-tope research data in actual vegetation type in Seoul, is measured and analyzed using Microsoft office excel 2003.

3.2.2   Classification of Urban Green Types

The characteristics of nature, rareness, originating period/diversity, inhabitability and isolation are considered to estimate diversity, stabilize, habitat of wild birds and richness of species based on patch area. And types are classified as the core patch, base patch, and stepping stone patch.

Result of green type based on vegetation diversity, it is chosen that   the core patch is over 40ha which have good characteristics of nature, rareness, originating period patch and good patch which is 10~40ha with good characteristics of nature, rareness, originating period. Point patch is considered and chosen that over 40ha patch which has high stabilize (low characteristics of nature, rareness, originating period), and 10~40ha which has mid stabilize, characteristics of nature, rareness and originating period. Stepping stone type of patch is chosen the area which has 10~40ha which has more or less stabilize, and low value of nature, rareness, and originating period or less than 10ha patch. The result of value of wild birds habitat diversity, the core patch which has over 100ha with good diversity, inhabitability, isolation and the area between 10~100ha with good diversity, inhabitability are chosen. The stepping stone patch which has mover 100ha with low diversity, inhabitability, isolation or the area between 10~100ha which has mid stabilize, diversity, inhabitability, and isolation are chosen. The stepping stone type of patch has 10~100ha patch area which has more or less stabilize, low value of diversity, inhabitability, isolation or less than 10ha with low diversity, inhabitability, and isolation are chosen.

3.2.3   Estimating Connectivity

Connectivity estimation is calculated from each patch per basin district range and each relation was analyzed by gravity model applicated with patch index (estimation index value about the each patch by basin district range). In landscape ecology fields, gravity model similar with Newton's gravity formula has been used to estimate each patch relation (Forman and Godron, 1986; Sklar and Constanza, 1991).

$$F = G \frac{Pi \cdot Pj}{Dijb} \qquad (1)$$

where:
- •F is the magnitude of the gravitational force between the two point masses
- •G is the gravitational constant
- •Pi, Pj is the mass of two subject masses
- •Dij is the distance between the two point masses

4   Study Result

4.1   Classification of Urban Patch Type by Inhabitability of Living Creatures

4.1.1   Current Ecological Condition of Patch

In the survey of actual vegetation type, natural forest is 0.2~98.1%, Gangbuk-70(Namsan (Mt.)), Gangbuk-81(Bukhansan (Mt.)). Artificial forest is 6.6~100%. More than 50% areas are artificial forest. However, it is very high ratio in narrow patch area. The size of dominant tree per actual vegetation type can be used to estimate inhabitability. Natural forest's diameter at breast height(D.B.H) is 6.0~36cm and artificial forest's D.B.H is 13.3~30cm. Narrow area's D.B.H is 15~20cm. Large area's D.B.H is over 20cm. The average D.B.H size in pitch in the north of Han River is over 20cm.

The area ratio per actual vegetation type is used to analyse succession stage. The artificial forest and *Pinus densiflora* are considered as early succession. *Quercus spp.* is considered as mid succession. *Carpinus laxiflora, Carpinus cordata* are considered as late succession. Decideous tree forest such as *Alnus japonica, Betula davurica Pall.* are correspond with later succession stage. Considering the area ratio per types, the area ratio dominated by artificial forest such as *Robinia pseudo-acacia, Fontanesia phyllyreoides*, appeared to early succession phase, are 1.92~100%. More than 50% of patch among 52, excluding 32 patches, have same result. The areas which is dominated by Pinus densiflora are 0.05~98%. The areas dominated by Quercus spp., appeared mid succession phase, are 0.85~65.33% with less than 50% excluding 4 patches. The areas dominated by Decideous tree forest, appeared late succession phase, are 0.12~12.84% with narrow area. While there are artificial forest such as *Robinia pseudo-acacia*,

Fontanesia phyllyreoides, *Pinus koraiensis* largely distributed in patch, north of Hangang (River), it is considered that *Quercus spp.* is early succession period because of small area. However, in some area, Deciduous tree forest such as *Carpinus laxiflora*, *Alnus japonica*, *Betula davurica Pall.* are appeared and this reason should be needed more study.

It is analyzed with extract sampling from trees by increment borer in Bukhansan(Mt.), Namsan (Mt.) and Choansan (Mt.). Excluding (22.5 year old) and *Quercus acutissima* (28.5 year old) which have less than 20cm of D.B.H in natural forest, *Pinus densiflora*, the age range of *Fraxinus rhynchophylla*, *Quercus mongolica* are 33.5~78.4 year old. Excluding *Pinus koraiensis* (23.5 year old) which has less than 20cm of D.B.H, in artificial forest, the age range of *Pinus rigida*, *Robinia pseudo-acacia* are 31.7~91 year old.

After all these vegetation status research in Gangbuk, large patch area, Bukhansan (Mt.)(Gangbuk-81), Namsan (Mt.)(Gangbuk-70), and Bongsan (Mt.)(Gangbuk-4) are located in outskirts of the city. However, Ansan (Mt.) (Gangbuk-18), Baegyeonsan (Mt.) (Gangbuk-22) are separated from rear green space and located inside of city. The small area such as Seongsan (Mt.) (Gangbuk-11), Wau neighbourhood park (Gangbuk-12), Nogosan (Mt.)(Gangbuk-13) are isolated in urbanized area.

Reviewing the result of actual vegetation status which affect to nature, there are more than 50% of artificial forest such as *Robinia pseudo-acacia* in the small patch area with bad nature. However, decideous tree forest such as *Quercus spp.* are in large patch area with good condition of nature. The layer structure and succession phase can effect to rareness. Excluding 3 patches, layer structures have simple structure with artificial and natural forest with less than 50%. In the succession phase, artificial forest such as *Robinia pseudo-acacia*, *Fontanesia phyllyreoides*, *Alnus hirsuta*, *Pinus rigida* are dominated. However, the most of *Quercus spp.* are less than 20% which shows early succession phase. Total trees' age, standards of estimating originating period, is more than 30 years excluding *Pinus densiflora* (22.5 year old) and *Quercus acutissima* (28.5 year old), less than 20cm D.B.H. Actual vegetation type, standard of estimating diversity to estimate the wild birds' inhabitability, are showing that 40 patches have more than 4 types. The north of Han River has small patch with bad nature. However, *Quercus spp.* are dominated in large area with good nature. All trees in natural and artificial forest have more or less 20cm of D.B.H. which is standard of estimating inhabitability.

4.1.2 Estimation and Classification of Patch Type

In the result of diversity of vegetation, patches, over 40ha, have stabilization in outer and inner of urban place even there is environmental change. Excluding some cases, most of patches which are less than 40ha are estimated as mid or less stabilization. The rareness showing disturbance degree followed by nature and succession phase got low value of nature and rareness. Because there are large introduced species dominated excluding Bukhansan (Mt.)(Gangbuk-81) and Namsan (Mt.)(Gangbuk-70). By the originating period estimated by age of dominant tree, trees between 20~50 years tree are dominated. However, patch which has mid value with artificial forest such as *Robinia pseudo-acacia*, *Pinus rigida* has The origination period estimated by age of dominant tree is the largest group. Based on the above research result of estimation of vegetation diversity value, core patch 3, strategic patch 16 and stepping stone patch 63 are classified.

The result of value of wild birds' inhabitability, the area to maintain diversity of species is over 100ha of stabilized patches not relating with outer environmental change and disturbance. The most of patches between 10~100ha are unstable. The inhabitability analysis by diversity and D.B.H of dominant trees showing spontaneity of vegetation and differentiate degree of layer structure, shows that the introduced species are dominated largely excluding massive patches located in the city limit of north of Seoul and it is estimated with less value (less than 50%) excluding 3 patches.

The isolation showing the distance between surrounding patches exist within 200m from background patch which has large area with good nature to project patch blocked by road. Extinct patch by urbanization act has larger than extinct by road. However it is interpreted that area within 1000m will not effect on wild birds' moving route. After all these results, core patch 7, strategic patch 24, and stepping stone patch 51 are classified.

5   Conclusion

Seoul has conducted park patch expansion 5 year plan and planting ten million preserver trees for expansion of patch area. To improve the quality of urban eco-system, current Bio-tope research and evaluation of those patterns were conducted. To develop eco-friendly urban places, there are 3 things have to be done for building eco-network plan. Firstly, in-depth study about the patch distribution condition in urban area has to be preceded. Secondly, through the ecosystem, vegetation and wild animal, research, evaluation of life inhabitability and site selection has to be done. Thirdly, selecting target species in each patch, providing improvement patch structure and connection plan will be desirable.

The purpose of this study is that valuating the connection of mountain type of urban patch and proposing the connection techniques for building eco-network using with existing Bio-tope map and data. It is desirable that proposing the connection techniques through in-depth analysis in each site. Considering evaluation of vegetation diversity, the search would be reliable because this research was done with Bio-tope attribute data done by Seoul. However, the data for wild birds' inhabitability was used for former evaluation research based on vegetation data. It could be less accurate than using current data. In the next research after this, the study of vegetation diversity and wild birds' inhabitability to build the most accurate standard of patch in urban area have to be conducted.

From now, conducting eco-network research in existing urban area, it is considered that the research of site selecting standard for decision and evaluation has to be conducted. To propose connectivity techniques, research and analysing about the character of Bio-Tope, land use, actual vegetation type, and wild birds habitat character have to be done. Based on these research, deciding target species in the site and patch expansion plan should be proposed. Therefore, to propose connection techniques about proposed eco-network site in this research, the basic study about vegetation and wild animal in entire site has to be conducted.

References

1. Brown, L.: Building a sustainable society. Norton & Company, New York (1981)
2. Ferreras, P., Gaona, P., Palomares, F., Delibes, M.: Restore habitat or reduce mortality? Implications from a population viability analysis of the Iberian lynx. Animal Conservation 4(3), 265–274 (2001)
3. Forman, R.T.T., Godron, M.: Landscape Ecology. John Wiley & Sons, Inc., New York (1986)
4. Forman, R.T.T.: Land mosaics: the ecology of landscape and regions, p. 632. Cambrige University Press, Cambrige (1995)
5. Guthrie, D.A.: Suburban bird populations in southern California. Am. Midl. Nat. 92, 461–466 (1974)
6. Harris, L.D.: The fragmented forest: Island biogeography theory and the preservation of biotic diversity. University of Chicago Press, Chicago (1984)
7. Hayama, Y.: Fundamental Studies for the Rilationship between Vegetation and Avifauna in the Urban Forest at Breeding Season. Journal of the Japanese Institute of Landscape Architects 57(5), 229–234 (1994)
8. Hiroyoshi, H., Yozo, T., Shin-ichi, H., Takeda, M.: The Relationship Between Forest Area and the Number of Bird Species. Wild Bird Society of Japan STRIX 1, 70–79 (1982)
9. Hough, M.: City form and natural process. Routledge, London (1989)
10. Jansson, G.: Scaling and habitat proportions in relation to bird diversity in managed boreal forests. Forest Ecology and Management 157, 77–86 (2002)
11. Jedicke, E.: Biotopverbund: grundlagen und maßnah neuen, Ulmer, Germany (1994)
12. Jeong, J.C.: The Analysis Method of Landscape Fragmentation using Normalized Difference Vegetation Index. Journal of the Korean Association of Geographic Information Studies 2(3), 16–22 (1999)
13. Kim, I.T.: The Strategies for Planning Ecopolis. Urban Administration Review 13, 105–132 (1998)
14. Park, C.R.: Establishment and Management of Urban Forests for the Inhabitation of Wild Birds. M.S. dissertation, p. 73. Seoul National University (1994)
15. Peterken, G.F.: A method for assessing woodland flora for conservation using indicator species. Biological Conservation 6, 239–245 (1974); Primack, P. B.: A Primer of Conservation Biology. Sinauer Associate Inc., Sunderland (1995)

Environmental Impact Assessment (EIA) and Photo-Manipulation Techniques

Kyung Jin An[1] and Hoon Ko[2]

[1] School of Architecture, Planning and Landscape, University of Newcastle upon Tyne,
United Kingdom
[2] Knowledge Engineering & Decision Support Research Group (GECAD),
Institute of Engineering-Polytechnic of Porto (ISEP/IPP), Portugal

Abstract. Recently, it becomes common process to implement photo manipulation techniques in Environmental Impact Assessment process. With the benefits and support of computer generated photomontages, EIA can be more flexible and scientifically credible. In the past, conventional media such as maps, plans, illustrations, sections, and physical models have been used. Yet due to technical advances and falling costs, the potential for photo-manipulation has much improved and has been increasingly adopted within the EIA process. The research employs case study as a methodology. Based on a critical review of existing literature, this research explores in particular the issues of credibility, realism and costs of production. The research findings illustrate the importance of the credibility of photomontage, a topic given insufficient consideration within the academic literature. Whereas the realism of visualisations has been the focus of much previous research, the results of the case study. Although visualisations will always be a simplification of reality and their level of realism is subjective, there is still potential for developing guidelines or protocols for image production based on commonly agreed standards. These findings suggest there needs to be a balance between scientific protocols and artistic licence in the production of photomontages.

Keywords: Environmental Impact Assessment, Landscape Visual Impact Assessment, Photo-manipulation, Photomontage.

1 Introduction

Within the UK planning processes of development management, consultation and assessments are often required which feed into Environmental Impact assessment (EIA) and Landscape Visual Impact Assessments (Wilson, 2009). These processes often involve computerised visualisation such as photomontage. During this process it is also necessary for the planning actors involved to consider spatial information, appreciate spatial transformations and various future scenarios (Tahvanainen et al., 2001). For instance, photomontages are widely implemented in Landscape Visual

T.-h. Kim et al. (Eds.): MulGraB/BSBT/IUrC 2012, CCIS 353, pp. 360–368, 2012.

Impact Assessment (LVIA) process in the UK. They provide vital comparisons on a development with before and after scenarios and the effects of mitigation measures and screening options.

However, photomontages, though inexpensive, suffer the limitation of requiring early selection of fixed viewpoints and offer no ability to change the nature of the proposal without starting again. Whereas, animation sequences follow predetermined paths and that considerable time to amend and re-render if changes to the chosen route are required.

This study critically evaluates the use and potential of photo manipulation techniques within the Environmental Impact Assessment process. Reflecting this need the research is employed case study analysis.

This study is divided into six sections. Section 1 introduces the background, research questions, and overall organisation of the research. Section 2 attempts to conceptualise photo manipulation techniques in planning and Section 3 also reviews EIA the legislative backgrounds and definitions. Thereafter, research methodology describes in the Section 4; whereas, Section 5 illustrates findings. Finally Section 6 provides research conclusions.

2   Photo-Manipulation Technique

There are a number of potential benefits of employing photo-manipulation techniques in the planning process. Notable, these can be summarised into two main themes: consultation (public participation and stakeholder groups) and various assessments including EIA and landscape Visual Impact Assessments. Firstly, the consultation and participation process has become an essential part of UK development management due to its discretionary system. Already a number of researches have suggested (Perkins and Barnhart, 2005) that use of computer visualisation in public participation is beneficial to the planning process.

As the long history of art shows how humans have attempted to illustrate and visualise the world for others. The history of actual visualisation could go back to a prehistoric age such as paintings found in Altamira Cave which are estimated to have been drawn between 16,000 and 9,000 BC (Johnson, 1996) and Lascaux's complex of caves in France where paintings have been estimated to be 17,300 years old. Since then, there have been numerous human attempts −as far as they remain and are recorded − to express the world environment: drawing, carving etc.

Traditional visualisation techniques for the representation of concepts in planning and design are plans, sections, sketches, perspective drawings, photomontages, and physical models (Lange and Bishop, 2005). The most practical example of using visualisation in environmental planning is provided by Humphrey Repton's before and after representation.

Fig. 1. Repton's Illustration which shows before and after scenes, source (Loudon, 1839)

In the 18th century, Repton's before and after approach became a classic to reproduce proposals in planning and design process. It is composed with a simple picture to show the existing site conditions and another picture to illustrate proposals, both of which were presented to Repton's clients to convey ideas of transformation. This is a basic drawn form of photomontage and using computerised methods has become a popular media to convey proposals to clients.

Such approaches started with artists' impression based on manual sketches and so on. However, these days computer technology enables the production of highly detailed photomontages.

3   UK Planning and Photomontage

Within development management process, as a planning applicant's point of view, the utilisation of computer visualisation is dependent on planning applications and stages of implementation. Planning applications are notably Landscape and Visual Impact Assessment (usually within Environmental Impact Assessment), public participation, public enquiry, stakeholder consultation, appealing decisions, and final submissions. As a private consultant, various computer visualisations can be utilised from initial design and conceptual development stages. This includes sketches, study models, interactive drawings and etc. However, most of visualisation media are implemented formally within process of assessments such as LVIA and consultations.

For example, landscape consultants prepare photomontages for a LVIA within an EIA. The produced photomontages can be used for a public consultation and any other stakeholder participation; however, it usually produced for landscape visual mitigations measures rather than reviewing initial proposals.

Within consultation stages, private consultants are often asked to prepare computer visualisation in order to receive stakeholders' opinion or public outlook on certain projects. For this reason, level of realism and credibility needs to meets appropriate level for the purpose in order not to mislead consultees and general public.

In summary, computer visualisation within development management process is utilised as an communication tool between stakeholders and general public – for both non and planning professionals – and the media used contain certain level of realism, interactivity, and credibility which determined by stages of planning.

3.1   Environmental Impact Assessment

Environmental Impact Assessment has been used internationally since 1970 as an environmental management tool. Its main process involves identification, prediction and evaluation of key environmental effects of a development. EIA is a technique and process by which information about the anticipated environmental effects of a project are collected, both by a developer and from other sources, and taken into account by a planning authority in forming their judgement on whether or not a development should proceed.

EIA is based on The EC Directive 'The Assessment of the Effects of Certain Public and Private Projects on the Environment' adopted 27 June 1985. In England, the EC Directive was brought into force in the UK through the implementation of: Town and Country Planning (Assessment of Environmental Effects) Regulations 1988 amended 1999.

The regulations require that certain types of projects, which are likely to have significant environmental effects, should not proceed until these effects have been systematically assessed. The regulations apply to two separate lists of projects:

- Annex/Schedule 1 Projects: EIA is required in every case.
- Annex/Schedule 2 Projects: EIA is required only if the particular project in question is judged likely to give rise to significant environmental effects.

During the appeals procedures of a planning decision – i.e. a public enquiry or technical and expert evidence, planning professions such as landscape architects may have to prepare a written precognition stating the landscape case on behalf of their clients, and/or illustrative material about visual or landscape matters and an environmental impact assessment. After the appeal decision, landscape architects may advise on reasons for refusal or implementation of landscape conditions.

As a member of the planning profession in appearing on behalf of either the local authority or the appellant, a professional witness is not meant to be an advocate but required to give evidence in 'good faith', that is, be able to present, declare and distinguish between generally accepted ideas and individual theories. If testimony is not given in good faith, then there may be a 'failure of candour' – true reasons may be being withheld because it is thought they may not gain wider agreement or further the client's case (Garmory et al., 2007).

3.2 Landscape and Visual Impact Assessment (LVIA)

LVIA is usually part of an Environmental Assessment of a development when there are likely to be negative effects on landscape. The technique of landscape and visual impact assessment is used to assess the effects of change on the landscape. For example, a new road or wind farm proposal, or a plan for forest felling and restocking. It is used to help locate and design the proposed change, so that negative landscape effects are avoided, reduced or offset. The two aspects of the assessment – landscape and visual effects – are independent but related.

Landscape and visual impact assessment is also an evolving practice that continues developing to take account of new issues and assessment techniques. These include, among others, the continued importance of landscape character assessment and the greater emphasis on process and public participation, the development of systems for assessing environmental and 'quality of life' capital, and the increased use of Strategic Environmental Assessment (The Landscape Institute and Institute of Environmental Management & Assessment, 2003).

However, Landscape and Visual Impacts are related but separate, different concepts. Landscape Impacts are on the fabric, character and quality of the landscape. They are concerned with landscape components, character and special interests such as designations, conservation sites and cultural associations. Whereas, Visual Impacts are the effects on people of the changes in available views through intrusion or obstruction and whether important opportunities to enjoy views may be improved or reduced.

Landscape and visual impacts do not necessarily coincide. Landscape impacts can occur in the absence of visual impacts, for instance where a development is wholly screened from available views, but nonetheless results in a loss of landscape elements, and landscape character within the site boundary. Similarly, some developments, such as a new communications mast in an industrial area, may have significant visual impacts, but insignificant landscape impacts. However, such cases are very much the exception, and for most developments both landscape and visual impacts will need to be assessed.

4 Methodology

The aim of this thesis is to understand and reflect on photo manipulation technique in current EIA process. This will be explored by considering how photo manipulation technique in the UK has been implemented at different levels, examine the photomontage production processes, and suggest some of the implications of the experience of photomontage for the EIA process. In order to achieve these aims, two main research questions were established in Chapter 1; *how photo manipulation technique has been utilised within EIA process? and what are the challenges faced when implemented photomontage within EIA?* To answer the questions, an appropriate methodology must be employed.

Accordingly, in order to answer those questions about implementation and current challenges in EIA, this research is employing case study methodology. The case study methodology is to examine the implementation of photo manipulation technique in EIA process. The case study was selected based on EIA and photomontage utilised.

In order for a case study to provide an insight it is important to understand what it is a case study of. One approach to the selection of cases is through a typical case approach to case study selection (Gerring, 2007). The typical case exemplifies what is considered to be a typical set of values, given some general understanding of a phenomenon. In this study, in order to investigate the implementation of photomontage in planning, typical planning applications include assessments (i.e. EIA and LVIA).

4.1   Holland House EIA

In the period between 2005 and 2006, landscape design consultants, White Young Green (WYG), carried out Environmental Impact Assessment for Holland House, Leeds. As a part of EIA, Landscape and Visual Impact Assessment was carried out and consequently, a set of photomontage was produced. In principle, every viewpoint consist with before and after photographs and Landscape Visual Impact Assessment were carried out based on site survey and photomontage produced.

Table 1. Facts for Holland House Case Study

Project	Holland House Development Landscape and Visual Impact Assessment
Date/Duration	2005-2006
Author's Role	Production of Photomontages including viewpoint selection involvement, site survey, modelling, and rendering.
Nature of Work	The development includes extension of facilities and erection of new fencing near Leeds. AS a part of EIA and Landscape and Visual Impact Assessment, the photomontages were presented to the residents adjacent and submitted to Local Planning Authority.

The methodology used to produce the photomontages involves a three stage process. The first stage is the production of a 3D computer model of the fence mesh and stanchions and applying the correct colour and texture to the computer model, e.g. the correct RAL colour. The mesh and stanchions are then pieced together and replicated to form a length of fence.

The site base plan is inserted into the model and the fence positioned in the proposed location. A camera is then located in the position from which the original photograph was taken. A snapshot of the fence is taken from the camera position which excludes all information in the 3D model apart from the fence.

The fence can then be superimposed over the original photograph image using sophisticated photomontage and image manipulation software. This enables the location of the fence between existing site elements, in this case in front of the existing mature tree cover and behind the existing hedge.

Fig. 2. Holland House Photo-montage – 3 Viewpoints (before/after)

5   Results and Findings

Recently, demanding utilisation of photomontage has brought its own issues such as credibility, realism and cost. In particular, credibility became significant when photomontage was implemented in the EIA process and a planning decision could be affected by the form that the photomontages took when they are implemented the processes. Realism and cost are equally important.

This study has also provided a better understanding of the use of photo manipulation technique in EIA and makes some recommendations for the improvement of its usage through the case study analysis.

The case study has brought into focus the dynamic interactions between the technology, perception and implementation behind EIA process. The findings also suggested that photomontages were considered to be the most accessible technology in planning such as EIA (LVIA). Moreover, they are formally recognised in development management processes in the UK.

The research also finds that scepticism exists in production of photomontages even though there is some published guidance. In the UK, photomontage techniques are only formally recognised in the planning process through ODPM [1] guidelines. Moreover, there are some guidelines for the production of photomontages currently available. Table 2 indicates current guidelines in the UK.

Table 2. Current Guidelines for Photomontage

	Guidelines	Year	Prepared by
1	Visual Representation of Windfarms: Good Practice Guide	2006	Scottish Natural Heritage, The Scottish Renewables Forum and the Scottish Society of Directors of Planning
2	Guidelines for Landscape and Visual Impact Assessment	2002 (2nd edition)	The Landscape Institute, Institute of Environmental Management and Assessment
3	Photography and photomontage in landscape and visual impact assessment: advice note	2011	Landscape Institute

6   Conclusion

The aim of this thesis is to understand and reflect on photo manipulation in current EIA process. This was explored by considering how photomontage in the UK has been implemented, examine the production processes, and suggest some of the implications of the experience of photomontage for EIA and LVIA process.

In order to tackle the research questions, the methodology has been developed from a case study. Throughout the research has adopted the lens of the landscape practitioner, which has focused on the process of photomontage design and implementation as part of EIA application.   This perspective has uncovered the practicalities of the actual usage of photomontage and the challenges emerging identified as the key questions within this study.

The rapid growth in the utilisation of photomontage in the EIA process within the last 10 years represents a technical revolution in the technology as a whole. Photo manipulation studies in planning have advanced from debating whether to employ new digital technology in order to assist the planning process. However, what remains largely unexplored is the question of what are the main factors affecting their usage

---

[1] Office for Deputy Prime Minister.

and how their usage affects planning decisions. This study has synthesised previous work on technological studies and literature in computer visualisation. It can therefore not only describe modern media of planning but also provide a prescription for the implementation of the technology. Thus it is hoped that this study will advance our understanding of the theoretical issues of modern computer technology within planning practice.

Then a further study on the relationship between all sorts of computer visualisation and EIA must be followed. With no official survey published about this specific issue, it was hard to estimate the precise scale of available technologies and their usage in planning in the UK. Therefore, together with the study on the technological aspects of the media, a planning analysis of the implementation must be taken.

Acknowledgement. This work is supported by FEDER Funds through the "Programa Operacional Factores de Competitividade - COMPETE" program and by National Funds through FCT "Fundação para a Ciência e a Tecnologia" under the project: FCOMP-01-0124-FEDER-PEst-OE/EEI/UI0760/2011.

References

1. Garmory, N., Tennant, R., Winsch, C.: Professional Practice for Landscape Architects. Architectural Press, London (2007)
2. Gerring, J.: Case Study Research Principles and Practices. Cambridge University Press, Cambridge (2007)
3. Johnson, M.S.: Altamira Cave Paintings. North Park University (1996)
4. Lange, E., Bishop, I.: Communication, Perception and Visualisation. In: Bishop, I., Lange, E. (eds.) Visualisation in Landscape and Environmental Planning. Taylor and Francis, London (2005)
5. Loudon, J.C.: The Landscape Gardening and Landscape Architecture of the Late Humphry Repton. Whitehead and Co., London (1839)
6. Perkins, N.H., Barnhart, S.: Visualisation and Participatory Decision Making. In: Bishop, I., Lange, E. (eds.) Visualisation in Landscape and Environmental Planning. Taylor and Francis, London (2005)
7. Tahvanainen, L., Tyrvainen, L., Ihalainen, M., Vuorela, N.: Forest management and public perceptions -visual versus verbal information. Landscape and Urban Planning 53, 53–70 (2001)
8. Wilson, S. (ed.): Guidelines for Landscape and Visual Impact Assessment. Taylor and Francis, London (2009)

Secure Information Sharing Using Personal Biometric Characteristics

Marek R. Ogiela, Urszula Ogiela, and Lidia Ogiela

AGH University of Science and Technology
Al. Mickiewicza 30, PL-30-059 Krakow, Poland
{mogiela,ogiela,logiela}@agh.edu.pl

Abstract. In this publication will be proposed a new algorithm for secure information sharing using personal or biometric information. In classic cryptographic threshold schemes used for secret splitting or sharing there aren't any connection between generated shares and particular participants of communication protocol. Sometimes it may be worth to generate personalized shadows, which allow not only recovery the original information or secret data, but also to identify who exactly took part in the secret reconstruction procedure. In the paper will be described the way of extraction some personal or biometric characteristics using cognitive information systems, as well as the algorithm of application such personal information for shadow generation in threshold schemes. Such new approach may play a great role in intelligent distributed computing or secure urban life.

Keywords: security of distributed information, cryptography, Urban Life, personal identification processes, information sharing.

1   Introduction

There are various methods of concealing (classifying) information and protecting it from being accessed by persons not authorised to learn it. They include secret splitting techniques. In this paper, the secret will consist of individual human biometrics, which include physical features. The most important physical features used for the biometric/identification analysis are the features of the iris, the shape of fingerprints, of hand/foot bones [6, 7], anatomical features of the face, the structure of blood vessels (including coronary ones) [5] and the DNA code [11].

The basic components of biometric analyses adopted in this paper are the features of the iris, which also determine the eye colour which is material for the verification analysis in biometric systems. The following factors determine the eye colour:

- the melanin content of pigments in the iris epithelium,
- the melanin content of the stroma of the iris,
- the density of cells in the stroma of the iris.

The melanin content of the iris can be a component for recognition processes executed as part of processes of information concealment (by splitting information into parts of the secret) after the stage of the proper personal verification.

T.-h. Kim et al. (Eds.): MulGraB/BSBT/IUrC 2012, CCIS 353, pp. 369–373, 2012.

2   Information Splitting and Sharing

In their research, the authors of this paper have assumed that the information sharing methods are based on the use of one of the following three algorithm types [1-4, 8-13]:

- vector algorithm,
- Asmuth-Bloom algorithm,
- Karnin-Greene-Hellman algorithm.

Information sharing protocols, in turn, are split into the following groups [4, 8-11]:

- information sharing without the involvement of a trusted person,
- message sharing without disclosing one's parts,
- message sharing with disclosure prevention,
- message sharing with cheaters,
- message sharing with testing,
- message sharing with a share withdrawal.

Information splitting algorithms dealing with concealing biometric information contained in the iris can be executed by two mutually independent ways of data splitting – both by a layer split and by a hierarchical split. The former means splitting the information between n secret holders and its reproduction by n-m trustees of the secret (from the same group). The latter case means that the secret is split between n holders of the secret, but the information can be reproduced by superior groups of secret holders within which the specific secret has been split into k parts (k < n). Thus the splitting methods depend on the purpose for which the information is split and concealed. In the case of personal identification systems or recognition systems, the methods of biometric data splitting most frequently used are layer splits (Fig. 1).

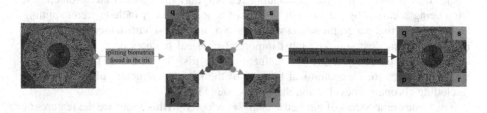

Fig. 1. Biometric information splitting

The presented information splitting and sharing methods and algorithms are based on the use of mathematical algorithms for data analysis and transmission. The information constituting the secret and the confidential information is analysed and interpreted by way of cryptographic information analyses.

3   Linguistic Coding in DNA Cryptography

Linguistic coding processes are based on the use of mathematical linguistic formalisms, particularly grammatical formalisms to record and interpret the meaning of the analysed biometric data. Linguistic coding processes are used because of the ability to execute generalised information coding as in DNA cryptography. In the traditional DNA coding model, one- or two-bit coding is used (utilising one of the four nitrogen bases, i.e. A, C, G, T or of the A-T and G-C bridges). DNA cryptography used to generate keys based on DNA codes and genetic/personal information can be combined with biometric features. The nucleotide polymer (DNA) is made up of purine bases are bonded in pairs [5]:

$$A\text{-}T,\ G\text{-}C,\ T\text{-}A,\ C\text{-}G$$

The bonding between purine and pyrimidine basses allows the DNA code to be written in an unanimous form, and the DNA code itself can be used for personal biometric characteristics.

In linguistic coding, it is possible to code longer bit sequences containing more than 2 bits of information. This coding is done using terminal symbols introduced in this grammar, and lengthening the coded blocks directly proportionally contributes to accelerating information splitting and reproduction, as well as to increasing the secret component containing information on the grammar used. The formal notation of a sequential grammar used to split information about the iris biometrics is as follows [11]:

$$G_{bi} = (N_{bi},\ T_{bi},\ P_{bi},\ ST)$$

where:
N_{bi} = {IRIS, BIT, 1B, 2B, 3B, 4B, 5B, 6B, ..., NB} – non-terminal symbols,
T_{bi} = {1b, 2b, 3b, 4b, 5b, 6b, ..., nb, Ø} – terminal symbols containing defined n-bit
        blocks,
{Ø} – an empty symbol,
ST = IRIS – the start symbol,
P_{bi} – the production set:

        1. IRIS → BIT BIT
        2. BIT → 1B | 2B | 3B | 4B | 5B | 6B, ... | NB
        3. BIT → Ø
        4. 1B → 1b {0, 1}
        5. 2B → 2b {00, 01, 10, 11}
        6. 3B → 3b {000, 001, 010, 011, 100, 101, 110, 111}
        7. 4B → 4b
        8. ....
        9. NB → nb
        10. b → {0, 1}

Linguistic information splitting and coding methods are presented in Fig. 2.

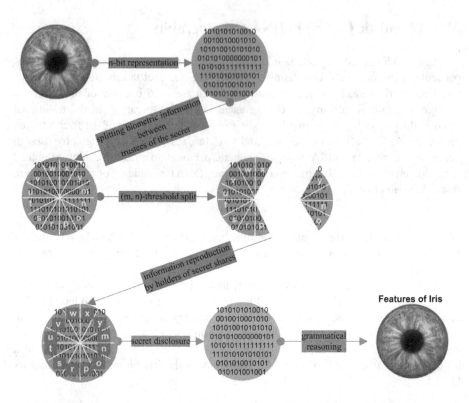

Fig. 2. Linguistic coding in the process of biometric information splitting

The coded biometric information recorded in the form of an n-bit representation is split using a selected information splitting algorithm. The (m, n)-threshold split allows this information to be reproduced by combining at least *m* of all *n* shares of the secret. Combining m shares of the secret causes the information to be reproduced in a coded version which can be fully understood only after executing its semantic analysis consisting in a grammatical reasoning carried out for the coded data set.

4 Conclusion

Processes of concealing (classifying) data are currently used in many fields of life, science and research. Employing linguistic coding methods in the concealment processes offers the full capability of using semantic processes for the identification and grammatical reasoning. Concealing biometric data (specific for every person) constitutes a very important problem because it is highly probable that personal data will be taken over by unauthorised persons. The individual DNA code, fingerprints, iris features and many other biometrics represent protected data and as such a valuable source of information not just about the specific person, but also their origin (genetic information), environment, interests, habits etc. Methods of concealing biometric information concerning the iris can also be used to split and conceal other sets of personal/biometric data due to the universal nature of linguistic methods.

Acknowledgement. This work has been supported by AGH University of Science and Technology research Grant No. 11.11.120.612.

References

1. Adleman, L.M., Rothemund, P.W.K., Roweiss, S., et al.: On applying molecular computation to the Data Encryption Standard. Journal of Computational Biology 6(1), 53–63 (1999)
2. Blakley, G.R.: Safeguarding Cryptographic Keys. In: Proceedings of the National Computer Conference, pp. 313–317 (1979)
3. Chomsky, N.: Syntactic Structures, London Mouton (1957)
4. Menezes, A., van Oorschot, P., Vanstone, S.: Handbook of Applied Cryptography. CRC Press, Waterloo (2001)
5. Ogiela L.: Semantic Analysis and Biological Modelling in Cognitive Categorization Systems. Mathematical and Computer Modelling (in press, 2013)
6. Ogiela, L., Ogiela, M.R.: Cognitive Techniques in Visual Data Interpretation. SCI, vol. 228. Springer, Heidelberg (2009)
7. Ogiela, L., Ogiela, M.R.: Advences in Cognitive Information Systems. COSMOS, vol. 17. Springer, Heidelberg (2012)
8. Ogiela, M.R., Ogiela, U.: Security of Linguistic Threshold Schemes in Multimedia Systems. In: Damiani, E., Jeong, J., Howlett, R.J., Jain, L.C. (eds.) New Directions in Intelligent Interactive Multimedia Systems and Services - 2. SCI, vol. 226, pp. 13–20. Springer, Heidelberg (2009)
9. Ogiela, M.R., Ogiela, U.: Shadow Generation Protocol in Linguistic Threshold Schemes. In: Ślęzak, D., Kim, T.-H., Fang, W.-C., Arnett, K.P. (eds.) SecTech 2009. CCIS, vol. 58, pp. 35–42. Springer, Heidelberg (2009)
10. Ogiela, M.R., Ogiela, U.: The use of mathematical linguistic methods in creating secret sharing threshold algorithms. Computers and Mathematics with Applications 60(2), 267–271 (2010)
11. Ogiela, M.R., Ogiela, U.: DNA-like linguistic secret sharing for strategic information systems. International Journal of Information Management 32, 175–181 (2012)
12. Ogiela, M.R., Ogiela, U.: Linguistic Protocols for Secure Information Management and Sharing. Computers and Mathematics with Applications 63(2), 564–572 (2012)
13. Shamir, A.: How to Share a Secret. Communications of the ACM, 612–613 (1979)
14. Tang, S.: Simple Secret Sharing and Threshold RSA Signature Schemes. Journal of Information and Computational Science 1, 259–262 (2004)

Visual Image Biometric Identification in Secure Urban Computing

Lidia Ogiela and Marek R. Ogiela

AGH University of Science and Technology
Al. Mickiewicza 30, PL-30-059 Krakow, Poland
{logiela,mogiela}@agh.edu.pl

Abstract. In this publication will be proposed a new technique of personal identification based on non-standard biometric patterns in the form of selected medical visualization. The proposed solutions will be illustrated on the example of using intelligent CPIAIS cognitive information systems for extraction an unique personal feature vector which next will be used for personal identity analysis. Such procedure will allow to support the identification processes based on several types of biometrics patterns, as well as using feature vector in cryptographic procedures. While image analysis a cognitive procedures will be based on hand layouts parameters, evaluated for particular persons during medical examination.

Keywords: cryptography, CPIAIS systems (Cognitive Personal Identification & Authentication Information Systems), semantic analysis, personal identification processes.

1   Introduction

A new techniques of personal authentication and identification based on non-standard biometric patterns in the form of selected medical visualization was proposed for a new class of cognitive systems. The essence of cognitive systems consists in the semantic analysis of images being interpreted, and particularly of medical images portraying lesions, pathologies of different organs [4-12]. Cognitive systems for analysis medical images for identification and personalization processes represent a special class of CPIAIS systems (Cognitive Personal Identification & Authentication Information Systems). This class of cognitive systems can be used to semantically analyse pathologies of human organs and personalisation and identification analyses (Fig. 1).

CPIAIS systems carry out personal verification and identification processes with the addition of medical image analysis and hand bones and heart arteries lesion detection.

Semantic analysis is carried out in systems founded on cognitive resonance [9, 11] which identifies the compliance between the set of expectations generated by the system (based on the expert's knowledge) of the analysed data set and the knowledge collected in the system, which knowledge forms the basis for executing the comparative analysis (Fig.2.).

T.-h. Kim et al. (Eds.): MulGraB/BSBT/IUrC 2012, CCIS 353, pp. 374–380, 2012.
© Springer-Verlag Berlin Heidelberg 2012

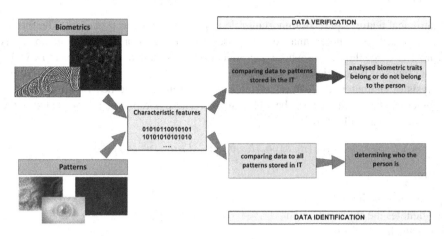

Fig. 1. Personal verification and identification processes

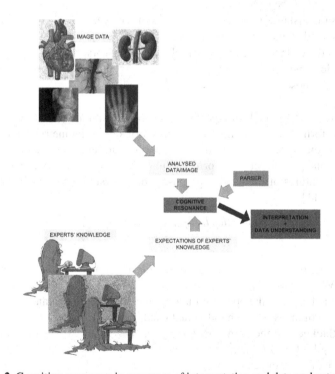

Fig. 2. Cognitive resonance in processes of interpretation and data understanding

2   Biometrics Features in Identification Process

Systems that semantically analyse medical images are essentially based on the use of linguistic formalisms grammar – can be a graph, a tree or a sequential grammar.

Anatomical features play an important role in personal analysis processes. The former are subjected to complex analysis processes which are to produce an unambiguous identification of the person whose anatomical features were analysed. The most wide-spread types of biometric analyses include analyses of the face, hand and voice. In the analysis of characteristic features of the face, it is important to describe and interpret parameters that can help describe a human face. These parameters are presented in the set P_f defined as follows [8]:

$$P_f = \{h_f, h_{fh}, h_n, h_{el}, h_{er}, d_{ee}, d_{el}, d_{eer}, w_m, w_n\}$$

where:

h_f – denotes the height face,
h_{fh} –denotes the forehead height,
h_n – is the height nose,
h_{el} – is the height of the left eye,
h_{er} – is the height of the right eye,
d_{ee} – denotes the distance between inter corners of the eye,
d_{el} – denotes the distance between outer corners of the eye,
d_{eer} – denotes the distance between external ends of the ears,
w_m – is the width mouth,
w_n – is the width nose.

The proposed P_f set for analysing personal features of human face has also been used to propose a formal description of the analysis of others biometric features. These features, with the added elements of the semantic data analysis, make an extended identification analysis possible. A formal solution based on defining a set of biometric characteristic features of the hand is proposed for analysing the biometric features of hand bones [8, 11]:

$$BL_h = \{th_{ij}, l_{ij}, s_{ij\text{-}ij}, th_{mi}, l_{mi}, s_n, p_i, o_j\}$$

where:

th_{ij} – denotes the thickness of the bones of the ith finger and the jth phalanx $i = \{I, II, III, IV, V\}, j = \{1, 2, 3\}$,
l_{ij} – denotes the length of the bones of the ith finger and the jth phalanx,
$s_{ij\text{-}ij}$ – is the size of areas between individual hand bones,
th_{mi} – is the thickness of the ith metacarpus bone,
l_{mi} – is the length of the ith metacarpus bone,
s_n – is the size of wrist bones,
p_i – denotes the print of the ith finger of the hand (from one to five),
o_j – is the shape of one of the three biometric prints of the palm.

The BL_h set (Fig. 3.) defines the biometric features and shapes of handprints as well as the shape of fingerprints, which make it possible to conduct a biometric analysis. Data on biometric features stored in the CPIAIS system supports personal identification and personal verification.

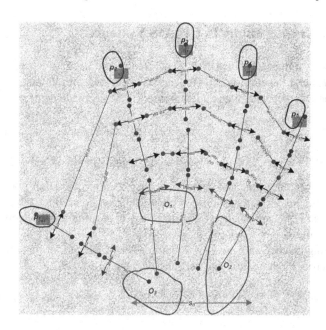

Fig. 3. Elements of the set BL_h

In biometrics analysis also it's possible to analyse medical 3D images portraying lesions in large heart vessels – coronary arteries [12]. Images of this type are acquired, inter alia, in heart disease diagnostics used to assess the lesions of the cardiac muscle and also of coronary vessels.

3D medical image data is analysed in cognitive data analysis systems on the basis of defined linguistic formalisms. In the case of analysing lesions found in coronary vessels, context-free graph grammars have been used to semantically analyse the lesions observed – G_R for the right coronary artery and the R_L for the left coronary artery [12]. Such work was aimed at proposing grammar formalisms powerful enough for analysing 3D images of coronary arteries and vessels [12]. Images of arteries, just like other multi-dimensional images showing lesions in human organs, can be subjected to a semantic analysis due to the diversity of lesions occurring. The most frequent lesions of large vessels include persistent Botall's arterial duct, trilogy, tetralogy and pentalogy of Fallot, pulmonary artery stenosis (a congenital defect), coronary artery sclerosis, congenital as well as acquired heart defects contributing to changes (or lesions) in the structure of coronary arteries.

In the data analysis process [1-3, 11, 13], the identification of the lesion occurring, its location, size and the frequency of its occurrence makes it possible to determine the significance and the impact of the analysed lesion on the subsequent diagnostic and treatment process.

3   DNA Cryptography in CPIAIS Systems

CPIAIS systems enhanced with DNA cryptography and used to generate keys based on DNA codes and genetic information can be combined with biometric features described by the BLh set. The nucleotide polymer (DNA) is made up of purine bases are bonded in pairs:

$$A\text{-}T, G\text{-}C, T\text{-}A, C\text{-}G$$

(Adenine-Thymine, Guanine-Cytosine, Thymine-Adenine, Cytosine-Guanine)

The bonding between purine and pyrimidine basses allows the DNA code to be written in an unanimous form, and the DNA code itself can be used for biometric analyses. The encoded DNA information forms the basis of cryptographic, identification and verification analyses.

This bonding has been adopted for defining a set which can for be used for executing the biometric, identification and verification analysis:

$$GEN\text{-}BL_h\text{-}P_f\text{-}CA(G_R, G_L) = \{\text{DNA CODE (A-T G-C T-A C-G)}, th_{ij}, l_{ij}, s_{ij\text{-}ij}, th_{mi}, l_{mi}, s_n,$$
$$p_i, o_j, h_f, h_{fh}, h_n, h_{el}, h_{er}, d_{ee}, d_{el}, d_{eer}, w_m, w_n, G_R, G_L\}$$

The $GEN\text{-}BL_h\text{-}P_f\text{-}CA(G_R, G_L)$ set with the coded form of genetic information takes the following form:

$$GEN(\text{CODE})\text{-}BL_h\text{-}P_f\text{-}CA(G_R, G_L) = \{01011001100010100, th_{ij}, l_{ij}, s_{ij\text{-}ij}, th_{mi}, l_{mi}, s_n, p_i,$$
$$o_j, h_f, h_{fh}, h_n, h_{el}, h_{er}, d_{ee}, d_{el}, d_{eer}, w_m, w_n, G_R, G_L\}$$

As a result of DNA information coding, the personal identification and the cognitive analysis carried out by CPIAIS systems, the feature vectors assigned to a given person in biometric data analysis systems can contain information about (Fig. 4):

- the DNA code,
- individual (physical) features (e.g. face features),
- standard biometric features,
- non-standard biometrics e.g. coronary archeries layouts (deformations, pathologies).

Figure 4 presents a description of the operation of biometric data analysis systems supplemented with elements of the semantic analysis of image data. This type of analysis makes it possible to assign a given person his/her genetic information in a coded form, biometric data, physical features and possible lesions. This multi-stage process of personal identification significantly reduces the possibility of an error due to the incorrect process of reasoning and personal verification.

The above vectors may also contain information on other lesions of a given person, e.g. those in coronary arteries, lesions/deformation in internal organs. Such information can be used for an in-depth data analysis which is not carried out by traditional verification systems, but which can, in individual cases, be used for complex personal identification problems.

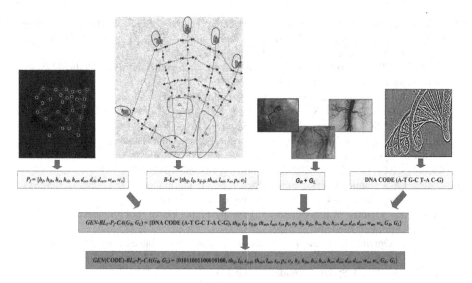

Fig. 4. A biometric data analysis system in CPIAIS systems

4   Conclusion

The idea of biometric data analysis in personal identification and verification systems carried out using CPIAIS cognitive systems presented here allows analysing and interpreting complex (very extensive) data sets. Systems of this kind can analyse various data sets (personal, physical and biometric features plus selected organs pathologies). This variety of data also allows various analysis methods to be employed. The ability to collect information on individual human organs and personal features, the occurrence of lesions as well as the DNA code in the knowledge bases of cognitive systems offers opportunities of enhancing CPIAIS systems with freely chosen data set.

Processes of modelling data stored in CPIAIS systems allow the personal data kept in cognitive systems to be made completely secret.

Acknowledgement. This work has been supported by the National Science Centre, Republic of Poland, under project number N N516 478940.

References

1. Cohen, H., Lefebvre, C. (eds.): Handbook of Categorization in Cognitive Science. Elsevier, The Netherlands (2005)
2. Duda, R.O., Hart, P.E., Stork, D.G.: Pattern Classification, 2nd edn. A Wiley-Interscience Publication John Wiley & Sons, Inc. (2001)
3. Meystel, A.M., Albus, J.S.: Intelligent Systems – Architecture, Design, and Control. A Wiley-Interscience Publication John Wiley & Sons, Inc., Canada (2002)

4. Ogiela, L.: Syntactic Approach to Cognitive Interpretation of Medical Patterns. In: Xiong, C.-H., Liu, H., Huang, Y., Xiong, Y.L. (eds.) ICIRA 2008, Part I. LNCS (LNAI), vol. 5314, pp. 456–462. Springer, Heidelberg (2008)
5. Ogiela, L.: UBIAS Systems for Cognitive Interpretation and Analysis of Medical Images. Opto-Electronics Review 17(2), 166–179 (2009)
6. Ogiela, L.: Computational Intelligence in Cognitive Healthcare Information Systems. In: Bichindaritz, I., Vaidya, S., Jain, A., Jain, L.C. (eds.) Computational Intelligence in Healthcare 4. SCI, vol. 309, pp. 347–369. Springer, Heidelberg (2010)
7. Ogiela, L.: Cognitive Informatics in Automatic Pattern Understanding and Cognitive Information Systems. In: Wang, Y., Zhang, D., Kinsner, W. (eds.) Advances in Cogn. Informatics. SCI, vol. 323, pp. 209–226. Springer, Heidelberg (2010)
8. Ogiela, L.: Semantic Analysis and Biological Modelling in Cognitive Categorization Systems. Mathematical and Computer Modelling (in press, 2013)
9. Ogiela, L., Ogiela, M.R.: Cognitive Techniques in Visual Data Interpretation. SCI, vol. 228. Springer, Heidelberg (2009)
10. Ogiela, L., Ogiela, M.R.: Semantic Analysis Processes in Advanced Pattern Understanding Systems. In: Kim, T.-h., Adeli, H., Robles, R.J., Balitanas, M. (eds.) AST 2011. CCIS, vol. 195, pp. 26–30. Springer, Heidelberg (2011)
11. Ogiela, L., Ogiela, M.R.: Advences in Cognitive Information Systems. COSMOS, vol. 17. Springer, Heidelberg (2012)
12. Trzupek, M., Ogiela, M.R.: Data aggregation techniques in heart vessel modelling and recognition of pathological changes. In: IMIS 2012 The Sixth International Conference on Innovative Mobile and Internet Services in Ubiquitous Computing, Palermo, Italy, July 4-6, pp. 69–72 (2012)
13. Foundations of Intelligent Systems. In: Zhong, N., Raś, Z.W., Tsumoto, S., Suzuki, E. (eds.) 14th International Symposium, ISMIS, Maebashi City, Japan (2003)

General Bayesian Network in Performing Micro-reality Mining with Mobile Phone Usage Data for Device Personalization

Seong Wook Chae[1], Jungsik Hwang[1], and Kun Chang Lee[2,*]

[1] Sungkyunkwan University, Seoul 110-745, Republic of Korea
[2] SKK Business School and Department of Interaction Science
Sungkyunkwan University, Seoul 110-745, Republic of Korea
{seongwookchae,jungsik.hwang,kunchanglee}@gmail.com

Abstract. Personalization is an emerging issue in the digital age, where users have to deal with many kinds of digital devices and techniques. Moreover, the complexities of digital devices and their functions tend to increase rapidly, requiring careful attention to the questions of how to increase user satisfaction and develop more innovative digital products and services. To this end, we propose a new concept of micro-reality mining in which users' micro behaviors, revealed through their daily usage of digital devices and technologies, are scrutinized before key findings from the mining are embedded into new products and services. This paper proposes micro-reality mining for device personalization and examines the possibility of adopting a GBN (general Bayesian network) as a means of determining users' useful behavior patterns when using cell phones. Through comparative experiments with other mining techniques such as SVM (support vector machine), DT (decision tree), NN (neural network), and other BN (Bayesian network) methods, we found that the GBN has great potential for performing micro-reality mining and revealing significant findings.

Keywords: Reality mining, Personalization, General Bayesian Network, Mobile phone, Usage pattern.

1 Introduction

We are living in a world of digital technologies. Many people use various kinds of digital devices, such as mobile phones and laptop computers. However, since most digital devices tend to become commodities, the success of these devices critically depends on how much manufacturers understand users' micro usage patterns and embed their understanding into the design of the devices' key functions, user interface, outward appearance, and other features. This mining activity is called micro-reality mining and refers to "the system's ability to extract a set of trivial but meaningful rules of action from individuals' behavior data" [1].

---

* Corresponding author.

T.-h. Kim et al. (Eds.): MulGraB/BSBT/IUrC 2012, CCIS 353, pp. 381–388, 2012.
© Springer-Verlag Berlin Heidelberg 2012

Among the wide array of digital devices in use, we focus on mobile phones because they have become ubiquitous. Therefore, this paper investigates the effect of micro-reality mining for the personalization of mobile phones. By means of micro-reality mining, a cell phone could provide a personalized interface that benefits its user. There are many methods available for micro-reality mining, such as the Bayesian network (BN), the decision tree (DT), the support vector machine (SVM), and the neural network (NN). This paper specifically examines the usefulness of a general Bayesian network (GBN) for performing micro-reality mining on mobile phone usage data. A GBN can provide a set of meaningful causal relationships for the target nodes (or variables). Moreover, GBNs are very useful in suggesting what-if and goal-seeking experiments. This paper assumes that the two key features of GBNs — causal relationships and what-if/goal-seeking experiments — may be critical in adding a sense of reality to the micro-reality mining results. A mobile phone usage data set was selected for the micro-reality mining experiment.

2   Related Works

2.1   Mobile Phone Personalization

Park et al. [2] presented a map-based personalized recommendation system based on user preference. A BN was used to model user preferences using profile and context information obtained from mobile devices. Yan and Chen [3] introduced the AppJoy system, which provides personalized application recommendations to its users. Lee and McKay [4] investigated a personalized keypad layout for mobile phones. They employed a genetic algorithm (GA) to match a suitable keypad layout to each user. GA-based optimization of mobile keypads can also be found in the work of How and Kan [5] and Moradi and Nickabadi [6]. Olwal et al. [7] investigated customization of mobile devices for elderly users and presented a prototype framework, OldGen. Mishra et al. [8] presented a method for personalized search on mobile phones based on the user's location. Rosenthal et al. [9] introduced personalized mobile phone interruption models that automatically adjust phone volume to avoid phone interruptions.

2.2   Micro-reality Mining

The term "micro-reality mining" was first suggested by Chae et al. [1], who described it as a system's capabilities to extract trivial but meaningful information from data. The concept is based on the fact that such trivial rules of action determine an individual's macro behavior. According to Fayyad et al. [10], data mining is the process of applying specific algorithms to find patterns or construct models from data and plays a critical role in the process of knowledge discovery [10]. There are many representations of data mining, including decision trees, artificial neural networks, and rule bases. There are also a variety of techniques for data mining, such as classification, regression, density estimation, and clustering [11].

2.3   Bayesian Network

A Bayesian network is a strong tool for modeling decision making under conditions of uncertainty [12-13], meaning that decision makers facing uncertainty can rely on a BN to get robust decision support with respect to the target problem.

A BN is composed of nodes, links, and conditional probability tables and applies the Bayes rule to probability theory. This rule specifies how existing beliefs should be modified mathematically with the input of new evidence. A BN consists of a directed acyclic graph (DAG) and a corresponding set of conditionals (conditional probability tables) [14]. The DAG shows the causal relationship between the variables and the nodes, where each node represents a variable that has an associated conditional probability distribution.

Researchers have studied BNs in earnest since the naïve Bayesian network (NBN) was presented. A NBN has the simplest shape of all BNs —a class node linked with all the other nodes — and does not explain the causal relationships between the child nodes. It has been shown to have relatively high accuracy [15]. NBNs have been shown to be surprisingly accurate in many domains when compared with alternatives such as rule learning, decision tree learning, and instance-based learning [16]. The tree-augmented NBN (TAN) is an extended version of the NBN in which the nodes form the shape of a tree. Experiments have indicated that it significantly outperforms the NB in classification accuracy [17]. To improve classification performance, Cheng and Greiner [18] suggested a general Bayesian network (GBN). In comparison with NBNs and TANs, GBNs can be structured very flexibly. Given a class node (or target node), a set of relevant explanatory nodes can be linked with each other [19].

2.4   Other Classifiers

There are many other classifiers used in data mining, including NN, SVM, and DT classifiers. A NN classifier mimics a neuronal structure of the human brain that performs classification with knowledge stored in connections between nodes in the network [20]. The SVM classifier is "a binary classifier which looks for an optimal hyperplane as a decision function in a high-dimensional space" [21]. A DT classifier is also a binary tree in which every non-leaf node is related to a predicate [22].

3   Research Methodology and Experiment

3.1   Data

In our study, we used a data set collected by the Reality Mining Group at MIT Media Lab [23]. From the many variables provided, we carefully selected those related to mobile phone usage patterns. Then, we organized the variables into individual units for one month's worth of data instead of using the full nine months of data. Consequently, the total number of data elements in our analysis was 80. The 20 variables included in the analysis are summarized in Table 1.

Table 1. Variables

Variable Name	Description
*call_N_in	Number of incoming calls
*call_N_missed	Number of missed calls
*call_N_out	Number of outgoing calls
*call_N_inOut	Sum of number of incoming and outgoing calls
*call_N_total	Sum of number of incoming, missed, and outgoing calls
*call_du_in	Sum of duration (seconds) of incoming calls
*call_du_out	Sum of duration (seconds) of outgoing calls
*call_du_inOut	Sum of duration of incoming and outgoing calls
**call_du_avg_in	Average duration of an incoming call
**call_du_avg_out	Average duration of an outgoing call
**call_du_avg_inOut	Average duration of a call
**vcDuOutPref	call_du_out / (call_du_out+ call_du_in) * 100
**vcOutter	call_N_out / call_N_in
**vcIncommer	call_N_in / call_N_out
**vcOutPref	call_N_out / (call_N_out+ call_N_in) * 100
*smIncoming	Number of incoming SMS
*smOutgoing	Number of outgoing SMS
*smTotal	Number of incoming and outgoing SMS
**smOutPref	smOutgoing / (smOutgoing + smIncoming) * 100
***caVCpref	call_N_out / (call_N_out+ smOutgoing) * 100

*   Observed variable.

**   Manipulated variable.

*** Target variable.

3.2   Experiments

We used WEKA version 3.6.7 (Waikato Environment for Knowledge Analysis) [24] to extract rules from the dataset. Seven different classifiers were examined: NBN, TAN, GBN-K2, GBN-Hill Climb (GBN-HC), NN, DT, and SVM. To construct the GBN-K2 and GBN-HC classifiers, we set the maximum number of parent nodes to 5. In addition, the BAYES scoring metric was used for Bayesian classifiers. To construct other classifiers, the default settings in WEKA were used. Because WEKA can handle nominal variables only, we discretized a range of numeric variables by using 3 equal-width bins. Table 2 shows the prediction accuracies of the classifiers.

Table 2. Prediction accuracies of classifiers

	NBN	TAN	GBN-K2	GBN-HC	NN	SVM	DT
Mean(S.D.)	85.30	88.42	**89.25**	86.87	86.48	86.77	**84.20**
	(5.96)	(4.89)	(4.74)	(6.95)	(4.81)	(5.18)	(6.32)

To determine classification performance, a one-way ANOVA followed by a post-hoc test using Dunnet T3[1] procedures was conducted on the mean scores of the 7 classifiers. Table 2 shows the mean values of the prediction accuracy[2] for the 7

---

[1] Tests of homogeneity of variances (Levene's test) showed that in all cases variances were significantly heterogeneous (Levene statistic = 5.134, p < 0.001).

[2] The classification performance was measured 100 times.

classifiers. ANOVA yielded statistically significant mean differences (F(6,693) = 9.376, p < 0.001), indicating that the mean accuracy performance was significantly different among the 7 classifiers. Based on the numbers in Table 2, the GBN-K2 classifier was regarded as demonstrating the best classification performance (m = 89.25, S.D. = 4.74), and the TAN classifier was ranked second (m = 88.42, S.D. = 4.89); the DT classifier demonstrated the worst performance (m = 84.20, S.D. = 6.32). However, the post-hoc test results indicated that there was no significant difference among the GBN-K2, TAN, and GBN-HC classifiers. In sum, the results from ANOVA demonstrated that the GBN-K2 and TAN classifiers demonstrated significantly better performance than the other classifiers.

4   Simulation

4.1   Selecting Classifier for Simulation

It is necessary to select an appropriate classifier to simulate the model. In the previously described classifier accuracy test, both the GBN-K2 and TAN classifiers demonstrated better performance than any other classifiers. For research purposes, we selected the GBN-K2 classifier for our simulation because a GBN is a full-fledged BN in which causal relationships between the class node and all other nodes are flexibly formulated. These characteristics of a GBN make it possible to conduct the scenario simulation in various ways while making interpretation of the results more fruitful.

Fig. 1 illustrates the constructed Bayesian network. The causal relationships between variables are depicted as directed arches and the probability distribution of each node is shown. As shown in Fig. 1, there were causal relationships between the target node caVCpref and descriptive variables such as call_N_in, call_N_missed, call_N_out, call_N_inOut, call_N_total, call_du_in, call_du_out, call_du_inOut, call_du_avg_in, call_du_avg_out, call_du_avg_inOut, vcDuOutPref, vcOutter, vcIncommer, vcOutPref, smIncoming, smOutgoing, smTotal, and smOutPref. In addition, the causal relationship between the descriptive variables was observable, demonstrating the advantages of using a general Bayesian network.

4.2   Sensitivity Analysis

To examine the possibility of employing micro-reality mining for mobile phone personalization, we simulated the models constructed from the selected classifier, GBN-K2. We then considered two scenarios, what-if and goal-seeking, and performed a sensitivity analysis for each, taking advantage of the causal relationships suggested by Fig. 1.

Scenario 1. (What-if analysis) *If call_N_in is set to low, smIncoming is set to high, and no other variables are changed, what changes occur in caVCpref and the other variables?*

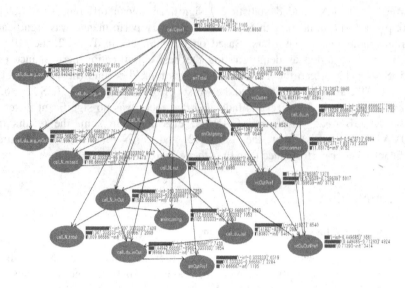

Fig. 1. Constructed Bayesian Network Model with caVCpref as a target node

In Scenario 1, we were able to obtain an idea of an individual's outgoing call preference based on the individual having a small number of incoming calls and a large number of incoming SMS (text) messages. Before we changed the values of call_N_in and smIncoming, the target node (degree of outgoing call preference, or caVCpref) was high, as shown in Fig. 1, indicating that, in general, people are more likely to make an outgoing call than to send a text message. These results indicate that people who have a small number of incoming calls and a large number of incoming SMS messages tend to make voice calls rather than sending texts.

Scenario 2. (Goal-seeking analysis) *To make caVCpref high, what other factors should be changed?*

We also conducted a goal-seeking analysis using the following scenario: For a user who prefers sending SMS messages to calling (low degree of outgoing call preference), what mobile usage patterns are observed? When the target node (caVCpref) was manipulated according to the scenario, the probability distribution of other variables changed. We focused primarily on two variables: sum of duration of incoming calls (call_du_in) and sum of duration of outgoing calls (call_du_out). A user who prefers sending SMS messages to calling might use a mobile phone more actively and frequently compared to other users. This type of user would have longer duration incoming and outgoing calls compared with users who prefer calling to sending SMS messages.

The usage pattern, which seemed meaningless before analysis, demonstrated that there was indeed a pattern or a model. Micro-reality mining can be used to extract several rules. For example, Soto et al. [25] investigated the relationship between individuals' socioeconomic levels and their cell phone records, constructing predictive models using SVM and random forests. As Soto et al. [25] stated, trivial acts can indeed determine macro user behavior.

5   Concluding Remarks

This paper investigated the effect and applicability of micro-reality mining for device personalization and the possibility of employing a GBN as a means of deriving causal relationships from mobile phone usage patterns. The results demonstrated that the valid causal relationships of the GBN can be used to provide new insights into users' micro behaviors when using mobile phones. In addition, these users' micro behaviors could be analyzed to predict users' macro behaviors.

Consequently, the present study not only showed the importance of micro-reality mining, but also suggested the implications for future study. By means of micro-reality mining, individuals' trivial behavior data could be used to reveal meaningful rules of actions. These insights, in turn, can be used in the personalization of mobile devices. By analyzing user's cell phone usage patterns (micro behaviors), the mobile devices can be tailored to meet user's requirements (macro behaviors). Especially, we hope that potentials of GBN may be recognized much more in future studies of personalizing smartphone user-interface, and upgrading user satisfaction.

Acknowledgment. This research was supported by WCU (World Class University) program through the National Research Foundation of Korea funded by the Ministry of Education, Science and Technology (Grant No. R31-2008-000-10062-0).

References

1. Chae, S.W., Hahn, M.H., Lee, K.C.: Micro Reality Mining of a Cell Phone Usage Behavior: A General Bayesian Network Approach. In: 2011 International Conference on Ubiquitous Computing and Multimedia Applications (UCMA), pp. 119–122 (2011)
2. Park, M.-H., Hong, J.-H., Cho, S.-B.: Location-Based Recommendation System Using Bayesian User's Preference Model in Mobile Devices. In: Indulska, J., Ma, J., Yang, L.T., Ungerer, T., Cao, J. (eds.) UIC 2007. LNCS, vol. 4611, pp. 1130–1139. Springer, Heidelberg (2007)
3. Yan, B., Chen, G.: AppJoy: personalized mobile application discovery. In: Proceedings of the 9th International Conference on Mobile Systems, Applications, and Services (MobiSys 2011), pp. 113–126. ACM, New York (2011)
4. Lee, J., McKay, B.: Optimizing a Personalized Cellphone Keypad. In: Lee, G., Howard, D., Ślęzak, D. (eds.) ICHIT 2011. LNCS, vol. 6935, pp. 237–244. Springer, Heidelberg (2011)
5. How, Y., Kan, M.-Y.: Optimizing Predictive Text Entry for Short Message Service on Mobile Phones. In: Human Computer Interfaces International, HCII 2005 (2005)
6. Moradi, S., Nickabadi, A.: Optimization of Mobile Phone Keypad Layout Via Genetic Algorithm. In: Information and Communication Technologies, ICTTA 2006, 2nd edn., pp. 1676–1681 (2006)

 7. Olwal, A., Lachanas, D., Zacharouli, E.: Oldgen: Mobile Phone Personalization for Older Adults. In: Proceedings of the 2011 Annual Conference on Human Factors in Computing Systems (CHI 2011), pp. 3393–3396. ACM, New York (2011)
 8. Mishra, V., Arya, P., Dixit, M.: Improving Mobile Search through Location Based Context and Personalization. In: 2012 International Conference on Communication Systems and Network Technologies, pp. 392–396 (2012)
 9. Rosenthal, S., Dey, A.K., Veloso, M.: Using Decision-Theoretic Experience Sampling to Build Personalized Mobile Phone Interruption Models. In: Lyons, K., Hightower, J., Huang, E.M. (eds.) Pervasive 2011. LNCS, vol. 6696, pp. 170–187. Springer, Heidelberg (2011)
10. Fayyad, U., Piatetsky-Shapiro, G., Smyth, P.: The Kdd Process for Extracting Useful Knowledge from Volumes of Data. Communications of the ACM 39(11), 27–34 (1996)
11. Heckerman, D.: Bayesian Networks for Data Mining. Data Mining and Knowledge Discovery 1(1), 79–119 (1997)
12. Cowell, R.G., Dawid, A.P., Lauritzen, S.L., Spiegelhalter, D.J.: Probabilistic Networks and Expert Systems. Springer, New York (1999)
13. Jensen, F.V.: Bayesian Networks and Decision Graphs. Springer, New York (2001)
14. Shafer, G.: Probabilistic Expert Systems. Society for Industrial and Applied Mathematics, Philadelphia (1996)
15. Langley, C.J., Holcomb, M.C.: Creating Logistics Customer Value. Journal of Business Logistics 13(2) (1992)
16. Langley, P., Sage, S.: Induction of Selective Bayesian Classifiers. In: Proceedings of the 10th Conference on Uncertainty in Artificial Intelligence, pp. 339–406 (2006)
17. Friedman, N., Geiger, M., Goldszmidt, M.: Bayesian Network Classifiers. Machine Learning 29(2), 131–163 (1997)
18. Cheng, J., Greiner, R.: Learning Bayesian Belief Network Classifiers: Algorithms and System. In: 14th Canadian Conference on Artificial Intelligence, pp. 141–151 (2001)
19. Silander, T., Myllymäki, P.: A Simple Approach for Finding the Globally Optimal Bayesian Network Structure. In: Proceedings of 22nd Conference on Uncertainty in Artificial Intelligence (2006)
20. Liao, K., Paulsen, M.R., Reid, J.F., Ni, B.C., Bonifacio-Maghirang, E.P.: Corn Kernel Breakage Classification by Machine Vision Using a Neural Network Classifier. Transactions of the ASAE (American Society of Agricultural Engineers) 36(6), 1949–1953 (1993)
21. Cristianini, N., Shawe-Taylor, J.: Introduction to Support Vector Machines. Cambridge University Press (2000)
22. Jin, R., Agrawal, G.: Effcient Decision Tree Construction on Streaming Data. In: SIGKDD Conference on Knowledge Discovery and Data Mining (KD), pp. 571–576 (2003)
23. Eagle, N., Pentland, A.S.: Reality Mining: Sensing Complex Social Systems. Personal and Ubiquitous Computing 10(4), 255–268 (2006)
24. Hall, M., Frank, E., Holmes, G., Pfahringer, B., Reutemann, P., Witten, I.H.: The Weka Data Mining Software: An Update. ACM Special Interest Group on Knowledge Discovery and Data Mining (SIGKDD) Explorations Newsletter 11(1), 10–18 (2009)
25. Soto, V., Frias-Martinez, V., Virseda, J., Frias-Martinez, E.: Prediction of Socioeconomic Levels Using Cell Phone Records. In: Konstan, J.A., Conejo, R., Marzo, J.L., Oliver, N. (eds.) UMAP 2011. LNCS, vol. 6787, pp. 377–388. Springer, Heidelberg (2011)

How Do Stress Management and Personal Characteristics Improve the Quality of Life?

Youngmi Baek[1], Kun Chang Lee[2,*], and Seong Wook Chae[3]

[1] Department of Interaction Science, Sungkyunkwan University, Seoul 110-745,
Republic of Korea
[2] SKK Business School, WCU Professor at Department of Interaction Science,
Sungkyunkwan University, Seoul 110-745, Republic of Korea
[3] Sungkyunkwan University, Seoul 110-745, Republic of Korea
{kunchanglee,seongwookchae}@gmail.com

Abstract. This paper investigates stress management and related health issues with smartphones, especially possible relationships among stress, well-being, and intention to purchase health-related apps. Using 98 valid questionnaire and GBN (General Bayesian Network), we analyzed survey data to extract meaningful lessons. First, people suffering from stress show high intention to purchase health-related mobile apps. Second, GBN is very effective in inducing rich interpretations from the experiments results.

Keywords: Stress, well-being, quality of life, General Bayesian Network, health-related apps.

1 Introduction

In today's daily life, stress management is a significant factor to improve personal health and work efficiency. The competitive working environment and the external and internal personal characteristics affect individuals' mental stability and well-being so that the effect of stress is critically related to the effectiveness of personal performance. Therefore, diverse perspectives were applied to research stress management in the psychological, sociological, medical and business research fields. In this study, we focus on the relationship between stress management and the personal quality of a healthy life.

Although stress was defined in the various views of past researchers, this study focused on psychological thought. This study started with the assumption that well-being is closely connected to the individual's psychological status and emotion and that well-being in modern society couldn't exist without stress management. Therefore, this study examined how stress management would improve individuals' well-being (quality of life) directly and indirectly through the general Bayesian network. In addition, we tried to identify the effect of external and internal variables on individuals' well-being, and to analyze the mutual relation with each variable. In addition, leisure activities contribute to health and well-being in the general

---

* Corresponding author.

T.-h. Kim et al. (Eds.): MulGraB/BSBT/IUrC 2012, CCIS 353, pp. 389–396, 2012.

population [1]. Therefore, this study tried to identify how leisure helps the stress management and quality of life.

The purpose of this study is to determine the relationship among psychological stress, demographic variables, leisure, intention of health care apps and well-being through the General Bayesian Network analysis. The specific aims of this study are (1) to examine the efficiency of health care apps in stress management and individuals' well-being, and (2) to identify how much leisure is important to improve the well-being of Koreans.

2   Background

2.1   Well-Being

Definitions of well-being and happiness can be seen from subjective and objective perspectives. The subjective definitions are grouped into three categories. First, well-being is defined by external criteria such as virtue or holiness. Secondly, well-being has come to be labeled as life satisfaction and relies on the respondent's standards to determine what the good life is. Third, subjective well-being emphasizes pleasant emotional experiences [2].

According to the World Health Organization (WHO) [3], quality of life is defined as "the individual perception of their life position in the context of the culture and value, and in relation to their goals, expectations, standards and concerns." On the other hand, social science defines quality of life as life satisfaction, morale, and happiness. However, other perspectives view quality of life as emotional well-being and life satisfaction.

2.2   Stress

Perceived stress is commonly considered a subjective appraisal of events or situations in one's life that exceed one's abilities and resources to cope with these situations [4–5]. Schwartz and Garamoni (1989) suggested the state of mind (SOM), which is divided into five categories [6]. Schwartz (1997) replaced the reformulated balanced state of mind (BSOM) measured by depression, anxiety, anger, stress, and psychological well-being (satisfaction and happiness) and showed that autonomic thought was positively related to satisfaction and happiness [7]. On the other hand, it was negatively related to anger, depression, anxiety, and perceived stress [8]. In the perspective related to the workplace, job is stress among the kinds of stress based on the burden of controlling the individual's own work and limited opportunity for cooperation and fellowship with others [9].

2.3   Leisure

Leisure activities contribute to health and well-being in the general population [1]. In past literature, leisure activities have been related to positive cognition function [10], better mental health [11], improved quality of life [12], coping with stress [13], and reduced risk of dementia [11, 14]. Coleman and Iso-Ahola's stress-buffer model [15] provides a foundation for empirical study of leisure as an instrument for buffering stress and possibly suppressing the effect of some stressors. In addition, Hutchinson and Kleiber (2005) considered leisure as a resource for coping with negative life events that serves as a buffer from the "immediacies of stress" [16]. Recently, Bedini et al.'s (2011) research verified that leisure is associated with perceived stress and perhaps may relieve the effect of stress on quality of life in female health care workers [1].

2.4   Mobile Application

As of the end of 2011, more than 91 million Americans own a smartphone, according to a recent ComScore report [17]. In a report "Global Mobile Health Market Report 2010–2015," research2guidance, a prominent mobile research specialist, there will be an estimated 1.4 billion smartphone users in the world within five years [18]. Especially healthcare smartphone users are expected to number 500 million people in 2015. In the current apps market, 17,000 mobile health apps were launched and 74 percent of them adhere to the paid business model. Both health care providers and consumers are embracing mobile apps as a means for improving health care. If the health care apps business generally adopts the paid model, the profit in the mobile health care market will be enormous in the near future.

2.5   Bayesian Network

The Bayesian network (BN) is a powerful formalism to represent a joint probability distribution. Its directed acyclic graphs (DAG) allow for efficient and effective representation of joint probabilistic distributions over a set of random variables. BN can infer the probability of any combination of variables without having to represent the joint probabilities of the variables. BN can be used as a classifier when users want to determine whether the exact probability of an event is above or below a certain threshold. GBN (general Bayesian network) is a full-fledged (unrestricted) BN in which casual relationships between the class node and all other nodes are flexibly formulated using an efficient network construction technique based on conditional independence tests.

3   Research Methodology and Experiment

3.1   Measures

In order to analyze the relationship with factors affecting individual well-being, we built the questionnaire and surveyed South Koreans based on the past literature's measures and methodology. Additionally, we added the individual health status data gathered by the Healthmax Co. Cady online system (http://healthmax.co.kr). Our questionnaire comprised largely five scales that measured aspect of stress, demographics, well-being, leisure, and application usage. First, five items regarding psychological stress were adopted from a quality of employment survey [19] that measured physical and psychological stress [20]. Secondly, we used Bedini et al.'s (2011) study for measuring demographic variables – age, the level of education, and physical health status. Third, well-being was measured by items from the Oxford happiness questionnaire [21] that are known to correlate with well-being. Fourth, leisure was adopted from leisure participation (LP) among the Bedini et al. (2011) measures. Fifth, mobile apps (health care related) purchase intention was measured by the behavioral intention used in Lu et al.'s (2005) study [22]. Lastly, to measure job, marital status, leave alone, and illness, we also used the Bedini et al. (2011) demographic profile.

3.2   Sampling and Sample Characteristics

In order to analyze the relation among the stress, leisure, mobile apps purchase intention, well-being, and some demographics variables, we gathered 98 samples from a questionnaire survey and measured some characteristics. In order to find the specialties, we categorized age and education level with four categories and gender and marital status with two categories. The general characteristics of the samples are summarized in Table 1.

Table 1. Descriptive demographic statistics

Category	Gender	Age	Education level	Job	Marital status
1	56 (57%)	7	8 (8.2)	13	95 (97%)
2	42 (43%)	66	37 (37.8)	40	2 (2%)
3		24	40 (40.8)	1	
4		0	13 (13.3)	36	
missing		1	0	8	1

Gender – 1: male; 2: female
Age – 1: 10–19; 2: 20–29; 3: 30–39; 4: 40–49
Education level – 1: high school graduate; 2: college student; 3: college graduate; 4: postgraduate degree
Job – 1: blue collar; 2: white collar; 3: housewife; 4: no job
Marital status- –1: married; 2: single

3.3   Test Result

The Cronbach's alpha indices of all variables appeared over .800 so the reliability of all variables was verified. To analyze the validity of the construct, we conducted a principal component analysis of five variables measured by more than two questionnaires. When the Eigen value became near 1, the five variables were selected. The variables represent each variable's meaning and the factor loading index appeared more than .700. All the Cronbach's alpha values are greater than 0.8, and the AVE was greater than 0.7.

According to the result of the general Bayesian network (GBN) analysis with three algorithms (K2, hill-climber, and lagged hill-climber), each algorithm showed the different causal relations among the variables. The following picture show the path models when the analysis was applied to K2, hill-climber, and lagged hill-climber algorithms.

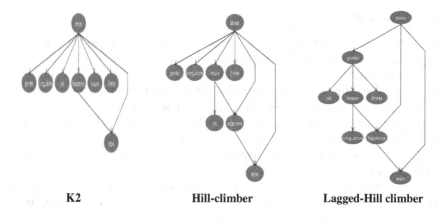

Fig. 1. Three types of GBN results

Comparing the model fit indices of analysis results, hill-climber was verified as the best model. Therefore, this study would describe the test result based on results of the hill-climber algorithm (see Table 2). First, the analysis result of the Bayesian network showed the following causal relation: stress directly affected illness, gender, leisure, happiness, living alone, and intention to purchase health-related smartphone apps. At the same time, stress indirectly affected intention to purchase health-related apps via happiness and job via leisure. To identify the significance of the causal path, we used the Warp PLS 2.0 program. In the path analysis, the P values of average path coefficient (APC), and average R-squared (ARS) were less than 0.05 and average variance inflation factor (AVIF) index showed much less than 5, so that the model using the hill-climber algorithm satisfied the model fit index. Among the path relations, the direct influences from stress to happiness, illness, and intention to purchase health-related apps were-0.518, 0.297, and 0.225, respectively. Each significance showed less than 0.05. Therefore, on the 95% confidence level, the direct path effects were verified as significant. In addition, the coefficient and significance from leisure to happiness showed 0.228 and 0.015, respectively, so leisure affected happiness significantly.

Table 2. Path analysis result- Hill-climber

variables	stress		happiness		leisure	
	coefficient	P value	coefficient	P value	coefficient	P value
happiness	-0.518	0.000			0.228	0.015
apps	0.225	0.013	-0.053	0.275		
illness	0.297	0.002				
gender	0.132	0.071				
living alone	-0.039	0.303				
job					-0.069	0.260
leisure	0.000	0.475				

Note: APC=0.154, P=<0.001, ARS=0.064, P=0.012, AVIF=1.184, Good if < 5.

3.4   Discussion

This study primarily tried to find how stress affects well-being and the consumer's intention to buy health-related mobile apps. Simultaneously, our aim was to identify the effect of leisure on the people's well-being. Therefore, we tried to find eight variable relations with various Bayesian algorithms and finally chose three algorithms to analyze the causal relation among the variables empirically.

First, stress was verified to decrease personal well-being and increase the extent of illness. This negative relationship between stress and well-being corresponds to the past [1, 8, 23]. The positive relation between stress and illness also was supported by prior researchers [24–25].

Second, leisure also was verified to affect individual happiness. This result also corresponds to the previous literature's empirical result [10]. However, even though leisure is an important factor to decrease stress and recent research also showed that leisure was associated with perceived stress and reduced the effect of perceived stress on the quality of life [1], this study result couldn't find any relation between stress and leisure via the general Bayesian network analysis.

Third, stress was identified to affect intention to buy health-related apps directly and indirectly. This reflects that mobile phone users, who have high stress in their daily life, are interested in the health-related application contents. The mobile phone is a handheld tool, which people carry all the time, so it is the easiest and fastest way to find the solution to get rid of stress and have fun.

4   Concluding Remarks

Stress management is very significant to the current population's exposure to the fast-moving and competitive environment. Diverse products are provided related to stress management and well-being in the food, cosmetic, health, and other industries in the main cities all over the world. South Korea is one of the fastest transforming areas, and especially mobile telecommunication technology is developing at the highest rate in the world. For this reason, this study examines stress management and health-related mobile apps.

In order to find the relation among stress, well-being, and other variables, we adopted the general Bayesian network. Based on the path gotten set by the Bayesian network analysis, we tested each path's relation empirically. According to the test result, stress affected illness positively, well-being negatively, and the purchase intention of health-related mobile apps directly and indirectly at the same time. This reflects the importance of the relationship between stress and well-being, and finally the significance of mobile apps through smartphones. This result especially means that stressed people have high intention to buy health-related mobile apps if they are exposed to the various health management apps. Additionally, this research showed leisure affected people's well-being.

However, the relationship result couldn't show the optimal path among variables so that some causal relations appeared insignificant even though they are important in the general thought. Therefore, it would be useful to analyze the relationship among the variables through a different methodology and then compare it to the result of the general Bayesian network in future research.

Acknowledgment. This research was supported by WCU(World Class University) program through the National Research Foundation of Korea funded by the Ministry of Education, Science and Technology   (Grant No. R31-2008-000-10062-0).

References

1. Bedini, L.A., Gladwell, N.J., Dudley, W.N., Clancy, E.J.: Mediation analysis of leisure, perceived stress, and quality of life in informal caregivers. Journal of Leisure Research 43, 153–175 (2011)
2. Diener, E.: Subjective Well-Being. Psychological Bulletin 95, 542–575 (1984)
3. The WHOQOL Group: The World Health Organization Quality of Life assessment (WHOQOL): Development and general psychometric properties. Social Science & Medicine 46(12), 1569–15825 (1998)
4. Cohen, H., Benjamin, J., Geva, A.B., Matar, M.A., Kaplan, Z., Kotler, M.: Autonomic dysregulation in panic disorder and in post-traumatic stress disorder: application of power spectrum analysis of heart rate variability at rest and in response to recollection of trauma or panic attacks. Psychiatry Research 96, 1–13 (2000)
5. Edwards, J.R.: A cybernetic theory of stress, coping, and well-being in organizations. Academy of Management Review, 238–274 (1992)
6. Schwartz, R.M., Caramoni, G.L.: Cognitive balance and psychopathology: Evaluation of an information processing model of positive and negative states of mind. Clinical Psychology Review 9, 271–294 (1989)
7. Schwartz, R.M.: Consider the simple screw: cognitive science, quality improvement, and psychotherapy. Journal of Consulting and Clinical Psychology 65, 970 (1997)
8. Wong, S.S.: Balanced states of mind in psychopathology and psychological well-being. International Journal of Psychology 45, 269–277 (2010)
9. Frankenhaeuser, M.: Quality of Life: Criteria for Behavioral Adjustment. International Journal of Psychology 12, 99–110 (1997)
10. Weuve, J., Kang, J.H., Manson, J.A.E., Breteler, M.M.B., Ware, J.H., Grodstein, F.: Physical activity, including walking, and cognitive function in older women. Journal of the American Medical Association 292, 1454–1461 (2004)
11. Everard, K.M., Lach, H.W., Fisher, E.B., Baum, M.C.: Relationship of activity and social support to the functional health of older adults. The Journals of Gerontology Series B: Psychological Sciences and Social Sciences 55(4), S208–S212 (2000)
12. Gabriel, Z., Bowling, A.: Quality of life from the perspectives of older people. Ageing and Society 24(5), 675–691 (2004)
13. Iwasaki, Y.: Roles of leisure in coping with stress among university students: A repeated-assessment field study. Anxiety, Stress & Coping 16, 31–57 (2003)
14. Verghese, J., Lipton, R.B., Katz, M.J., Hall, C.B., Derby, C.A., Kuslansky, G., Ambrose, A.F., Sliwinski, M., Buschke, H.: Leisure activities and the risk of dementia in the elderly. New England Journal of Medicine 348, 2508–2516 (2003)
15. Coleman, D., Iso-Ahola, S.E.: Leisure and health: The role of social support and self-determination. Journal of Leisure Research 25, 111–111 (1993)
16. Hutchinson, S.L., Kleiber, D.A.: Gifts of the ordinary: Casual leisure's contributions to health and well-being. World Leisure Journal 47, 2–16 (2005)

17. comScore: comScore Reports November 2011 U.S. Mobile Subscriber Market Share (September 17, 2012), http://www.comscore.com/Press_Events/ Press_Releases/2011/12/comScore_Reports_November_2011_U.S._ Mobile_Subscriber_Market_Share

18. Mikalajunaite, E.: 500m people will be using healthcare mobile applications in 2015, Global Mobile Health Market Report 2010-2015 (November 2010), http://www.research2guidance.com/500mpeople-will-be-using- healthcaremobile-applications-in-2015/

19. Quinn, R.P., Staines, G.L.: The 1977 quality of employment survey. Institute for Social Research, The University of Michigan, Ann Arbor, Mich (1979)

20. Choi, J.P.: Work and Family Demands and Life Stress among Chinese Employees: The Mediating Effect of Work-Family Conflict. International Journal of Human Resource Management 19, 878–895 (2008)

21. Hills, P., Argyle, M.: The Oxford Happiness Questionnaire: A compact scale for the measurement of psychological well-being. Personality and Individual Differences 33, 1073–1082 (2002)

22. Lu, H.P., Hsu, C.L., Hsu, H.Y.: An empirical study of the effect of perceived risk upon intention to use online applications. Information Management & Computer Security 13, 106–120 (2005)

23. Danna, K., Griffin, R.W.: Health and well-being in the workplace: A review and synthesis of the literature. Journal of Management 25, 357–384 (1999)

24. Collins, K.S., Schoen, C., Joseph, S., Duchon, L., Simantov, E., Yellowitz, M.: Health concerns across a woman's lifespan: The Commonwealth Fund 1998 Survey of Women's Health

25. Schulz, R., Beach, S.R., Lind, B., Martire, L.M., Zdaniuk, B., Hirsch, C., Jackson, S., Burton, L.: Involvement in caregiving and adjustment to death of a spouse. Journal of the American Medical Association 285, 3123–3129 (2001)

Coverage Verification Algorithm
for Sensor Networks

Aleksander Ćwiszewski and Piotr Wiśniewski*

Faculty of Mathematics and Computer Science
Nicolaus Copernicus University
Toruń, Poland
{aleks,pikonrad}@mat.uni.torun.pl

Abstract. The paper deals with the problem of coverage of domains in $\mathbb{R}^2$ by a network of sensors. It is related to a recent paper by de Silva and Ghrist. We provide a coverage verification algorithm, based on homotopy equivalent reductions of the Rips simplicial complex associated to the sensor network. The algorithm does not involve any computation in homology spaces of the Rips simplicial complex.

1 Introduction

A sensor is a device which measures some feature in the surrounding region and can return information (e.g. detection of movement, environmental features). Sensor networks has become a subject of recent intensive studies, see e.g. [5] and the references therein. One of most vital issue is the coverage problem. That is we ask whether a randomly scattered set of sensors covers the whole domain (without any holes in its coverage). In [4] de Silva and Ghrist consider a coordinate-free model in which sensors broadcast their unique ID signals and detect other sensors within radius r_b as well as cover with their sensing properties the region of radius r_c. Our paper is inspired by their criterion for coverage verification expressed in terms of homology spaces of Rips simplicial complexes built out of connection graphs. We work under the similar assumptions as in [4]. We assume that

(H1) Nodes from $\mathbb{X}$ broadcast their unique ID numbers. Each node detects other nodes within distance r_b and can also return their ID's.

(H2) Each node from $\mathbb{X}$ covers with its sensing properties the area within radius $r_c \geqslant r_b/\sqrt{3}$.

(H3) Nodes from $\mathbb{X}$ lie in a compact connected domain $\mathbb{D} \subset \mathbb{R}^2$ whose boundary $\partial\mathbb{D}$ is piecewise-linear and consists of disjoint closed polygonal curves without self-intersections $\gamma_0, \gamma_1, \ldots, \gamma_l$ and that $\gamma_1, \ldots, \gamma_l$ are contained in the domain bounded by γ_0.

* Supported by the Polish National Science Centre grant 2011/01/B/ST6/03867.

T.-h. Kim et al. (Eds.): MulGraB/BSBT/IUrC 2012, CCIS 353, pp. 397–405, 2012.

(H4) There are nodes in all the vertices of the boundary polygonal curves. Each fence node knows the identities of its neighbors on $\partial \mathbb{D}$ and these neighbors lie within distance r_b.

The main idea is to consider an abstract simplicial complex, the so-called Rips complex $\mathcal{R}$, whose simplices are built of the nodes which lie within distance r_b of each other with the distinguished boundary complex $\mathcal{F}$. An example for the set $\mathbb{X} := \{1, 2, 3, 4, 5, 6, 7, 8\}$ with the hexagon 123456 as the boundary γ_0 and $r_b = \sqrt{3} r_c$ is shown in Figure 1 where in (a) we see a covering $\{\mathbb{B}(1, r_c), \ldots, \mathbb{B}(6, r_c)\}$ and in (b) one has the Rips complex $\mathcal{R}$ with $\mathcal{F} := \{1, 2, 3, 4, 5, 6\}$ ([1]). It is embedded into $\mathbb{R}^3$ as the points 4, 5, 7 and 8 lie within distance r_b of each other, i.e. they determine a 3-dimensional simplex in the complex $\mathcal{R}$.

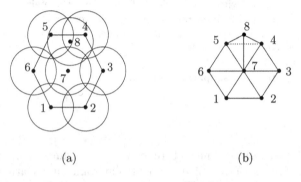

(a)   (b)

Fig. 1.

The relation between the structure of the Rips complex and the sensor coverage hinges on a simple geometric property that states: *if three points lie within distance r_b of each other, then, for any $r_c \geqslant r_b/\sqrt{3}$, the open discs of radius r_c centered at these points cover the triangle spanned by them.* De Silva and Ghrist give a general criterion for the network covering. Namely they show that the sensor network covers the domain $\mathbb{D}$ if the relative homology space $H_2(\mathcal{R}, \mathcal{F})$ contains a nontrivial element whose boundary is nonvanishing. The idea behind gave rise to many other sensor network related problems – see [1, 4–7] and the references therein.

In this paper we apply a similar approach to that from [4], however our algorithm itself does not perform computation in homology spaces of the Rips complex. Instead we distinguish special simplices, that we call boundary ones, and in consecutive steps remove them from the Rips complex reducing it to the homotopy equivalent one. If we manage to reduce the flag complex to a point, this means that the coverage does not leave uncovered holes. As mentioned, our algorithm does not use homology objects and does not need computations in homologies, which may be viewed as an advantage. Although the proof of

---

[1] We use the following notation: $\mathbb{B}(x, r) := \{y \in \mathbb{R}^2 \mid |y - x| < r\}$ where $|\cdot|$ stands for the Eucledean norm in $\mathbb{R}^2$.

its correctness is closely related to that due to de Silva and Ghrist in [4]. It is noteworthy that we also solve the problem when the domain to be covered has disconnected boundary. In this case, the above reduction algorithm without any modification would fail, since it would 'see' the holes in the domain as uncovered by the network and would not reduce the Rips complex to a point even if the domain was indeed covered. Therefore, to overcome the problem, we artificially fill these holes with simplices and proceed as before. Then if the modified complex is reduced to a point, we can deduce that the whole domain must be covered by the network.

Let us mention that methods based on Rips complexes may provide a sufficient condition, but one can not expect a necessary one. The reason for that is illustrated in Figure 2, where, for $r_c := r_b/\sqrt{3}$ we see two coverings in pictures (a) and (b) with the same Rips complex in (c) (the boundary of the square 1234). The covering in (a) does not cover the whole square 1234 (since the square side length is between $r_b\sqrt{2/3}$ and r_b), while that in (b) does (as the side length lies between $r_b/\sqrt{2}$ and $r_b\sqrt{2/3}$).

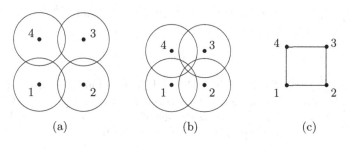

(a)   (b)   (c)

Fig. 2.

The paper is organized as follows. In Section 2 we introduce the general concepts of boundary simplex and reduction of simplicial complex. In Section 3 we recall the construction of Rips complex, describe the algorithm and prove its correctness. Section 4 is devoted to the implementation of the algorithm and its computational complexity.

2   Flag Complex of Coverings and Reduction Procedure

A set s is called a k-*simplex* (or *simplex of dimension* k) in a normed linear space $\mathbb{E}$ if it is a convex hull of $k + 1$ distinct points $v_0, v_1, \ldots, v_k$ spanning a k-dimensional hyperplane of $\mathbb{E}$. The points $v_0, \ldots, v_k$ are called vertices of the k-simplex s and k is the dimension of the simplex s. Hence each k-simplex is uniquely determined by the set of its vertices. Any simplex defined by an l-element subset of the set of vertices $\{v_0, v_1, \ldots, v_k\}$ is called a l-*face* (or *face*) of the simplex s.

Recall that a finite set $\mathcal{R}$ of simplices (in some normed linear space $\mathbb{E}$) is called a *simplicial complex* if the following conditions hold

(a) any face of a simplex in $\mathcal{R}$ belongs to $\mathcal{R}$;

(b) for $s, s' \in \mathcal{R}$ either $s \cap s' = \emptyset$ or $s \cap s'$ is a common face for both s and s'.

The *underlying space* of a simplicial complex $\mathcal{R}$ is the union of all simplices from $\mathcal{R}$ and is denoted by $|\mathcal{R}|$.

Suppose now that $\mathcal{R}$ is an arbitrary simplicial complex. The following concept of *boundary simplex* plays a crucial role in our reduction procedure.

Definition 21. We say that a k-simplex $s \in \mathcal{R}$ is a *boundary simplex* of $\mathcal{R}$ if there exists a unique $(k+1)$-simplex $\bar{s}$ in $\mathcal{R}$ such that s is a face of $\bar{s}$.

Definition 22. Given a boundary simplex $s \in \mathcal{R}$. The *s-reduced complex* is the simplicial complex $\text{Red}_s(\mathcal{R})$ obtained by removing in $\mathcal{R}$ the simplices $\bar{s}$ and s.

Proposition 23. *For any boundary simplex s of a simplicial complex $\mathcal{R}$, the topological spaces $|\mathcal{R}|$ and $|\text{Red}_s(\mathcal{R})|$ are homotopy equivalent.*

Proof: Let $\{v_0, \ldots, v_{k-1}\}$ be the vertices of s. Since s is a boundary simplex, there, due to the definition, there exists the unique vertex v_k in $\mathcal{R}$ such that the $\bar{s}$ is spanned by $\{v_0, \ldots, v_{k-1}, v_k\}$. Hence any point $x \in \bar{s}$ can be uniquely expressed as $x = \sum_{i=0}^{k} x_i v_i$ where $x_i \geq 0$ for $i \in \{0, 1, \ldots, k\}$ and $\sum_{i=0}^{k} x_i = 1$. For $j = 0, \ldots, k-1$, put

$$s_j := \{x \in |s| \mid x_i \geq x_j \ \forall \, i \in \{0, 1, \ldots, k-1\}\}.$$

It is clear that $|\bar{s}| = \bigcup_{j=0}^{k-1} s_j$. We claim that $|\mathcal{R}|$ can be continuously deformed to the s-reduced complex $|\text{Red}_s(\mathcal{R})|$ in such a way that each set s_j, $j \in \{0, 1, \ldots, k-1\}$, is mapped onto the face of $\bar{s}$ spanned by the set of vertices $\{v_0, v_1, \ldots, v_k\} \setminus \{v_j\}$. Precisely, we define a homotopy $h : |\mathcal{R}| \times [0, 1] \to |\mathcal{R}|$ by

$$h(x, t) := \begin{cases} x + tkx_j(v_k - \bar{x}) & \text{if } x \in s_j \text{ for some } j = 0, \ldots, k-1, \, t \in [0, 1], \\ x & \text{if } x \in |\text{Red}_s(\mathcal{R})|, \, t \in [0, 1], \end{cases}$$

where $\bar{x}$ stands for the baricentric center of s, i.e. $\bar{x} = \frac{1}{k} \sum_{i=0}^{k-1} v_i$. It can be directly checked that h is continuous,

$$h(x, t) = x \text{ for all } x \in |\text{Red}_s(\mathcal{R})|, t \in [0, 1],$$
$$h(x, 0) = x \text{ for all } x \in \mathcal{R},$$
$$h(|\mathcal{R}| \times \{1\}) \subset |\text{Red}_s(\mathcal{R})|,$$

which means that $|\text{Red}_s(\mathcal{R})|$ is a strong deformation retract of $|\mathcal{R}|$. This implies, in particular, that the two spaces are homotopy equivalent (see [3]). $\square$

3   Rips Complex and Coverage Verification Algorithm

Given a domain $\mathbb{D} \subset \mathbb{R}^2$ with the boundary $\partial \mathbb{D}$ consisting of polygonal cycles $\gamma_0, \gamma_1, \ldots, \gamma_l$, where $\gamma_1, \ldots, \gamma_l$ lie in a region bounded by γ_0 and a finite set of nodes $\mathbb{X} = \{x_\alpha\}_\alpha$ satisfying assumptions $(H1) - (H4)$. Recall the construction of the Rips complex.

Definition 31. (cf.[4]) Given a set $\mathbb{X} = \{x_\alpha\}_{\alpha \in A}$ in a metric space and $\varepsilon > 0$. The *Rips complex* of $\mathbb{X}$, is the abstract simplicial complex $\mathcal{R}_\varepsilon(\mathbb{X})$ whose k-simplices correspond to $(k+1)$-element subsets of $\mathbb{X}$ such that the distance between each pair of its elements is less than ε.

Let $\mathcal{R}$ be the Rips complex $\mathcal{R}_{r_b}(\mathbb{X})$ of $\mathbb{X}$. The complexes consisting of simplices corresponding to the polygonals γ_j denote by Γ_j, $j = 0, 1, \ldots, l$. We extend the complex $\mathcal{R}$ with the simplicial complexes $\mathcal{R}^{(j)}$, $j = 1, \ldots, l$, obtained by dividing the polygons $\mathbb{D}_j$ bounded by γ_j into triangles with vertices from among the vertices of γ_j. Let $\mathcal{R}_0$ be the simplicial complex being the union of $\mathcal{R}$ and all $\mathcal{R}^{(j)}$, $j = 1, \ldots, l$. By $\sigma_0 : |\mathcal{R}_0| \to \mathbb{R}^2$ we denote the natural continuous mapping sending the vertices of $\mathcal{R}_0$ into the corresponding nodes in $\mathbb{X}$ and the k-simplices of $\mathcal{R}_0$ onto the planar k-simplices being the convex hulls of corresponding nodes. The simplicial complex in the image denote by $\sigma_0(\mathcal{R}_0)$. Observe that in this way we get

$$\sigma_0 \text{ maps homeomorphically } |\Gamma_j| \text{ onto } \gamma_j, \text{ for } j = 0, 1, \ldots, l, \tag{1}$$

$$\sigma_0(|\mathcal{R}^{(j)}|) \subset \mathbb{D}_j, \text{ for } j = 1, \ldots, l.$$

We shall use the reduction procedure (from the previous section) to verify whether the complex $\mathcal{R}_0$ reduces to a 0-simplex in the following algorithm.

Algorithm 32

1. *Construct the Rips complex $\mathcal{R} = \mathcal{R}_{r_b}(\mathbb{X})$.*
2. *For each $j = 1, \ldots, l$, build a simplicial complex $\mathcal{R}^{(j)}$ containing triangles covering the interior of the polygon bounded by γ_j.*
3. *Put $\mathcal{R}_0 := \mathcal{R} \cup \left(\bigcup_{j=1}^{l} \mathcal{R}^{(j)} \right)$.*
4. *Find a boundary simplex s in $\mathcal{R}_0$ and put $i := 1$.*
5. *Put $\mathcal{R}_i := \mathrm{Red}_s(\mathcal{R}_{i-1})$.*
6. *If there is a boundary simplex $s \in \mathcal{R}_i$, then put $i := i+1$ and go to step 5 otherwise go to step 7.*
7. *If $\mathcal{R}_i$ is a point, then stop and inform that the whole domain $\mathbb{D}$ is covered by $\{\mathbb{B}(x_\alpha, r_c)\}_\alpha$ otherwise stop and inform that the covering problem can not be resolved.*

Proposition 33. *Algorithm 32 stops after a finite number of steps.*

Proof: It is immediate, since the number of all simplices in $\mathcal{R}_i$ after each step decreases and the algorithm stops when there is no boundary simplex left. $\square$

Example 34. Consider a sensor network with $\mathbb{X} := \{1, 2, 3, 4\}$ from Figure 2 with its Rips complex of the form $\mathcal{R}_0$ as in Figure 3 (this occurs when each of the balls $\mathbb{B}(1, r_b)$, $\mathbb{B}(2, r_b)$, $\mathbb{B}(3, r_b)$ and $\mathbb{B}(4, r_b)$ contains $\mathbb{X}$). Figure 3 shows the reduced complexes $\mathcal{R}_1, \mathcal{R}_2, \ldots, \mathcal{R}_5$. Observe that the simplex spanned by $\{2,3,4\}$ in $\mathcal{R}_0$ is boundary and the $\{2,3,4\}$-reduced complex $\mathrm{Red}_{\{2,3,4\}}(\mathcal{R}_0)$ is $\mathcal{R}_1$ from the figure. Further we get the following reductions with respect to boundary simplices

$$\mathcal{R}_2 = \mathrm{Red}_{\{2,4\}}(\mathcal{R}_1),$$
$$\mathcal{R}_3 = \mathrm{Red}_{\{3,4\}}(\mathcal{R}_2),$$
$$\mathcal{R}_4 = \mathrm{Red}_{\{4\}}(\mathcal{R}_3),$$
$$\mathcal{R}_5 = \mathrm{Red}_{\{2,3\}}(\mathcal{R}_4),$$
$$\mathcal{R}_6 = \mathrm{Red}_{\{3\}}(\mathcal{R}_5),$$
$$\mathcal{R}_7 = \mathrm{Red}_{\{2\}}(\mathcal{R}_6) = \{1\},$$

i.e. the algorithm stops with a 0-simplex. This according to step 7 of Algorithm 32 would mean that the sensors from $\mathbb{X}$ cover the whole domain $\mathbb{D}$.   □

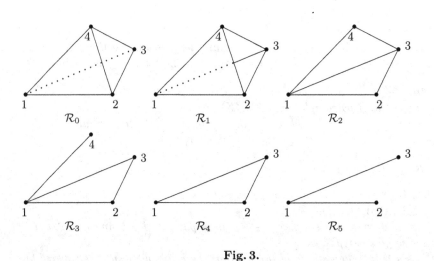

Fig. 3.

Now we pass to the correctness of the algorithm.

Theorem 35. *If the output $\mathcal{R}_i$ of Algorithm 32 consists of a 0-simplex (i.e. a point), then $\mathbb{D} \subset \bigcup_\alpha \mathbb{B}(x_\alpha, r_c)$.*

The result is intuitively clear and its proof is rather standard. It uses the ideas from [4].

Lemma 36. *(See [4, Lem. 2.2]) If free points $x_0, x_1, x_2 \in \mathbb{R}^2$ lie within distance r_b of each other, then for any $r_c \geqslant r_b/\sqrt{3}$ the triangle spanned by x_0, x_1, x_2 is contained in $\bigcup_{i=0}^2 \mathbb{B}(x_i, r_c)$.*

Proof of Theorem 35: Suppose to the contrary that there exists $x_0 \in \mathbb{D}$ such that $x_0 \notin \bigcup_\alpha \mathbb{B}(x_\alpha, r_c)$. Note that $x_0 \in \text{int}\,\mathbb{D}$, since by assumption the boundary is covered by the network. Due to Lemma 36, we infer that x_0 does not belong to any triangle in the simplex $\sigma_0(\mathcal{R}_0)$. Therefore, taking into account (1), one has the following commutative diagram of maps

$$
\begin{array}{c}
(|\mathcal{R}_0|, |\Gamma_0|) \\
{\scriptstyle \tilde{\sigma}_0} \nearrow \qquad \downarrow {\scriptstyle \sigma_0} \\
(\mathbb{R}^2 \setminus \{x_0\}, \gamma_0) \xrightarrow[incl]{} (\mathbb{R}^2, \gamma_0)
\end{array}
$$

where $\tilde{\sigma}_0(x) := \sigma_0(x)$, $x \in |\mathcal{R}_0|$. By using the long exact sequences of homologies (see e.g. [3] or [2]) for the pairs $(|\mathcal{R}_0|, |\Gamma_0|)$ and $(\mathbb{R}^2, \gamma_0)$, we get a diagram

$$
\begin{array}{c}
H_2(|\mathcal{R}_0|, |\Gamma_0|) \xrightarrow{onto} H_1(|\Gamma_0|) \longrightarrow H_1(|\mathcal{R}_0|) = \{0\} \\
{\scriptstyle H_2(\tilde{\sigma}_0)} \swarrow \quad \downarrow {\scriptstyle H_2(\sigma_0)} \qquad \downarrow {\scriptstyle iso} \\
H_2(\mathbb{R}^2 \setminus \{x_0\}, \gamma_0) \longrightarrow H_2(\mathbb{R}^2, \gamma_0) \xrightarrow{iso} H_1(\gamma_0) \longrightarrow H_1(\mathbb{R}^2) = \{0\}.
\end{array}
$$

Here we use Proposition 23 to see that $|\mathcal{R}_0|$ is homotopic to a point and, in consequence, its homologies spaces are isomorphic to those of a point, i.e. in particular $H_1(|\mathcal{R}_0|) \cong \{0\}$. Furthermore, since $x_0 \in \text{int}\,\mathbb{D}$ and γ_0 is homeomorphic to a circle, we deduce from the long exact sequence that $H_2(\mathbb{R}^2 \setminus \{x_0\}, \gamma_0) \cong \{0\}$ $(H_n(\gamma_0) \cong H_n(S^1) \cong \mathbb{Q}$ for $n \in 0, 1$ and $H_n(\gamma_0) \cong \{0\}$ for all the other n's). Therefore it follows from the left triangle in the diagram above that $H_2(\sigma_0) = 0$, which contradicts the commutativity in the square part of the diagram as $H_1(\gamma_0) \cong H_1(S^1) \cong \mathbb{Q}$. $\qquad \square$

4   Implementation

Data Structures. Suppose that node ID's are positive integers. The input has the form of a sequence of lists containing ID's. Each list starts with a chosen node ID, say `ID`, and next enumerates the ID's of all those nodes that lie within distance r_b of the node `ID` and has its ID smaller than `ID` (for each node one list is provided). Actually each list can be easily obtained from the information emitted by each sensor. We may also assume that the input is sorted with respect to first elements `ID` of the lists (one can always sort the data in time $n \log n$).

Each simplex is represented as a structure called `Simplex` that contains:

- the ordered sequence of **vertices** spanning the simplex (made of appropriate ID's),
- the simplex size (dimension) **size** (the length of **vertices**),

– the list SubList of all its faces (in all dimensions),
– the list UpList of simplices containing the given one as a face.

The list SubList may seem redundant, nevertheless it is convenient in our implementation (when the complex is reduced).

A structure representing complexes is denoted by Complex and is built of:

– the list SimplexList of all simplices sorted with respect to size and next by the lexycographical order,
– the list of boundary simplices BoundaryList.

When UpList of a simplex is modified, the simplex is tested if it is a boundary one or not and if necessary it is added to or removed from the BoundaryList.

Construction of Rips Complex. For any simplex $s \in \mathcal{R}$ by Ver(s) we denote the set of all vertices of s. Let ls be a list of simplices, and lv be a set of some ID's of vertices. We use a function chooseSpanned (ls,lv) that returns a list of all simplices s from ls such that Ver(s) $\subset$ lv. And by simplexSpan(lv) we denote a function generating the simplex spanned by all the vertices from lv. Assume that the set of all ID's is equal to $\{1, 2, 3, \ldots, n\}$ where $n \geqslant 1$. We process the input lists and construct the Rips complex in SimplexList as follows.

Data: input - sequence of list of ID's
SimplexList← [ ]
for idlist in input do
    id ←idlist[0];
    SimplexList.append(0-simplex(id));
    for s in chooseSpanned(SimplexList,idlist[1:]) do
    | SimplexList.append(simplexSpan(Ver(s)+[id]))
    end
end

Algorithm 1. Rips complex construction

Total Computational Cost. The first component of cost is related to the preparation of the input data made out of an unsorted list of pairs of ID's, that is $n \log(n)$. The Rips complex construction could make theoretically an exponential cost in a pessimistic case, i.e. when all the sensors see each other and the Rips complex contains 2^n simplices. However, usually in practice one tends to scatter the sensors uniformly so that each vertex belongs to a number of simplices which is estimated by a certain fixed upper bound, for instance 20. Then the practical cost may be $n \log(n)$. The operations in the main loop make a $\log(n)$ cost due to the list operations. The internal loop does not contibute much to the total cost as the idlist length is estimated by the number of simplics containing a common vertex. As for the the reduction procedure in Algorithm 32, note that every step of the reduction is of $log(n)$ cost. So in practice the total cost may be $n \log(n)$, in analogy to the cost estimation for the Rips complex construction, and, theoretically, in a pessimistic case it can be 2^n.

Table 1. Example of Rips complex construction

Step no.	idlist	chooseSpanned(SimplexList,idlist[1:])	Simplices added in the step
1.	1	-	(1)
2.	2,1	(1)	(2), (1,2)
3.	3,1,2	(1), (2), (1,2)	(3), (1,3), (2,3), (1,2,3)
4.	4,2,3	(2), (3), (2,3)	(4), (2,4), (3,4), (2,3,4)
5.	5,1,2,3	(1), (2), (3),(1,2) (1,3), (2,3), (1,2,3)	(1,5), (2,5), (3,5), (1,2,5), (1,3,5), (2,3,5), (1,2,3,5)

References

1. Dłotko, P., Ghrist, R., Juda, M., Mrozek, M.: Distributed computation of coverage in sensor networks by homological methods. Applicable Algebra and Engineering, Communication and Computing, Special Issue on Computer Algebra in Algebraic Topology and its Applications, 29–58 (2012)
2. Dold, A.: Lectures on Algebraic Topology. Springer (1995)
3. Hatcher, A.: Algebraic topology. Cambridge University Press (2002)
4. de Silva, V., Ghrist, R.: Coordinate-free coverage in sensor networks with controlled boundaries via homology. Intl. J. Robotics Research 25(12), 1205–1222 (2007)
5. de Silva, V., Ghrist, R.: Homological sensor networks. Notices Amer. Math. Soc. 54(1), 10–17 (2007)
6. Tahbaz-Salehi, A., Jadbabaie, A.: Coordinate-Free Distributed Coverage Verification and Intruder Detection in Dynamic Sensor Networks. In: Proceedings of Forty-Fifth Annual Allerton Conference on Communication, Control and Computing, pp. 417–422
7. Ghrist, R., Muhammad, A.: Coverage and hole-detection in sensor networks via homology. In: IPSN 2005 Proceedings of the 4th International Symposium on Information Processing in Sensor Networks (2005) Article No. 34

Author Index